Records
Management

AUTHORS

Judith Read
Instructor & Department Chair
Computer Information Systems
Portland Community College
Portland, Oregon

Mary Lea Ginn, Ph.D.
Coordinator, Institutional Review Board
Union Institute & University
Cincinnati, Ohio

Editorial Consultant
Cincinnati, Ohio

CONTRIBUTING AUTHORS

Virginia A. Jones, Ph.D.
VAJones Associates
Newport News, Virginia

Dianne S. Rankin
Educational Media Development
Monticello, Kentucky

8e

THOMSON

SOUTH-WESTERN

Australia · Brazil · Canada · Mexico · Singapore · Spain · United Kingdom · United States

Records Management, Eighth Edition
Judith Read and Mary Lea Ginn

VP/Editorial Director:
Jack W. Calhoun

VP/Editor-in-Chief:
Karen Schmohe

Acquisitions Editor:
Jane Phelan

Project Manager:
Penny Shank

Production Project Manager:
Darrell E. Frye

Marketing Manager:
Valerie A. Lauer

Marketing Coordinator:
Kelley Gilreath

Manufacturing Coordinator:
Charlene Taylor

Art Director:
Linda Helcher

Photo Researcher:
Darren Wright

Consulting Editors:
Dianne S. Rankin
Carol L. Ruhl

Production House:
Graphic World Inc.

Printer:
RR Donnelley
Willard, OH

Internal and Cover Designer:
Diane Gliebe

Cover Images:
©Getty Images

For more information about our products, contact us at:

Thomson Higher Education
5191 Natorp Boulevard
Mason, Ohio 45040
USA

Preface

RECORDS MANAGEMENT, Eighth Edition, continues the strong tradition of serving as an introduction to the increasingly comprehensive field of records and information management. New information continues to grow at a rapid rate, which causes the field of records and information management to be in a state of flux. This edition emphasizes principles and practices of effective records management for manual and electronic records systems. This approach offers practical information to students as well as to professionals at managerial, supervisory, and operating levels. Emphasis is placed on the need to understand the changes occurring with the volume of information, the need for compliance to government regulations, and advances in technology.

As a text for students in post-secondary institutions, RECORDS MANAGEMENT, Eighth Edition, may be used for short courses or seminars emphasizing filing systems or longer courses such as quarter or semester plans. Basic manual systems concepts and the concepts needed for understanding electronic records storage and retrieval methods are discussed and applied.

As a reference book, this latest edition of RECORDS MANAGEMENT serves several purposes. It presents sound principles of records and information management that include the entire range of records—paper, image records, and electronic media used in computerized systems. Although the key management functions as they relate to records management are introduced, emphasis is placed upon control for ensuring that the records system achieves its stated goals. Professionals who direct the operation of records systems will find this edition to be valuable because the rules in the textbook agree with the latest standard filing rules presented by ARMA International.

How the Text Is Organized

The text consists of four parts organized into 12 chapters.

- Part 1 introduces the student to the expanding area of records management.
- Part 2 centers on alphabetic storage and retrieval methods for manual and electronic systems. Transferring records from active storage according to established records retention schedules is also discussed.
- Part 3 presents a detailed description of adaptations of the alphabetic storage and retrieval method; namely, subject, numeric, and geographic storage methods.

- Part 4 covers records and information management technology, which includes an update of image systems and the technology that integrates the computer with other automated records systems. In addition, the need for controlling paperwork and electronic records problems are reviewed for both large and small offices. The records audit, the records and information manual, knowledge management, and developing and implementing a disaster recovery plan conclude the discussion of a comprehensive records and information management program.

Key Features

The eighth edition of RECORDS MANAGEMENT was completely redesigned for easy reading and maximum retention.

- Each chapter begins with easy-to-understand **learning objectives** so you know exactly what your goals are as you read and study the chapter.
- **Key terms** are bolded the first time they are used and conveniently listed at the end of the chapter and in the **glossary** for improved vocabulary building.
- Eye-catching, full-color **illustrations and photos** provide realistic examples of filing supplies, file drawers, filing systems, and electronic records.
- **Marginal notes** in the form of questions lead you through the major points in each chapter.

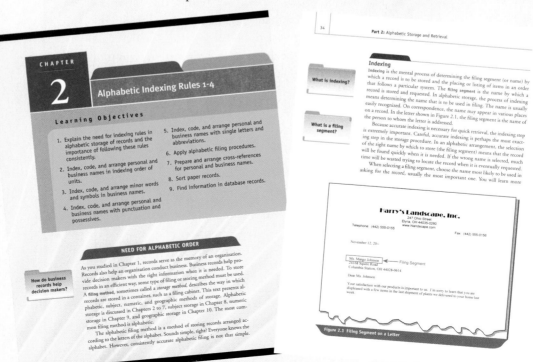

- **My Records,** a personal records management feature, provides valuable information about managing personal records.

- **Career Corner** features careers in records management, job descriptions, and interviews with professionals that add realism.

- **Chapter review and applications** sections include points to file and retrieve, important terms, review and discussion questions, applications, and links to simulation and Internet activities.

- **Folder icons**—such as Access Activity, Collaboration, Critical Thinking, Data CD, Internet—may appear by the applications at the end of each chapter.

- Optional **Access tutorial** to learn and strengthen basic software skills; plus, one or more **Access activities** are provided in each chapter's application activities to reinforce skills being learned.

- **Internet activities** are included to bring real-world work situations into the classroom.

Simulation

A filing simulation, entitled RECORDS MANAGEMENT SIMULATION, Eighth Edition, is available for use with the textbook. The simulation provides realistic activities for filing and retrieval of both paper and electronic records in a business environment and is also compatible with standard ARMA International guidelines. This set of realistic learning materials consists of 13 filing jobs in which students practice correspondence filing in alphabetic, subject, consecutive numeric, terminal-digit numeric, and geographic filing systems. In addition, students will practice requisition/charge-out and transfer procedures. A data CD includes report sheets to be filled out by students after they complete each job, finding test forms, simulated e-mail messages, and files for use with database applications.

Study Guide

A Study Guide, which is designed to reinforce the material covered in the textbook, includes review of important terms, sample test questions, and several practical activities to supplement the textbook exercises assigned by the instructor. Solutions, or answers, to exercises and activities are given at the end of each chapter to provide immediate feed-back.

Data CD

A data CD—included in the back of the student text—contains files to complete the self-check activities in Chapters 2, 3, and 4 and end-of-chapter applications. Because an understanding of our government's hierarchy is helpful when applying alphabetic indexing rules to government names, a file that provides an overview of the structure of the U.S. local, state, and federal government is also included. Throughout the text, an icon identifies applications that require the data CD. An *Access* Basics tutorial is also included on the data CD. This tutorial teaches the basic features of *Microsoft® Access* software used in completing the database activities.

Instructor's Manual

The instructor's manual that accompanies RECORDS MANAGEMENT, Eighth Edition, provides instructors with suggested methods of instruction, teaching aids, and time schedules for various teaching situations. Teaching suggestions are also provided for each chapter as well as the answers to the review and discussion questions, solutions to the end-of-chapter applications, and the self-check activities that appear in Chapters 2, 3, and 4. The Simulation Manual section of the Instructor's Manual includes an overview of the simulation, teaching suggestions, solutions for all simulation jobs, and finding tests and their solutions. Finding-test forms for student use are provided on the data CD that comes with the simulation. Finding tests, finding-test forms, and solutions are also available on the web site for instructors.

Electronic Test Package

A flexible, easy-to-use test bank and test generator software contains objective questions for each test. The ExamView® software enables instructors to modify questions and add instructor-written questions. Questions are included for 12 chapter tests.

(NEW!) WebTutor WebTUTOR

WebTutor™ for WebCT and Blackboard combines easy-to-use course management tools, as well as chapter overviews and outlines, vocabulary flash cards, quizzes (including a Beat the Clock challenge quiz), reinforcement activities, discussion topics, Access tutorial drills, and additional content from this text's rich companion web site. Ready to use as soon as you log on—or, customize WebTutor ToolBox with web links, images, and other resources.

(NEW!) Product Web Site

A web site related to this textbook is available at http://read.swlearning.com. On this site, students can access data files, vocabulary flash cards, games that review chapter concepts, supplemental activities, and links to other web sites. Resources such as a course syllabus; sample solutions; transparency masters; finding tests, finding-test forms, and solutions to accompany the simulation; a placement test and alphabetic filing test and solutions; and an *Access* tutorial are also provided for instructors.

Acknowledgments

We are grateful to many companies and individuals who assisted in completing this extensive revision of RECORDS MANAGEMENT, Eighth Edition. Furthermore, we appreciate the help of the filing equipment and supplies manufacturers and vendors who gave time and information to the authors in their efforts to update this edition effectively.

We are especially grateful to the following individuals who served as contributing authors on this edition:

Virginia A. Jones, CRM, FAI
VAJones Associates
Newport News, VA

Dianne S. Rankin
Educational Media Development
Monticello, KY

We are also grateful to the following reviewers and instructors who offered valuable suggestions and support:

Beatriz V. Castillo
Associate Master Instructor
University of Texas
Brownsville, TX

David P. Heffley
Academic Dean
Lansdale School of Business
North Wales, PA

Sissy Copeland
Office Systems Technology Instructor
Piedmont Technical College
Greenwood, SC

Marlyce Johnson
Instructor, Office Technology
Milwaukee Area Technical College
West Allis, WI

Bruce W. Dearstyne
Professor, College of Information
  Studies
University of Maryland
College Park, MD

Donna Love
Instructor, Office Systems Technology
Gaston College
Dallas, NC

Cheryl Reindl-Johnson
Department Chairperson, Business
  Information Systems
Sinclair Community College
Dayton, OH

Trina M. Dendy
Business Technology Instructor
East Mississippi Community College
Mayhew, MS

Patricia Fredenberg
Office Technology Instructor
Milwaukee Area Technical College
Milwaukee, WI

Betty Wanielista
Office Administration Program
  Manager
Valencia Community College
Orlando, FL

In addition, special appreciation is extended to our families, friends, coworkers, and each other whose encouragement and direction have been invaluable in completing this revision. The result, we believe, is an easily understandable, instructive, up-to-date introduction to the field of records and information management.

Judy Read
Mary Lea Ginn

Contents

PART 3 Subject, Numeric, and Geographic Storage and Retrieval

PART 4 Technology and the RIM Program

The Field of Records Management

| Chapter 1 | What Is Records Management? |

Part 1 defines the field of records management and the nature and purpose of records. As you study this part, you will learn what records are and how records are used and classified. These questions and more are answered in this first part:

- How has information grown lately?
- What are records?
- How are records used and classified?
- What is the history of records management?
- What is the next stage of evolution for records and information management?
- What are the legal considerations for records management?
- What are the records management functions in organizations?
- What are some careers in records management?

What Is Records Management?

Learning Objectives

1. Discuss the challenges of the information explosion to records managers.

2. Describe the importance of records management to an organization.

3. Describe how records are classified and used in businesses.

4. Discuss relevant legislation that affects records management.

5. Describe the management functions necessary to operate a records management program effectively.

6. Identify possible careers in records management.

7. Access the web site that provides related information for this textbook.

HOW HAS INFORMATION GROWN?

Today's workers are increasing their use of information. This time in our history is frequently called the *Information Age.* Computers, so much a part of today's world, play a key role in information systems.

Did you know that the amount of new information in the world has almost doubled in the past 3 years? How much new information do you receive every day from the newspaper, radio, television, mail, electronic-mail, the Internet, magazines, and telephones? It is hard to quantify how much information comes and goes from all the listed sources! You could say that the world is in the middle of an information explosion in the Information Age.

Researchers at UC Berkeley's School of Information Management and Systems[1] wanted to find out how much information was new in 2002 compared

[1]School of Information Management and Systems, University of California, Berkeley, "How Much Information? 2003," October 27, 2003, <http://www.sims.berkeley.edu/research/projects/how-much-info-2003/execsum.htm#report> (accessed June 5, 2005).

© Getty Images/PhotoDisc

Figure 1.1 Many records are stored on optical media such as DVDs.

to a previous study completed for 1999. Findings from the study show an amazing growth of information:

How much new information was created from 1999 to 2002?

1. Print, film, magnetic, and optical storage media produced about 5 exabytes[2] of new information in 2002. Ninety-two percent of the new information was stored on magnetic media, mostly on hard disks.
2. Estimates show that the amount of new information stored on paper, film, magnetic, and optical media has about doubled in the past 3 years.
3. Information flowing through electronic channels—telephone, radio, TV, and the Internet—contained almost 18 exabytes of new information in 2002, three and a half times more than is recorded in storage media. Ninety-eight percent of this total is the information sent and received in telephone calls—including both voice and data on both fixed lines and wireless.

The proliferation of information, recent legislation, and storage of information all contribute to a growing problem for individuals, organizations, institutions, businesses, and countries: How is information managed to meet the needs of the people who need it? With so much information produced daily, how is specific information accessed when needed? Records and information management involves organizing information for retrieval. The first section in this chapter answers the question, "What is records management?"

---

[2]An exabyte contains 1,000,000,000,000,000,000 bytes or 10^{18} bytes. 2 Exabytes: Total volume of information generated in 1999. 5 Exabytes: All words ever spoken by human beings.

WHAT IS RECORDS MANAGEMENT?

What is management?

What is records management?

Management is the process of using an organization's resources to achieve specific goals through the functions of planning, organizing, leading and controlling. Information is an important and valuable business resource. To survive, businesses and organizations must have up-to-date information in the right form, at the right time, and in the right place to make management decisions.

Records management is the systematic control of all records from their creation or receipt, through their processing, distribution, organization, storage, and retrieval, to their ultimate disposition. Because information is such an important resource to organizations, the records management function also includes information management. Therefore, records management is also known as *records and information management (RIM)*.

Records management is not new. Records management has been taking place in organizations for many years. In recent years, the tragedies of the terrorist attacks on the United States and the well-known corporate scandals have affected the profession of records and information management. These events have forced senior managers in corporate America and the government to reconsider how information and records management processes should be updated and improved.

Digital Vision

Figure 1.2 Managers must consider how information and records management processes can be updated and improved.

The role of records in recent business scandals affects the business climate. Searching for remedies, Congress has enacted legislation that affects the management of records. Compliance with the new rules and new auditing standards are now part of doing business in the United States. Records managers carry out these complex responsibilities in cooperation with the Information Technology and Legal Departments in an organization.

ISO (the International Organization for Standardization) is a worldwide federation of national standards organizations. **ISO 15489** is a standard for records management policies and procedures. The purpose of this standard is to ensure that appropriate attention and protection applies to all records, and that the evidence and information they contain can be retrieved efficiently and effectively using standard practices and procedures.[3] These international standards help the records management function of an organization clarify its purpose and prove its value by managing important information.

Traditional records management is being transformed because of changes in technology. Records management is also affected by legislation related to how businesses must operate and keep records. This textbook deals with records in business organizations; however, the principles you learn should also help you understand how to use records efficiently in other types of organizations and in your personal life.

WHAT ARE RECORDS?

The term **record** has a specific meaning in records management. **ARMA International** (an association for information management professionals) defines a record as stored information, regardless of media or characteristics, made or received by an organization that is evidence of its operations and has value requiring its retention for a specific period of time.[4]

ISO 15489 defines a record as follows:

> A record is information created, received, and maintained as evidence and information by an organization or person, in pursuance of legal obligations or in the transaction of business.[5]

Records are not just any document an organization produces or receives. Some experts estimate that of all the documents an organization creates, only 10 to 15 percent qualify as records. Records management procedures for each

What is a record?

---

[3]International Organization for Standardization, *ISO 15489-1:2001, Information and Documentation—Records Management, Part 1: General* (Geneva, Switzerland: ISO, 2001).
[4]Definitions throughout this textbook are consistent with those in the *Glossary of Records and Information Management Terms* (ANSI/ARMA 10-1999) by ARMA International and *A Glossary for Archivists, Manuscript Curators, and Records Managers,* compiled by Lewis J. Bellardo and Lynn L. Bellardo (Chicago: The Society of American Archivists, 1992).
[5]Ibid: *ISO 15489-1:2001, Information and Documentation—Records Management, Part 1: General.*

organization specify which documents or information become records based on classification of records.

HOW ARE RECORDS CLASSIFIED?

Common records, such as correspondence (letters and memos), reports, forms, and books, can appear on paper, on optical or digital storage media, or on an organization's intranet pages. An organization may receive these records through regular mail, electronic mail, facsimile machines (fax), special couriers, or by accessing computer networks including the Internet and company intranets.

Other types of records to consider are oral records that capture the human voice and are stored on cassettes and other magnetic media. Records also are stored on film, CDs, DVDs, videotapes, photographs, and microfilm. Records

Figure 1.3 Computer data is a common record form.

Corbis

are valuable property, or resources, of a firm; and, like all other resources, they must be managed properly.

Usually, records are classified in three basic ways: (1) by the type of use, (2) by the place where they are used, and (3) by the value of the records to the firm.

Classification by Use

Classification according to records use includes transaction documents and reference documents. A **transaction document** is a record used in an organization's day-to-day operations. These documents consist primarily of business forms which can be created manually, electronically, or generated via e-commerce systems on the Internet. Examples are invoices, requisitions, purchase and sales orders, bank checks, statements, contracts, shipping documents, and personnel records such as employment applications, time sheets, and attendance reports.

A **reference document,** on the other hand, contains information needed to carry on the operations of a firm over long periods. These records are referenced for information about previous decisions, quotations on items to purchase, statements of administrative policy, and plans for running the organization. Common reference documents, the most frequently used category of records maintained in an office, are business letters, reports, and interoffice e-mail. Other examples include catalogs, price lists, brochures, and pamphlets.

How are records classified?

Classification by Place of Use

Classification by place of use of the records refers to external and internal records. An **external record** is created for use outside an organization. Examples of such records are letters, faxes, or e-mail sent to a customer, client, supplier, or to the various branches of the government.

Internal records are a larger group of records classified by their place of use. An **internal record** contains information needed to operate an organization. Such a record may be created inside or outside an organization. Many internal records are created through the use of e-commerce systems using databases and web server applications. Examples are communications between a firm and its employees (payroll records, bulletins, newsletters, and government regulations) and communications among a firm's departments (inventory control records, interoffice memos or e-mail, purchase requisitions, and reports).

What is the difference between external and internal records?

Classification by Value of the Record to the Firm

From an inventory and analysis of the use of each major record category, a manager determines the value of the record to the firm. This evaluation is used to develop a records retention schedule specifying how long to keep the records in an organization. Recent legislation makes records retention of critical importance. You will learn more about this in Chapter 7: Storing, Retrieving, and Transferring Records.

Some records are so valuable to a firm that they require special measures of protection. Each record maintained by a firm falls into one of four categories used to determine how records should be retained and the level of protection they require. These categories are (1) vital, (2) important, (3) useful, and (4) nonessential as shown in Figure 1.4.

WHY RECORDS ARE USED

Records serve as the memory of a business. They document the information needed for complying with regulations and the transactions of an organization. For example, management policies are developed and recorded to furnish broad guidelines for operating a business. Each department (for example, Finance, Marketing, Accounting, and Human Resources) bases its entire method of operations upon records. Usually, records are used and retained because they have one or more of the following values to a firm as shown in Figure 1.5 on page 9.

Category	Examples
Vital Records	
▪ Necessary for the continuing operation of the organization ▪ Usually not replaceable ▪ Highest degree of protection necessary	Legal papers, articles of incorporation, titles to property, reports to shareholders
Important Records	
▪ Assist in performing business operations ▪ Usually replaceable but at great cost ▪ High degree of protection necessary	Personnel records, sales records, financial and tax records, selected correspondence and reports, contracts
Useful Records	
▪ Helpful in conducting business operations ▪ Usually replaceable at slight cost ▪ Low to medium degree of protection	General correspondence and bank statements
Nonessential Records	
▪ Records have no predictable value after their initial use ▪ Lowest degree of protection	Announcements and bulletins to employees, acknowledgments and routine telephone/ e-mail messages

Figure 1.4 Records Categories

Value and Record Type	Examples
Administrative	
Records that help employees perform office operations	• Policy and procedures manuals • Handbooks • Organizational charts
Fiscal records used to document operating funds and other financial processes	• Tax returns • Records of financial transactions: purchase and sales orders, invoices, balance sheets, and income statements
Legal	
Records that provide evidence of business transactions	• Contracts • Financial agreements that are legally binding • Deeds to property owned • Articles of incorporation
Historical	
Records that document the organization's operations and major shifts of direction over the years	• Minutes of meetings • Corporate charter • Public relations documents • Information on corporate officers

Figure 1.5 Record Values and Types

From a personal standpoint, why do you keep your diploma, birth certificate, the title of ownership to your car, or the promissory note that provided you with the money to attend college? The answer is simple: In today's complex world, people cannot get along without records. They need records for the information records contain.

WHAT IS THE HISTORY OF RECORDS MANAGEMENT?

What are the earliest records of civilization? Hieroglyphics drawn on rock walls and caves reflect ancient humanity's need to tell stories. Museums of the world tell the story of ancient civilizations with artifacts and relics. How have records evolved from the beginning of time?

My Records

Do You Know Where Your Records Are?

Think quickly—where is your birth certificate? Where is the title to your car?

If you are like most people, you might not know exactly where your important records are. Do you know where you keep each of these records?

- Birth certificate
- Marriage license
- Marriage certificate
- Passport
- Diploma
- Auto insurance policy
- Life insurance policy
- Property deeds

- Tax returns for previous years
- Will
- Automobile title
- Renter's or homeowner's insurance policy
- Divorce decree
- Adoption or naturalization papers

- Military discharge papers
- Vaccination records for all family members
- Medical histories for all family members
- Pay stubs from current and previous jobs
- Stock purchases and other investment records

Each of the records listed above are either vital or important records. What degree of protection have you provided for each record? Are your records in a fire resistant container or in a safe deposit box? Follow these suggestions for keeping your vital and important records safe:

- Identify a single location to store all vital papers and information related to your financial transactions.
- Create copies of your vital records. Some of the copies may need to be certified as official copies.
- Put important original documents in plastic sheet protectors to protect and easily identify them.
- Notify family members or friends not living with you where important information will be located if disaster strikes.
- Inventory the records you and/or your financial institutions keep only on computers. Include account numbers and passwords on your inventory. Keep the inventory safe.
- Make backups of your computer records. If possible, store the backups at another location.
- Once a month, update your stored information. Has anything changed? Make another backup.

EARLY RECORDS

Most of the business records before 1600 were based upon simple trade transactions that provided evidence of money received and spent, lists of articles bought and sold, and simple contracts. These records and any copies were created by hand until the printing press and later the typewriter were invented.

Until the 1950s when computers were first used in business, records were almost entirely paper documents. The most important emphasis during this stage in history was getting the records properly placed in the files. Emphasis on retrieval surfaced later. Little importance or status was granted to records and to records management functions at this time.

Before World War II, management directed its main business efforts toward work performed in factories and plants. Usually the plant workforce was large compared with the office staff. Consequently, managers gave their main attention to the factory because the factory produced the salable products that resulted in profits and against which expenses were charged. In this setting, management assumed that records should be the sole responsibility of the office staff and not managed as an important resource.

> **What was the common form for most records until the 1950s?**

TODAY'S EVOLVING RECORDS

Starting in the early 1970s, manufacturing's proportion of the U.S. Gross Domestic Product (GDP) started to fall. Since that time, more of the GDP is produced by information services. This is a significant change from the 1950s industrial-based economy. As discussed earlier, the world is in an information explosion. The majority of business records are no longer just records of accounting transactions. Correspondence and information about customers are prevalent because these records are an important resource about the customer who buys the products or services a company sells. Records are stored on magnetic media, microforms, and optical media as well as in paper form. Fast, accurate retrieval helps a business meet customer needs.

The process of creating records, the media on which records are stored, and the ways records are used have changed greatly since the 1980s. Changes in technology facilitate changes in business methods. Additionally, technology has helped create a global marketplace, making it easier for people around the world to exchange goods and services. The scope of managing information in this environment is creating new challenges and opportunities. The next section discusses some of these trends—merely the next phase in the evolution of records and information management.

TRENDS IN RECORDS AND INFORMATION MANAGEMENT

Even though more businesses than ever are investing in new technologies, paper usage continues to be a fact of office life. This can be attributed to the increased use of equipment that enables employees to create paper records from electronic media. Copiers, printers, and facsimile machines all have the ability to interface with office computer systems to produce large volumes of paper documents.

Other reasons for continued popularity of paper are more personal and individual: paper requires no additional equipment for viewing; people can write on and annotate paper documents; and paper is easily transportable.

People who have grown up reading from a screen are comfortable with that medium. Will this comfort of reading from a screen change the dependence on printed documents? This change in work and learning methods could help reduce paper records in the future. As a consequence of the current information explosion, records managers must deal with increasing numbers of records—both paper and electronic.

Do you like to read from a computer screen?

Electronic Records

An **electronic record** is a record stored on electronic media that can be readily accessed or changed. A piece of equipment is required to view and read or listen to electronic records. With the development and use of application software on personal computers, letters, memos, and reports were created electronically; however, the purpose of these systems was to facilitate the creation of paper records. As technology has advanced, true electronic records are in use today; i.e., records created, distributed, used, and stored in electronic form. The contents of these records are accessible by machine.

The challenge for the records manager is to ensure that all records are what they appear to be. Increases in fraud and theft of electronic records have left records and information managers desperate to ensure the safety and security of the organization's valuable resources.

To that end, each person responsible for electronic records follows the records management storage and retrieval procedures set up for the office. Consistently following procedures helps protect the company in legal actions. The same benefits of following proper records management procedures for paper records also apply to electronic records: The information is available at the right time to help make effective decisions.

Electronic Mail

Electronic mail (e-mail) is a system that enables users to compose, transmit, receive, and manage electronic documents and images across networks. A variety of electronic mail systems allow users to write and send messages via computers and software.

What is electronic mail?

E-mail is now the primary mode of communication between employees in corporations and most governmental agencies. The many advantages of using e-mail include its ease of use and short delivery time. The message-delivery process of e-mail is nearly instantaneous on some networks. Unfortunately, e-mail has a potential for abuse and disaster. Records and information managers have developed policies related to electronic records for their organizations. Employees must follow the policies developed for effective and efficient management of electronic records.

Many questions related to records management and e-mail must be addressed by records managers. E-mail can be used in a court of law. What procedures are in place to respond to a court order to produce e-mail records? How do you maintain the integrity of a record? Can you keep it confidential? How long do you keep an electronic mail message? These questions are only a few of the ones that must be answered as more and more messages are sent and received electronically. Records and information managers work with Information Technology departments to determine the feasibility of storage. Many organizations are changing their archiving policies because the volume of e-mail is expanding.

Document Imaging

Document imaging is an automated system for scanning, storing, retrieving, and managing images of paper records in an electronic format. A paper document is scanned into a computer file, thus creating an electronic image of the

> **What is document imaging?**

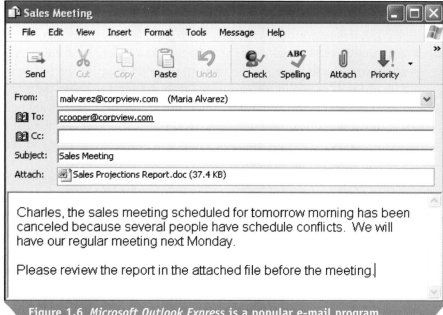

Figure 1.6 *Microsoft Outlook Express* is a popular e-mail program.

document. Scanned files are usually large; consequently, optical disk storage (discussed in Chapter 11) is recommended.

Textual data can be converted electronically using optical character recognition (OCR) software. Lists of key words are created for each scanned file. An image and text database is developed enabling a search by key words to find a document in a matter of seconds. Once found, the document can be sent to the requester by fax, computer-to-computer communication, or a hard (printed) copy. Chapter 11 includes a discussion of this technology.

The Internet and Electronic Commerce

The **Internet** is a worldwide network of computers that allows public access to send, store, and receive electronic information over public networks. The multimedia center of the Internet, the **World Wide Web,** is a worldwide hypermedia system (a network of computers that can read documents containing hyperlinks) that allows browsing in many databases. Companies, organizations, and individuals create locations, called web sites, that can be accessed by anyone who has an Internet connection.

Companies use these sites to share information about themselves and their products. They also conduct business using these sites. A broad definition of **e-commerce** is an electronic method to communicate and to transact business over networks and through computers. In other words, e-commerce is the buying and selling of goods and services using the Internet and other digital communications such as electronic funds transfer, smart cards, and digital cash.

Complex, sophisticated e-commerce systems use a combination of technology: the organization's databases, server applications, and browser software to display the transaction. For example, when you decide to buy something from an e-commerce site, you create an account. Your account information is entered into a database—you, as the user, are creating a record for the company. The record is stored in the company's database until the next time you look at the company's web site. Companies utilize "cookies," which are embedded information stored on your computer. When you visit the company site again, the cookie sends information about you to the site so that you can add purchases or edit your account.

As you buy more products, the company tracks your particular taste in products. If you haven't purchased anything for a while, an e-mail may be automatically generated to let you know of new products that match your previous purchases. The company is able to generate new business based on previous business. This process is called niche marketing, and it's available in an all-electronic format. Amazon.com is an example of a sophisticated e-commerce system with which you may be familiar.

Management of e-commerce bridges the gap between information technology, records and information management, and the company's legal departments.

> **Have you used e-commerce?**

Cooperation between and among these departments ensures a smooth flow of customer service, sales, and evidence of the transactions.

Electronic File Transfer and Data Interchange

The business processes of electronic file transfer and data interchange are another way that organizations use digital communications.

Electronic fund transfer (EFT) provides for electronic payments and collections. It is safe, secure, efficient, and less expensive than paper check payments and collections. Many organizations deposit their employees' pay by using EFT.

Electronic data interchange (EDI) is a communication procedure between two companies that allows the exchange of standardized documents (most commonly invoices or purchase orders) through computers. If the two companies have compatible systems, the computers talk to each other through a connection. For example, Company A sends a purchase order to Company B by EDI. When Company B ships the order to Company A, an invoice is created and sent to Company A, again through EDI. Company A can then pay Company B by electronic funds transfer. Thus, no paper documents are exchanged. Records and information managers should ensure that the records transmitted in this business process are authentic, correct, and usable.

The next section tells about newer technologies and processes that organizations are implementing as a way to enhance the effectiveness of records creation, distribution, storage and retrieval.

Enterprise Content Management

"**Enterprise content management (ECM)** is the term used to describe the technologies, tools, and methods used to capture, manage, store, preserve, and deliver *content* or *information* across an enterprise or organization."[6] This term and definition comes from AIIM, a global enterprise content management association. An enterprise is a business venture or company. Systems have long been in place for electronic document management (EDM) and business process management (BPM). The broader term of ECM is an attempt to deal with the complex world of information technology where one technology can become outdated and be replaced with several new ones.

What is enterprise content management?

The value of ECM is not only in its technology, but also in the activities that involve people and processes. Organizations need a solution that enables their users to share documents and provides collaborative features (such as discussion threads, calendar items, and additional project information) in a secure manner.

Many organizations realize that implementing and managing an integrated process is a challenge. Organizations must invest in risk assessments, policy

[6]"EMC Roadmap 2005," AIIM web site, <http://www.aiim.org.uk/publications/ecmroadmap/2005/index.asp> (accessed May 6, 2005).

development, training, management strategies, and other activities, as well as technology. This involves several departments in an organization that work together to make ECM work in the organization.

As with all records, ECM acknowledges that not all records are created equal. The records have business, operation, legal, and/or regulatory value as discussed earlier. ECM also works well on unstructured information that exists outside the confines of database systems. The vast majority of information in most organizations comes from e-mail, word processing documents, digital images, and PDF (portable document format) files. Industry experts place this type of information at 80 percent of all information created for a company.[7]

ECM is an up-and-coming process that will help an enterprise benefit in efficiency and effectiveness because of the combination of people, processes, and technology. Because of the information explosion, most new information is stored on some type of electronic media. Records and information management professionals are concerned about the management of these records. In the next section, you will learn about the legal considerations for records management.

What is unstructured information?

WHAT ARE THE LEGAL CONSIDERATIONS FOR RECORDS MANAGEMENT?

In 1947, concerns about the amount of paperwork generated for the federal government prompted the creation of the General Services Administration (GSA). Since that time, the GSA has been responsible for improving government practices and controls in records and information management.

The federal government's pioneer studies in records management were widely acclaimed. They provided the example and motivation needed by business, industry, and lower levels of government to study the need for records and for setting up programs for their management.

What three rights are addressed by legislation?

As the number of records increases dramatically, legislation to balance and protect an individual's right to privacy, the public's access to information, and the quest for national security also increases. When individuals' rights to privacy have been violated, the public's access to information denied, or the national security has been breached, steps need to be taken to protect these three important rights in a democratic society. These three rights are kept in balance by legislation.

Figure 1.7 on pages 17 and 18 contains a summary of key legislation related to the field of records and information management. Records and information managers are responsible for implementing phases of these laws.

How does the Privacy Act impact you?

As companies rely increasingly on information stored on a variety of media, records managers must be certain that their companies' recordkeeping

[7]Barclay T. Blair, "An Enterprise Content Management Primer," *The Information Management Journal,* September/October 2004, pp. 64-66.

Legislation and Amendments	Outcome and/or Intended Solution
General Services Administration (GSA) 1947	Improve government practices and control in records management
Freedom of Information Act, 1966 Privacy Act, 1974, 1994	Individuals have a right to see information about themselves Imposes strict rules on the government's use of records collected about individuals, requiring government agencies to permit individuals to: <ul><li>Control disclosure of information in their records</li><li>Retain records of information that is disclosed</li><li>Review and have a copy of information in their records</li><li>Request amendment of information in their records</li></ul>
Copyright Act, 1976 Intellectual Property Protection and Court Amendments of 2004	Provides copyright protection for many forms of print and media works
Right to Financial Privacy Act, 1978	<ul><li>Prevents financial institutions from requiring customers to authorize the release of financial records as a condition of doing business</li><li>States that customers have a right to access a record of all disclosures</li></ul>
Paperwork Reduction Act, 1980, 1995	To have Federal agencies become more responsible and publicly accountable for reducing the burden of Federal paperwork on the public and for other purposes
Video Privacy Protection Act, 1988	A criminal law that prohibits disclosure about videotapes individuals have rented without the informed, written consent of the individual
Computer Matching and Privacy Protection Act, 1988	<ul><li>Establishes procedural requirements for government agencies to follow when engaging in computer-matching activities</li><li>Provides matching subjects with opportunities to receive notice and to refute adverse information before having a benefit denied or terminated</li><li>Requires that agencies engaged in matching activities establish Data Protection Boards to oversee those activities</li></ul>
Electronics Signature in Global and National Commerce Act (E-SIGN), 2000	Eliminates legal barriers to the use of electronic technology to form and sign contracts, collect and store documents, and send and receive notices and disclosures
Fair Credit Reporting Act	<ul><li>Designed to promote accuracy and ensure the privacy of the information used in consumer reports</li><li>Allows controlled access to credit bureau files</li></ul>

Figure 1.7 Legislation Related to Records Management

Continued.

Legislation and Amendments	Outcome and/or Intended Solution
Health Insurance Portability and Accountability Act, Privacy Rule (HIPAA), 2001	▪ Creates national standards to protect individuals' medical records and other personal health information ▪ Gives patients more control over their health information ▪ Sets boundaries on the use and release of health records ▪ Establishes appropriate safeguards that health care providers and others must achieve to protect the privacy of health information
Patriot Act, 2001 (In response to the terrorist attacks on September 11, 2001)	▪ Allows investigators to use the tools already available to investigate possible terrorist activities ▪ Facilitates information sharing and cooperation among government agencies ▪ Updates the law to reflect new technologies and new threats
Sarbanes-Oxley Act, 2002	Passed in response to a number of major corporate and accounting scandals, this law ▪ Enhances standards for all U.S. public company boards, management, and public accounting firms ▪ Strengthens corporate governance

Figure 1.7 Continued.

systems are legally acceptable to governmental agencies and courts of law. Compliance issues are a concern to many organizations. Records management professionals are working together in organizations such as ARMA International and AIIM to optimize the effectiveness of records and information management to their organizations.

WHAT ARE RECORDS MANAGEMENT FUNCTIONS IN ORGANIZATIONS?

As noted earlier, management is the process of using an organization's resources to achieve specific goals through the functions of planning, organizing, leading, and controlling.

What are the four functions of management?

- **Planning** involves establishing goals or objectives and the methods required to achieve them.
- With the firm's goals in mind, **organizing** involves arranging the tasks, people, and other resources needed to meet the goals set in the planning stage.
- **Leading** refers to managerial behavior (such as training, supervising, and motivating) that supports the achievement of an organization's goals.
- Finally, **controlling** involves measuring how well the goals have been met.

Keep these four functions in mind when you study the management of records. Also, observe how you manage because you, too, perform these steps when you manage your study time, money, and social and professional life.

THE LIFE CYCLE OF RECORDS

As a manager, you must see the whole picture, which involves understanding the four managerial functions discussed earlier and how each relates to the other. In the same way, managing records involves clearly understanding the phases making up the life cycle of a record.

As Figure 1.8 shows, the **record life cycle** is the life span of a record as expressed in the five phases of creation, distribution, use, maintenance, and final disposition. The phases of the life cycle often overlap. Note how this cycle is carried out.

Whenever a letter is produced, an e-mail written, a form completed, or a pamphlet printed, a record is created. This record is then distributed (sent) to the person responsible for its use. Records are commonly used in decision

What are the phases of the record life cycle?

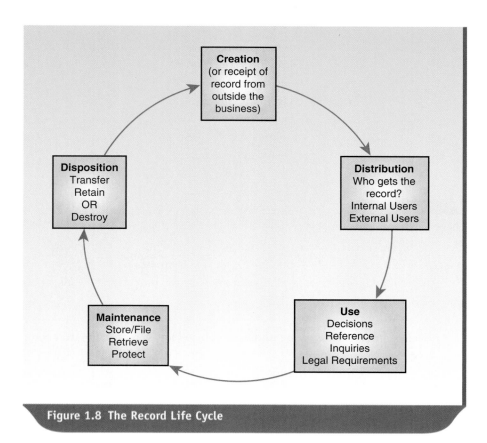

Figure 1.8 The Record Life Cycle

making, for documentation or reference, in answering inquiries, or in satisfying legal requirements.

When a decision is made to keep the record for use at a later date, it must be stored, retrieved, and protected—three key steps in the maintenance of records. During this phase, the records must be stored (filed), which involves preparing and placing records into their proper storage place. After a record is stored, a request is made to retrieve (find and remove) it from storage for use. When the retrieved record is no longer needed for active use, it may be re-stored and protected, using appropriate equipment and environmental and human controls to ensure record security. Also involved in the maintenance phase are activities such as updating stored information and throwing away obsolete records that are no longer useful or that have been replaced by more current ones.

The last phase in the record life cycle is disposition. After a predetermined period of time has elapsed, records to be kept are transferred to less expensive storage sites within the firm or to an external records storage facility. At the end of the number of years indicated in the retention schedule, the records are disposed of, either by destruction or by transfer to a permanent storage place. The facilities where records of an organization are preserved because of their continuing or historical value are called the **archives.** The records retention schedule is discussed in detail in Chapter 7.

The record life cycle is an important concept for you to understand. It shows, for example, that filing is only one part of records and information management. Many interrelated parts must work together for an effective records and information management program. Knowing the meaning and importance of each part of the entire record life cycle, you will be able to understand what is needed to manage all records—those on paper and those stored on other media such as magnetic media or microforms.

Why is filing only one part of records and information management?

PROGRAMS FOR MANAGING RECORDS

As mentioned earlier, a records program must be in place to manage all phases in the record life cycle. Although the contents of records and information management programs vary, such programs generally have these features:

1. Well-defined goals that are understood by all workers (See Figure 1.9 on page 21 for an example.)
2. A simple, sound organizational plan
3. Efficient procedures for managing each of the five stages in the record life cycle (See Figure 1.8. You will study these procedures in detail in Chapter 12.)

XYZ COMPANY

GOALS OF THE RECORDS AND INFORMATION MANAGEMENT PROGRAM

1. To provide accurate, timely information whenever and wherever it is needed.

2. To provide information at the lowest possible cost.

3. To provide the most efficient records systems, including space, equipment, and procedures for creating, storing, retrieving, retaining, transferring, and disposing of records.

4. To protect information by designing and implementing effective measures for records control.

5. To determine methods for evaluating all phases of the records and information management program.

6. To train company personnel in the most effective methods of controlling and using records.

Figure 1.9 Goals of a Records and Information Management Program

4. A well-trained staff (See the "Careers in Records Management" section later in this chapter.)

Sometimes, the program is **centralized** (records are physically located and controlled in one area); in other cases, it is **decentralized** (records are physically located in the departments where they are created and used). Each plan offers advantages and disadvantages that managers should consider carefully before deciding on an organizational plan. In large firms where work can be specialized, computers and other information systems, as shown in Figure 1.10 on page 22, play a major role in records and information management.

PROBLEMS IN RECORDS SYSTEMS

The programs for managing records discussed earlier achieve their goals through the operation of an organization's records system. In this sense, a **records system** is a group of interrelated resources—people, equipment and supplies, space, procedures, and information—acting together according to a plan to accomplish the goals of the records and information management program. Anything that interferes with the operation of one or more of these resources, either individually or in combination, creates a problem in the records

> **What are common problems in records systems?**

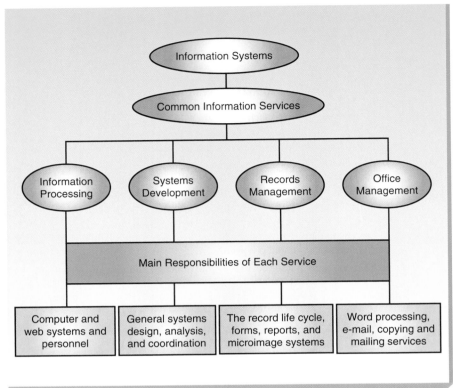

Figure 1.10 Location of Records Management in a Large Organization

system and, therefore, hinders the effectiveness of the records and information management program. Common problems in records systems and typical symptoms of such problems are listed in Figure 1.11 on page 23.

To resolve such problems, managers frequently turn to various forms of information technology. Solutions may include company-wide computer systems, microfilm systems, and image systems. These systems, however, are not a panacea for records-related problems. Nor do they eliminate the use of paper. Companies still rely on paper, and this situation will continue because of the ease of producing paper copies with computers and copying machines.

The paper records system is the best place to begin a study of records management. Good records and information management principles are universal. They can and should be applied to electronic systems as well. Additionally, the tangible nature of paper records, the fact that paper records are familiar to most people, and that such records can be located easily make the study of paper records the logical introduction to the records and information management field. From such study, you need to understand alphabetic storage and retrieval systems discussed in Part 2 along with subject, numeric, and geographic storage and retrieval systems explained in Part 3.

Problem	Symptoms
Management	▪ No overall plan for managing records problems ▪ No plan for retaining or destroying records ▪ No standards for evaluating workers
Human problems	▪ Lack of concern about the importance of records ▪ Hoarding of records ▪ Assuming that people know how to use the files for storage and retrieval of records
Inefficient filing procedures	▪ Computer files not organized into folders ▪ Overloaded and poorly labeled drawers and folders ▪ Failure to protect records ▪ Misfiles resulting in lost records or slow retrieval ▪ Records removed from and placed in files without proper authorization
Poor use of equipment	▪ No equipment standards ▪ No use of fire-resistant equipment ▪ Improper type of storage containers for records ▪ Lack of or improper use of automated systems
Inefficient use of space	▪ Crowded working conditions ▪ Poor layout of storage area ▪ Resistance to the use of magnetic media
Excessive records costs	▪ Inefficiency due to the above problems

Figure 1.11 Common Problems in Records Systems

CAREERS IN RECORDS MANAGEMENT

Opportunities to work with records exist in every type and size of office. In a small office with one administrative assistant and an owner/manager, working with records occupies much of the time of both people. In this setting, opportunities for records work are unlimited. The classified ads section of daily newspapers lists many general positions in small offices.

> **What opportunities for work exist for records management?**

Another potential career connected to records and information management is the marketing of records supplies and storage equipment. Offices need the paper, folders, file cabinets, shelves, and other supplies and equipment that are necessary for records storage and retrieval. Office supply vendors are an important resource to a records and information management department. A career as a marketing service representative for an office supplies company offers growth opportunities.

Larger firms with more specialized staff often employ records supervisors who direct the work of several records clerks. In major corporations or other large administrative headquarters, you can find levels of records workers as shown in Figure 1.12 and described below.

1. **Managerial level,** where the top position is the records manager who is responsible for directing the entire program.
2. **Supervisory level,** which includes specialists responsible for operating the records center, supervising the design and use of business forms, and directing the creation and use of microfilm records.
3. **Operating level,** which includes those workers responsible for routine filing and retrieving tasks, and assisting with vital records and records retention work. Because this is the level of work emphasized in this textbook, you will concentrate on the basic principles involved in storing and retrieving records.

Companies that place a high value on their information resources have created a new position to oversee all information-related departments, including Records and Information Management. These new positions are variously titled "Chief Information Officer" (CIO) or "Chief Knowledge Officer" (CKO).

Many experienced records and information management professionals have become Certified Records Managers (CRMs) by taking and passing a multipart test administered by members of the Institute of Certified Records Managers (ICRM). This certification represents a standard by which persons involved in records and information management can be measured, accredited, and recognized according to criteria of experience and capability established by their peers. Each individual is experienced in active and inactive

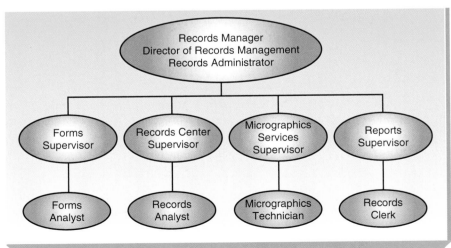

Figure 1.12 Typical Job Levels and Job Titles in Records Management

records systems and related areas such as archives, computer technology, micrographics, and optical disk technology. The CRM designation is earned by meeting both educational and work experience requirements and by passing the required examinations.[8]

In times of economic downsizing, many organizations are outsourcing portions of their records and information management services such as inactive records storage. Because inactive records may be kept for a long period of time but may not be referenced often, records storage facilities are usually located offsite in lower rent districts. Many companies offer storage and retrieval services for several types of businesses. Career opportunities exist in these records and information management service businesses.

You can easily locate information on the records and information management profession by checking the publications and web sites of the various professional associations specializing in the records and information management

CAREER CORNER

Interview with Josh Butler, Records Management Customer Service Associate

Josh Butler is a Records Management Customer Service Associate for Iron Mountain Incorporated at the Portland, Oregon, office. When Josh accepted a position from Iron Mountain, he was attracted by the company's reputation and mission. Josh's background includes a Bachelor of Science degree.

He started attending the Oregon Chapter of ARMA International to learn more about records management. The educational programs from ARMA were helpful to Josh. He filled in as the treasurer of the chapter, and now he's the president of the Oregon Chapter for 2005.

When asked about current issues in records and information management, Josh responded, "The amount of new information is amazing. People are starting to realize the need to better manage electronic records. Integration of paper and electronic records is the next big issue in records and information management."

Josh advises students to join ARMA and to learn as much as they can about the importance of records. He noted that students should have an understanding of both paper and electronic records.

---

[8]Visit the Institute of Certified Records Managers web site for more information about the ICRM and the CRM examination. You can find a link to this site at web site for this textbook at <http://read.swlearning.com>.

What is ARMA International?

profession. ARMA International is an important professional group interested in improving educational programs in schools and industry and providing on-the-job knowledge about records and information management. ARMA members receive subscriptions to *The Information Management Journal.* Learn more about ARMA International at the organization's web site. You can find a link to this site at the web site for this textbook at http://read.swlearning.com.

Information on records management jobs can be found in the *Occupational Outlook Handbook.* This handbook is published by U.S. Bureau of Labor Statistics and is available online. O*NET, the Occupational Information Network, is a comprehensive database of worker attributes and job characteristics. As the replacement for the *Dictionary of Occupational Titles* (DOT), O*NET is the primary source of occupational information in the United States. O*NET may also be accessed online. You can find links to these two sites at the web site for this textbook.

AIIM is the international authority on enterprise content management, the tools and technologies that capture, manage, store, preserve, and deliver content in support of business processes. AIIM provides subscriptions to two electronic publications, *E-DOC Magazine* and *M-iD Magazine—Managing Information and Documents.* Learn more about AIIM at their web site. You can find a link to this site at the web site for this textbook.

AHIMA (American Health Information Management Association) is specifically for health and related industry records and information managers. AHIMA provides members subscriptions to the *Journal of AHIMA* as well as information about careers, schools, and online courses. Learn more about AHIMA at the organization's web site. You can find a link to this site at the web site for this textbook. Records and information management is universal in its concepts; however, medical records procedures are unique. This text does not cover managing medical records.

Chapter Review And Applications

POINTS TO FILE AND RETRIEVE

- The information age is in an information explosion.

- Records and information management is the systematic control of all records from creation to disposition.

- Records are used to document information needed for complying with regulations and transactions of an organization.

- Legislation balances and protects an individual's right to privacy, the public's access to information, and the quest for national security.

- Management functions include planning, organizing, leading, and controlling.

- The life cycle of records includes creation, distribution, use, maintenance, and disposition.

- Career opportunities in records and information management are available in small, medium, and large offices.

IMPORTANT TERMS

archives
ARMA International
document imaging
e-commerce
electronic data interchange (EDI)
electronic fund transfer (EFT)
electronic mail (e-mail)
electronic record
enterprise content management
  (ECM)
external record
important records
internal record

Internet
ISO 15489
management
nonessential records
record
record life cycle
records management
records system
reference document
transaction document
useful records
vital records
World Wide Web

REVIEW AND DISCUSSION

1. Describe the information explosion. (Obj. 1)

2. What is the role of records and information management in an organization? (Obj. 2)

3. What is the purpose of ISO 15489? (Obj. 2)

4. What are the main classifications for records? What types of records are commonly found in each classification? (Obj. 3)

5. Why are records used in businesses? (Obj. 3)

6. What is the intended outcome of the Sarbanes-Oxley Act? (Obj. 4)

7. List the phases in the record life cycle and describe the activities that occur during each phase. What phases, if any, do you eliminate in your own personal records cycle? Why? (Obj. 5)

8. What are some common problems found in records systems? (Obj. 5)

9. How can you best prepare for work and advancement in records and information management positions? (Obj. 6)

10. Describe two benefits available for members of ARMA International. (Obj. 6)

APPLICATIONS

1-1 CLASSIFYING RECORDS (OBJ. 3)

COLLABORATION

DATA CD

1. Work in a team with two or three classmates to complete this application. Visit a business. Ask the person you visit to share with you five examples of the records of the business.

2. Open the *Microsoft® Word* file *1-1 Classification* from the data files. Record each business record by name in the first chart in the data file. Working with your teammates, decide how each record should be classified—by use, by place of use, or by value to the firm. Key an **x** in the appropriate column on the chart for each record.

3. List the records again in the second chart in the data file. Working with your teammates, decide how each record should be classified—vital, important, useful, or nonessential. Key an **x** in the appropriate column on the chart for each record.

4. Compare your charts and records with another team in the class. Discuss the reasons for any differences in the way you classified the records.

5. Analyze the records from the business. Why did the business develop each record? How will each record help that company conduct business?

1-2 RECORDS MANAGEMENT WEB SITE DISCOVERY (OBJ. 3)

The publisher of this textbook maintains a site on the World Wide Web where you can access data files, supplementary activities, and links to other sites you need to visit as you complete applications. You will explore this site in this application.

INTERNET

1. Access the Internet and go to http://read.swlearning.com.

2. Add this site to your Favorites or Bookmarks list. Use the Favorites or Bookmarks link for quick access to this site in later activities.

3. Browse the site to become familiar with it. Where do you find the data file needed for Chapter 1?

4. Where do you find the links to related sites?

5. Where do you find the supplemental activities to enhance your learning?

6. Submit the answers to questions 2, 3, and 4 in an e-mail to your instructor.

1-3 USING TECHNOLOGY (OBJ. 1)

INTERNET

1. Access a search engine on the Internet. Search using the key words *information explosion*.

2. Follow at least three links in the search results list. Read and summarize the article or other information you find at each of the three sites.

3. Send an e-mail to your instructor that contains the summary of your findings.

ACCESS BASICS

As you complete later chapters of this textbook and the related simulation, you will use *Microsoft® Access* database software for electronic records management. Before completing these activities, you should complete the *Access Basics* tutorial (found on the CD in the back of this textbook and on the web site for this textbook). This tutorial will allow you to review or learn the basics of using *Access*. The tutorial is provided in PDF files. You will need a program such as *Adobe® Acrobat® Reader®* to view or print the tutorial. A link is provided on the web site for this textbook that will take you to a site where you can download *Acrobat Reader*.

Access data files for use in completing the tutorial and other applications are provided on the CD in the back of this textbook and on the web site for this textbook. To use an *Access* data file, you should first copy the file from the CD or web site to a working folder on a hard drive or a removable storage device. Directions for copying files using *Microsoft® Windows® Explorer* are provided in the *Access Basics* tutorial.

If you are an experienced *Access* user, read the tutorial to review *Access* concepts. Follow the instructions provided to learn to use any *Access* features with which you are not familiar. If you have little or no experience using *Access*, read and complete each lesson carefully to learn to use the basic features of *Access*.

FOR MORE ACTIVITIES GO TO **http://read.swlearning.com**

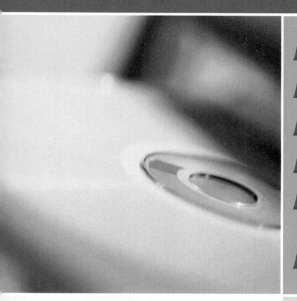

Alphabetic Storage and Retrieval

Part 2 highlights the rules for alphabetic storage and retrieval systems. The ten rules studied in Chapters 2, 3, and 4 are based on the ARMA International general alphabetic indexing rules. Chapter 5 discusses managing electronic records. Chapter 6 presents the equipment, supplies, and procedures used in correspondence records management systems. Principles and procedures for storing, retrieving, and transferring records are discussed in Chapter 7.

Corbis

2

Alphabetic Indexing Rules 1-4

Learning Objectives

1. Explain the need for indexing rules in alphabetic storage of records and the importance of following these rules consistently.

2. Index, code, and arrange personal and business names in indexing order of units.

3. Index, code, and arrange minor words and symbols in business names.

4. Index, code, and arrange personal and business names with punctuation and possessives.

5. Index, code, and arrange personal and business names with single letters and abbreviations.

6. Apply alphabetic filing procedures.

7. Prepare and arrange cross-references for personal and business names.

8. Sort paper records.

9. Find information in database records.

NEED FOR ALPHABETIC ORDER

How do business records help decision makers?

As you studied in Chapter 1, records serve as the memory of an organization. Records also help an organization conduct business. Business records help provide decision makers with the right information when it is needed. To store records in an efficient way, some type of filing or storing method must be used. A **filing method,** sometimes called a *storage method,* describes the way in which records are stored in a container, such as a filing cabinet. This text presents alphabetic, subject, numeric, and geographic methods of storage. Alphabetic storage is discussed in Chapters 2 to 7, subject storage in Chapter 8, numeric storage in Chapter 9, and geographic storage in Chapter 10. The most common filing method is alphabetic.

The alphabetic filing method is a method of storing records arranged according to the letters of the alphabet. Sounds simple, right? Everyone knows the alphabet. However, consistently accurate alphabetic filing is not that simple.

Look in the telephone books of two major cities, and you will find major discrepancies in the order of the listings. Another example is filing under the letters *Mc*. *Mc* is not one of the 26 letters of the alphabet; however, it is included in some alphabetic filing systems and not in others.

Filing Rules

The most important filing concept to remember is that all filing is done to facilitate retrieving information when it is needed. To retrieve information efficiently, a set of rules must be followed. Different businesses have different needs for information retrieval. Businesses do not all follow a universal set of rules for alphabetic filing because the goals and needs of businesses vary. ARMA International has published *Establishing Alphabetic, Numeric, and Subject Filing Systems,*[1] containing standard rules for storing records alphabetically. By using ARMA International's alphabetic indexing rules, businesses have a place to start setting up an efficient alphabetic storage system. The rules in this textbook are written to agree with the standard filing rules presented in *Establishing Alphabetic, Numeric and Subject Filing Systems* published by ARMA International.

Procedures for storing records alphabetically vary among organizations and among departments within organizations. Therefore, the filing procedures to be used in any *one* office must be determined, recorded, approved, and followed with no deviation. Without written rules for storing records alphabetically, procedures will vary with time, changes in personnel, and oral explanations. Unless those who maintain the records are consistent in following storage procedures, locating records will be difficult. The real test of an efficient records storage system is being able to find records quickly once they have been stored.

Why are written rules needed for filing?

If you thoroughly understand the rules in this textbook, you will be able to adjust to any exceptions encountered in the specific office where you may work. Records managers who adopt these rules for their offices will find them understandable, logical, workable, and comprehensive enough to provide answers to the majority of storage questions that arise.

Alphabetic filing procedures involve inspecting, indexing, coding, cross-referencing, sorting, and storing documents. In this chapter, you will practice four of the steps: indexing, coding, cross-referencing, and sorting. In Chapter 6 you will learn to complete the other steps for alphabetic filing procedures.

---

[1]ARMA International, *Establishing Alphabetic, Numeric and Subject Filing Systems* (Lenexa, KS: ARMA International, 2005), pp. 17-22.

Indexing

Indexing is the mental process of determining the filing segment (or name) by which a record is to be stored and the placing or listing of items in an order that follows a particular system. The **filing segment** is the name by which a record is stored and requested. In alphabetic storage, the process of indexing means determining the name that is to be used in filing. The name is usually easily recognized. On correspondence, the name may appear in various places on a record. In the letter shown in Figure 2.1, the filing segment is the name of the person to whom the letter is addressed.

Because accurate indexing is necessary for quick retrieval, the indexing step is extremely important. Careful, accurate indexing is perhaps the most exacting step in the storage procedure. In an alphabetic arrangement, the selection of the right name by which to store (the filing segment) means that the record will be found quickly when it is needed. If the wrong name is selected, much time will be wasted trying to locate the record when it is eventually requested.

When selecting a filing segment, choose the name most likely to be used in asking for the record, usually the most important one. You will learn more

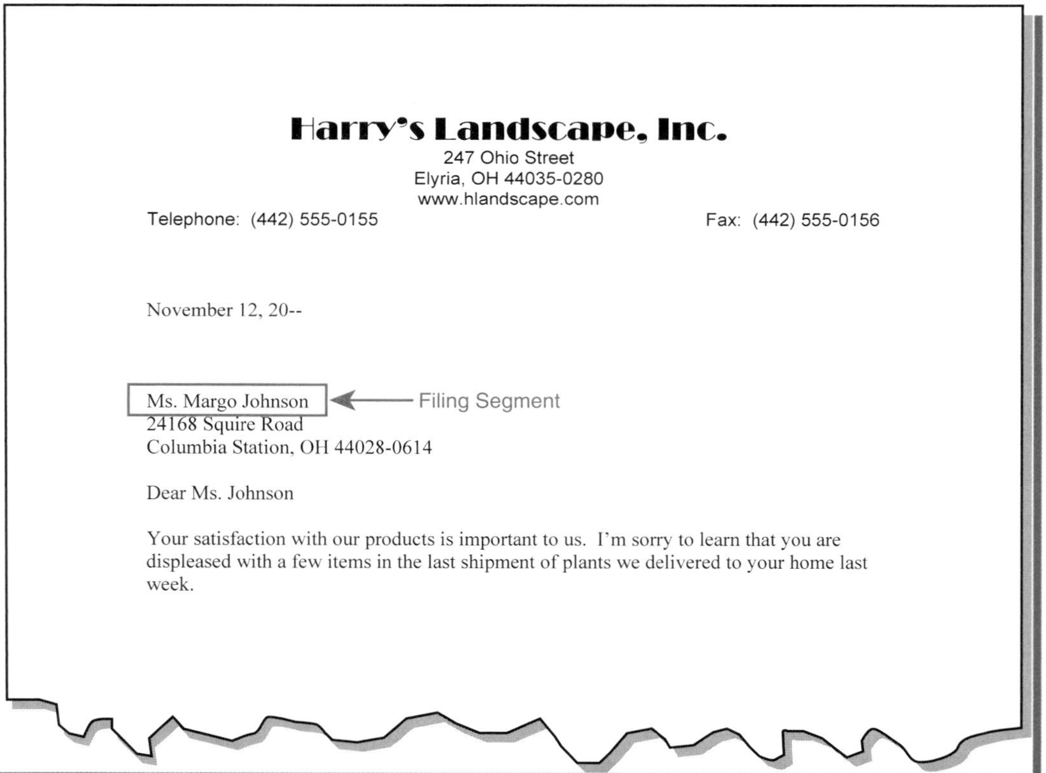

What is indexing?

What is a filing segment?

Harry's Landscape, Inc.

247 Ohio Street
Elyria, OH 44035-0280
www.hlandscape.com

Telephone: (442) 555-0155   Fax: (442) 555-0156

November 12, 20--

Ms. Margo Johnson   ◄——— Filing Segment
24168 Squire Road
Columbia Station, OH 44028-0614

Dear Ms. Johnson

Your satisfaction with our products is important to us. I'm sorry to learn that you are displeased with a few items in the last shipment of plants we delivered to your home last week.

Figure 2.1 Filing Segment on a Letter

about choosing the filing segment for documents in Chapter 6. Take a look at the examples shown in Figure 2.2. Each part of the name is labeled with a unit designation *(Key Unit, Unit 2, Unit 3,* or *Unit 4).* These units are the **indexing units** of the filing segment; in other words, the indexing units are the various words that make up the filing segment.

The **key unit** is the first unit of a filing segment. It is the part of the segment considered first when determining where the record will be stored. Units 2, 3, 4, and so on are the next units by which the placement of the record is further determined. The order in which units of the filing segment are considered is called the **indexing order.** Identifying the key and succeeding units makes a complex process simpler and easier to handle. Marking these units is the next step in the process.

Coding

Coding is the act of assigning a file designation to records as they are classified. For paper records, coding is marking a record to indicate the filing segment (name, number, or subject) by which it is to be stored and indicating the indexing units. Coding is a physical act, as contrasted with indexing, which is a mental determination.

What is coding?

Coding procedures for this book for paper records are to place diagonals (/) between the parts of the filing segment, underline the key unit, and then number each succeeding unit (i.e., 2, 3, 4), which you have mentally identified in the indexing process. The filing segments shown in Figure 2.2 are coded in this manner.

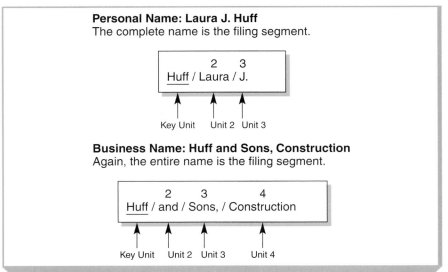

Personal Name: Laura J. Huff
The complete name is the filing segment.

$$\text{Huff} / \text{Laura} / \text{J.}$$
Key Unit Unit 2 Unit 3

Business Name: Huff and Sons, Construction
Again, the entire name is the filing segment.

Huff / and / Sons, / Construction
Key Unit Unit 2 Unit 3 Unit 4

Figure 2.2 Coded Filing Segments for Personal and Business Names

To code properly, a set of rules for alphabetic storage must be faithfully followed. **Indexing rules** are the written procedures that describe how the filing segments are ordered. The indexing rules that follow give you a good start in following appropriate alphabetic storage procedures.

ALPHABETIC INDEXING RULES

What is an effective way to study alphabetic indexing rules?

In this section, rules for alphabetic storage are presented with examples to help you understand how to apply the rules. Study each rule and the examples of its application carefully; above all, be sure you understand the rule.

Follow these guidelines to study the indexing rules effectively:

- Read the rule carefully. Make sure you understand the meaning of the words used to state the rule.
- Look at the examples. Note that the complete filing segment (the name and other words, such as a title) is given at the left. Then the filing segment is separated into indexing units at the right according to the rule you are studying.
- Be sure you understand why the filing segment has been separated as it has.

In determining alphabetic order, compare the units in the filing segments for differences. If the key units are alike, move to the second units, the third units, and succeeding units until a difference occurs. The point of difference determines the correct alphabetic order, as shown here. Compare the three filing segments shown in units and note the correct order.

Filing Segment	Key Unit	Unit 2	Unit 3
Diane Ruhl	Ruhl	Diane	
Diane M. Ruhl	Ruhl	Diane	M
Dianne Ruhl	Ruhl	Dianne	

In an office, filing records goes much more quickly when filers are able to determine the proper indexing order of personal and business names on the records. Filing records based on incorrect indexing order can result in lost records or additional time required when users want to retrieve records.

When working with paper documents, the next step in the filing process is sorting. **Sorting** is arranging records in the sequence in which they are to be stored (placed in filing cabinets or other storage containers). In this chapter, you will practice sorting slips of paper that simulate paper documents.

Examples are provided for each alphabetic indexing rule. In the examples, you will find an underscore in one of the indexing units for each filing segment except the first one. This underscore indicates the letter of the unit that determines alphabetic order. Examples are numbered for ease in referring to them. Indexing units are shown in mixed case. Marks that appear over or under some letters in different languages are disregarded (such as Señora, Marçal, René, Valhallavägen). Be sure you understand each rule before going to the next.

Rule 1: Indexing Order of Units

A. Personal Names

A personal name is indexed in this manner: (1) the surname (last name) is the key unit, (2) the given name (first name) or initial is the second unit, and (3) the middle name or initial is the third unit. If determining the surname is difficult, consider the last name written as the surname. (You will learn how to handle titles that appear with names in a later rule.)

A unit consisting of just an initial precedes a unit that consists of a complete name beginning with the same letter—*nothing before something*. Punctuation is omitted. Remember, the underscored letter in the example shows the correct order. For example, 1 and 2 below have the same Key Unit *(Sample)*. The underscored "D" in *Darin* shows the alphabetic difference between the two names.

> **What does "nothing before something" mean?**

Examples of Rule 1A

Filing Segment	Indexing Order of Units		
Name	**Key Unit**	**Unit 2**	**Unit 3**
1. Charlene Sample	Sample	Charlene	
2. Darin Sample	Sample	Darin	
3. Darlene A. Samples	Samples	Darlene	A
4. Jeff Simmons	Simmons	Jeff	
5. Neil S. Simon	Simon	Neil	S
6. Paula Simon	Simon	Paula	
7. Neil S. Simone	Simone	Neil	S
8. Michelle Skrzynski	Skrzynski	Michelle	
9. Robert Sunderland	Sunderland	Robert	
10. Roberta Sunderland	Sunderland	Roberta	
11. Andrew Taylor	Taylor	Andrew	
12. Andy Taylor	Taylor	Andy	
13. Anne M. Taylor	Taylor	Anne	M
14. Armand R. Taylor	Taylor	Armand	R
15. Joyce Utterbock	Utterbock	Joyce	

B. Business Names

What does "as written" mean?

Business names are indexed *as written* using letterheads or trademarks as guides. Each word in a business name is a separate unit. Business names containing personal names are indexed as written.

Examples of Rule 1B

Filing Segment	Indexing Order of Units		
Name	**Key Unit**	**Unit 2**	**Unit 3**
1. Samantha Seger Designs	Samantha	Seger	Designs
2. Secure Design	Secure	Design	
3. Secure Digital Networks	Secure	Digital	Networks
4. Sester Farms Inc.	Sester	Farms	Inc
5. Settlement Professionals Inc.	Settlement	Professionals	Inc
6. Shelly Sherman Photography	Shelly	Sherman	Photography
7. Sherman Auto Sales	Sherman	Auto	Sales
8. Silver Pizza Co.	Silver	Pizza	Co
9. Silverwood Apartments	Silverwood	Apartments	
10. Silvin Painting Inc.	Silvin	Painting	Inc

Rule 1 Self-Check

DATA CD

1. Open the *Word* file *2 Check Rule 1* found in the data files or write the names below on a piece of paper. Identify the units in the filing segments (names). Place diagonals between the units. Underline the key unit and number the remaining units. See the example below.

>   2   3
> Alice / S. / <u>Roberts</u>

a. Thi Dien Personnel Inc.

b. Latasha Gregory

c. Edward Simmons

d. Greg Simmons Car Company

e. Albert Brown Suit Shop

f. Elbert Albert

g. Thi Dien

h. T. F. Simmons

i. Dien Dry Cleaners

j. Anna C. Dien

2. Compare the key units and the other units, if needed, to determine the correct alphabetic filing order for the names. Indicate the correct filing order by writing or keying numbers 1 through 10 beside the names.

3. Are the two names in each of the following pairs in correct alphabetic order? If not, explain why they are not.

a. Dahlin Clothing Store
   Charlotte Dahling

b. Rose Andrews
   Rose Garden Nursery

c. Rayburn Law Office
   Rayborn Electrical Co.

d. Little Pond Productions
   Lyle A. Little

e. David Allen
   Allen Furniture Company

f. Rosalie Simmons
   Rod Simmons

g. Kent Wade
   Wade Eves Designs

h. Red Robin Restaurant
   Red Robin Bait Shop

i. Tewksbury Ornamental Plants
   Olivia Tewksbury

j. Gerald Minton
   G. L. Minton

4. Are the names in each group listed in correct order? If not, show the correct order by rearranging the numbers. See the example below.

```
            2
 1. Michael / Brown
            2        3
 2. Michael / Brown / Consulting
            2        3
 3. Brown's / Shoe / Store
    Ans: 1, 3, 2
```

a. 1. Mark Joackims
   2. Vicky Jolly
   3. Ardis Johnson

b. 1. Zelda Bruss
   2. Bruss Flower Arranging
   3. Ryan T. Bruss

c. 1. Linda Podany
   2. Daniel Potter
   3. Maria Ponzi

d. 1. Miranda Moore
   2. Miranda's Hobbies
   3. Miranda A. Moore

e. 1. Richard Pope
   2. Popeye's Deli
   3. Theresa Pope

f. 1. Carroll Guest
   2. Edgar Guest
   3. Ella May Guest

5. The answers to this exercise are shown in the *Word* file *2 Check Answers* found in the data files. Compare them with your answers.

My Records

What is Identity Theft?

Beware! Identity theft is on the rise. Might you be one of the estimated 7 to 10 million victims per year?

Identify theft is a serious crime in which an impostor obtains key pieces of information about you, such as your Social Security number (SSN) and/or driver's license number, and uses your information for his or her personal gain. Impostors use this information to impersonate their victims, spending as much money as they can in as short a time as possible before finding another victim's name and identifying information.

Account takeover identity theft occurs when a thief steals your existing credit account information and purchases products and services using either the actual credit card or simply the account number and the expiration date.

Application fraud identity theft occurs when a thief uses your SSN and other identifying information to open new accounts in your name. Victims of application fraud are not likely to learn about it for some time because the monthly account statements are mailed to an address used by the impostor.

Federal legislation holds victims of credit and banking fraud liable for no more than the first $50 of the loss. However, victims of identity theft can spend months or years clearing their good names and credit records. Victims may also lose job opportunities, be refused loans or housing, or even get arrested for crimes committed by the identity thief.[1]

[1] Adapted from the Federal Trade Commission—Your National Resource for ID Theft, <http://www.consumer.gov/idtheft/html> (accessed May 29, 2005).

What is identity theft?

Learn more about identity theft at the U.S. Department of Justice CyberCrime web site. You can find the URL in the Links section of the web site for this textbook. Preventing identity theft is the subject of My Records in Chapter 3, and recovering from identity theft is the subject of My Records in Chapter 4.

Figure 2.3 U.S. Department of Justice CyberCrime Web Site

Rule 2: Minor Words and Symbols in Business Names

Articles, prepositions, conjunctions, and symbols are considered separate indexing units. Symbols are considered as spelled in full. When the word *The* appears as the first word of a business name, it is considered the last indexing unit.

How are symbols indexed?

Articles: a, an, the
Prepositions: at, in, out, on, off, by, to, with, for, of, over
Conjunctions: and, but, or, nor
Symbols: &, ¢, $, #, % (and, cent *or* cents, dollar *or* dollars, number *or* pound, percent)

Examples of Rule 2

Filing Segment	Indexing Order of Units			
Name	**Key Unit**	**Unit 2**	**Unit 3**	**Unit 4**
1. A & A Drilling	A	and	A	Drilling
2. A Clean House	A	Clean	House	
3. The An Dong Market	An	Dong	Market	The
4. Dollar Drug Store	Dollar	Drug	Store	
5. The $ Shop	Dollar	Shop	The	
6. Golf By The Mountain	Golf	By	The	Mountain
7. Gone But Not Forgotten	Gone	But	Not	Forgotten
8. Gone To The Dogs	Gone	To	The	Dogs
9. Granger & Graves Yachts	Granger	and	Graves	Yachts
10. # One Copy Store	Number	One	Copy	Store

Rule 2 Self-Check

1. Open the *Word* file *2 Check Rule 2* found in the data files or write the names below on a piece of paper. Identify the units in the filing segments (names). Place diagonals between the units. Underline the key unit and number the remaining units.

   a. The Chimney Sweepers
   b. The Crazy Fox
   c. A Shop of Wonders
   d. An Honorable Store
   e. C & R Offerings

   f. Camp By The Sea
   g. C & R Company
   h. The Clip Joint
   i. $ Saver Cleaners
   j. Cybersurf By The Hour

2. Compare the key units and the other units, if needed, to determine the correct alphabetic filing order for the names. Indicate the correct filing order by writing or keying numbers 1 through 10 beside the names.

3. The answers to this exercise are shown in the *Word* file *2 Check Answers* found in the data files. Compare them with your answers.

Rule 3: Punctuation and Possessives

All punctuation is disregarded when indexing personal and business names. Commas, periods, hyphens, apostrophes, dashes, exclamation points, question marks, quotation marks, underscores, and diagonals (/) are disregarded, and names are indexed as written.

What do you do with punctuation marks when indexing?

Examples of Rule 3

Filing Segment		Indexing Order of Units		
Name	**Key Unit**	**Unit 2**	**Unit 3**	**Unit 4**
1. Grant & Reardon Sales	Grant	and	Reardon	Sales
2. Grant's Barber Shop, Inc.	Grants	Barber	Shop	Inc
3. Grant's Homestyle Eatery	Grants	Homestyle	Eatery	
4. I Do Windows!	I	Do	Windows	
5. I_can_do_it.com	Icandoitcom			
6. Ike & Sons Realty	Ike	and	Sons	Realty
7. Inter-Asia Services	InterAsia	Services		
8. Iron Mountain	Iron	Mountain		
9. Iron Mountain Mining Co.	Iron	Mountain	Mining	Co
10. Julia Jones-Zeta	JonesZeta	Julia		

Rule 3 Self-Check

DATA CD

1. Open the *Word* file *2 Check Rule 3* found in the data file or write the names below on a piece of paper. Identify the units in the filing segments (names). Place diagonals between the units. Underline the key unit and number the remaining units.

   a. In-and-Out Car Wash
   b. Imelda Irving-Brown
   c. The Flying Cow Dairy
   d. Inside/Outside Games, Inc.
   e. #s Away Diet Center
   f. The Ink-a-Do Stamp Store
   g. $ Saver Store
   h. In-Town Couriers
   i. Allison Love-Jarvis
   j. Lovely & Ripley Clothing

2. Compare the key units and the other units, if needed, to determine the correct alphabetic filing order for the names. Indicate the correct filing order by writing or keying numbers 1 through 10 beside the names.

3. Are the two names in each of the following pairs in correct alphabetic order? If not, explain why they are not.

   a. Yolanda's $ Saver
      Yolanda Doolittle
   b. Rod-N-Reel Store
      Rodney Associates, Inc.
   c. Do-Rite Pharmacy
      Do-Rite Builders
   d. Rob & Son Electric
      Rob & Sons Alignment
   e. Colt-Western Company
      Colt Industries
   f. Temp-A-Cure Company
      Temp-Control Mechanics
   g. Nor-West Growing Company
      Nor'Wester Novelties
   h. Ezekiel M. Swanson
      The Swan Dive Shop
   i. Heckman Law Firm
      Dennis Heckman
   j. Chi Kuo
      Ching-yu Kuo

4. The answers to this exercise are shown in the *Word* file *2 Check Answers* found in the data files. Compare them with your answers.

Rule 4: Single Letters and Abbreviations

A. Personal Names

Initials in personal names are considered separate indexing units. Abbreviations of personal names (Wm., Jos., Thos.) and nicknames (Liz, Bill) are indexed as they are written.

How do you index abbreviated personal names?

B. Business Names

Single letters in business and organization names are indexed as written. If single letters are separated by spaces, index each letter as a separate unit. An acronym (a word formed from the first, or first few, letters of several words, such as NASDAQ and ARCO) is indexed as one unit regardless of punctuation or spacing. Abbreviated words (Mfg., Corp., Inc.) and names (IBM, GE) are indexed as one unit regardless of punctuation or spacing. Radio and television station call letters (KDKA, WNBC) are indexed as one unit.

Examples of Rule 4

Filing Segment	Index Order of Units			
Name	Key Unit	Unit 2	Unit 3	Unit 4
1. A C T Realty	A	C	T	Realty
2. Ace Smile Dental Lab	Ace	Smile	Dental	Lab
3. Ackerson & Day Mfgs.	Ackerson	and	Day	Mfgs
4. KKRS Radio Station	KKRS	Radio	Station	
5. K-Nine Security	KNine	Security		
6. KOGO Television	KOGO	Television		
7. M A C Construction	M	A	C	Construction
8. MAC, Inc.	MAC	Inc		
9. U & I Nursery	U	and	I	Nursery
10. Ulys. A. Udey	Udey	Ulys	A	

Rule 4 Self-Check

1. Open the *Word* file *2 Check Rule 4* found in the data files or write the names below on a piece of paper. Identify the units in the filing segments (names). Place diagonals between the units. Underline the key unit and number the remaining units.
   a. IDEA Corporate Services
   b. I-Can-Fix-It Auto Body
   c. I C A Corp.
   d. I Dig It Services
   e. I Am Woman, Inc.
   f. I C Clearly Vision
   g. I Buy Antiques
   h. ICAP Inc.
   i. ID Booth Inc.
   j. IBT Associates

2. Compare the key units and the other units, if needed, to determine the correct alphabetic filing order for the names. Indicate the correct filing order by writing or keying numbers 1 through 10 beside the names.

3. The answers to this exercise are shown in the *Word* file *2 Check Answers* found in the data files. Compare them with your answers.

CROSS-REFERENCING

Some records of persons and businesses may be requested by a name that is different from the one by which it was stored. This is particularly true if the key unit is difficult to determine. When a record is likely to be requested by more than one name, an aid called a cross-reference is prepared. A **cross-reference** shows the name in a form other than that used on the original record, and it indicates the storage location of the original record. The filer can then find requested records regardless of the name used in the request for those records.

Both the filing segment used to determine the storage location for the record and the cross-reference notation are coded on the document as shown in Figure 2.4. A copy of the document may be stored in the cross-reference location or a cross-reference sheet may be prepared. Cross-reference sheets used with correspondence records are discussed in Chapter 6.

Cross-referencing must be done with discretion. Too many cross-references crowd the files and may hinder retrieval rather than help. Each

> **Why are cross-references needed?**

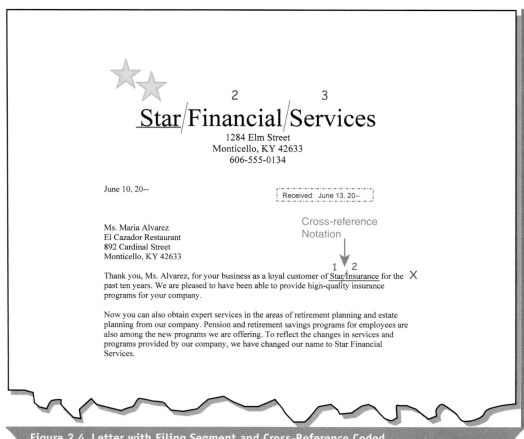

Figure 2.4 Letter with Filing Segment and Cross-Reference Coded

cross-reference requires valuable time to prepare, creates at least one additional sheet to be stored, and, therefore, requires additional space in a file.

Cross-references for data stored in an electronic database are often not needed. Because the search features of database software are extensive, a record can usually be found easily using any part of the filing segment. Also, entire records are often visible when a search result shows on the screen. There may be instances, however, when a cross-reference is needed under an entirely different name. In these instances a cross-reference database record can be created.

Four types of personal names should be cross-referenced:

1. Unusual names
2. Hyphenated surnames
3. Alternate names
4. Similar names

Also, nine types of business names should be cross-referenced. Two will be presented in this chapter; the remainder, in Chapters 3 and 4.

1. Compound names
2. Names with abbreviations and acronyms

An explanation of the procedure to be followed in cross-referencing each of these kinds of names follows. To practice coding and cross-referencing records in these early chapters, you will work with names arranged on pieces of paper to simulate paper documents. Later, in Chapter 6, you will code and file actual business documents.

Personal Names

Cross-references should be prepared for the following types of personal names.

What is an example of an unusual name?

1. **Unusual (easily confused) names.** When determining the surname is difficult, use the last name written as the key unit on the original record. Prepare a cross-reference with the first name written as the key unit. On the original correspondence for Charles David, *David* (last name) is the key unit, and *Charles* (first name) is the second unit. However, a request might be made for *David Charles*. In a correspondence file, the cross-reference sheet would show *Charles* as the key unit and *David* as the second unit. Someone looking under C for Charles would find the cross-reference directing the filer to look under D for David. Study the following examples.

Coded Filing Segment	Cross-Reference
2 Charles / <u>David</u>	2 Charles / David SEE David Charles
2 Gee-Hong / <u>Cheung</u>	2 GeeHong / Cheung SEE Cheung GeeHong
2 Keooudon / <u>Sayasene</u>	2 Keooudon / Sayasene SEE Sayasene Keooudon

2. **Hyphenated surnames.** Hyphenated surnames often are used by married women. With hyphenated surnames, a request for records could be in either of the two surnames. A cross-reference enables retrieval in either case. An example is *Wendy Reardon-Bruss* shown below.

How do you cross-reference a hyphenated surname?

Many men use hyphenated surnames that are their family names, and they are known only by their hyphenated surnames. A cross-reference is not necessary. Some men choose to adopt a hyphenated surname when they marry and may, in that case, be known by more than one name. A cross-reference is needed for accurate retrieval of records when a man changes his surname to a hyphenated surname. See *Douglas Edwards-Read* shown below. You will be told when a cross-reference is needed for a man's name; otherwise, a cross-reference will not be required.

Coded Filing Segment	Cross-Reference	
2 Wendy / <u>Reardon-Bruss</u>	2 <u>Bruss</u> / Wendy / Reardon SEE ReardonBruss Wendy	3
2 Douglas / <u>Edwards-Read</u>	2 <u>Read</u> / Douglas / Edwards SEE EdwardsRead Douglas	3

3. **Alternate names.** When a person is known by more than one name, you need to make cross-references. Two examples are *Michelle Starkinsky* doing business as *Michelle Star* and *Faith Moran,* who is also known as *Faith Moran-Ripley, Mrs. Michael Ripley,* and *Mrs. Faith Ripley.* Note that three cross-references are required for Faith Moran.

Coded Filing Segment	Cross-Reference
2 Michelle / Star	2 Starkinsky / Michelle SEE Star Michelle

2
Faith / Moran
	2
	MoranRipley / Faith
	SEE Morgan Faith
	-- 	
	           2 3
	Ripley / Michael / Mrs
	SEE Moran Faith
	-- 	
	           2 3
	Ripley / Faith / Mrs
	SEE Moran Faith

4. **Similar names.** A variety of spellings exist for some names like *Brown* and *Johnson*. A SEE ALSO cross-reference is prepared for all likely spellings. If the name is not found under one spelling, the filer checks the SEE ALSO sheet for other possible spellings. In a correspondence file, there would likely be a permanent cross-reference (could be a guide) to show the different spellings for common names. Cross-reference guides are discussed in Chapter 6.

Coded Filing Segment	Cross-Reference
Brown SEE ALSO Browne, Braun, Brawn	Browne SEE ALSO Brown, Braun, Brawn -- Braun SEE ALSO Brown, Brawn, Browne -- Brawn SEE ALSO Brown, Browne, Braun
Johnson SEE ALSO Johnsen, Johnston, Jonson	Johnsen SEE ALSO Johnson, Johnston, Jonson -- Johnston SEE ALSO Johnson, Jonson, Johnsen -- Jonson SEE ALSO Johnson, Johnsen, Johnston

Business Names

Cross-references should be prepared for the following types of business names. The original name is the name appearing on the letterhead.

> **How many cross-references are needed for a business that includes three surnames?**

1. **Compound names.** When a business name includes two or more individual surnames, prepare a cross-reference for each surname other than the first.

Coded Filing Segment	Cross-Reference

2   3
Jarvis, / Rasmussen, / and /
  4   5
Sheraden / Antiques
	2 3
	Rasmussen / Sheraden / and /
	  4 5
	Jarvis / Antiques
	SEE Jarvis Rasmussen and Sheraden Antiques
	
	------------------------------ 	
	    2 3 4
	Sheraden / Jarvis / and / Rasmussen /
	  5
	Antiques
	SEE Jarvis Rasmussen and Sheraden Antiques

2. **Abbreviations and acronyms.** When a business is commonly known by an abbreviation or an acronym, a cross-reference is prepared for the full name. Examples are *MADD* (Mothers Against Drunk Driving) and *EZ Electronics* (Ewen and Zuker Electronics) shown below.

Coded Filing Segment	Cross-Reference
MADD	2 3 4 Mothers / Against / Drunk / Driving SEE MADD
2 EZ / Electronics (Ewen and Zucker Electronics)	2 3 4 Ewen / and / Zucker / Electronics SEE EZ Electronics ------------------------------ 2 3 4 Zucker / and / Ewen / Electronics SEE EZ Electronics

Cross-Referencing Self-Check

1. Open the *Word* file *2 Check CR* found in the data files or write the names below on a piece of paper. Identify the units in the filing segments (names). Place diagonals between the units. Underline the key unit and number the remaining units.
   a. WKKP Radio Station
   b. IBM (International Business Machines)
   c. Sideras and Shadduck Company
   d. Platika and Miller Investment Firm
   e. Joan Childress-Edwards
   f. The Riverside Terrace
   g. Akeo Saga
   h. Mauruka's Diner
   i. Smith, Childers, & Jones Inc.
   j. BBCC (Big Bend Community College)

2. Key or write cross-references for the names that require them. See the example below.

2	3	4		2	3	4
<u>Lundry</u> / and / Masur / Meats				<u>Masur</u> / and / Lundry / Meats		
				SEE Lundry and Masur Meats		

3. The answers to this exercise are shown in the *Word* file *2 Check Answers* found in the data files. Compare them with your answers.

Rules 1–4 Self-Check

1. Open the *Word* file *2 Check Rules 1–4* found in the data files or write the names below on a piece of paper. Identify the units in the filing segments (names). Place diagonals between the units. Underline the key unit and number the remaining units.

   a. Carolyn's Autos for Less
   b. Janet Crawford
   c. Crow's Nest Pass Inn
   d. Andrew Carstairs
   e. Crawford Law Firm
   f. Deseree Campbell
   g. George M. Caldwell
   h. Cross-Town Transit
   i. Linda E. Craft
   j. Cyrus Campbell

2. Compare the key units and the other units, if needed, to determine the correct alphabetic filing order for the names. Indicate the correct filing order by writing or keying numbers 1 through 10 beside the names.

3. The answers to this exercise are shown in the *Word* file *2 Check Answers* found in the data files. Compare them with your answers.

CAREER CORNER

Job Description for Student Records Transcript Clerk

The following job description is representative of a career opportunity in records management at a community college.

JOB TITLE

Student Records Transcript Clerk
Office Support Series, Job #4

SALARY RANGE

$24,400 to $37,400 per year

PRINCIPAL JOB DUTIES

- Review and/or prepare and process moderately complex documents and paperwork.
- Input and/or retrieve information from college mainframe and/or microcomputer or other computer networks. Create databases, download, edit, or convert computer files.
- Produce materials using a microcomputer.
- Answer phones; take and distribute messages.
- Set up and/or maintain detailed files and records.
- Perform other related duties as assigned.

MINIMUM QUALIFICATIONS

To be successful in this position, you must have a high school diploma or equivalent supplemented with two terms of college-level course work emphasizing business technology or other area of office occupations. Experience performing the duties described above for six months may substitute for the college level course work. Additional requirements:

- Keyboarding, filing, math and/or ten-key skills.
- Ability to use word processing, database and/or spreadsheet software.
- Good interpersonal, organization, and problem-solving skills.
- Ability to maintain accurate records; use office equipment such as fax, telephone and copy machines; and convey technical information to students, staff, and the public.

Chapter Review And Applications

POINTS TO FILE AND RETRIEVE

- A set of written rules helps make filing consistent.

- Indexing is the mental process of determining the filing segment (or name) by which the record is to be stored.

- Coding is the physical process of marking the filing segment into indexing units.

- Personal names are indexed by the surname, the given name, and then middle name or initial.

- Business names are indexed as written.

- Minor words and symbols in business names are indexed as written and are considered separate indexing units.

- Symbols in business names are spelled out.

- When the word "The" is the first word in a business name, it is considered the last indexing unit.

- Ignore all punctuation marks when indexing personal and business names.

- Single letters and abbreviations are indexed as written for both personal and business names. When single letters in a business name are separated by spaces, each letter is considered a separate indexing unit.

- Cross-reference personal names that are unusual, hyphenated surnames, alternate names, and similarly spelled names.

- Cross-reference business names that are abbreviations and acronyms and those that contain more than one surname.

- Sorting is the process of arranging records in the sequence in which they are to be stored.

IMPORTANT TERMS

coding	indexing order
cross-reference	indexing rules
filing or storage method	indexing units
filing segment	key unit
indexing	sorting

REVIEW AND DISCUSSION

1. Why is consistency in filing important? (Obj. 1)

2. Why are indexing rules important when filing names alphabetically? (Obj. 1)

3. In personal names, what is the key unit? (Obj. 2)

4. How is the key unit of a business name determined? (Obj. 2)

5. Code and arrange the following names in alphabetic order. Justify your arrangement. (Objs. 2 and 4)
   a. Randolph Thornton
   b. Randy's Painting Company
   c. Rachelle Thornton
   d. Randall Printing Company

6. Code and arrange the following names in alphabetic order. Justify your arrangement. (Objs. 2 and 3)
   a. Gardner & House Produce
   b. The Garden Deli & Restaurant
   c. G/T Delivery
   d. The $ Off Store

7. Code and arrange the following names in alphabetic order. Justify your arrangement. (Objs. 2, 3, and 4)
   a. Lindsey Morris-Hatfield
   b. Moore's Mercantile
   c. Lindsey's Copies, Inc.
   d. Morris and Moore Hardware Store

8. Code and arrange the following names in alphabetic order. Justify your arrangement. (Objs. 2 and 5)
   a. MLG, Inc.
   b. M L G Associates
   c. Will Jones
   d. Wm. S. Jones

9. Code and arrange the following names in alphabetic order. Justify your arrangement. (Objs. 2, 4, and 5)
   a. Janet Owens
   b. Owen's Mower Repair
   c. Lisa Ovey
   d. O T H Consulting

10. Can you have too many cross-references? Explain. (Obj. 7)

11. Give two examples of types of personal names that should be cross-referenced. (Obj. 7)

12. Give two examples of types of business names that should be cross-referenced. (Obj. 7)

APPLICATIONS

2-1 INDEX, CODE, AND SORT RECORDS (OBJS. 2-8)

DATA CD

CRITICAL THINKING

In this activity, you will use names on slips of paper to practice using alphabetic indexing rules 1-4 to index, code, and sort paper documents.

1. Open the *Word* file *2-1 Alphabetic* found in the data files. Print the file. Cut the sheets into slips of paper along the table lines to represent business correspondence and cross-reference sheets.

2. Index and code the filing segments as you have practiced earlier in this chapter. The names are also shown below for reference.

Names

1. Lydia Cavanaugh
2. Maria Christina Castro
3. Vagif Agayev
4. Jane Carter-Anderson
5. Chia Cha
6. Best-Lock Gate Company
7. C & R Inc.
8. Allison's Salon of Beauty
9. Julie Anderson
10. C A B Services
11. Bio-Logic Resources
12. Abbott, Brady, & Craig Attorneys
13. Anderson Hardware Store
14. Anderson and Carter Associates
15. Abbott Furniture Store
16. C/K Corporation
17. Anne Carter Brokerage
18. BioGems, Inc.
19. Be-U-Ti-Ful Salon
20. "Build-It" Construction Co.

---

3. Determine which names should have cross-references. Using the blank cross-references provided in the file, write the number of the original name plus an **X.** Then write the cross-reference. See the example below.

	2	3
4X	Anderson / Jane / Carter	
	SEE CarterAnderson Jane	

4. Arrange the slips of paper, including cross-references, in alphabetic order. On a separate sheet of paper, list the numbers of the slips of paper that you have now arranged in alphabetic order.

5. Save the slips of paper for use in Chapter 3.

2-2 INDEX, CODE, AND SORT RECORDS (OBJS. 2-8)

In this activity, you will use names on slips of paper to practice using alphabetic indexing rules 1-4 to index, code, and sort paper documents.

DATA CD

CRITICAL THINKING

1. Open the *Word* file *2-2 Alphabetic* found in the data files. Print the file. Cut the sheets into slips of paper along the table lines to represent business correspondence and cross-reference sheets.

2. Index and code the filing segments as you have practiced earlier in this chapter. The names are also shown below for reference.

Names

1. WRAP Television Station	13. Mary Underwood-Watson
2. TUT Games & Videos (Taylor, Underwood, and Travis)	14. Wanda Wells Bakery
	15. Ultra-Bright Skin Care
3. John Vanguard	16. Trent Taylor
4. U-Nique Business Solutions	17. Upper/Lower Deliveries, Ltd.
5. Wilson and Travis Consulting	18. San-li Truong
6. Watson's Electronics	19. WORK Radio Station
7. Tots-R-Us Pre-School	20. Tall/Big Clothing Store
8. Williams Business College	21. Watch Repair
9. Will's Construction Company	22. Lucinda Watson
10. The # One Printer	23. Jos. H. Warner
11. U-n-I Delivery Service	24. Ralph Ventura
12. U-R-Healthy Natural Foods	25. Laura Wilson

3. Determine which names should have cross-references. Using the blank cross-references provided in the file, write the number of the original name plus an **X.** Then write the cross-reference. See the example below.

	2	3	4
5X	Travis / and / Wilson / Consulting		
	SEE Wilson and Travis Consulting		

4. Arrange the slips of paper, including cross-references, in alphabetic order. On a separate sheet of paper, list the numbers of the slips of paper that you have now arranged in alphabetic order.

2-3 FIND INFORMATION IN DATABASE RECORDS (OBJ. 9)

Locate the *Access* file *2-3 Customers* in the data files. Copy the file to your working folder on a hard drive or removable storage device. Open the file. This file includes contact data for customers. It also includes the indexing units used to file paper records for the customer. If a paper record is requested by number, this database can be used to find the customer name and how the paper records should be coded for filing in the alphabetic filing system. This facilitates finding the records quickly. The database can also be used to find other information about the customers.

Open the Customer Form database form. Use the Find feature to find the answers to the following questions. Write or key the answers.

1. How many people or businesses are located in Illinois?

2. Where is the Sterling Investments, Inc., located?

3. Which record number contains data for Donna Saba?

4. A record with data for a storage company is included in the database. What is the exact name of this company?

5. How many beauty salons have records in the database? Give the name(s) of the beauty salons.

6. Are any of the people or businesses in the database from Alaska? If yes, list the record number(s).

7. One of the people listed in the database is from Hartford, Connecticut. What is the name of the person who lives there?

8. One of the records in the database is for any agency. What is the name of the agency?

9. In which city is the Satin-N-Lace Boutique located?

10. What is the Postal Code for the Sav-On Oil Company?

2-4 RESEARCH IDENTITY THEFT

1. Access a search engine on the Internet. Search using the key words *identity theft*. You are interested in learning about what identity theft is, not how to prevent it. In Chapter 3, you will research preventing identity theft.

2. Follow at least three links in the search results list. Read and summarize the article or other information you find at each of the three sites. Be sure to list each site as a reference.

3. Send an e-mail to your instructor that contains the summary of your findings.

RECORDS MANAGEMENT SIMULATION

JOB 1 ALPHABETIC FILING RULES 1-4

A simulation titled RECORDS MANAGEMENT SIMULATION, Eighth Edition, is available for use with this textbook. If you have been instructed to complete this simulation, you should begin to do so now.

Welcome to Auric Systems, Inc., a company that sells wireless communications devices and broadband access to individuals, companies, and government agencies. Read the Overview and examine the organization chart; then complete Job 1. All supplies necessary for completing Job 1 and all other jobs in RECORDS MANAGEMENT SIMULATION, Eighth Edition, are contained in the simulation packet.

FOR MORE ACTIVITIES GO TO **http://read.swlearning.com**

Alphabetic Indexing Rules 5–8

Learning Objectives

1. Index, code, and arrange personal and business names with titles and suffixes.

2. Index, code, and arrange personal and business names with articles and particles.

3. Index, code, and arrange business names with numbers.

4. Index, code, and arrange the names of organizations and institutions.

5. Apply alphabetic filing procedures.

6. Prepare and arrange cross-references for business names.

7. Sort paper records.

8. Create and find information in a database table.

ALPHABETIC INDEXING RULES (CONTINUED)

In this chapter, you will continue your study of alphabetic filing rules. Remember to follow these guidelines to study the indexing rules effectively:

- Read each rule carefully. Make sure you understand the meaning of the words used to state the rule.
- Look at the examples. Note that the complete filing segment (the name and other words, such as the title) is given at the left. Then the filing segment is separated into indexing units at the right according to the rule you are studying.
- Be sure you understand why the filing segment has been separated as it has.

Rule 5: Titles and Suffixes

A. Personal Names

A title before a name (Dr., Miss, Mr., Mrs., Ms., Professor, Sir, Sister), a seniority suffix (II, III, Jr., Sr.), or a professional suffix (CRM, DDS, Mayor, M.D., Ph.D., Senator) after a name is the last indexing unit.

Numeric suffixes (II, III) are filed before alphabetic suffixes (Jr., Mayor, Senator, Sr.). If a name contains a title and a suffix (Ms. Lucy Wheeler, DVM), the title *Ms* is the last unit.

Royal and religious titles followed by either a given name or a surname only (Princess Anne, Father Leo) are indexed and filed as written.

> **What are some suffixes for personal names?**

Examples of Rule 5A

Filing Segment	Indexing Order of Units			
Name	**Key Unit**	**Unit 2**	**Unit 3**	**Unit 4**
1. Father Paul	Father	Paul		
2. Ms. Noreen Forrest, CPA	Forrest	Noreen	CPA	Ms
3. Dr. Noreen Forrest	Forrest	Noreen	Dr	
4. Mr. Huyen Huong	Huong	Huyen	Mr	
5. Bishop Barnard Hyatt	Hyatt	Barnard	Bishop	
6. Benjamin D. Hyatt	Hyatt	Benjamin	D	
7. Benjamin D. Hyatt II	Hyatt	Benjamin	D	II
8. Benjamin D. Hyatt III	Hyatt	Benjamin	D	III
9. Benjamin Hyatt, Jr.	Hyatt	Benjamin	Jr	
10. Benjamin Hyatt, Sr.	Hyatt	Benjamin	Sr	
11. King Olaf	King	Olaf		
12. Ms. Naomi Luu, CRM	Luu	Naomi	CRM	Ms
13. Miss Naomi Luu	Luu	Naomi	Miss	
14. Mrs. Naomi Luu	Luu	Naomi	Mrs	
15. Sister Joy Miller	Miller	Joy	Sister	
16. Sister Kathryn	Sister	Kathryn		
17. Jeff Sneed, CRM	Sneed	Jeff	CRM	
18. Mr. Jeff Sneed	Sneed	Jeff	Mr	
19. Senator Kenneth Sneed	Sneed	Kenneth	Senator	
20. Dr. Kenneth Snyder	Snyder	Kenneth	Dr	

B. Business Names

Titles in business names (Capt. Hook's Bait Shop) are indexed as written. Remember, the word *The* is considered the last indexing unit when it appears as the first word of a business name.

Examples of Rule 5B

	Filing Segment	Indexing Order of Units			
	Name	Key Unit	Unit 2	Unit 3	Unit 4
1.	Capt. Hook's Bait Shop	Capt	Hooks	Bait	Shop
2.	Dr. Pane's Windows	Dr	Panes	Windows	
3.	Grandma's Cookie Shop	Grandmas	Cookie	Shop	
4.	Mister Hulk's Gym	Mister	Hulks	Gym	
5.	Mother Nature's Botanicals	Mother	Natures	Botanicals	
6.	Mr. Mom's Day Care	Mr	Moms	Day	Care
7.	Mr. Video Connection	Mr	Video	Connection	
8.	Ms. Salon of Beauty	Ms	Salon	of	Beauty
9.	Professor Little's Bookstore	Professor	Littles	Bookstore	
10.	The Prof's Tutorial Service	Profs	Tutorial	Service	The

Rule 5 Self-Check

1. Open the *Word* file *3 Check Rule 5* found in the data files or write the names below on a piece of paper. Identify the units in the filing segments. Place diagonals between the units. Underline the key unit and number the remaining units. See the example below.

> 4   2   3
> Mr. / Ryan / Marree, / DDS

a. Father Tom

b. Ms. Rosalie Torres, CRM

c. Mrs. Darlene Talbot, DVM

d. Doctor Dee's Delivery

e. Governor Talbot's Construction Co.

f. Father Steven Gerzinski

g. Grandfather Ben's Recycling

h. Queen Anne II

i. Mom's TLC Services

j. Ms. Karen Farthing, Ph.D.

2. Compare the key units and the other units, if needed, to determine the correct alphabetic filing order for the names. Indicate the correct filing order by writing or keying numbers 1 through 10 beside the names.

3. Are the two names in each of the following pairs in correct alphabetic order? If not, explain why they are not.

   a. The Magic Shop   f. Red Hot Tamales
      Maggie's $ Save   Red Hat Shop
   b. Robert Norberg, Sr   g. LMNO Shipping Co.
      Robert Norberg, Jr.   L & N Appliance Repair
   c. Mrs. Carmen Libby   h. Sharon's "Of Course"
      Lady Liberty Realty   Miss Sharon Oest
   d. ABC Rentals, Inc.   i. The Office King
      Allied Chemical Co.   The Office Doctor
   e. MVP Pizza Shop   j. I-Net, Inc.
      Mrs. Marvis Miller   I-Freenet Company

4. Are the names in each group listed in correct alphabetic order? If not, show the correct order by rearranging the numbers. See the example below.

   ```
             3       2
   1. Ms. / Kati / Berman
                 2        3
   2. Mom / Berman's / Brownies
        3      2
   3. Mr. / Michael / Berman
      Ans: 1, 3, 2
   ```

   a. 1. Closets by Elizabeth   b. 1. Senator Alex Hatfield
      2. Dr. Claudia Carter   2. Hatfield's Department Store
      3. Admiral Tristan Chandler   3. Ms. Margaret Hayes

5. The answers to this exercise are shown in the *Word* file *3 Check Answers* found in the data files. Compare them with your answers.

Rule 6: Prefixes, Articles, and Particles

A foreign article or particle in a personal or business name is combined with the part of the name following it to form a single indexing unit. The indexing order is not affected by a space between a prefix and the rest of the name (Alexander La Guardia), and the space is disregarded when indexing.

> **What are some examples of names with foreign articles and particles?**

CAREER CORNER

Job Description for Information Administrator

The following is typical of a job description for a corporate Information Administrator.

DEVELOPS AND IMPLEMENTS CORPORATE RECORDS MANAGEMENT SYSTEMS:

- Plans, develops, and implements corporate information management procedures and practices to standardize information organization, protect corporate information, ensure proper storage and accessibility, and create retention guidelines for all information, regardless of the storage medium.

- Develops and periodically reviews retention schedules and legal recordkeeping requirements to determine timetables for transferring active information to inactive storage, for implementing image reduction processes, or for destroying obsolete information.

- Recommends purchase of storage, retrieval, or disposal equipment based on knowledge of equipment capability, cost and user needs.

- Coordinates daily inactive information storage and retrieval activities, ensuring storage areas remain secure.

- Evaluates methods of protection for vital records and makes recommendations for business contingency needs.

DEVELOPS AND IMPLEMENTS CORPORATE FORMS MANAGEMENT SYSTEMS:

- Reviews forms to evaluate need for creation, revision, consolidation, or discontinuation.

- Confers with form users to gather recommendations for improvements, considering such characteristics as form necessity and design.

- Analyzes workflow and confers with users for the design of forms.

- Maintains information regarding form origin, function, necessity, usage, cost, and inventory level.

EXPERIENCE AND QUALIFICATIONS:

- B.A. in business management or related field.

- Two to four years related experience and/or training (or equivalent combination of education and experience).

- Ability to analyze and interpret general business periodicals, professional journals, technical procedures, or governmental regulations.

- Ability to write reports, business correspondence, and procedure manuals.

- CRM (Certified Records Manager) certification preferred.

Examples of articles and particles are: a la, D,' Da, De, Del, De La, Della, Den, Des, Di, Dos, Du, E,' El, Fitz, Il, L,' La, Las, Le, Les, Lo, Los, M,' Mac, Mc, O,' Per, Saint, San, Santa, Santo, St., Ste., Te, Ten, Ter, Van, Van de, Van der, Von, Von der.

Examples of Rule 6

Filing Segment		Indexing Order of Units		
Name	**Key Unit**	**Unit 2**	**Unit 3**	**Unit 4**
1. Michael D'Agostino, DMD	DAgostino	Michael	DMD	
2. D'Angelo's Pizza Parlor	DAngelos	Pizza	Parlor	
3. Ms. Penelope D'Cruz	DCruz	Penelope	Ms	
4. Mario De La Torres, MD	DeLaTorres	Mario	MD	
5. Theresa Del Favero, CPA	DelFavero	Theresa	CPA	
6. La Marte & McCaw Attys	LaMarte	and	McCaw	Attys
7. Dr. Terrence O'Donald	ODonald	Terrence	Dr	
8. O'Donald's Public House	ODonalds	Public	House	
9. Edward Saint Cyr	SaintCyr	Edward		
10. San Souci Resturant	SanSouci	Restaurant		
11. St. Edwina's Arts & Crafts	StEdwinas	Arts	and	Crafts
12. Ms. Mayme Ten Eyck	TenEyck	Mayme	Ms	
13. Ms. Lorraine TenPas, Ph.D.	TenPas	Lorraine	PhD	Ms
14. Lt. Enid Van de Haven	VandeHaven	Enid	Lt	
15. Van der Camp's Hobbies	VanderCamps	Hobbies		

Rule 6 Self-Check

1. Open the *Word* file *3 Check Rule 6* found in the data files or write the names below on a piece of paper. Identify the units in the filing segments. Place diagonals between the units. Underline the key unit and number the remaining units.
   a. D'Arcy & Davis Consultants
   b. Ms. Syndi LaJoi, RD
   c. McLean's Web Design
   d. Mr. James Van Dyke
   e. Pamela St. John, CPA
   f. Ms. Maureen O'Boyle
   g. Eleanor K. DeLacy
   h. Mr. Mitchell Ste. John
   i. Gov. Tom McCall
   j. McAdam's Paving Co.
2. Compare the key units and the other units, if needed, to determine the correct alphabetic filing order for the names. Indicate the correct filing order by writing or keying numbers 1 through 10 beside the names.
3. The answers to this exercise are shown in the *Word* file *3 Check Answers* found in the data files. Compare them with your answers.

My Records

Protect Yourself from Identity Theft

Identity theft is a serious problem. What can you do to reduce the chances that you will be a victim?

Although no one can guarantee that you are safe from identity theft, you can reduce your risks by following these guidelines.

- Create passwords and/or personal identification numbers (PINS) to protect your credit card, bank, and phone accounts. (Avoid using your mother's maiden name, your birth date, the last four digits of your Social Security number, your phone number, or a series of consecutive numbers.)

- Change passwords often and include upper- and lowercase letters, numbers, and symbols.

- Secure personal information at home in a locked, fire-resistant box.

- Shred charge receipts, credit records, checks, bank statements, and unwanted credit card offers before throwing them away.

- Update your computer's virus and spyware protection software regularly.

- Review a copy of your credit report each year to make sure no new credit cards or other accounts have been issued in your name without your authorization.

- Remove incoming mail daily from your mailbox and hold your mail at the post office until you return from a vacation.

- Mail letters or documents that contain personal data (such as tax forms or checks) at the post office or in an official postal service mailbox.

- React quickly if a creditor or merchant calls about charges you did not make.

- Show only your name and address on printed checks and deposit slips.

- Do not give out personal information on the phone, through the mail, or online unless you know the site is safe and you initiated the call or transaction.

- Do not carry your Social Security card, passport, or birth certificate on your person.

Are you pro-active in protecting yourself from identity theft?

Rule 7: Numbers in Business Names

Numbers spelled out (Seven Lakes Nursery) in business names are filed alphabetically. Numbers written in digits are filed before alphabetic letters or words (B4 Photographers comes before Beleau Building and Loan).

Names with numbers written in digits in the first units are filed in ascending order (lowest to highest number) before alphabetic names (229 Club, 534 Shop, First National Bank of Chicago). Arabic numerals are filed before Roman numerals (2 Brothers Deli, 5 Cities Transit, XII Knights Inn).

Names with inclusive numbers (20-39 Singles Club) are arranged by the first digit(s) only (20). Names with numbers appearing in other than the first position (Pier 36 Cafe) are filed alphabetically and immediately before a similar name without a number (Pier 36 Cafe comes before Pier and Port Cafe).

When indexing names with numbers written in digit form that contain *st, d,* and *th* (1st. Mortgage Co., 2d Avenue Cinemas, 3d Street Pest Control), ignore the letter endings and consider only the digits (1, 2, 3).

When indexing names with a number (in figures or words) linked by a hyphen to a letter or word (A-1 Laundry, Fifty-Eight Auto Body, 10-Minute Photo), ignore the hyphen and treat it as a single unit (A1, FiftyEight, 10Minute).

When indexing names with a number plus a symbol (55+ Social Center), treat it as a single unit (55Plus).

Which is filed first— numbers spelled out or numbers written as words?

Examples of Rule 7

Filing Segment	Indexing Order of Units			
Name	**Key Unit**	**Unit 2**	**Unit 3**	**Unit 4**
1. 7 Days Market	7	Days	Market	
2. 17th Avenue Fashions	17	Avenue	Fashions	
3. 21 Club, Inc.	21	Club	Inc	
4. 24 Caret Jewelry	24	Caret	Jewelry	
5. 50% Discounters	50Percent	Discounters		
6. 65+ Retirement Village	65Plus	Retirement	Village	
7. 405 Auto Body	405	Auto	Body	
8. 500-510 Princess Court	500	Princess	Court	
9. The 500 Princess Shop	500	Princess	Shop	The
10. 1111 Vacations	1111	Vacations		
11. 12500 McNary, Inc.	12500	McNary	Inc	
12. XXI Club	XXI	Club		
13. Fourth Dimension Printing	Fourth	Dimension	Printing	

Filing Segment	Indexing Order of Units			
Name	Key Unit	Unit 2	Unit 3	Unit 4
14. Highway 18 Café	Highway	18	Cafe	
15. I-90 Road Services	I90	Road	Services	
16. I-205 Towing, Inc.	I205	Towing	Inc	
17. #1 Pet Grooming	Number1	Pet	Grooming	
18. One Main Place	One	Main	Place	
19. Pier 99 Imports	Pier	99	Imports	
20. Sixty-Six Sunset Blvd. Apts.	SixtySix	Sunset	Blvd	Apts

Rule 7 Self-Check

1. Open the *Word* file *3 Check Rule 7* found in the data files or write the names below on a piece of paper. Identify the units in the filing segments. Place diagonals between the units. Underline the key unit and number the remaining units.

2. If the names are not in alphabetic order, show the correct order by rearranging the numbers. See the example below.

> 2 3
> 1. <u>1-2-3</u> / Go / Store
> 2 3
> 2. <u>#1</u> / Sandwich / Shop
> 2 3 4
> 3. <u>7</u> / Dwarfs / Mining / Co.
> Ans: <u>3, 1, 2</u>

a.
1. Lady Bug Enterprises
2. Denise J. LaMonte
3. LaMonte Beauty Shop

b.
1. 50% Discount Shop
2. V Roman Way
3. 21st Century & Beyond Shop

c.
1. Labels 4 All, Inc.
2. Lawrence LaBerge, DVM
3. Patricia La Belle

d.
1. Marsha Mc Beth
2. Marsha McBath
3. 10 Minute Lube Shop

e.
1. Mackenzie M. Minten
2. McKenzie 500 Realty
3. McKenzie and Eft Realty

f.
1. Ralph DaCosta, Sr.
2. 10 Minute Delivery
3. Ralph DaCosta, Jr.

g. 1. #1 Delivery Express
   2. A-1 Auto Sales
   3. 10# Line Shop

h. 1. One Dollar Store
   2. #1 Sports Gear
   3. 5-7-9 Petites 2 Go

i. 1. Daniel Van de Bos
   2. Venture Tours, Inc.
   3. Matthew Van der Sluys

j. 1. 4-5-6 Nursery
   2. Four Corners Bistro
   3. 4 Movers & A Truck

3. The answers to this exercise are shown in the *Word* file *3 Check Answers* found in the data files. Compare them with your answers.

Rule 8: Organizations and Institutions

Banks and other financial institutions, clubs, colleges, hospitals, hotels, lodges, magazines, motels, museums, newspapers, religious institutions, schools, unions, universities, and other organizations and institutions are indexed and filed according to the names written on their letterheads.

> **How are names of organizations and other institutions indexed?**

Examples of Rule 8

Filing Segment	Indexing Order of Units			
Name	**Key Unit**	**Unit 2**	**Unit 3**	**Unit 4**
1. 1st National Bank	1	National	Bank	
2. Archdiocese of Austin	Archdiocese	of	Austin	
3. Assembly of God Church	Assembly	of	God	Church
4. Associated Auctioneers	Associated	Auctioneers		
5. Bank of the West	Bank	of	the	West
6. The Bank of Wyoming	Bank	of	Wyoming	The
7. Billings Community College	Billings	Community	College	
8. College of the Rockies	College	of	the	Rockies
9. De Long Children's Center	DeLong	Childrens	Center	
10. Disabled American Veterans	Disabled	American	Veterans	

Filing Segment	Indexing Order of Units			
Name	Key Unit	Unit 2	Unit 3	Unit 4
11. Federated Farm Workers	Federated	Farm	Workers	
12. First United Methodist Church	First	United	Methodist	Church
13. Freeport Daily News	Freeport	Daily	News	
14. Institute for Traditional Medicine	Institute	for	Traditional	Medicine
15. Int'l Brotherhood of Boilermakers	Intl	Brotherhood of		Boilermakers
16. Irish Cultural Society	Irish	Cultural	Society	
17. Jewish Historical Society	Jewish	Historical	Society	
18. JFK High School	JFK	High	School	
19. Journal of Photography	Journal	of	Photography	
20. Lincoln High School	Lincoln	High	School	
21. Nagy Aerospace Research Lab	Nagy	Aerospace	Research	Lab
22. Pacific University	Pacific	University		
23. Public Employees Union	Public	Employees	Union	
24. Rotary Club of Denver	Rotary	Club	of	Denver
25. School of the Arts	School	of	the	Arts
26. Society of American Foresters	Society	of	American	Foresters
27. St. Vincent's Medical Center	StVincents	Medical	Center	
28. Temple Beth Israel	Temple	Beth	Israel	
29. University of Michigan	University	of	Michigan	
30. Western Pacific Trucking School	Western	Pacific	Trucking	School

Rule 8 Self-Check

1. Open the *Word* file *3 Check Rule 8* found in the data files or write the names below on a piece of paper. Identify the units in the filing segments. Place diagonals between the units. Underline the key unit and number the remaining units.

   a. National Business Education Association
   b. Immaculate Heart Catholic Church
   c. Church of Religious Science
   d. St. Paul's Episcopal Church
   e. St. Thomas's Lutheran Church
   f. Temple Sinai
   g. Quran Foundation
   h. ARMA International
   i. University of Utah Hospital
   j. New Mexico State University

2. Compare the key units and the other units, if needed, to determine the correct alphabetic filing order for the names. Indicate the correct filing order by writing or keying numbers 1 through 10 beside the names.

3. Are the names in each of the following pairs in correct alphabetic order? If not, explain why not.

   a. International Webmasters Association
      International Association of Organ Donation
   b. United Cerebral Palsy
      United Four Wheel Drive Associations
   c. Association of American Publishers
      American Society for Training & Development
   d. World Federation of United Nations Associations
      World Federation of Personnel Management Association
   e. Union of Needletrades, Textiles and Industrial Employees
      United Food and Commercial Workers International Union

4. The answers to this exercise are shown in the *Word* file *3 Check Answers* found in the data files. Compare them with your answers.

Rules 5–8 Self-Check

1. Open the *Word* file *3 Check Rules 5–8* found in the data files or write the names below on a piece of paper. Identify the units in the filing segments. Place diagonals between the units. Underline the key unit and number the remaining units.

   a. lst Methodist Church
   b. First National Bank
   c. First Baptist Church
   d. The St. Paul Chronicle
   e. The Savannah Union Tribune
   f. The New York Times
   g. Sisters of Charity
   h. The Seattle Post-Intelligencer
   i. Fountain of Youth Spa
   j. 1 Stop Dry Cleaners

2. Compare the key units and the other units, if needed, to determine the correct alphabetic filing order for the names. Indicate the correct filing order by writing or keying numbers 1 through 10 beside the names.

3. Are the two names in each of the pairs in correct alphabetic order? If not, explain why not.

   a. St. John's Academy
      St. John's Church
   b. 21ˢᵗ Century Gallery
      The 21 Club
   c. Astor Elementary School
      Astoria Community College
   d. Bai Tong Thai Cuisine
      Berbati Resaurant
   e. Center-Line Curtains
      Center Pointe Mill Works

   f. Dr. June DeSimone
      Design-A-Weld Inc.
   g. Green Acres Kennels
      Ms. Towanda Greco
   h. School of Arts and Crafts
      School of the Arts
   i. San Carlos Apartments
      Mr. Tatsumi Sanada
   j. Grisvold McEwen, LLP
      Dr. Kevin M. McEvoy

4. The answers to this exercise are shown in the *Word* file *3 Check Answers* found in the data files. Compare them with your answers.

Cross-Referencing Business Names (Continued)

In this chapter you prepared cross-references for two of the nine types of business names that should be cross-referenced:

1. Compound names
2. Names that are abbreviations and acronyms

In this chapter, you will learn to prepare cross-references for the following types of business names:

3. Popular and coined names
4. Hyphenated names
5. Divisions and subsidiaries
6. Changed names
7. Similar names

An explanation of the procedure to be followed in cross-referencing each of these types of names follows. The original record is stored in one place according to the alphabetic rules being used. A cross-reference is made, if necessary, for any of the reasons discussed here and in Chapter 2.

3. Popular and Coined Names

Often a business is known by its popular and/or coined name. A cross-reference will assist in retrieval. For example, the official name is shown as the coded filing segment. The popular or coined name is the name usually mentioned when retrieving anything for this business; therefore, a cross-reference with the popular name is helpful for retrieving. In the following examples, *Fred Meyer One Stop Shopping* is commonly known as *Freddy's*, and *Smiths Homestyle Eatery* is commonly known as *Smitty's*.

How is a company's popular name cross-referenced?

Coded Filing Segment	Cross-Reference
2 3 4 Fred / Meyer / One / Stop / 5 Shopping	Freddys SEE Fred Meyer One Stop Shopping
2 3 Smiths / Homestyle / Eatery	Smittys SEE Smiths Homestyle Eatery

4. Hyphenated Names

Many business names include hyphenated surnames. Like hyphenated personal names, business surnames with hyphens need to be cross-referenced for each surname combination. Three examples follow.

Coded Filing Segment	Cross-Reference
2 3 Jolly-Reardon / Consulting / Co.	2 3 ReardonJolly / Consulting / Co SEE JollyReardon Consulting Co
2 3 Heckman-O'Connor / Tour / Guides	2 3 OConnorHeckman / Tour / Guides SEE HeckmanOConnor Tour Guides
2 3 Bruss-Podany-Moore / Law / Firm	2 3 PodanyMooreBruss / Law / Firm SEE BrussPodanyMoore Law Firm --- 2 3 MooreBrussPodany / Law / Firm SEE BrussPodanyMoore Law Firm

5. Divisions and Subsidiaries

How is a cross-reference for a division of a company prepared?

When one company is a subsidiary or a division or branch of another company, the name appearing on the letterhead of the branch or subsidiary is the one indexed on the original record. A cross-reference is made under the name of the parent company. Two examples follow. Ricoh Business Systems is a division of Ricoh USA, and Micro-Weld Operations is a subsidiary of Kintech Corporation.

Coded Filing Segment	Cross-Reference
2 3 Ricoh / Business / Systems (a div. of Ricoh USA)	2 Ricoh / USA SEE Ricoh Business Systems
2 Micro-Weld / Operations (a subsidary of Kintech Corporation)	2 Kintech / Corporation SEE MicroWeld Operations

6. Changed Names

If an organization changes its name, how is the cross-reference prepared?

A company may change its name. Records must then be changed to indicate the name change and to ensure that the new name will be used for storage purposes. If only a few records are already in storage, they are usually re-filed under the new name, and the former name is marked as a cross-reference. If many records are filed under the former name, a permanent cross-reference is placed at the beginning of the records for the former name. Any new records are placed under the new name. In the examples, *AT&T Wireless* changed its name to *Cingular Wireless,* and *Hershey Foods Corporation* changed its name to *The Hershey Co.*

Coded Filing Segment	Cross-Reference
2 Cingular / Wireless	2 ATandT / Wireless SEE Cingular Wireless
3 2 The / Hershey / Co.	2 3 Hershey / Foods / Corporation SEE Hershey Co The

7. Similar Names

A SEE ALSO cross-reference is used to alert the filer to check other possible spellings for a business name. The complete business name is not cross-referenced—only the similar name. Similar names for a business include examples like *Northwest* or *North West*, *Southeast* or *South East*, *Goodwill* or *Good Will*, and *All State* or *Allstate*. If a name could be considered either as one unit or as two units, it is a good candidate for a cross-reference. Two examples follow.

When is a SEE ALSO cross-reference used?

Coded Filing Segment	Cross-Reference
2 3 Allstate / Insurance / Co.	2 All / State SEE ALSO Allstate
2 3 4 South / East / Distribution / Co.	Southeast SEE ALSO South East

Cross-Referencing Self-Check

DATA CD

1. Open the *Word* file *3 Check CR* found in the data files or write the names below on a piece of paper. Identify the units in the filing segments. Place diagonals between the units. Underline the key unit and number the remaining units.
   a. Napen-Crawford Fishing Gear
   b. Lettson-Ridgeway Antique Cars
   c. St. Peter's Episcopal Church
   d. Woody's Dog and Cat Grooming
   e. Tech-N-Go Co. (a div. of Systems Solutions Corp.)
   f. Northwest Computer Systems
   g. Anchorage Daily News
   h. Westpark Aquarium
   i. All State Supply Co.
   j. Thao Huong Distributing Company (changed its name to Huong Distribution, Inc.)

2. Key or write cross-references for the names that require them. See the example below.

2 SillsOrdway / Caterers	2 OrdwaySills / Caterers SEE SillsOrdway Caterers

3. The answers to this exercise are shown in the *Word* file *3 Check Answers* found in the data files. Compare them with your answers.

Chapter Review And Applications

- A title before a personal name or a professional suffix after a personal name becomes the last indexing unit.

- Business names with titles are indexed as written.

- A foreign article or particle in a personal or business name is combined with the part of the name following it to form a single indexing unit.

- Numbers spelled out in business names are filed alphabetically.

- Numbers written in digits are filed before alphabetic letters or words.

- Numbers written as digits are filed in ascending order.

- The name of an organization or institution is indexed and filed according to how its name is shown on its letterhead.

- Cross-reference business names that are popular and/or coined, hyphenated, divisions and subsidiaries, changed names, or similar names.

REVIEW AND DISCUSSION

1. Code and arrange the following names in alphabetic order. Justify your arrangement. (Obj. 1)
   a. Mr. Paul Childers, Jr.
   b. Ms. Paula Childers
   c. Mrs. Paul Childers, CRM
   d. Mr. Paul Childers, Sr.
   e. Father Paul Childers

2. Code and arrange the following names in alphabetic order. Justify your arrangement. (Obj. 1)
   a. Sister Ellen
   b. Sister Ellen McSorley
   c. Sister Elena
   d. Sisters of Mercy
   e. Ms. Ellen Mc Sorley

3. Code and arrange the following names in alphabetic order. Justify your arrangement. (Obj. 2)
   a. Frank LaBarre
   b. L-A-B Supply Service
   c. Frank S. LaBarre
   d. Joanna LaBarge
   e. LaBar's Web Design

4. Code and arrange the following names in alphabetic order. Justify your arrangement. (Objs. 1 and 2)
   a. Ms. Colleen McHenry, CRM
   b. Mr. Colin McHenry
   c. Mrs. Colin Mac Henry
   d. Colleen McHenry, M.D.
   e. Dean Colleen Mac Henry

5. Code and arrange the following names in alphabetic order. Justify your arrangement. (Obj. 3)
   a. 3 Rs Study Service
   b. 7 Gnomes Mining Co.
   c. 5 Star Hotels Association
   d. 205 Interstate Inn
   e. 1 Stop Shopping

6. Code and arrange the following names in alphabetic order. Justify your arrangement. (Objs. 1-3)
   a. 1-2-3 Go Store!
   b. 2 B-True Memories, Inc.
   c. 30 McNamara Suites
   d. Cardinal Joseph O'Neill
   e. One Stop Repair Mart

7. Code and arrange the following names in alphabetic order. Justify your arrangement. (Obj. 4)
   a. St. Peter's Orthodox Church
   b. St. Paul First National Bank
   c. The St. Paul Times
   d. St. Peter's Children's Home
   e. Abbot Paul's Chapel

8. Code and arrange the following names in alphabetic order. Justify your arrangement. (Objs. 1 and 4)
   a. 4 Seasons Hotel
   b. 4-Fold Way, Inc.
   c. Mr. Russell Forrett, CPA
   d. 444 Fountain Court Apts.
   e. Four Rivers Stadium

9. Which of the following items need cross-references? Explain why cross-references are needed and prepare the necessary cross-references. (Obj. 6)
    a. Carter-Watters Real Estate
    b. E'Lan Construction changed its name to Buildings by E'Lan
    c. Southwest Computer Institute
    d. Modular Housing, a subsidiary of St. Cyr Construction Company, Inc.
    e. PJs, a popular name of Pat Jennings Gourmet Bakery

10. What is the difference between a regular cross-reference and a SEE ALSO cross-reference? (Obj. 6)

APPLICATIONS

3-1 INDEX, CODE, AND SORT RECORDS (OBJS. 1-7)

DATA CD

CRITICAL THINKING

In this activity, you will use names on slips of paper to practice using alphabetic indexing rules 5–8 to index, code, and sort paper documents.

1. Open the *Word* file *3-1 Alphabetic* found in the data files. Print the file. Cut the sheets into slips of paper along the table lines to represent business correspondence and cross-reference sheets.

2. Index and code the filing segments as you have practiced earlier in this chapter. The names are also shown below for your reference.

Names	
21. 9 to 5 Uniform Shop	30. The Astoria Times
22. Albany Baptist Church	31. 21st Avenue Bistro
23. All State Packing Co.	32. Belleville Hospital
24. Mr. Elmer Darby, Jr.	33. Elmer Darby, Ph.D.
25. Big Rock Candies (a div. of Heavenly Sweets, Inc.)	34. The Badger Times
26. 2 B-True Pet Supply	35. Mr. Louis DeBois
27. Akron Foundation for the Blind	36. Beauty on Broadway
28. DBB Inc. (DeHart, Brady, & Baldwin, Inc.)	37. Albany Brotherhood of Iron Workers
29. Abraham Lincoln Museum	38. Ms. Andrea Adams, CRM
	39. Abbot & Anderson Law Firm
	40. All State Shopping Inc.

3. Determine which names should have cross-references. Using the blank cross-references provided in the data file, write the number of the original name plus an **X.** Then index and code the filing segments. Notice in the example below that three cross-references are needed for DBB, Inc. (DeHart, Brady & Baldwin, Inc.).

	2	3		2	3
28X	DeHart / Brady / and /	28X	Brady / Baldwin / and /		
	4 5		4 5		
	Baldwin / Inc.		DeHart / Inc.		
	SEE DBB Inc		SEE DBB Inc		

	2	3	4
28X	Baldwin / DeHart / and / Brady /		
	5		
	Inc.		
	SEE DBB Inc		

4. Arrange the slips of paper, including the cross-references, in alphabetic order. On a separate sheet of paper, list the numbers of the slips of paper that you have now arranged in alphabetic order.

5. Combine the slips of paper you created in Chapter 2 Application 2-1 with the papers you created for this application. Arrange the papers so all 40 names and their cross-references are shown in alphabetic order.

3-2 INDEX, CODE, AND SORT RECORDS (OBJS. 1-7)

In this activity, you will use names on slips of paper to practice using alphabetic indexing rules 5-8 to index, code, and sort paper documents.

1. Open the *Word* file *3-2 Alphabetic* found in the data files. Print the file. Cut the sheets into slips of paper along the table lines to represent business correspondence and cross-reference sheets.

DATA CD

CRITICAL THINKING

2. Index and code the filing segments as you have practiced earlier in this chapter. The names are also shown below for reference.

Names	
1. St. Theresa Lutheran Church	15. 5000 King's Court Suites
2. TTW Trucking (Travis, Trent, and Wilson Trucking)	16. Tours, Inc. (a div. of Travel America)
3. Ms. Julia Van der Hay, CRM	17. 1-2-3 Lawn Care Co.
4. Union Workers Federation	18. Southwest Airlines
5. Simon & Travis Consulting	19. Salem General Hospital
6. Clara St. Ambach, CRM	20. The Temple Institute
7. Teddy Roosevelt Prep School	21. James Ten Eyck, DVM
8. The St. Joseph Foundation	22. Daniel L. Smith Commercial Diving
9. Ms. Angela Stamp-VandeCamp	23. St. Genistus Village for Children
10. 1 Stop Shopping	
11. #1 Print Shop	24. Sam the Clown
12. 3 Square Meals, Inc.	25. Ms. Wilma Tescher, CPA
13. 100 Points of Light Co.	
14. Walla Walla Hospital	

3. Determine which names should have cross-references. Using the blank cross-references provided in the data file, write the number of the original name plus an **X.** Then index and code the filing segments. See the example below for Tours Inc. (a div. of Travel America).

	2
16X	<u>Travel</u> / America
	SEE Tours Inc

4. Arrange the slips of paper, including cross-references, in alphabetic order. On a separate sheet of paper, list the numbers of the slips of paper that you have now arranged in alphabetic order.

3-3 ENTER NAMES INTO A DATABASE (OBJS. 1–7)

ACCESS ACTIVITY

In Application 3-2 you practiced using alphabetic indexing rules 5–8 to file paper documents. In this application, you will use the same names in an electronic database. To compare the results of the two methods, you will enter the names as written (the filing segment) and by filing units.

1. Create a new *Access* database file named *3-3 Customers*.

2. Create a table in the database named **Customers.** Create these fields in the table: ID Number, Filing Segment, Key Unit, Unit 2, Unit 3, Unit 4, Unit 5. Select **AutoNumber** for the field type for the ID Number field. Select **Text** for the field type for all other fields. Set the ID Number field as the primary key.

3. Enter the names from Application 3-2 in the Customer table. In the Filing Segment field, enter the complete name as written. In the other fields, enter the data in all capitals and follow the alphabetic indexing rules 5-8 presented in this chapter. (Do not enter information shown in parentheses after a company name in the Units fields.)

4. Sort the records in the Customer table in ascending order by the Key Unit field. (Further sorting is not necessary because none of the key units are the same as another.) Does the order of the records in the sorted table match the order of the records you sorted manually in Application 3-2? If not, how does the order differ?

3-4 FIND INFORMATION IN DATABASE RECORDS (OBJ. 8)

ACCESS ACTIVITY

When filing paper documents, cross-references are created to help users find names that might be requested in different ways. In an *Access* database, the Find feature can be used to locate records using any part of a name. This eliminates the need for some types of cross-references. You will practice using the Find feature in this application.

Open the *Access* database file *3-3 Customers* that you created in Application 3-3. Select the **Customers** table but do not open it. Create an AutoForm based on the Customers table. Use the Find feature to answer the questions that follow. Close the form without saving it after answering the questions.

Hint: When searching, look in the Filing Segment field and match any part of the record.

1. What are the names in the database that are hospitals?

2. What is the name of the consulting company that is included in this database?

3. What are the names of the two people in the database who are Certified Records Managers (CRM)?

4. What is the complete name of the business whose name begins with 1-2-3?

5. What is the name of the church in the database?

3-5 RESEARCH IDENTITY THEFT PREVENTION

1. Access a search engine on the Internet. Search using the key words *preventing identity theft.*

INTERNET

COLLABORATION

2. Follow at least three links in the search results list. Read and summarize the article or other information you find at each of the three sites. Be sure to list each site as a reference.

3. Work as a team with two other students to compile a list of strategies for preventing identity theft. Share your findings as your instructor directs.

RECORDS MANAGEMENT SIMULATION

JOB 2 ALPHABETIC FILING RULES 5-8

Continue working with Auric Systems, Inc.
Complete Job 2.

FOR MORE ACTIVITIES GO TO **http://read.swlearning.com**

Alphabetic Indexing Rules 9–10

Learning Objectives

1. Index, code, and arrange personal and business names that are identical.

2. Index, code, and arrange government names.

3. Apply alphabetic filing procedures.

4. Prepare and arrange cross-references for foreign business and government names.

5. Sort paper records.

6. Select appropriate subject categories to be used within an alphabetic arrangement.

7. Create, sort, and query a database.

ALPHABETIC INDEXING RULES (CONTINUED)

In this chapter, you will continue your study of alphabetic storage rules. Follow these guidelines to study the indexing rules effectively:

- Read each rule carefully. Make sure you understand the meaning of the words used to state the rule.
- Look at the examples. Note that the complete filing segment is given at the left. Then the filing segment is separated into indexing units at the right according to the rule you are studying. Be sure you understand why the filing segment has been separated as it has.

Rule 9: Identical Names

Retrieving the correct record when there are identical names of people or businesses is easy when using a computer database. A records management database typically contains a unique field with information specific to a particular person or business name—often a phone number, a special identification number, or an assigned number generated by the database software. Because each person or business has a unique identifier, there is no need to look for other information to determine which person is which.

In correspondence files, determining which person or business is the correct one when there are others with identical names can be a challenge. When personal names and names of businesses, institutions, and organizations are identical (including titles as explained in Rule 5), the filing order is determined by the addresses. Compare addresses in the following order:

1. City names
2. State or province names (if city names are identical)
3. Street names, including *Avenue, Boulevard, Drive,* and *Street* (if city and state names are identical)
   a. When the first units of street names are written in digits (18th Street), the names are considered in ascending numeric order (1, 2, 3) and placed together before alphabetic street names (18th Street, 24th Avenue, Academy Circle).
   b. Street names written as digits are filed before street names written as words (22nd Street, 34th Avenue, First Street, Second Avenue).
   c. Street names with compass directions (North, South, East, and West) are considered as written (SE Park Avenue, South Park Avenue).
   d. Street names with numbers written as digits after compass directions are considered before alphabetic names (East 8th Street, East Main Street, Sandusky Drive, South Eighth Avenue).
4. House or building numbers (if city, state, and street names are identical)
   a. House and building numbers written as digits are considered in ascending numeric order (8 Riverside Terrace, 912 Riverside Terrace) and placed together before spelled-out building names (The Riverside Terrace).
   b. House and building numbers written as words are filed after house and building numbers written as digits (11 Park Avenue South, One Park Avenue).
   c. If a street address and a building name are included in an address, disregard the building name.
   d. ZIP Codes are not considered in determining filing order.

When names are identical, which indexing units are compared next?

Are ZIP Codes considered in determining filing order?

Examples of Rule 9

Names of Cities Used to Determine Filing Order

Filing Segment	Indexing Order of Units			
Name	Key Unit	Unit 2	Unit 3	Unit 4
1. Seaside Inn Oceanside, CA	Seaside	Inn	Oceanside	CA
2. Seaside Inn Oceanside, NJ	Seaside	Inn	Oceanside	NJ
3. Seaside Inn Oceanside, WA	Seaside	Inn	Oceanside	WA
4. Seaside Inn Ventura, CA	Seaside	Inn	Ventura	CA

Examples of Rule 9

Names of States and Provinces Used to Determine Filing Order

Filing Segment	Indexing Order of Units				
Name	Key Unit	Unit 2	Unit 3	Unit 4	Unit 5
1. Anita J. Spencer Fenwick, ON (Ontario)	Spencer	Anita	J	Fenwick	ON
2. Anita J. Spencer Fenwick, WV	Spencer	Anita	J	Fenwick	WV
3. Topper's Restaurant Clifton, AZ	Toppers	Restaurant	Clifton	AZ	
4. Topper's Restaurant Clifton, TN	Toppers	Restaurant	Clifton	TN	
5. Topper's Restaurant Clifton, TX	Toppers	Restaurant	Clifton	TX	
6. Topper's Restaurant Clifton, WI	Toppers	Restaurant	Clifton	WI	

Examples of Rule 9

Names of Streets and Building Numbers Used to Determine Filing Order

Filing Segment	Indexing Order of Units					
Name	Key Unit	Unit 2	Unit 3	Unit 4	Unit 5	Unit 6
1. Subs-2-Go 6570 8th St. Houston, TX	Subs2Go	Houston	TX	8	St	
2. Subs-2-Go 4560 48th St. Houston, TX	Subs2Go	Houston	TX	<u>48</u>	St	
3. Subs-2-Go 16450 Carter Ave. Houston, TX	Subs2Go	Houston	TX	<u>Carter</u>	Ave	
4. Subs-2-Go 12800 Carter St. Houston, TX	Subs2Go	Houston	TX	Carter	<u>St</u>	12800
5. Subs-2-Go 18800 Carter St. Houston, TX	Subs2Go	Houston	TX	Carter	St	<u>18800</u>
6. Subs-2-Go 255 SW 15th St. Houston, TX	Subs2Go	Houston	TX	<u>SW</u>	15	St
7. Subs-2-Go 576 SW Eighth St. Houston, TX	Subs2Go	Houston	TX	SW	<u>Eighth</u>	St
8. Subs-2-Go 6224 SW Pecan Dr. Houston, TX	Subs2Go	Houston	TX	SW	<u>Pecan</u>	Dr
9. Subs-2-Go 17 Tyler Way Houston, TX	Subs2Go	Houston	TX	<u>Tyler</u>	Way	17
10. Subs-2-Go 296 Tyler Way Houston, TX	Subs2Go	Houston	TX	Tyler	Way	<u>296</u>

Rule 9 Self-Check

1. Open the *Word* file *4 Check Rule 9* found in the data files or write the names below on a piece of paper. Identify the units in the filing segments. Place diagonals between the units. Underline the key unit and number the remaining units. Remember, house or building numbers are considered only if city, state, and street names are identical. An example follows.

DATA CD

```
              2          3
Pattaya / Thai / Restaurant
   8      6      7
400 / 55th / Street
      4          5
Spartanburg, / SC
```

a. United Methodist Church
    1250 SE Concord
    Salisbury, MA

    United Methodist Church
    2725 N 48th Street
    Salisbury, VT

b. Ms. Andrea Moore
    4550 SE Flavel St.
    Salem, OR

    Ms. Andrea Moore
    975 Cedar Street
    Salem, MA

c. The Granite Times
    One Martin Street
    Granite, OK

    The Granite Times
    371 Martin Street
    Granite, OK

d. The Burger Barn
    1015 17th Street
    Pittsburgh, PA

    The Burger Barn
    11500 8th Street
    Pittsburgh, PA

e. Mr. Daniel L. Gerson
    8th and Grand Streets
    Melbourne, FL

    Mr. Daniel L. Gerson
    16875 Carnation Way
    Madeira Beach, FL

f. Key West Bank
    210 N Elgin Blvd.
    St. Louis, MO

    Key West Bank
    150 S Elgin Ave.
    St. Louis, MO

2. Are the two names in each of the pairs in correct indexing order? If not, explain why they are not.

3. The answers to this exercise are shown in the *Word* file *4 Check Answers* found in the data files. Compare them with your answers.

My Records

Recovering from Identify Theft

Has your personal information or identity been stolen? What's the next step?

If your personal information has been stolen or if you become a victim of identity theft, you must act quickly to minimize the damage that may result from this theft of your records. Follow these four steps.

1. Notify the fraud units of the three credit reporting companies: Equifax, Experian (formerly known as TRW), and TransUnion.
   - Ask to be placed on fraud alert on your credit report. This alert tells creditors to contact you before opening any new accounts or making any changes to your existing accounts.
   - Ask for a free copy of your credit report. Scrutinize the report. Report any errors by writing to the credit bureaus.
   - The Federal Trade Commission (FTC) web site offers an online publication, "Take Charge: Fighting Back Against Identity Theft."
2. Close the accounts that you know or believe have been fraudulently opened.
   - Notify the security or fraud department of each company.
   - Follow up in writing and include copies of supporting documents.
   - Keep a log of phone calls and letters you send and receive.
3. Report the identity theft to your local police or sheriff's department.
   - Document the theft.
   - Make sure the police report lists the fraud accounts.
   - Obtain a copy of the police report, which is called an *identity theft report.*
4. Report the crime to the Federal Trade Commission.
   - Include your police report number.
   - Call the FTC's Identity Theft Hotline (877-438-4338).
   - Use the FTC's online identity theft complaint form.

Following the above guidelines will help you recover from identity theft. The best place to beat identity theft is to do all you can to prevent it. (Links to the web sites mentioned are available on the web site for this textbook.)

Rule 10: Government Names

As a citizen of a democratic society, you have rights and responsibilities. Governmental rules and regulations define the rights and responsibilities individuals and organizations enjoy. Documents from government entities are often vital records such as your birth certificate, Social Security card, or a marriage certificate. You also receive documents asking for payment of taxes or other obligations to the government.

DATA CD

The records that an organization may receive from various governmental agencies uphold the rights and responsibilities of an individual or a business. For example, an electronics company doing business with the city of Philadelphia and the state of Pennsylvania interacts with city, county, state and federal agencies by:

- Obtaining a business name and/or incorporating.
- Obtaining permits to do business within the city.
- Paying property taxes.
- Paying employer taxes.
- Complying with transportation regulations when shipping products.
- Complying with other regulations while operating a business.

An understanding of our government's hierarchy may be helpful when applying alphabetic indexing rules to government names. Open the *Word* file *4 Government* found in the data files to review the structure of the U.S. Government and learn how organizations interact with government agencies. You can also find links to federal governmental sites on the web site for this textbook.

Government names are indexed first by the name of the governmental unit—city, county, state, or country. Next, index the distinctive name of the department, bureau, office, or board. A discussion of local and regional, state, federal, and foreign government names is provided in this chapter.

A. Local and Regional Government Names

The first indexing unit is the name of the county, city, town, township, or village. *Charlotte Sanitation Department* is an example. *Charlotte* (a city) would be the first indexing unit. Next, index the most distinctive name of the department, board, bureau, office, or government/political division. In this case, *Sanitation* would be the most distinctive name of the department. The words *County of, City of, Department of, Office of,* etc., are retained for clarity and are considered separate indexing units. If *of* is not a part of the official name as written, it is not added as an indexing unit.

> **How are city government names indexed?**

Examples of Rule 10A

Filing Segment	Indexing Order of Units				
Name	Key Unit	Unit 2	Unit 3	Unit 4	Unit 5
1. County of Alameda Aquatic Center	Alameda	County	of	Aquatic	Center
2. City of Arlington Public Library	Arlington	City	of	Public	Library
3. City of Arlington Senior Center	Arlington	City	of	Senior	Center
4. Ashley County Dept. of Elections	Ashley	County	Elections	Dept.	of
5. Augusta City Water Works	Augusta	City	Water	Works	
6. Baker County Bureau of Licenses	Baker	County	Licenses	Bureau	of
7. City of Banks Water Dept.	Banks	City	of	Water	Dept
8. Barstow Municipal Court	Barstow	Municipal	Court		
9. Benton City Hall Benton, GA	Benton	City	Hall	Benton	GA
10. Mayor's Office Benton, GA	Benton	Mayors	Office	Benton	GA

Rule 10A Self-Check

DATA CD

1. Open the *Word* file *4 Check Rule 10A* found in the data files or write the names below on a piece of paper. Identify the units in the filing segments. Place diagonals between the units. Underline the key unit and number the remaining units. An example follows.

>   2   3   4   5   6
> Warren / County / Sheriff's / Department / Warren / OH

   a. Douglas City Library, Douglas, AL
   b. City of Douglas Water Bureau, Douglas, AZ
   c. Douglas County Emergency Services
   d. City of Douglas Human Resources Department, Douglas, MA

　　e. City of Douglas Public Library, Douglas, GA

　　f. Douglas County Public Works Department

　　g. Douglas City Hall, Douglas, MI

　　h. Douglas County Circuit Court

2. Compare the key units and the other units, if needed, to determine the correct alphabetic filing order for the names. Indicate the correct filing order by writing or keying numbers 1 through 8 beside the names.

3. The answers to this exercise are shown in the *Word* file *4 Check Answers* found in the data files. Compare them with your answers.

B. State Government Names

Similar to local and regional political/governmental agencies, the first indexing unit is the name of the state or province. Then index the most distinctive name of the department, board, bureau, office, or government/political division. The words *State of, Province of, Department of,* etc., are retained for clarity and are considered separate indexing units. If *of* is not a part of the official name as written, it is not added as an indexing unit.

> **How are state government names indexed?**

Examples of Rule 10B

Filing Segment	Indexing Order of Units					
Name	**Key Unit**	**Unit 2**	**Unit 3**	**Unit 4**	**Unit 5**	**Unit 6**
1. Michigan Dept. of Community Health	Michigan	Community	Health	Dept	of	
2. Michigan Dept. of Education	Michigan	Education	Dept	of		
3. Michigan Dept. of Labor	Michigan	Labor	Dept	of		
4. Michigan Natural Resources	Michigan	Natural	Resources			
5. Michigan State Attorney General	Michigan	State	Attorney	General		
6. Michigan Dept. of State	Michigan	State	Dept	of		
7. State of Michigan Dept. of Aging	Michigan	State	of	Aging	Dept	of
8. State of Michigan Civil Service Dept.	Michigan	State	of	Civil	Service	Dept
9. Secretary of Education, State of Michigan	Michigan	State	of	Education	Secretary	of
10. Michigan State Police	Michigan	State	Police			

Rule 10B Self-Check

1. Open the *Word* file *4 Check Rule 10B* found in the data files or write the names below on a piece of paper. Identify the units in the filing segments. Place diagonals between the units. Underline the key unit and number the remaining units. An example follows.

> 2   3   5   6   4
> State / of / <u>Hawaii</u> / Department / of / Tourism

   a. Washington State Employment Department
   b. State of Washington, Dept. of Transportation, Highway Division
   c. Washington Dept. of Justice, Child Support Division
   d. State of Washington, Governor's Office
   e. State of Washington, Dept. of Corrections, Walla Walla Prison
   f. Washington State Patrol
   g. Washington State Legislature, Ways and Means Committee
   h. Washington Veterans' Affairs Department
   i. State of Washington, Secretary of State
   j. Washington Dept. of Human Services
   k. Dept. of Services for the Blind, State of Washington
   l. Washington State Museum
   m. Washington State Law Library
   n. Office of the Attorney General, State of Washington
   o. Washington State Fire Marshal

2. Compare the key units and the other units, if needed, to determine the correct alphabetic filing order for the names. Indicate the correct filing order by writing or keying numbers 1 through 15 beside the names.

3. The answers to this exercise are shown in the *Word* file *4 Check Answers* found in the data files. Compare them with your answers.

C. Federal Government Names

How are federal government names indexed?

Use three indexing "levels" (rather than units) for the United States federal government. Consider *United States Government* as the first level. The second level is the name of a department; for example, *Department of Agriculture*. Level three is the next most distinctive name; for example, *Forest Service*. The words *of* and *of the* are extraneous and should <u>not</u> be considered when indexing. In the following examples, note that *United States Government* is the first level in all cases.

Examples of Rule 10C

Filing Segment		
	Level 1 United States Government	
Name	**Level 2**	**Level 3**
1. National Weather Service, Dept. of Commerce	Commerce Dept (of)	National Weather Service
2. Office of Civil Rights, Dept. of Education	Education Dept (of)	Civil Rights Office (of)
3. Dept. of Health and Human Services	Health and Human Services Dept (of)	
4. Energy Assurance Office, Dept. of Homeland Security	Homeland Security Dept (of)	Energy Assurance Office
5. Bureau of Reclamation, Dept. of the Interior	Interior Dept (of the)	Reclamation Bureau (of)
6. Federal Bureau of Investigation, Dept. of Justice	Justice Dept (of)	Investigation Federal Bureau (of)
7. Federal Bureau of Prisons, Dept. of Justice	Justice Dept (of)	Prisons Federal Bureau (of)
8. Global Affairs, Dept. of State	State Dept (of)	Global Affairs
9. Federal Aviation Adm., Dept. of Transportation	Transportation Dept (of)	Federal Aviation Adm
10. Internal Revenue Service, Dept. of the Treasury	Treasury Dept (of the)	Internal Revenue Service
11. Bureau of Public Debt, Dept. of the Treasury	Treasury Dept (of the)	Public Debt Bureau (of)
12. Veterans Health Adm., Dept. of Veterans Affairs	Veterans Affairs Dept (of)	Veterans Health Adm

DATA CD

Rule 10C Self-Check

1. Open the *Word* file *4 Check Rule 10C* found in the data files or write the names below on a piece of paper. Remember that the first level of federal government names is *United States Government*. Identify the levels (beginning with Level 2) in the filing segments. Place diagonals between the levels. Number the remaining levels. An example follows.

> Level 3   Level 2
> National Cemetery Adm, / Dept. (of) Veterans Affairs

   a. National Park Service, Dept. of the Interior
   b. Marshals Service, Dept. of Justice
   c. National Nuclear Security Adm., Dept. of Energy
   d. Fish & Wildlife Service, Dept. of the Interior
   e. Bureau of Land Management, Dept. of the Interior
   f. Federal Bureau of Prisons, Dept. of Justice
   g. Power Administrations, Dept. of Energy
   h. Drug Enforcement Administration, Dept. of Justice
   i. Alcohol, Tobacco, Firearms, and Explosives, Dept. of Justice
   j. Fossil Energy, Dept. of Energy

2. Compare the levels, if needed, to determine the correct alphabetic filing order for the names. Indicate the correct filing order by writing or keying numbers 1 through 10 beside the names.

3. The answers to this exercise are shown in the *Word* file *4 Check Answers* found in the data files. Compare them with your answers.

Resources

It is not always easy to find the correct department, bureau, division, or office of your city, county, or federal government, but there are resources readily available. Several are listed here.

What sources could you use to find information about the local government where you live?

- Many cities and states have Internet web sites to help keep citizens informed. The city of Pittsburgh and the Commonwealth of Pennsylvania are two examples.
- Telephone directories list city and county offices and federal government services in a special section.
- The *United States Government Manual* (USGM), published by the U.S. Government Printing Office, provides the correct hierarchical order of the departments, bureaus, offices, etc., within our government. The same information is available online. You can the link to the main page of the *United States Government Manual* at the web site for this textbook.

D. Foreign Government Names

The name of a foreign government and its agencies is often written in a foreign language. When indexing foreign names, begin by writing the English translation of the government name on the document. The English name is the first indexing unit. Then index the balance of the formal name of the government, if needed, or if it is in the official name (China Republic of). Branches, departments, and divisions follow in order by their distinctive names. States, colonies, provinces, cities, and other divisions of foreign governments are followed by their distinctive or official names as spelled in English.

How are foreign government names indexed?

Examples of Rule 10D

Foreign Government Name	English Translation in Indexed Order			
Name	Unit 1	Unit 2	Unit 3	Unit 4
1. Govern d'Andorra	<u>A</u>ndorra	Government		
2. Republik of Österreich	<u>A</u>ustria	Republic	of	
3. Druk-yul	<u>B</u>hutan	Kingdom	of	
4. Bundesrepublik Deutschland	<u>G</u>ermany	Federal	Republic	of
5. Jamhuri ya Kenya	<u>K</u>enya	Republic	of	
6. Al-Joumhouriya al-Lubnaniya	<u>L</u>ebanon	Republic	of	
7. Fuerstentum Liechtenstein	<u>L</u>iechtenstein	Principality	of	
8. Republicii Moldova	<u>M</u>oldova	Republic	of	

Rule 10D Self-Check

DATA CD

1. Open the *Word* file *4 Check Rule 10D* found in the data files or write the names below on a piece of paper. Identify the units in the English translation filing segments. Place diagonals between the units. Underline the key unit and number the remaining units.

Foreign Government Name	English Translation
a. République de Guinée	Republic of Guinea
b. Lietuvos Respublika	Republic of Lithuania
c. Republika Hrvatska	Republic of Croatia
d. República del Ecuador	Republic of Ecuador
e. Nippon	Japan
f. Respublikasinin Azərbaycan	Republic of Azerbaijan

2. Compare the key units and the other units, if needed, to determine the correct alphabetic filing order for the names. Indicate the correct filing order by writing or keying numbers 1 through 6 beside the names.
3. The answers to this exercise are shown in the *Word* file *4 Check Answers* found in the data files. Compare them with your answers.

Resources

Countries, Dependencies, Areas of Special Sovereignty, and Their Principal Administrative Divisions, published by the U.S. Department of Commerce, National Bureau of Standards, provides a list of geographic and political entities of the world and associated standard codes. The *World Almanac and Book of Facts,* updated annually, includes facts and statistics on many foreign nations, and is helpful as a source for the English spellings of many foreign names. The Central Intelligence Agency (CIA) maintains an online World FactBook. You can find a link to this site at the web site for this textbook.

> **What source will help you find the English spelling of a foreign country?**

Cross-Referencing Business Names (Continued)

In Chapters 2 and 3, you prepared cross-references for seven of the nine types of business names that should be cross-referenced:

1. Compound names
2. Names that are abbreviations and acronyms
3. Popular and coined names
4. Hyphenated names
5. Divisions and subsidiaries
6. Changed names
7. Similar names

In this chapter, you will learn to prepare cross-references for the last of the nine types of business names:

8. Foreign business names
9. Foreign government names

An explanation of the procedure to be followed in cross-referencing each of these types of names follows. The original record is stored in one place according to the alphabetic rules being used. A cross-reference is also made, if necessary, for any of the reasons discussed in Chapters 2 and 3.

8. Foreign Business Names

The original spelling of a foreign business name is often written in the foreign language, which is then translated into English for coding. When working with foreign business names, take special note of the correct spellings and markings because they may differ greatly from the English form.

Write the English translation of the foreign business name on the document to be stored, and store the document under the English spelling. Prepare a cross-reference sheet using the foreign spelling as written in its native language, using the first word as the key unit. When a request for a record is written in the native language, the filer will find that a cross-reference sheet bearing the original spelling is an aid in finding the record. Two examples follow.

> **In what language is the original record of a foreign business name filed?**

Coded Filing Segment	Cross-Reference
2 Humboldt / University	Humboldt-Universität SEE Humboldt University
2 Venezuelan / Line	2 3 Venezolana / de / Navegacion SEE Venezuelan Line

9. Foreign Government Names

The name of a foreign government and its agencies, like foreign businesses, is often written in a foreign language. Write the English translation of the government name on each document to be stored. Store all documents under the English spelling. Prepare a cross-reference sheet using the foreign spelling as written in its native language, using the first word as the key unit. Two examples follow.

> **In what language is a cross-reference prepared for a foreign government name?**

Coded Filing Segment	Cross-Reference
2 3 4 Federal / Republic / of / Brazil	2 3 4 República / Federativa / do / Brasil SEE Brazil Federal Republic of
2 3 Kingdom / of / Bhutan	Druk-yul SEE Bhutan Kingdom of

Job Description for Office Automation Clerk

CAREER CORNER

The following job description is an example of a career opportunity in records management with the U.S. Federal Government. This job description was adapted from a posting on USAJOBS, the official job site of the U.S. Federal Government.[1] A link to this web site is provided at the web site for this textbook. Follow the link to learn about other career opportunities with the federal government.

VACANCY ANNOUNCEMENT

Agency Name: USDA Forest Service
Area of Consideration: U.S. Citizens
Position Title, Series, Grade: Office Automation Clerk
Duty Location: Arlington, VA
Work Schedule: Full time
Appointment: Permanent
Salary: $25,702.00—$29,507.00
Duties

- Receives and directs callers and visitors.

- Provides information about the organization, its functions, activities, and personnel.

- Arranges displays of informational materials in the reception area.

- Orders and maintains publications for public distribution.

- Performs filing work, including the establishment, maintenance, control, protection, and disposition of records.

- Performs work related to acquiring and developing resource materials in support of the policy development or technical activities of an organization.

- Performs office automation work requiring the use of software applications and computer equipment.

- Prepares correspondence, reports, technical documents, graphs/charts, forms, and other office support materials.

- Monitors and reports time and attendance and maintains appropriate records.

[1]USAJOBS, U.S. Office of Personnel Management, <http://www.usajobs.opm.gov/> (accessed on June 22, 2005).

CAREER CORNER

(continued)

MINIMUM FEDERAL QUALIFICATION REQUIREMENTS

Qualifying experience for the GS-4 level includes one (1) year of general experience in clerical, office, or other work which indicates ability to acquire the particular knowledge and skills needed to perform the duties of the position, or two (2) years of education above the high school level.

SUBSTITUTION OF EDUCATION FOR EXPERIENCE

The experience requirements for the GS-4 level may be met by completion of two (2) full years of full-time academic study in an accredited business, secretarial or technical school, junior college, college, or university.

COMBINING EDUCATION AND EXPERIENCE

Equivalent combinations of successfully completed post high school education and general experience may be used to meet the total experience requirements.

PROFICIENCY REQUIREMENT

Applicant must be able to type 40 words per minute.

BENEFITS

Benefits include a variety of health insurance plans, a retirement system with investment options, paid holidays, paid sick and annual (vacation) leave, life insurance, incentive systems, subsidized transportation, a flexible work schedule, training and development opportunities, and a family/worklife program.

Cross-Referencing Self-Check

1. Open the *Word* file *4 Check CR* found in the data files or write the names below on a piece of paper. Identify the units in the filing segments of the English translation. Place diagonals between the units. Underline the key unit and number the remaining units.

Foreign Name	English Translation
a. Hotel Vier Jahreszeiten	Four Seasons Hotel
b. Repubblika ta' Malta	Republic of Malta
c. Société Européene des Satellite	European Society of Satellites
d. Republica Bolivariana de Venezuela	Bolivarian Republic of Venezuela
e. Ristorante do Leoni	The Two Lions Restaurant
f. Kongeriket Norge	Kingdom of Norway

2. Key or write cross-references for the names that require them, using the cross-reference examples in this chapter as a guide.

3. The answers to this exercise are shown in the *Word* file *4 Check Answers* found in the data files. Compare them with your answers.

SUBJECTS WITHIN AN ALPHABETIC ARRANGEMENT

In what situation would you find records grouped by subject in an alphabetic file?

Within an alphabetic arrangement, records may sometimes be stored and retrieved more conveniently by a subject title than by a specific name. Beware, however, of using so many subjects that the arrangement becomes primarily a subject arrangement with alphabetic names as subdivisions. A few typical examples of acceptable subjects to use within an otherwise alphabetic name arrangement are:

- **Applications.** All records pertaining to job openings are kept together under the job title. The job for which individuals are applying is more important than are the names of the applicants.
- **Bids or projects.** All records pertaining to the same bid or the same project are kept together under the project or bid title.
- **Special promotions or celebrations.** All records relating to a specific event are grouped together by subject.

The filing procedure for the subject storage method is explained in detail in Chapter 8. Its application in this chapter consists of writing the subject title on the record if it does not already appear there.

When coding a record, the main subject is the key unit. Subdivisions of the main subject are considered as successive units. The name of the correspondent (individual or company name) is considered last. For example, on all records pertaining to applications, the word *Applications* is written as the key unit. The specific job applied for is a subdivision of that main subject and is the next unit (*Assistant,* for example). The applicant's name is coded last.

Examples of Subjects Within an Alphabetic Arrangement

Indexing Order of Units in Names				
Key Unit	**Unit 2**	**Unit 3**	**Unit 4**	**Unit 5**
1. Applications	Assistant	Bianchi	Jason	
2. Applications	Assistant	Fung	Brenda	
3. Applications	Cashier	Corbett	Lucy	
4. Applications	Cashier	Jennings	Kenneth	
5. Applications	Data	Entry	Neally	Joyce
6. Applications	Data	Entry	Rodrigez	Luis
7. Applications	Records	Clerk	Adamson	Cody
8. Applications	Records	Clerk	Osuna	Jamella
9. Applications	Records	Clerk	Tisio	Angelo
10. Applications	Records	Supervisor	Kakazu	Nancy
11. Applications	Records	Supervisor	Wasserman	Robert
12. Applications	Records	Supervisor	Wu	Vivian
13. Applications	Sales	Representative	Fusilli	Brian
14. Applications	Sales	Representative	Gagliardo	Carmella
15. Applications	Sales	Representative	Gains	Sara

Chapter Review And Applications

POINTS TO FILE AND RETRIEVE

- When filing identical names of persons, businesses, and organizations, filing is determined by the city names, state or province names, street names, and house or building numbers.

- Index local and regional governments first by the name of the government unit; then index the most distinctive name of the department, board, bureau, or office.

- Index state or province government first by the name of the state or province. Next, index the descriptive name of the department, division, or office.

- Use three indexing "levels" for U.S. federal governmental agency names. The first level of indexing is *United States Government*. The second level is the department name; and the third level is the name of the bureau, service, administration, or office.

- Index the distinctive English name for foreign government names. Next, index the balance of the formal name of the government.

- Index the English translation of a foreign business name.

- Cross-reference foreign business or government names.

- Within an alphabetic file, subject files are appropriate for applications, bids or projects, and special promotions or celebrations.

REVIEW AND DISCUSSION

1. Code and arrange the following names in alphabetic order and explain your arrangement. (Obj. 1)
   a. The Longview Times, Longview, MN
   b. The Longview Times, Longview, TX
   c. The Longview Times, Longview, IL
   d. The Longview Times, Longview, NC

2. Code and arrange the following names in alphabetic order and explain your arrangement. (Obj. 1)
   a. Chad Davis, CRM, Ludlow, SD
   b. Dr. Chad Davis, Ludlow, SD
   c. Mr. Chad Davis, Ludlow, CA
   d. Chad Davis, CPA, Ludlow, VT

3. Code and arrange the following names in alphabetic order and explain your arrangement. (Obj. 1)
   a. John Miller, 425 Mayberry Street, Independence, OR
   b. John Miller, 145 Lakeshore Dr., Independence, MO
   c. John Miller, 375 E. Washington Street., Independence, KY
   d. John Miller, 2650 Cedar Street, Independence, MO

4. When arranging city, county, province, or state government names, what are the key units? (Obj. 2)

5. Code and arrange the following names in alphabetic order and explain your arrangement. (Obj. 2)
   a. City of Rice, City Manager, Rice, TX
   b. City of Rice, Police Department, Rice, VA
   c. City of Rice, Fire Department, Rice, MN
   d. City of Rice, Mayor's Office, Rice, WA

6. Code and arrange the following names in alphabetic order and explain your arrangement. (Obj 2)
   a. Board of Commissioners, Beaver County
   b. Information Technology Department, Beaver County
   c. Department of Emergency Services, Beaver County
   d. Community Services Department, Beaver County

7. Identify the levels of the filing segments and arrange the following federal government names in alphabetic order. Justify your arrangement. Remember that the first level is *United States Government*. (Obj. 2)
   a. Animal and Plant Health Inspection, Department of Agriculture
   b. California Operations Office, Environmental Protection Agency
   c. Coast Guard, Department of Homeland Security
   d. Bureau of Export Administration, Department of Commerce
   e. Maritime Administration, Department of Transportation
   f. Bureau of Engraving and Printing, Department of the Treasury
   g. Bureau of Public Affairs, Department of State
   h. Department of the Navy, Department of Defense
   i. Research, Education, and Economics, Department of Agriculture
   j. Vocational and Adult Education, Department of Education

8. Code and arrange the following state government names in alphabetic order and explain your arrangement. (Obj. 2)
   a. Illinois State Police
   b. Department on Aging, State of Illinois
   c. Office of Management and Budget, State of Illinois
   d. Illinois General Assembly
   e. Department of Labor, State of Illinois
   f. Department of Children and Family Services, State of Illinois
   g. Office of the Governor, State of Illinois
   h. Office of the State Treasurer, State of Illinois
   i. Department of Human Services, State of Illinois
   j. Historic Preservation Agency, State of Illinois

9. Explain why cross-references are needed and prepare the necessary cross-references for each item. (Obj. 4)
   a. Respublika Byelarus' (Republic of Belarus)
   b. Slovenska Republika (Slovak Republic)
   c. Latvijas Republika (Republic of Latvia)
   d. Preahreacheanacha Kampuchea (Kingdom of Cambodia)

10. Why are subject categories sometimes used in an alphabetically arranged name file? Give two examples of subjects that might be found in an alphabetic file. (Obj. 6)

APPLICATIONS

4-1 INDEX, CODE, AND SORT RECORDS (OBJS. 1-5)

DATA CD

CRITICAL THINKING

In this activity, you will use names on slips of paper to practice using alphabetic indexing rules 9–10 to index, code, and sort paper documents.

1. Open the *Word* file *4-1 Alphabetic* found in the data files. Print the file. Cut the sheets into slips of paper along the table lines to represent business correspondence and cross-reference sheets.

2. Index and code the filing segments as you have practiced earlier in this chapter. For your reference, the names are also shown below.

Names
41. Royaume de Belgique (French) Koninkrijk Belgie (Dutch) Kingdom of Belgium
42. Minority Business Development Agency, Department of Commerce (federal government)
43. Dept of Emergency Services, Allegany County
44. Ashland City Hall, Ashland, WI
45. Secretary of Education, State of Colorado
46. Rural Utilities Service, Dept. of Agriculture (federal government)
47. Community College System, Education Department, State of Colorado
48. Ashland City Hall, Ashland, OR
49. Patent & Trademark Office, Dept. of Commerce (federal government)
50. Board of Commissioners, Allegany County
51. Information Technology Agency, Technology Department, State of Colorado
52. Ashland City Hall, Ashland, ME
53. Zhonghua Renmin Gongheguo (People's Republic of China)
54. Ashland City Hall, Ashland, NE
55. Secretary of Public Safety, State of Colorado

56. Environmental Management, Department of Energy (federal government)
57. Fiscal Services, Allegany County
58. Department of Environment Services, State of Colorado
59. Ashland City Hall, Ashland, KY
60. Centers for Disease Control and Prevention, Dept. of Health & Human Services (federal government)

2. Determine which names should have cross-references. Using the blank cross-references provided in the file, write the number of the original name plus an **X.** Then index and code the filing segments. An example follows.

	2	3
53X	Zhonghua / Renmin / Gongheguo	
	SEE China Peoples Republic of	

3. Arrange the slips of paper, including the cross-references, in alphabetic order. On a separate sheet of paper, list the numbers on the cards that you have now arranged in alphabetic order.

4. Combine the slips of paper you created in Chapters 2 and 3 (Applications 2-1 and 3-1) with the papers you created for this application. Arrange the papers so all 60 names and their cross-references are shown in alphabetic order.

4-2 INDEX, CODE, AND SORT RECORDS (OBJS. 1-5)

In this activity, you will use names on slips of paper to practice using alphabetic indexing rules 9-10 to index, code, and sort paper documents.

1. Open the *Word* file *4-2 Alphabetic* found in the data files. Print the file. Cut the sheets into slips of paper along the table lines to represent business correspondence and cross-reference sheets.

2. Index and code the filing segments as you have practiced earlier in this chapter. For your reference, the names are also shown on page 104.

DATA CD

CRITICAL THINKING

Names

1. Al Mamlakah al Arabiyah as Suudiyah (Kingdom of Saudi Arabia)
2. Dept. of Criminal Justice, State of Texas
3. Fire Dept., Shelby, AL
4. Records Clerk Applications, Heather Zane
5. Board of Supervisors, Washington County, Fort Edward, NY
6. Office of Disability Employment Policy, Department of Labor (federal government)
7. Records Clerk Applications, Tom Snell
8. City of Shelby, Fire Department, Shelby, NC
9. Court of Appeals, State of Texas
10. Dept. of Elections, Washington County, Hillsboro, OR
11. Konungariket Sverige (Kingdom of Sweden)
12. Political Affairs, Dept. of State (federal government)
13. Records Clerk Applications, Angela Berg
14. Shelby Fire Dept., Shelby, IN
15. Governor's Office, State of Texas
16. Emergency Services, Washington County, Blair, NE
17. Records Clerk Applications, Elias Boljuncic
18. Texas State Board for Education Certification
19. Bureau of Public Debt, Dept. of the Treasury (federal government)
20. Records Clerk Applications, Pei-Fang Hung
21. Fire Department, Shelby, MS
22. Research & Innovative Technology Administration, Dept. of Transportation (federal government)
23. Records Clerk Applications, Leslie Strickland
24. Office of Community Development, Dept. of Agriculture (federal government)
25. Police Dept., Shelby, OH

3. Determine which names should have cross-references. Using the blank cross-references provided in the file, write the number of the original name plus an **X.** Then index and code the filing segments.

4. Arrange the slips of paper, including cross-references, in alphabetic order. On a separate sheet of paper, list the numbers on the cards that you have now arranged in alphabetic order.

4-3 CREATE AND QUERY A DATABASE (OBJ. 6-7)

ACCESS ACTIVITY

You have been hired as records clerk for a new Catchy-Containers store scheduled for opening in the spring. The store owner has asked you to create a database table to keep track of all the people who have applied for jobs.

1. Open *Access* and create a new database named *4-3 Applicants*.

2. Create a table named **Applicants** with the following fields: Date, Position, First Name, Last Name, Phone. Select **Date** as the field type for the Date field. Select **Text** as the field type for the other fields. Select the **Phone** field as the primary key.

3. Enter the following information into the table. Enter the current year in the dates (instead of 20--).

Date	Position	First Name	Last Name	Phone
1/3/20--	Cashier	Jennifer	Smith	541-555-0101
1/4/20--	Stocker	Forrest	Bayly	541-555-0122
1/4/20--	Cashier	Susan	Mcintyre	541-555-0131
1/5/20--	Manager	Barry	Gamble	541-555-0125
1/5/20--	Cashier	Joshua	Neslund	541-555-0030
1/6/20--	Stocker	Erin	Gonzales	541-555-0127
1/6/20--	Manager	Laura	Reynolds	541-555-0129
1/7/20--	Cashier	Amy	Pederson	541-555-0124
1/7/20--	Cashier	Serena	Worcester	541-555-0126
1/7/20--	Stocker	Philip	Raymond	541-555-0133
1/8/20--	Cashier	Bryan	Crider	541-555-0108
1/8/20--	Manager	Sara	Reyes	541-555-0115
1/8/20--	Stocker	Lauren	Hurst	541-555-0128
1/9/20--	Manager	Jennifer	Smith	541-555-0154
1/9/20--	Stocker	Tom	Reitz	541-555-0114
1/9/20--	Cashier	Kelly	Tumpane	541-555-0111

4. Even when a database contains identical names, retrieving the correct record is easy when a unique field is used to identify records. In this database, the Phone field is the unique field/primary key. The store owner said to you, "I need to return a call from an applicant, but the message has only her first name and phone number: 541-555-0154. What is the applicant's full name and for what position did she apply?" Use the Find feature with the Applicants table to find this information.

5. The owner has asked you to create a list of applicants sorted in ascending order first by the position and then by the last name. Create a query based on the Applicants table. In the query results, display all fields and sort the data as requested. Save the query as **Position Sort Query.** Run the query and print the results table.

4-4 RESEARCH THE FEDERAL EXECUTIVE BRANCH

INTERNET

COLLABORATION

Earlier in this chapter, you reviewed the *Word* file *4 Government* found in the data files. You learned that the three branches of state and federal government are Executive, Legislative, and Judicial. In this activity, you will research one aspect of the executive branch of the federal government.

1. Access the Internet and go to http://read.swlearning.com. Find the links for this chapter. Follow the link to the Federal Executive Branch site.

2. Work as a team with another student to answer the following questions:
   a. What is one of the principal purposes of the President's Cabinet?
   b. How many members does the current Cabinet include?
   c. What are the names of the executive departments within the Cabinet? What are the names of the current secretaries of those departments?
   d. What is the primary responsibility of the Secretary of Defense? Of the Secretary of Transportation?

3. Share your findings as your instructor directs.

RECORDS MANAGEMENT SIMULATION

JOB 3 ALPHABETIC FILING RULES 9-10

Continue working with Auric Systems, Inc.
Complete Job 3.

FOR MORE ACTIVITIES GO TO **http://read.swlearning.com**

Electronic File Management

Learning Objectives

1. Describe elements found in an electronic database.

2. Enter and sort data in an electronic database.

3. Describe how databases can be used in records management and e-commerce.

4. Describe the differences in how records are sorted manually and by computers.

5. Describe the life cycle for electronic records.

6. Describe and apply electronic file management.

ELECTRONIC RECORDS AND FILES

Sorting data and records in electronic files and organizing electronic files and folders are important aspects of managing electronic records. Electronic files, also called records, can be created using many software applications. You have probably created electronic files using word processing, spreadsheet, and presentation programs. If you completed the applications for Chapters 2, 3, and 4, you have created or edited electronic files using a database program, *Microsoft Access*. As with paper records, electronic files should be managed so the data can be retrieved quickly when needed. In Chapters 2, 3, and 4, you focused on learning alphabetic indexing rules for use in indexing, coding, sorting, and storing paper records. In this chapter, you will learn about how computers sort electronic data and how to organize electronic files.

DATABASES

An electronic **database** is a collection of related data stored on a computer system. The data can be used with various applications but managed independently of them. For example, records in a database that contain names and addresses can be used to create personalized letters with a word processing program. Databases are organized especially for rapid search and retrieval of specific data. People have been using databases on large mainframe computers for over 50 years. A variety of database programs are available for personal computers as well. If you completed the applications in Chapters 2, 3, and 4, you have used a popular database program, *Microsoft Access. Access* is typical of modern database programs. A database contains **tables** that hold the data. Data in a table is organized in fields and records. A **field** is a set of one or more characters treated as a unit of information. The combination of characters forms words, numbers, or a meaningful code. For example, your first name, middle name, and last name could each be entered in a separate field. Your date of birth, social security number, telephone number, the year you started school, and the month and year you finished high school are all examples of facts about you. Each fact could be entered in a separate field.

What is a field?

All the fields related to one person or organization make up a **record** (sometimes called a *computer record* to distinguish it from a paper record). Records related to one subject or topic (customers, students, orders) are usually stored in one or more related tables. A database can also contain several other objects such as forms and reports. Figure 5.1 shows a database created with *Microsoft Access.*

What is a record?

A field has a unique name and a specified number of characters, and it contains a defined type of information. Commonly used field types are text fields (sometimes called alphanumeric fields for letters, numbers, symbols, and punctuation) and number fields (for numbers, punctuation characters, and symbols). Other typical field types are date fields, logical fields, and memo fields.

Fields are arranged in columns

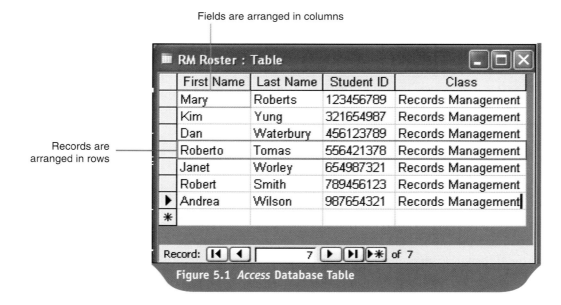

Records are arranged in rows

RM Roster : Table

	First Name	Last Name	Student ID	Class
	Mary	Roberts	123456789	Records Management
	Kim	Yung	321654987	Records Management
	Dan	Waterbury	456123789	Records Management
	Roberto	Tomas	556421378	Records Management
	Janet	Worley	654987321	Records Management
	Robert	Smith	789456123	Records Management
▶	Andrea	Wilson	987654321	Records Management
*				

Record: ◀◀ ◀ 7 ▶ ▶◀ ▶* of 7

Figure 5.1 *Access* **Database Table**

When using database software, the user can assign a field as a primary key. The database will not allow the same data to be entered in the primary key field for two or more records. The primary key creates a unique identifier for each record. For example, when you change a service to your telephone, the person making the change asks for your phone number (which is unique to you). Your phone number is entered as the search criteria in the database. The database then finds and displays your personal information.

Word processing and spreadsheet software can contain simple databases. A relational database program such as *Microsoft Access, MySQL*®, or *Oracle*® allows more flexibility in working with the information in the database. When a document is set up in database form with fields (whether the document is in a word processing, spreadsheet, or database program) sorting on any field is possible. The procedures vary depending on the software. Usually a field or column is selected. The type of sort is defined: ascending (A-Z, 1-10) or descending (Z-A, 10-1). The sort command is carried out, and the list is placed in alphabetic or numeric order by the chosen field. Several words can be entered in the same field and the correct alphabetic order is maintained.

Can you use a word processing program to create a database?

Finding Information in a Database

Finding a specific piece of information in a database is easy. Use the Find feature to enter the data you want to find such as a name, address, or phone number. Tell the database to search all fields or selected fields, give the command to start the search, and the information will display on the screen within seconds. What if you don't know the exact name you wish to find? In this case, you can enter the first few letters of the last name. When that information displays on the screen, scroll through the records until you find the correct one. You may need other information to validate that the name is the correct one.

On which field can you sort data?

A database is useful for sorting various fields alphabetically. As you learned in Chapters 2, 3, and 4, an alphabetic listing of customer names makes it much easier to look up a particular customer. Database software can sort records using fields in a database. If you want to sort the database by the city in which customers live, simply sort on the City field. If you want to sort the database by the Postal Code for a large customer mailing, sort on the Postal Code field. If you want to sort the database by the city then alphabetically by customer, the database will return this information with the proper query. Remember that the purpose of sorting data is for retrieval—finding and using information again. A **query** is a database object used to instruct the program to find specific information. For example, Figure 5.2 on page 110 shows the design view of a query in *Microsoft Access* and the resulting query table.

What is a query?

Figure 5.3 on page 111 shows a portion of a report based on the query shown in Figure 5.2. Customers are grouped alphabetically by city, and then

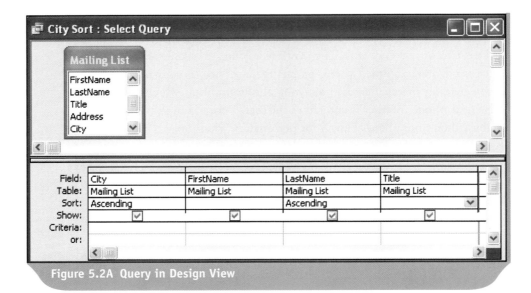

Figure 5.2A Query in Design View

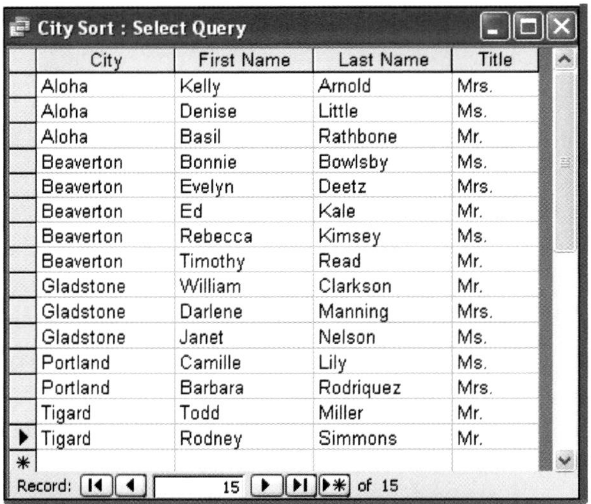

Figure 5.2B Query Results Table

sorted by name. Queries also help a user summarize information. For example, a video store has a database of customer names, addresses, phone numbers, video rentals organized by types of movies, and the dates of rentals. The store manager wants to know which category of movies had the most rentals last month. The query would ask the database to sort the Movie Category field, and then identify the beginning and ending dates of the last month in the Date Rented field. The database would return a list of customers in sorted order by the Movie Category field for the last month.

City Sort

City	Last Name	First Name	Title
Aloha	Arnold	Kelly	Mrs.
Aloha	Little	Denise	Ms.
Aloha	Rathbone	Basil	Mr.
Beaverton	Bowlsby	Bonnie	Ms.
Beaverton	Deetz	Evelyn	Mrs.
Beaverton	Kale	Ed	Mr.
Beaverton	Kimsey	Rebecca	Ms.
Beaverton	Read	Timothy	Mr.
Gladstone	Clarkson	William	Mr.
Gladstone	Manning	Darlene	Mrs.
Gladstone	Nelson	Janet	Ms.
Portland	Lily	Camille	Ms.
Portland	Rodriquez	Barbara	Mrs.
Tigard	Miller	Todd	Mr.
Tigard	Simmons	Rodney	Mr.

Figure 5.3 *Access Report*

How could this information be used? The store manager could count the number of rentals for a specific category of movie. If comedies were rented more often than dramatic movies, the manager could obtain more comedies. Keeping track of the rental dates will help the store manager know which days are the busiest. Would you guess Fridays and Saturdays? The database will return a listing of days of the week so that the store manager has solid data to use in making decisions.

Using Databases in Records Management and E-Commerce

Many records departments create a database index of their paper and/or non-paper records. For example, a database is created that contains the names, addresses, and telephone numbers of customers of the symphony. An electronic database allows rapid creation of mailing labels to notify customers of special concerts or other events to help generate more sales.

In Chapter 1 you learned about e-commerce and how RIM professionals work with IT professionals to manage electronic records created via the

CAREER CORNER

The Certified Records Manager (CRM) professional designation is conferred on candidates who have passed the six-part test administered by the Institute of Certified Records Managers. The examination is offered twice a year, and candidates must apply to take the exam. A candidate's educational background and professional work experience is also taken into consideration for the CRM.

Parts 1-5 of the examination include 100 multiple choice questions on each part. The passing score for each part is 70 percent. Each part contains different subject matter and the broad categories are listed below. The last part, Part 6 Case Studies, is taken after the candidate has passed the first five parts.

1. Management principles and the records and information program
2. Records creation and use
3. Records systems, storage, and retrieval
4. Records appraisal, retention, protection, and disposition
5. Facilities, supplies, and technology

Earning the right to use *CRM* as a professional title is a respected and professional accomplishment. People with a CRM designation usually have a higher salary than those in similar jobs who do not. The Institute of Certified Records Managers web site lists jobs for which the CRM designation is required.

Internet. E-commerce is another way of doing business using electronic resources. Most large organizations have a web presence and many allow some type of dynamic interaction with the visitors to their web sites. The dynamic interaction usually involves filling out a form, clicking the Send button, and receiving some type of response on the web page.

HTML (HyperText Markup Language) is the language that Internet browsers (such as *Microsoft® Internet Explorer* or *Netscape®*) interpret and display. The server computer that houses the web pages sends instructions from the HTML document to web server application software which in turn queries or displays the database.

What is the relationship between a form on a web page and an organization's database?

The application server software acts as a translator between the form on the web page and the data in the database. Filling out a form and clicking the Send button causes the server application software to create a new record in the database. If you signed up for an electronic newsletter, for example, a record is created indicating your e-mail address. When the newsletter is sent the next time, you will receive a copy in your e-mail inbox. If you change your e-mail address, you fill out another form on the web page. Clicking on the Send button updates your record in the database.

If you were to contact the organization in person or over the phone, the customer service representative would access the same database. Your record would be found by searching using a unique field. In the case of the newsletter example, the unique field would be your e-mail address.

A bigger role for databases in e-commerce is played when the actual transaction for services or merchandise is completed. The dynamic form on the web page not only accesses the database, but also starts the procedure for products to be "picked" off the warehouse floor, sent to shipping, and then sent to the customer. The payment part of the transaction is completed via electronic fund transfer (EFT). The customer receives the product and a credit card is charged for the amount of the product. The customer receives a credit card statement showing the bill for this product.

HOW COMPUTERS SORT DATA

A computer performs sorting operations quickly and can store a great amount of data in a small space. It pays great attention to detail and can retrieve information faster and more accurately than humans if the input is accurate. You should be aware, however, that computers sort data differently than you would sort records manually. When you sort records manually, you look at each letter, number, or symbol. You understand each one to have a different meaning. When sorting, for example, you know that key indexing units that begin with numbers are placed before key indexing units that begin with letters. You know that the letter *A* comes before the *E*. Computers understand only numbers. Computer programs use character codes to represent the symbols, numbers, and letters in the data you enter.

Character Standards

In Chapter 1 you learned about the International Organization for Standardization (ISO). The American National Standards Institute (ANSI) is a member of the ISO. Remember that the volume of information is growing. Standards help all computers interpret data in the same way. Data standards work on the computer so that it is readable on all machines using the English language or any other language. As more information is displayed on the Internet, standardization is even more important to global communication.

For the United States, ANSI uses the American Standard Code for Information Interchange (**ASCII,** pronounced "Ask E") for compliance to the ISO

> According to the ASCII values, which comes first—an uppercase A or a lowercase a?

standard. ASCII is a character code that was developed as a standard and logical way to recognize character data on computers. ASCII assigns specific numeric values to the first 128 characters of the 256 possible character combinations. ANSI, an expanded version of the code, is used for other characters. Notice the order of the decimal numbers and the ASCII characters in the ASCII Values Chart shown in Figure 5.4.

Decimal Number	ASCII Character	Decimal Number	ASCII Character	Decimal Number	ASCII Character
*32	Space	64	@	96	'
33	!	65	A	97	a
34	"	66	B	98	b
35	#	67	C	99	c
36	$	68	D	100	d
37	%	69	E	101	e
38	&	70	F	102	f
39	'	71	G	103	g
40	(	72	H	104	h
41	)	73	I	105	i
42	*	74	J	106	j
43	+	75	K	107	k
44	,	76	L	108	l
45	-	77	M	109	m
46	.	78	N	110	n
47	/	79	O	111	o
48	0	80	P	112	p
49	1	81	Q	113	q
50	2	82	R	114	r
51	3	83	S	115	s
52	4	84	T	116	t
53	5	85	U	117	u
54	6	86	V	118	v
55	7	87	W	119	w
56	8	88	X	120	x
57	9	89	Y	121	y
58	:	90	Z	122	z
59	;	91	[	123	{
60	<	92	\	124		
61	=	93	]	125	}
62	>	94	^	126	~
63	?	95	_	127	DEL

*The first 31 decimal numbers are reserved for non-printing characters, sometimes known as control characters.

Figure 5.4 ASCII Values Chart

Each character you enter in an electronic record is represented by a unique number in the character code. For example, in ASCII, the code number for letter *C* is 67. The code number for letter *W* is 87. When a computer program sorts data, it uses the character code numbers assigned to the symbols, numbers, and letters you have entered. The resulting sort order may be quite different from the way you would sort the same records manually.

The Company Name Computer Sort column of Figure 5.5 below shows a computer sort of example names. The names were keyed into the computer as they were written. The Indexing Order Manual Sort column shows the same list of names (with no punctuation) keyed in indexing order (as would be used for manual filing) and sorted. Notice the difference in the order of the examples. What causes the difference? Part of the difference is due to placing the names in indexing order. Part of the difference is due to the way computers sort data.

Sort Order

When you manually sort a list of names, you look at the letters to determine the order. When a computer sorts data, it reads each character as a value in the character code. Because these values are numbers, the computer places the lowest value, or number, first. The sort order will depend on the character code used by the computer and possibly on other settings that have been selected. For example, some computer applications ignore the case of letters when sorting. *Microsoft Word* and *Microsoft Excel*® have options the user can set to determine whether the sort is case sensitive. The default setting is no checkmark in the case sensitive box. Figure 5.6 shows the options for selecting *Case Sensitive* for sorting in *Word* and in *Excel. Access* ignores the case when sorting on a particular field. If *Access* encounters two identical values, for example, one uppercase and the other lowercase, *Access* lists them in the order in which they were entered. For example, if a record with the value **jones** in the Last Name

> **Why is Case Sensitive not checked in either *Word* or *Excel?***

Company Name Computer Sort	Indexing Order Manual Sort
# Off Diet Center	3 Rs Nursery School
$ Value Store	26 Highway Service
"A-OK" Smart Shop	405 Shopping Center
26 Highway Service	AOK Smart Shop
3 Rs Nursery School	Dollar Value Store
405 Shopping Center	Labelle Fashion Boutique
LaBelle Fashion Boutique	Larrys Restaurant
Larry's Restaurant	Pounds Off Diet Center

Figure 5.5 Comparison of Sort Orders

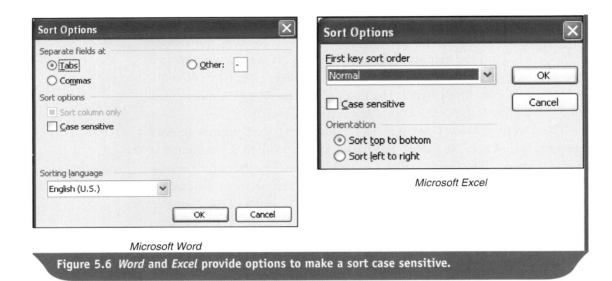

Figure 5.6 *Word* and *Excel* provide options to make a sort case sensitive.

field was entered before a record with the value **Jones** in the same field, the record containing **jones** will be displayed before the record containing **Jones.**

In *Access,* the user can select a default language sort order. The option selected will affect how data is sorted. The *General* option, shown in Figure 5.7, is appropriate for a variety of languages, including English.

The sort order of electronic data can be affected by general settings selected for the computer. For example, for computers that use the *Microsoft Windows*® operating system, settings can be selected on the Regional and Language Options in the Control Panel as shown in Figure 5.8.

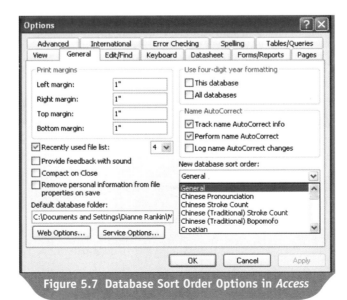

Figure 5.7 Database Sort Order Options in *Access*

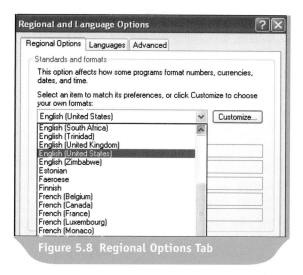

Figure 5.8 Regional Options Tab

Other Sorting Differences

When you are entering records for computerized storage, careful attention to detail and knowledge of how a computer processes data are important points to remember. You have learned that computers sort records in a particular way depending on the character code used and other settings specified by the user. This section points out some other specific differences you may find between how a computer sorts records and how the records would be sorted for manual filing.

Titles and Suffixes

Names with titles and suffixes are indexed for paper records according to Rule 5, Chapter 3. Numeric suffixes (I, II) are filed before alphabetic suffixes (CPA, Jr., Sr.). The computer reads Roman numerals as letters and sorts them after numbers. Figure 5.9 shows examples of names with suffixes sorted by a com-

> **How does a computer sort Roman numerals?**

Example 1 Computer Order			Example 2 Manual Order		
Last Name	**First Name**	**Title/Suffix**	**Last Name**	**First Name**	**Title/Suffix**
Jones	Allen	CPA	Jones	Allen	II
Jones	Allen	II	Jones	Allen	III
Jones	Allen	III	Jones	Allen	CPA
Jones	Allen	Jr	Jones	Allen	Jr
Jones	Allen	Mayor	Jones	Allen	Mayor
Jones	Allen	Mr	Jones	Allen	Mr
Jones	Allen	Sr	Jones	Allen	Sr

Figure 5.9 Comparison of Sort Order for Suffixes

puter and sorted for manual filing. Note the differences in the sort order. In Example 1, CPA is filed before Roman numeral II.

Numbers in Business Names

As mentioned earlier, a computer program may not sort numbers in a text field in consecutive order. Most people know that 2 comes before 10 in a listing of numbers. To a computer, which reads from left to right, 1 comes first, then 10 through 19, then 2, followed by 20 through 29, continuing to 99. Be aware that numbers in text fields may not sort in consecutive order. However, numbers in a database number field can be sorted in consecutive order.

> **How many leading zeros are entered for the number 7 in a list containing numbers 10, 505, and 1330?**

Numbers in a database such as customer IDs, invoice numbers, or product numbers are sometimes keyed with **leading zeros** so that all numbers are the same number of digits and can be sorted consecutively even in a text field. This works well with numbers a company can control or assign. Figure 5.10 shows examples of numbers with and without leading zeros.

Spacing and Punctuation

When filing paper records, spaces are disregarded in some situations. For example, in last names such as *De La Torres* or *Van de Hoef,* the spaces are disregarded when filing paper records. When keying these names in computer records, the spaces will be considered and the filing order will be different than it would be for paper records.

When filing paper records, punctuation is disregarding in determining filing order. When records are keyed in a database, punctuation is not ignored. Therefore, the same names will sort in a different order than that used for manual filing of paper records.

When filing paper records, the word *The* at the beginning of a business name is considered the last indexing unit. When keying such a name in a computer database, the name stays in its original order with *The* as the first word. Therefore, the same names will sort in a different order than that used for manual filing of paper records.

Example 1 Without Leading Zeros		Example 2 With Leading Zeros	
Customer ID (Text field)	Last Name	Customer ID (Text field)	Last Name
1	Allen	001	Allen
11	Jones	002	Thomas
111	Perez	011	Jones
2	Thomas	022	Leon
22	Leon	111	Perez
222	Chin	222	Chin

Figure 5.10 Comparison of Sorted Numbers with and without Leading Zeros

Indexes for Paper Records

In some cases, you may want to change the way you enter records into a computer to achieve the same sorted order as when related paper records are sorted. For example, you might have an index of company names in an electronic database that corresponds to paper records. In this case, you might want the electronic index to show the same sort order as that used for the paper records. An easy way to achieve this would be to add an Indexing Order field to the database table. The company name would be entered in the Company Name field as it is written. This field would be used for tasks such as creating mailing labels where the name should appear as written. In the Indexing Order field, the name would be keyed in indexing order according to manual filing rules. When sorted electronic records are needed to match sorted paper records, the Indexing Order field can be used for the sort.

ELECTRONIC RECORD LIFE CYCLE

Electronic records are being created at an increasing rate. As the number of computer files increases, the need to organize these files is more important than ever. In this section, you will learn how the record life cycle is applied to electronic file management. Figure 5.11 shows the record life cycle for electronic files. Notice the distribution and use phases are shown as one for electronic records. Each phase of the electronic record life cycle is described below.

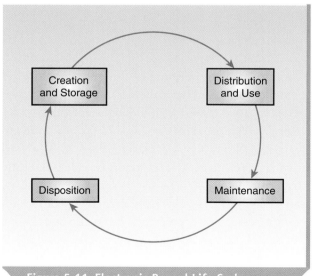

Figure 5.11 Electronic Record Life Cycle

Creation and Storage

How are electronic files created?

Electronic files are created in specific software applications such as *Word, Excel, Access,* and many others. When the application is opened, the user starts keying the needed information in a new document. Creating and storing (saving) the document is the first step in the records life cycle. One way to save a document the first time is to choose Save or Save As from the File menu. When the Save As dialog box opens, navigate to the proper drive and folder. Then, key a filename that is meaningful to the task you are performing. A **filename** is a unique name given to a file stored for computer use that must follow the computer's operating system rules. If the user doesn't change the drive or folder, many programs will automatically save a new document to the My Documents folder on the hard drive for computers that use *Microsoft Windows.*

Electronic documents are stored as bytes on some type of computer storage device. Chapter 11 goes into more detail about storage devices and their media. In many offices, electronic files are stored on a stand-alone computer's hard drive or on shared drives on a local area network (LAN). Some workers might use external storage devices. Removable external storage devices include devices such as floppy disks (although they will be obsolete soon), CDs, tape drives, magnetic hard drives, and USB Flash drives. These devices are removable; thus, the user can take a device from one computer and use it on another computer. You will learn more about external storage devices in Chapter 11. Whatever type of storage device is used, the data should be stored using meaningful filenames and in a logical structure of folders or directories to facilitate retrieving the data.

Folder Structure

What is an operating system?

Dividing storage space into folders is an important part of managing electronic information. A **folder** or **directory** is a subdivision of storage space created by the operating system of a computer. An **operating system** is an organized collection of software that controls the overall operations of a computer. A folder can contain many files. For example, you might have a folder for this class named *Records Management.* You might save a file in the folder named *Chapter 4 Review Questions.* The full path to this document would be *C:\Records Management\Chapter 4 Review Questions.* Notice that a backward diagonal (\) is used to separate the drive, the folder, and filename. This notation, called the **path**, indicates where the file is stored.

Creating folders on any storage device is easy. As with many operations on a computer, different procedures can be used to achieve the same result. Figure 5.12 on page 121 shows the *Windows Explorer* application that comes with the *Microsoft Windows* operating system. To create a new folder using this program, the user can choose File from the menu bar and select New, Folder. The

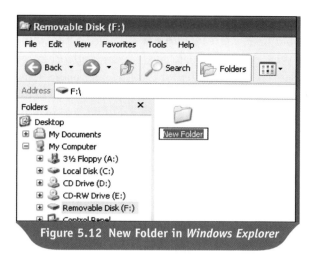

Figure 5.12 New Folder in *Windows Explorer*

new folder appears with the name *New Folder*. The user can change the name of the folder to a meaningful name.

Folders (sometimes called subfolders) can be created within other folders. This allows the user to create a folder structure. For example, suppose you work for Safety First, a company that sells smoke alarms, fire extinguishers, and other fire prevention products. You handle routine correspondence to customers who regularly buy Safety First products. Safety First has a LAN where shared folders are available for any of the office workers. Figure 5.13 shows a partial listing of customer folders.

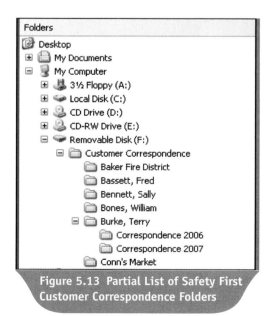

Figure 5.13 Partial List of Safety First Customer Correspondence Folders

Using the example in Figure 5.13, if you wanted to retrieve a letter you sent to Fred Bassett, you would open the *Customer Correspondence* folder, the *Bassett, Fred* subfolder, and then the appropriate file. Correspondence for a new customer would necessitate creating a folder for the customer name. Correspondence such as letters to the new customer would be stored in the customer's folder. When many files are stored in one customer's folder, it may be helpful to create subfolders to organize the files by dates such as by year. These subfolders are shown in Figure 5.13 in the *Burke, Terry* folder.

Folder structure should be designed to facilitate finding files quickly. A shallow folder structure has many folders at the same level. This may mean that the user has to look through a long list of folders to find the one needed. A deep folder structure has folders within folders within folders. Seeing the logic of the folder structure can be difficult when too many levels of folders are used. A folder structure that is neither too shallow nor too deep is ideal. The structure should have enough levels of folders to organize files in a meaningful way, but not so many levels that the structure is hard to understand. Choose meaningful names for folders and files for quick retrieval of files.

> **Which is the most effective type of folder structure?**

Filenames

Using meaningful filenames is an important part of managing electronic files. An organization may have procedures in place for naming files and folders. If no procedures or guidelines exist, think about how the data might be requested when you need to retrieve it later. Using the earlier Safety First example, suppose you write to Conn's Market to answer a question about changing the company's credit terms. You might name the document *Conn's Market credit terms 5-6-06*. The document would be stored in the customer's folder. The complete path would be *F:\Customer Correspondence\Conn's Market\ Conn's Market credit terms 5-6-06*. Using a date in the filename will help distinguish different files about the same topic within the customer's folder.

In Chapters 8, 9, and 10 you will learn about subject, numeric, and geographic order. Any of these methods are appropriate for organizing your electronic files and folders.

Use and Distribution

The next phase of the record cycle is distributing and using the information contained in the electronic folders and files. Distribution can be through electronic channels described below; or files can be printed and sent by regular mail, by facsimile, or by courier.

My Records

Backing Up Data

What back-up operations are needed for your computer records? Do you know how to restore data on the computer system?

Storage disk failure is a matter of *when* rather than *if.* The software loaded on your computer can be re-installed if the hard drive fails; thus, backing up the software applications is usually not necessary. Three types of back-up operations are needed on your personal computer (PC).

WINDOWS SYSTEM RESTORE

The purpose of this utility is to allow you to undo harmful changes to your computer. For example, suppose you loaded some software that is not as compatible with your system as you thought it would be. Restoring the system through *Microsoft Windows* allows you to go back to an earlier time (called a restore point) and restore the settings in effect at that time. *Windows* will automatically set restore points. You can also create a restore point before you install a new hardware device or a new program. Make sure the *Windows System Restore* is turned on.

SPECIFIC PROGRAM AND DATA BACKUP

Some financial programs such as *Microsoft® Money* or *Quicken®* allow users to create a backup of the data used in the program. For example, *Quicken* requests a backup when you close the program. *Quicken* stores your data in its own folder on your hard drive and provides instructions to make a backup on another drive or folder. Make the back-up copy on removable storage such as a rewritable compact disk or a flash drive. This type of backup ensures that the data is safe even if the hard drive on the computer fails. For these types of programs, plan and schedule backups at least once a week. Store the back-up copy in another location so it will be safe from fire or other disasters that may occur at your office.

BACK UP DATA

Regularly schedule and back up data on your hard drive. For example, suppose you are in college and are completing homework assignments using software on your computer. Make a back-up copy of the homework assignments on removable storage devices. When the hard drive fails, you will be able to read your data from removable storage.

E-Mail

Documents can be created in *Word, Excel, Access,* and other programs and then attached to an e-mail message for distribution. The user can also key the information in a program such as *Word* and copy and paste the information into an e-mail. Electronic mail is the most common type of internal communication for large companies. Depending on the e-mail software used, folders can be created to help organize messages. Using the example of the Safety First business, you could send correspondence within the company via e-mail to communicate with people in other departments such as the Shipping or Accounting Department. If you receive an inquiry from a customer, you could access the order number from the company database and know which stage of processing has been completed. You could then send an e-mail to the department that is currently working on the order. When your inquiry is answered, you could forward the information to the customer.

For customers who order many products from the company, create a customer name folder into which you store all e-mails to and from the customer. If you have a few customers who only order once or twice a year, you can create a folder named *A* for all customers whose names begins with an *A.* The procedures for setting up files to hold paper correspondence are given in Chapter 6. With a little adaptation, the same procedures can be followed for e-mail folders.

All the phases of the record life cycle can be completed using e-mail software. For example, Figure 5.14 shows a folder structure in *Microsoft Outlook®* organized by customer names. In this program, folders can be created by right-clicking on the Inbox icon and then keying the name you want the folder to have.

> **What is the most common type of written internal communication for businesses?**

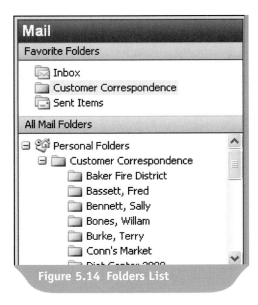

Figure 5.14 Folders List

Intranets

Many organizations post internal documents such as procedure manuals, reference documents, a personnel directory, and correspondence on a secure intranet site where employees see and use distributed information. Browser software, such as *Internet Explorer,* interprets and displays HTML documents. Users may also be allowed to download documents to their computers. The Information Technology (IT) Department may work with RIM professionals to update and manage the intranet site. An intranet site allows employees access through password-protected user names. Some companies do not allow access to the intranet site unless you are using a company computer on the premises of the business. Many companies do not print and distribute manuals to everyone in the organization but, instead, post the information on an intranet site. Because the information is available on the intranet and updated regularly, the documents are not made available in printed form, and the company saves the cost of printing. An individual could print the data from the intranet site if desired.

An intranet site is usually organized by the subject method of storage which you will learn about in Chapter 8. Search engines are available on most large company intranets so the user can find the appropriate information. An IT Department is usually in charge of a company intranet site. However, IT works with a team of workers from all departments of the company to help test the site and help guide its evolution.

What is the main advantage of using an intranet site?

Shared Folders on a LAN

Another place for distribution and use of electronic documents is on shared drives or folders on the company's local area network. The LAN may be set up so that certain departments have use of a particular shared drive. For example, department workers have the right to create, save, edit, modify, and delete files and folders on the shared drive. Some shared drives are available to everyone in the company. Confidential information is usually on a restricted drive available only to employees who are cleared to access confidential information.

Cooperation and coordination between IT and RIM professionals determine the procedures for creating, maintaining, and disposing of folders and files on shared drives.

Find/Search Features

Programs or features that allow users to search for files on a computer drive, LAN drives, or intranet are important tools for electronic records management. On a computer that uses *Microsoft Windows,* for examples, users can search by filename, date, or text on any drive on the computer and/or any drives to which the computer connects. Search Companion options for *Windows Explorer* are shown in Figure 5.15.

Which *Windows* program can help you find a file?

Figure 5.15 *Windows Explorer* **Search Companion Options**

Maintenance

The next phase of the record life cycle is maintenance of the files. In Chapter 1, you learned that a records retention schedule is used to specify how long to keep the records in an organization. Based on retention schedules, maintenance of electronic files follows regularly scheduled times to keep or dispose of the files.

Moving Files and Folders

> **What is the difference between the Move and Copy commands?**

Files and folders can be moved from one folder to another as part of managing electronic records. Moving electronic files that are over a year old, for example, to a different folder leaves fewer files in the original folder so that the more active files are easier to find. At the Safety First business, customer files older than a year are moved to removable storage devices. On the removable drive, the same alphabetic system with the customer name for the folder is used. The dates are noted in the folder name also.

Copying Files and Folders

The Copy command in programs such as *Windows Explorer* is used to create a duplicate of a file or a folder. The copy may have a different name than the original file or folder or it may have the same name if it is stored in a different folder. Copying allows files to be available in two or more locations. For example, a worker can copy a file to a removable storage device and then edit the file on his or her home computer. When the worker returns to work, the updated file is copied to the work computer. Having files readily available can be a convenience to the worker. However, keeping unnecessary copies of files should be avoided to make the best use of storage capacity on hard drives or other devices. Figure 5.16 shows the Copy option in *Windows Explorer.* The Move option works in a similar manner.

Backing Up and Restoring Data

A **backup** is a copy of electronic files and/or folders as a precaution against the loss or damage of the original data. Users should follow a regular schedule to back up vital and important electronic records. Many LANs use software that automatically makes copies of some or all of the data on the network on a regular schedule.

If data is lost or damaged, it can be restored using backup copies. The process of restoring backup copies ensures that the electronic files can be used again without interruption to the flow of business.

Disposition

Several disposition methods are available for electronic records. In Chapter 7, you will learn about records retention and disposition in more detail.

Data Migration

Data migration is used to copy electronic folders and files onto new media as it becomes available. In the 1980s, floppy disks 8 inches in size were commonly used. Today, disk drives that can read the 8-inch floppy disks are no longer commonly used. Implementing a data migration procedure ensures that today's electronic storage can be read with new devices in the future.

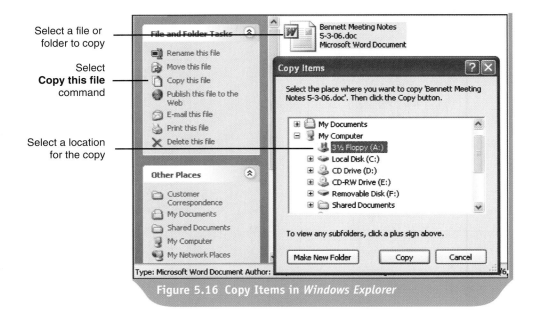

Figure 5.16 Copy Items in *Windows Explorer*

Deleting Files

When electronic records reach the end of their retention period, the information can be deleted. RIM professionals work with users to help manage disposition of electronic records. When files are deleted from a hard drive, users may be able to recover the data if the sectors where the data were stored have not been written over with new data. When deleting confidential information, use a special program such as *Wipe Info,* found in *Nortion AntiVirus*® software, that makes the data unrecoverable. CDs and DVDs used to store confidential data should be completely destroyed when the records are to be destroyed.

What is a PDA?

Managing Data on Handheld Computers and Smart Phones

Electronic file management is necessary for smaller digital devices such as cell phones and personal digital assistants. A **personal digital assistant (PDA)** is a handheld computer that is portable, easy to use, and capable of sharing information with a desktop or notebook computer. PDAs can be used manage contact data for business associates and friends. They can connect to the Internet, act as global positioning system (GPS) devices, and run various types of software. The newest models of PDAs have combined technology with cell phones, multimedia players, or digital cameras to add even more usefulness. Figure 5.17 shows a PDA and a smart phone.

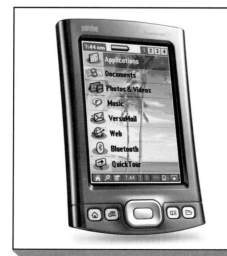 

Courtesy of Palm, Inc.

Figure 5.17 Handhelds and smart phones allow users to organize and share data.

Tools

Many types of software, such as word processing, spreadsheet, games, and graphics, are available for PDAs. They may come with the PDA or be purchased separately and loaded on the PDA. PDAs come with personal information management (PIM) software already loaded. The programs or features allow users to do tasks such as those listed below. Some of the tasks, such as connecting to the Internet, may require subscription services or special features such as a wireless connection to implement.

- Store names, addresses, phone numbers, e-mail addresses
- Make to-do lists
- Take notes
- Track appointments using a calendar feature
- Set reminders for appointments
- Perform calculations
- Synchronize with personal computers
- Connect to the Internet
- Send and receive e-mails

Synchronization with Personal Computers

Synchronization is the process bringing items into agreement, usually in relation to time or rates. In the case of PDAs and personal computers, this means updating the data on the PC and the PDA so that both contain the same data. For example, suppose you use *Microsoft Outlook* on your desktop computer to enter contact data for business associates and to schedule appointments. While at a meeting, you use your PDA to take notes, enter data for a new business contact, and schedule an appointment. Once the meeting is over and you return to your desktop PC, you need to upload the information from your PDA to *Outlook* on your PC.

> **How often should you synchronize your PDA and PC?**

Synchronization software on the PDA works with software that you install on your PC when you purchase a PDA. On your PC, you also need an application similar to *Microsoft Outlook* that stores information on your computer.

Most PDAs have a cable that connects the PDA to a USB port on a PC. Many PDAs can send data to another PDA or to a PC through wireless transmissions. Once the PDA and PC are connected, select the synchronization button or command on the PDA. Follow the instructions to upload and download information from one device to the other. An advantage of synchronizing regularly is that you always have a backup copy of your data on the PDA or on your desktop or notebook computer. Plan to synchronize your PDA and your PC at least once daily.

Chapter Review And Applications

POINTS TO FILE AND RETRIEVE

- Sorting data and records in electronic files and organizing electronic files and folders are important aspects of managing electronic records.

- An electronic database is a collection of related data stored on a computer system. In a database, data is stored in tables containing fields and records.

- The Find or Query feature of database software can be used to find information. Reports can be made from the data in a table or query results.

- Databases are an integral part of e-commerce. Web server and web application software use a form on a web page to create or append records.

- In an e-commerce transaction for services or merchandise, the dynamic form on a web page not only accesses the database but also starts the procedure for products to be sent to the customer. The payment part of the transaction is completed via electronic fund transfer (EFT).

- Computers sort data by using a standard character code values such as ASCII values. The sort order may be different than the sort order that would be used for the same records in a manual filing system.

- General settings selected for a computer (such as language) and options chosen in a particular program may affect the sort order for electronic data.

- Leading zeros may be added to numbers written as digits in a text field to change the sort order.

- Electronic records have a life cycle as do paper records. The stages of the electronic record cycle include creation and storage, use and distribution, maintenance, and disposition.

- Tools (such as *Windows Explorer*) are available on computers to manage all phases of the record life cycle.

- Using meaningful filenames is an important part of managing electronic files.

- Electronic file management is necessary for smaller digital devices such as cell phones and personal digital assistants.

IMPORTANT TERMS

ASCII	operating system
backup	path
database	personal digital assistant (PDA)
directory	query
field	record
filename	synchronization
folder	table
leading zero	

REVIEW AND DISCUSSION

1. Describe the relationship among a database and its tables, records, and fields. (Obj. 1)

2. What is the purpose of a database query? (Obj. 1)

3. Describe how a database is used during an e-commerce transaction. (Obj. 3)

4. How does a character code used by a computer, such as ASCII, affect how the computer sorts data? (Obj. 4)

5. What settings on a computer or program might affect the sort order of electronic records? (Obj. 4)

6. Describe the life cycle for electronic records. (Obj. 5)

7. What is a computer folder or directory? (Obj. 6)

8. You are taking the following classes: WR 121 English Composition, SOC 104 Introduction to Sociology, HST 201 History of Western Civilization, and BA 244 Records Management. List the folder names you will create for your disk to store files for each of your classes. (Obj. 6)

9. How can you assure that confidential data deleted from a computer hard drive or from a CD or DVD cannot be recovered?

10. What is synchronization as it applies to PDAs and desktop or notebook computers? (Obj. 6)

APPLICATIONS

5-1 CREATE A LOGICAL FOLDER STRUCTURE (OBJ. 6)

1. Copy the folder named *Sheraden Investment Services* found in the data files to your hard drive or other storage device.

2. Study the list of files contained in the folder. The files are also listed below. Open some of the files to see the type of data they contain. Determine how to organize the files into a meaningful folder structure.

3. Create a logical folder structure with appropriate folders and subfolders. Move appropriate files to their folders.

4. Submit your work as your instructor directs.

Filenames

Abbott Kenneth 2004	McAllister Vicky Annual
Abbott Kenneth 2005	Reston Brenda 2004
Abbott Kenneth Annual	Reston Brenda 2005
Abbott Paul 2004	Reston Brenda Annual
Abbott Paul 2005	St Amand Dennis 2004
Abbott Paul Annual	St Amand Dennis 2005
Annual Appointment Letter	St Amand Dennis Annual
Demarco David 2004	TenPass Margaret 2004
Demarco David 2005	TenPass Margaret 2005
Demarco David Annual	TenPass Margaret Annual
Investment Summary	Thatcher Linda 2004
McAllister Vicky 2004	Thatcher Linda 2005
McAllister Vicky 2005	Thatcher Linda Annual

5-2 INPUT AND SORT RECORDS (OBJ. 2)

1. Open *Access* and create a new database named *5-2 Customers*.

2. Create a table named **Customers** with the following fields: Customer ID, Business, First Name, Middle Name, Last Name, Title, and Suffix. Select **Number** as the field type for the Customer ID field. Select **Text** as the field type for all other fields. Select the **Customer ID** field as the primary key.

3. Enter the following data into the table.

Customer ID	Name
4114	"Demand the Best" Co.
1122	1 Way Direct
3163	180 Stations, Inc.
1159	2001 Net Works
4135	360 Dish, Inc.
3149	99 TV & Appliance
4108	B-N Handy Company
4122	Catch-A-Dish, Inc.
2115	Early Bird Installers
3109	Earnest Satellite Installations
2107	K. A. Abbott III
2690	KATZ Communications
3127	KBOS Television Station
2980	Keep It Beaming!
1102	KPDX Radio Station
4970	Miss Elena A'Breau
1101	Mr. Archie Abbott
3119	Mr. Daniel De La Torres

4. Create a query to list only the customers that are businesses. Show the Business and the Customer ID fields in the query results. Sort in ascending order using the Business field. Remember to enter an asterisk (*) in the Criteria row for the Business field so that only records with data in this field will display. Print the query results table.

5. You need to locate the customer name for the company or person with customer ID 2115. Use the Find feature with the Customers table to locate this record. What is the company or person's name?

5-3 RESEARCH PERSONAL DIGITAL ASSISTANTS (OBJ. 4)

INTERNET

CRITICAL THINKING

You've just been given a $300 scholarship for purchasing a PDA. Your benefactor will give you the money when you have justified your choice of PDA.

1. Make a list of the features or programs you want on your PDA.

2. Access a search engine on the Internet. Search using the key words *personal digital assistant*.

3. Choose three PDA devices that match your list of features. Compare and contrast the brands and models of the PDAs. Recommend a device to purchase.

4. Send the summary of your findings in an e-mail to your instructor.

RECORDS MANAGEMENT SIMULATION

JOB 4 ALPHABETIC FILING RULES 1-10

Continue working with Auric Systems, Inc.
Complete Job 4.

FOR MORE ACTIVITIES GO TO **http://read.swlearning.com**

Alphabetic Records Management, Equipment, and Procedures

Learning Objectives

1. Explain terms used in correspondence records management systems.

2. Identify the basic types of equipment and supplies for correspondence records storage.

3. Explain considerations for selecting storage equipment and supplies.

4. Discuss the advantages and disadvantages of the alphabetic method of records storage.

5. Describe types of information that should be determined before selection and design of an alphabetic records system.

6. Explain how color can be used in correspondence records storage.

7. Apply procedures for storing correspondence.

8. Explain how a tickler file is used.

9. Prepare folder labels using *Access*.

CORRESPONDENCE RECORDS STORAGE

As you studied earlier chapters of this textbook, you learned to index, code, and cross-reference names and addresses. Beginning with this chapter, you will learn other considerations for working with correspondence—the type of records found in all kinds of businesses. Business letters, forms, reports, and memorandums are all part of the daily correspondence that businesses transact.

What is business correspondence?

As noted in an article for *Inside Self Storage,* "Regardless of the impact technology will have on business as we move into the future, the pure mass of paper records is increasing every year."[1] Business offices continue to use paper as a medium for all or part of their records. Thus, the discussion in this chapter focuses on the use of equipment and supplies for paper records. Chapter 11 discusses electronic systems used in records management.

[1]Cary F. McGovern,"Jump-Start a Records-Management Business," *Inside Self Storage,* <http://www. insideselfstorage.com/articles/1c1recor.html> (accessed June 21, 2005).

As you complete this chapter, you will apply the ten alphabetic indexing rules learned from Chapters 2, 3, and 4 to indexing, coding, and cross-referencing correspondence. In addition, you will learn three other steps in alphabetic storage procedures: inspecting, sorting, and storing.

Information requirements make systematic storage and retrieval of records increasingly important. Businesses use records to complete transactions, to communicate with customers or clients, and to document compliance with laws and regulations. You have discovered that a set of written rules for alphabetic indexing provides consistency for storing and retrieving records. Consistent application of the alphabetic indexing rules is only one part of an efficient records management program. Using effective, appropriate equipment and supplies is another. This chapter introduces a variety of available records storage equipment and supplies and describes selection criteria.

You are familiar with some of the specific terms and meanings pertaining to the storage and retrieval of records. The following terms and definitions will help you understand the information in this chapter:

- **Records management** is the systematic control of all records from their creation, or receipt, through their processing, distribution, organization, storage, and retrieval to their ultimate disposition. The goal of records management is to get the right record to the right person at the right time at the lowest possible cost.
- **Storage** is the actual placement of records, according to a plan, on a shelf, or in a file drawer. Also, storage can be electronically saving a record to a medium readable by a computer. The term *filing* may be used to mean storage, but filing is usually associated with paper records only.
- A **storage method** is a systematic way of storing records according to an alphabetic, subject, numeric, geographic, or chronologic plan. A specific system for organizing and arranging records can be referred to as a records management system or filing system. Often these terms are used synonymously.
- **Alphabetic records management** is a method of storing and arranging records according to the letters of the alphabet.
- **Storage procedures** are a series of steps for the orderly arrangement of records as required by a specific storage method or records management system.

The storage method or system discussed here and in previous chapters is alphabetic. Records and information management (RIM) professionals do not agree on the number of records storage methods. Some professionals say there are just two: alphabetic and numeric. Subject and geographic methods are not considered separate methods because the subjects and geographic names are filed alphabetically. Other records professionals add alphanumeric as a third

How many storage methods are used to file records?

method. Still others add a fourth—chronologic. In this text, alphabetic, subject, numeric, and geographic are considered as four RIM methods. With the exception of chronologic storage, each of these methods uses alphabetic concepts in its operation. Subject, numeric, and geographic records are described in detail in Chapters 8, 9, and 10.

RECORDS STORAGE EQUIPMENT AND SUPPLIES

You have probably heard the adage, "A place for everything, and everything in its place." The records manager or person in charge of purchasing the equipment and supplies for the records center must certainly heed this advice. To have a proper place for various types of records requires knowledge of equipment for records processing and storage. What type of equipment and supplies are used most often in offices? What is the specific vocabulary for RIM equipment and supplies? To help answer these questions, you can use an Internet search engine to locate web sites for vendors of filing equipment and supplies. Viewing information on these web sites can help familiarize you with the array of available RIM equipment and supply products. This section of the chapter describes characteristics of these different types of products and their uses.

Storage Equipment

Types of storage equipment commonly used for paper records are: (1) vertical file cabinets, (2) lateral file cabinets, (3) shelf files, and (4) mobile shelving. Other types of storage equipment and their special uses for RIM are discussed in later chapters.

Vertical File Cabinets

A **vertical file cabinet** is storage equipment that is deeper than it is wide. Generally, the arrangement of folders in the file drawers is from front to back. A **folder** is a container used to hold and protect the contents of a file together and separate from other files. Vertical file cabinets, as shown in Figure 6.1 on page 138, are the conventional storage cabinets in one- to five-drawer designs. Two rows of vertical file cabinets may be placed back to back in a large central storage area with aisle space on either side. The type and volume of records to be stored will determine the width, depth, number, and size of drawers. The two-drawer file is desk height and sometimes used beside a desk for additional workspace, as well as for ready access to frequently used records. The most common widths of vertical file cabinet drawers are appropriate for letters or legal-size documents.

The HON Company

Figure 6.1 Vertical File Cabinets

Lateral File Cabinets

A **lateral file cabinet** is storage equipment that is wider than it is deep—records are accessed from the side (horizontally). Records can be arranged in the drawers from front to back or side to side. Because the long (narrow) side opens, lateral file cabinets are particularly well suited to narrow aisle spaces. They are available in a variety of sizes, depending on the number and depth of the drawers. Figure 6.2 on page 139 shows a lateral file cabinet with roll-back drawer fronts and one with pull-out drawers.

Shelf Files

A **shelf file** is open-shelving equipment in which records are accessed horizontally from the open side. Shelf files may be an open style or have roll-back or roll-down fronts. They may be stationary shelves (see Figure 6.3 on page 139) or shelves arranged in rotary form. Rotary shelf files have a rotating bank of shelves so that records can be stored and accessed from both sides of the shelves.

The HON Company

Figure 6.2 Lateral File Cabinets

The HON Company

Figure 6.3 Shelf Files

Courtesy of TAB Products Co., LLC

Mobile Shelving

Areas with limited space may use mobile banks of shelves that can be moved as needed for storage and retrieval. **Mobile shelving** is a series of shelving units that move on tracks attached to the floor for access to files (Figure 6.4). In some movable shelving equipment, the shelves slide from side to side. The records on shelves behind the moved shelves are then exposed for use. The units may operate with electric power or may be moved manually by the operator. Because aisle space is not constantly maintained between each unit, mobile shelving can approximately double the storage capacity of an area.

Motorized rotary storage is a unit that rotates shelves in the unit around a central hub to bring the files to the operator. Such systems may have an automated keypad-driven retrieval system. This system uses overhead storage with the rotation of the files moving horizontally around a central core to bring files to the operator, and it provides access at a height that can accommodate persons with a disability requiring a wheelchair. Figure 6.5 on page 141 shows a system of no-walk carousels with banks of vertical shelves rotating for access by an operator.

Figure 6.4 Mobile Shelving

The Smead Manufacturing Company

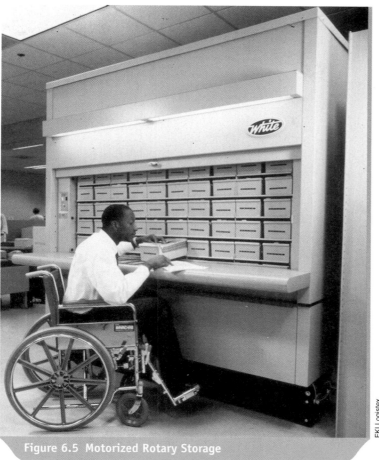

Figure 6.5 Motorized Rotary Storage

FKI Logistex

File Capacity and Space Requirements

When choosing storage cabinets or shelves, a comparison of file capacity and floor space requirements helps determine cost effectiveness. An estimated capacity for a standard four-drawer file cabinet is about 10,000 records (calculated at about 100 sheets per linear inch including guides and folders). Three to four inches of space should be left as working space at the end of a file drawer or shelf section to allow easy removal and replacement of file folders. A letter-size vertical cabinet drawer measures 15 by 28 inches and, therefore, holds about 25 linear inches of records. A lateral file drawer is 18 by 36 inches with a file capacity of 33 linear inches. Pull-out drawer space for vertical files requires about two feet; lateral file drawers use approximately one foot of pull-out space. Shelf files require less floor space because they need no drawer-pull space, are not as deep as file cabinets, and hold records that can be readily accessed up to seven shelves high. Figure 6.6 on page 142 illustrates the capacity and floor space requirements for these three types of storage equipment.

> **Which type of cabinet requires the least amount of aisle space?**

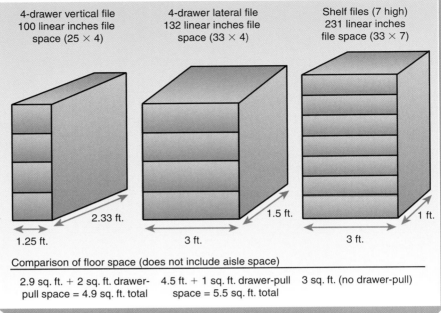

Figure 6.6 Filing Equipment Storage Capacity

Shelf files save filer time as well as floor space because there are no drawers to open before records can be accessed; however, open-shelf filing for confidential or vital records must be placed in a records vault for security. File drawers and closed-front cabinets can be purchased with locks. Fire protection is a safety consideration. Vital records can be duplicated and kept in off-site storage. Fireproof storage cabinets can be purchased for important records; these cabinets are heavier and higher in cost than standard file cabinets.

Storage Supplies

Efficient storage and retrieval requires the use of the right equipment and the right supplies. The principal supplies used in manual storage of paper records are discussed briefly in this section.

Guides

A **guide** is a rigid divider used to identify a section in a file and to facilitate reference to a particular record location. Guides are made of heavy material such as pressboard, manila, or plastic. A **tab** is a projection for a caption on a folder or guide that extends above the regular height or beyond the regular width of the folder or guide. Some guides have reinforced tabs of metal or acetate to

What purpose do guides serve?

give added strength for long wear. Tabs and tab cuts are discussed in detail later in this chapter.

The proper placement of guides eliminates the need to spend time searching through similar names to find the part of the alphabet needed. The same set of guides may be used year after year with no change, or they may be added to or changed as the quantity of records increases. Because of their thickness and sturdy construction, guides also serve to keep the contents of a container (drawer or box) upright. Keeping contents upright promotes efficient storage and retrieval. Guides serve as signposts and speed location of records. Too few guides result in unnecessary time spent looking for the correct place to store or find a record. Too many guides that are unevenly distributed throughout the files can slow storage and retrieval because the eye must look at so many tabs to find the right storage section. Using about 20 guides for each file drawer or for each 28 linear inches of stored records will facilitate efficient storage and retrieval in a typical system.

Primary Guides

A **primary guide** is a divider that identifies a main division or section of a file and always precedes all other material in a section. In Figure 6.7 on page 144, the NAMES WITH NUMBERS, A, and B guides in first position (at the left) are primary guides. Remember Rule 7 about business names beginning with numbers? Numbers are filed before letters of the alphabet; the NAMES WITH NUMBERS guide and NAMES WITH NUMBERS folder are filed before the A guide. A small volume of stored correspondence with many individuals or firms requires only primary guides to indicate the alphabetic sections. Systems that use color extensively may use only primary guides with the letters of the alphabet because blocks of colored folders act as a visual guide to a section of the alphabet.

Guide sets that divide the alphabet into many different segments are available from manufacturers of filing supplies. The simplest set is a 23- or 25-division set, the latter having a tab for each letter from A to W, a tab labeled *Mc,* and a last tab with the combination *XYZ.* Figure 6.8 on page 145 compares an 80-division and a 120-division breakdown of guides printed by manufacturers.

The number of alphabetic guides furnished by different manufacturers can vary even though each plan may divide the alphabet into 40 subdivisions. Manufacturers may elect to omit Mc, subdivide letters differently, or combine different letters. Before purchasing a set of guides, the records manager should examine the manufacturer's alphabetic subdivisions to see if the subdivisions fit specific office requirements. Alphabetic guides can be purchased with preprinted tabs or tabs with slotted holders for the insertion of labels.

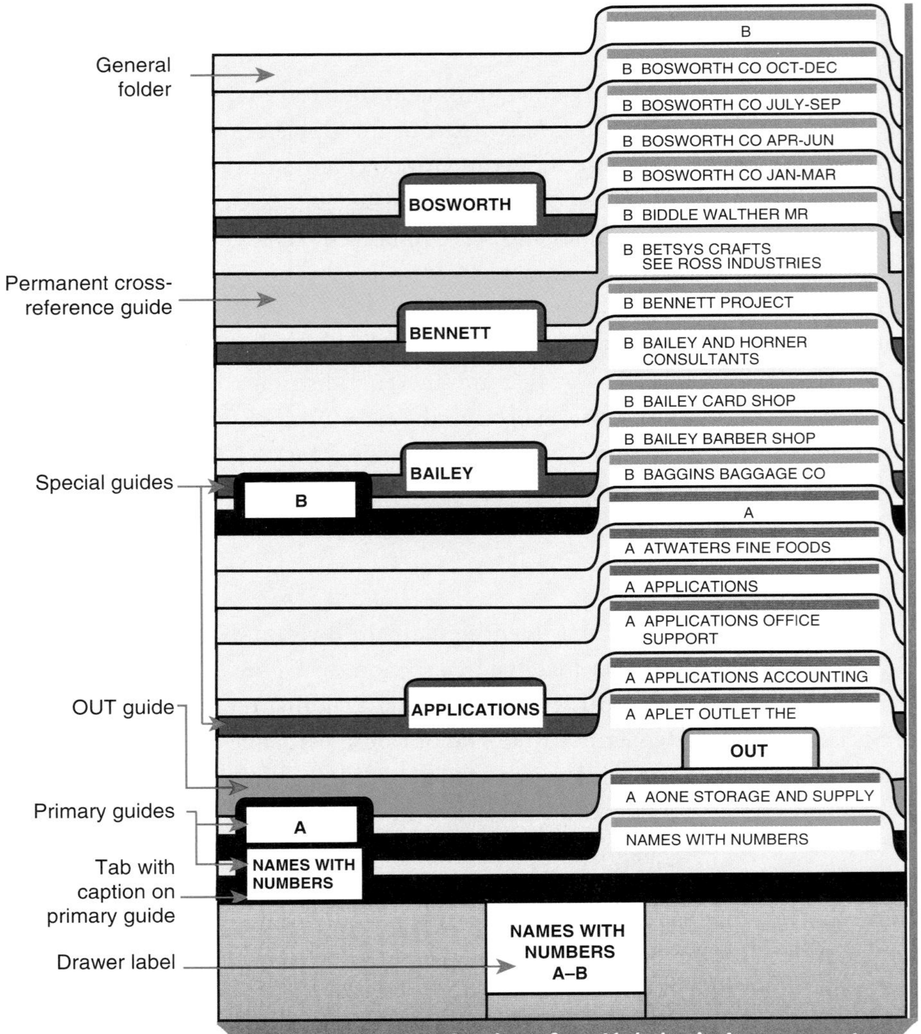
General folder
Permanent cross-reference guide
Special guides
OUT guide
Primary guides
Tab with caption on primary guide
Drawer label
B
B BOSWORTH CO OCT-DEC
B BOSWORTH CO JULY-SEP
B BOSWORTH CO APR-JUN
B BOSWORTH CO JAN-MAR
BOSWORTH
B BIDDLE WALTHER MR
B BETSYS CRAFTS SEE ROSS INDUSTRIES
B BENNETT PROJECT
BENNETT
B BAILEY AND HORNER CONSULTANTS
B BAILEY CARD SHOP
B BAILEY BARBER SHOP
BAILEY
B BAGGINS BAGGAGE CO
B
A
A ATWATERS FINE FOODS
A APPLICATIONS
A APPLICATIONS OFFICE SUPPORT
A APPLICATIONS ACCOUNTING
APPLICATIONS
A APLET OUTLET THE
OUT
A AONE STORAGE AND SUPPLY
A
NAMES WITH NUMBERS
NAMES WITH NUMBERS
NAMES WITH NUMBERS A–B

Figure 6.7 One Section of an Alphabetic Arrangement

Special Guides

A **special (auxiliary) guide** is a divider used to lead the eye quickly to a specific place in a file. Use special guides to:

1. Indicate the location of an individual or a company folder with a high volume of correspondence. In Figure 6.7, the guides labeled *BENNETT* and *BOSWORTH* are special (auxiliary) name guides.
2. Introduce a special section of subjects, such as Applications, Bids, Conferences, Exhibits, Projects, or Speeches. Figure 6.7 shows a special subject guide, APPLICATIONS, placed in alphabetic order in the A section. Correspondence concerning applications for positions in accounting and office support is stored behind APPLICATIONS, in properly labeled folders.

80 Div. A to Z				120 Div. A to Z					
A	1	L	41	A	1	Gr	41	Pe	81
An	2	Le	42	Al	2	H	42	Pi	82
B	3	Li	43	An	3	Han	43	Pl	83
Be	4	Lo	44	As	4	Has	44	Pr	84
Bi	5	M	45	B	5	He	45	Pu	85
Bo	6	Map	46	Bar	6	Hen	46	Q	86
Br	7	McA	47	Bas	7	Hi	47	R	87
Bro	8	McH	48	Be	8	Ho	48	Re	88
Bu	9	McN	49	Ber	9	Hon	49	Ri	89
C	10	Me	50	BI	10	Hu	50	Ro	90
Ce	11	Mi	51	Bo	11	I	51	Rog	91
Co	12	Mo	52	Br	12	J	52	Ru	92
Coo	13	N	53	Bre	13	Jo	53	S	93
Cr	14	O	54	Bro	14	K	54	Sch	94
D	15	P	55	Bu	15	Ke	55	Scho	95
De	16	Pl	56	C	16	Ki	56	Se	96
Do	17	Q	57	Car	17	Kl	57	Sh	97
Dr	18	R	58	Ce	18	Kr	58	Shi	98
E	19	Re	59	Ci	19	L	59	Si	99
En	20	Ro	60	Co	20	Lar	60	Sm	100
F	21	S	61	Corn	21	Le	61	Sn	101
Fi	22	Sch	62	Cop	22	Len	62	Sp	102
Fo	23	Se	63	Cr	23	Li	63	St	103
G	24	Sh	64	Cu	24	Lo	64	Sti	104
Ge	25	Si	65	D	25	M	65	Su	105
Gi	26	Sm	66	De	26	Map	66	T	106
Gr	27	St	67	Di	27	McA	67	Th	107
H	28	Sti	68	Do	28	McD	68	Tr	108
Har	29	Su	69	Du	29	McH	69	U	109
Has	30	T	70	E	30	McN	70	V	110
He	31	To	71	El	31	Me	71	W	111
Her	32	U	72	Er	32	Mi	72	Wam	112
Hi	33	V	73	F	33	Mo	73	We	113
Ho	34	W	74	Fi	34	Mu	74	Wh	114
Hu	35	We	75	Fo	35	N	75	Wi	115
I	36	Wh	76	Fr	36	Ne	76	Wil	116
J	37	Wi	77	G	37	No	77	Wim	117
K	38	Wo	78	Ge	38	O	78	Wo	118
Ki	39	X-Y	79	Gi	39	On	79	X-Y	119
Kr	40	Z	80	Go	40	P	80	Z	120

Figure 6.8 Comparison of Guide Sets for A to Z Indexes

3. Identify a section reserved for names with the same first indexing unit. In Figure 6.7, the BAILEY special name guide leads the eye to the section with numerous folders labeled with BAILEY as the first indexing unit.

The tabs on guides for open-shelf equipment are at the side as shown in Figure 6.9. Because materials stored in open-shelf equipment are visible at one edge instead of across the top (as is true in drawer files), the alphabetic or other divisions must extend from the side of the guide so that they can be seen easily. The printing on these side-guide tabs may be read from either side.

Folders

Folders are containers used to hold and protect the records in a file. Folders are usually made of heavy material such as manila, plastic, or pressboard and can have either top or side tabs in varying sizes. Folders are creased approximately in half; the back is slightly higher than the front. A folder may be reinforced across the top of the back edge because that is the place receiving the greatest wear, as a folder is usually grasped by that edge.

A tab is a projection for a caption on a folder or guide that extends above the regular height or beyond the regular width of the folder or guide. Folder and guide tabs are available in different sizes or cuts. A **tab cut** is the length of the tab expressed as a proportion of the width or height of the folder or guide. A **straight cut tab** extends across the complete width of a folder. A **one-third cut tab** extends only one-third the width of a folder and may be in any of three positions as shown in Figure 6.10 on page 147.

Position refers to the location of the tab across the top or down one side of a guide or folder. First position means the tab is at the left; second position

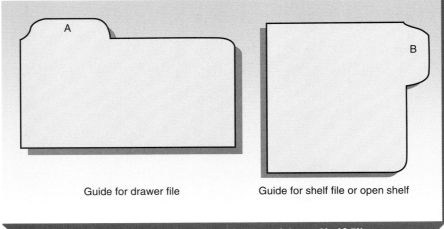

Guide for drawer file   Guide for shelf file or open shelf

Figure 6.9 Guides Used in Drawer Cabinets and Open-Shelf Files

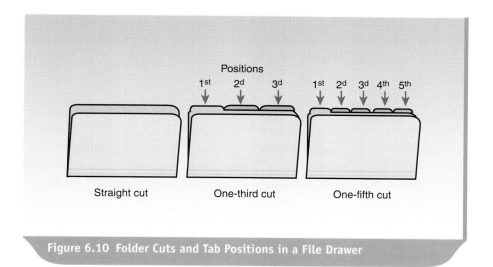

Figure 6.10 Folder Cuts and Tab Positions in a File Drawer

means the tab is second from the left; and so on. **Straight-line arrangement** is a system that aligns folder tabs in one position; for example, all folder tabs are third position (see Figure 6.7 on page 144). **Staggered arrangement** is a system that follows a series of several different positions of folder tabs from left to right according to a set pattern. Straight-line position is preferred because of ease in reading label captions; the eye travels faster in a straight line than when it jumps back and forth from left to right. The most efficient position for folders is third, with third-cut tabs; and the most efficient position for guides is either first or second with fifth-cut tabs as shown in Figure 6.7.

Tabs on folders for open-shelf equipment are on the side edge (Figure 6.11) in various positions according to the manufacturer's system or the customer's preference.

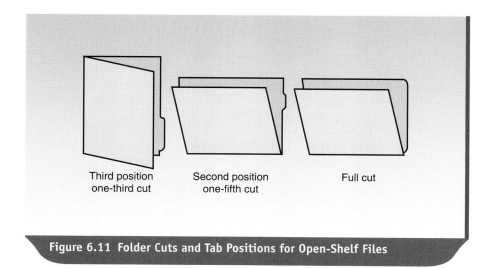

Figure 6.11 Folder Cuts and Tab Positions for Open-Shelf Files

Folders behind every guide are used to keep like records together. The three main types of folders used in alphabetic storage are general folders, individual folders, and special folders.

General Folders

Every primary guide has a corresponding general folder, bearing the same caption as that on the guide. A **general folder** is a folder for records to and from correspondents with a small volume of records that does not require an individual folder or folders. In Figure 6.7, the A folder is a general folder and is the last folder in that section. General folders often are color coded for greater visibility.

Records are arranged inside a general folder alphabetically by the correspondents' names. Then, the most recently dated record is placed on top within each correspondent's records as shown in Figure 6.12.

Individual Folders

An **individual folder** is a folder used to store the records of an individual correspondent with enough records to warrant a separate folder. Records are arranged chronologically within an individual folder with the most recently dated record on top. In Figure 6.7, all individual folders are one-third cut, third position. Records pertaining to one correspondent are removed from the general folder and placed in an individual folder when the number of records accumulates to a predetermined number. Individual folders are placed in alphabetic order between the primary guide and its general folder.

> **What is a general folder? An individual folder? A special folder?**

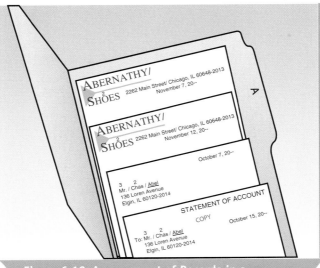

Figure 6.12 Arrangement of Records in a General Folder

Special Folders

A **special folder** is a folder that follows a special guide in an alphabetic arrangement. In Figure 6.7, three special folders are shown: two behind APPLICATIONS and one behind BENNETT. Within the APPLICATIONS ACCOUNTING folder, all records pertaining to accounting positions are arranged first by the names of the applicants. If an applicant has more than one record in the folder, those records are arranged by date with the most recent date on top. Within the BENNETT PROJECT folder, records are arranged by date, the most recent one on top.

Care of Folders

Proper care of folders will help make stored records readily accessible. When records start to "ride up" in any folder, too many papers are in the folder. The number of records that will fit into one folder obviously depends on the thickness of the papers. Records should never protrude from the folder edges and should always be inserted with their tops to the left. The most useful folders have score marks. Score marks are indented or raised lines or series of marks along the bottom edge of a folder to allow for expansion (Figure 6.13). As it becomes filled, the folder is refolded along a score mark and expanded to give it a flat base on which to rest. Most folders can be expanded from ¾ to 1 inch. Refolding a folder at the score marks reduces the danger of folders bending and sliding under others, avoids curling papers, and results in a neater file.

A folder lasts longer and is easier to use if it is not stuffed beyond its capacity. If too many papers are in an individual folder, prepare a second folder for that correspondent. Then label the folders to show that the records are arranged chronologically in them (see the four BOSWORTH CO folders in Figure 6.7). Sometimes papers in a folder are redistributed by adding subject folders instead of subdividing by dates, as is the case with APPLICATIONS in Figure 6.7.

> **Why are score marks on file folders?**

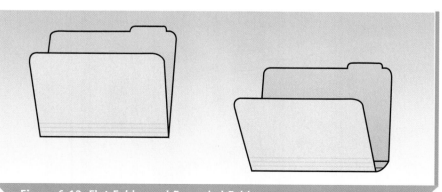

Figure 6.13 Flat Folder and Expanded Folder

New folders may be needed because:

When are new folders needed?

- A new group of names is to be added to a file.
- Older folders have become full, and additional ones must be added to take care of the overload.
- Enough records have accumulated for certain correspondents so that their records can be removed from the general folders and put into individual folders.
- Folders have worn out from heavy use and must be replaced.
- The scheduled time has arrived for replacing folders and transferring infrequently used folders to inactive storage. Chapter 7 further explains records transfer.

Types of Folders

Other folders frequently used in offices are a suspension or hanging folder, a bellows folder, and a pocket folder. These folder types can be useful for particular types of records within a RIM system.

The **suspension (hanging) folder** is a folder with built-in hooks on each side that hang from parallel metal rails on each side of a file drawer or other storage equipment (Figure 6.14). The main advantage of hanging folders over conventional folders is their added support for holding records in a neat, upright position due to support of both the front and back of the folder with hooks on the drawer rails. If your file cabinet does not have built-in rails for hanging folders, you can purchase drawer frames with rails that adjust for letter or legal-size files. Hanging folders have up to ten slots across the upper edge for placement of insertable plastic tabs and can hold several interior folders to subdivide a file.

Esselte Corporation

Figure 6.14 Hanging or Suspension File Folders

Generally, hanging folders should not leave a file drawer. Placing the contents of these folders in interior conventional-type folders or interior folders that are shorter than traditional file folders provides records protection and facilitates removal or placement of records. In addition, some hanging folders have a pocket for small items like computer disks, notes, or receipts.

A **bellows (expansion) folder** is a folder that has a top flap and sides to enclose records in a case with creases along its bottom and sides that allow it to expand. These folders usually come with dividers inside for subdividing the records and are used when the volume of stored records is small. In Figure 6.15, the bellows folder is on the left.

A **pocket folder** is a folder with partially enclosed sides and more expansion at the bottom than an ordinary folder (Figure 6.15, right). A pocket folder is useful for transporting as well as for storing records. Also, these folders can be used to store records such as bound reports or other records media with more bulk than can be easily fitted into a traditional file folder.

Follower Blocks or Compressors

Failing to use proper means to hold drawer contents upright causes folders to bend and slide under one another. The proper number of guides and correct use of a follower block behind the guides and folders keeps folders upright. A **follower block (compressor)** is a device at the back of a file drawer that can be moved to allow contraction or expansion of the drawer contents (Figure 6.16 on page 152). A follower block that is too loose will allow the drawer contents to sag; one that is too tight will make filing and retrieving a folder difficult. In an over-compressed drawer, as in an overcrowded drawer, locating and removing a single sheet of paper is difficult. Instead of follower blocks, some file drawers have slim steel upright dividers placed permanently throughout the

> **What is the purpose of a follower block in a file drawer?**

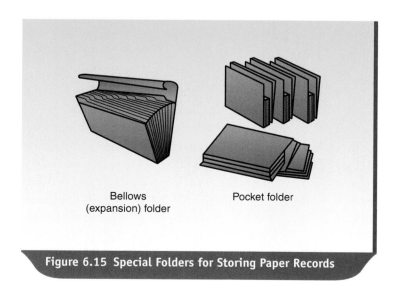

Bellows
(expansion) folder

Pocket folder

Figure 6.15 Special Folders for Storing Paper Records

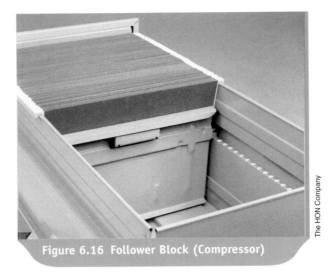

The HON Company

Figure 6.16 Follower Block (Compressor)

file drawer to keep the contents vertical. Also, shelf files use a series of metal upright dividers to hold records upright. A lateral or vertical file with metal rails and hanging folders does not require the use of a follower block; the suspension of each folder on the drawer rack holds records upright.

OUT Indicators

An **OUT indicator** is a control device that shows the location of borrowed records. These indicators contain a form for recording the name of the person borrowing the record, the date it was borrowed, a brief statement of the contents of the record, and the due date for return to storage. When a borrowed record is returned to storage, the OUT indicator is removed, to be reused, thrown away, or saved and later used to check the activity at the files or to determine which records are active or inactive. Commonly used indicators are OUT guides, OUT folders, and OUT sheets.

OUT Guides

An **OUT guide** is a special guide used to replace any record that has been removed from storage and to indicate what was taken and by whom. When the borrowed record is returned, the filer can quickly find the exact place from which the record was taken. An OUT guide is made of the same sturdy material as other guides with the word OUT printed on its tab in large letters and a distinctive color. In Figure 6.7 on page 144, an OUT guide is located between the AONE STORAGE AND SUPPLY and the APLET OUTLET THE individual folders. The guides can have preprinted charge-out forms on both sides or a plastic insert pocket to hold a charge-out form. Some OUT guides have a pocket for temporarily holding documents to be replaced in the folder when it is returned to the file.

What is the purpose of an OUT indicator?

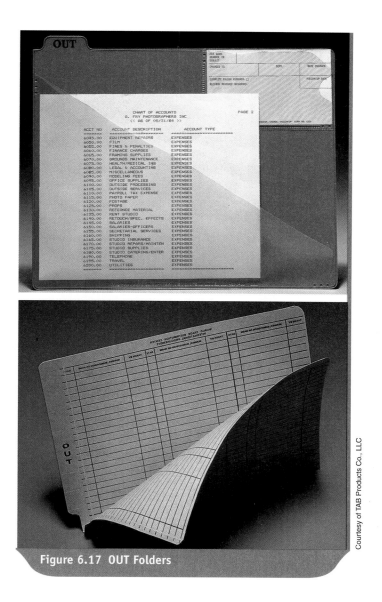

Figure 6.17 OUT Folders

Courtesy of TAB Products Co., LLC

OUT Folders

An **OUT folder** is a special folder used to replace a complete folder that has been removed from storage. This folder has a pocket or slot into which a small card is placed bearing the same information concerning who took the folder, the date it was taken, its contents, and the date the folder should be returned to storage. The OUT folder remains in the file as a temporary storage place for records that will be transferred to the permanent folder when it is returned to storage.

OUT Sheets

An **OUT sheet** is a form that is inserted in place of a record removed from a folder. An OUT sheet is often the same size and color as an OUT guide, but its thickness is that of a sheet of paper. An OUT sheet remains in the file folder until replaced with the returned record.

Labels

Containers, guides, and folders that help filers store records efficiently must be labeled to guide the eye to the appropriate storage location. A **label** is a device that contains the name of the subject or number assigned to the file folder or section contents. It may have other pertinent information, be color-coded to denote its place in an overall filing system, or have a bar code. A **caption** is a title, heading, short explanation, or description of a document or records.

Container Labels

The labels on drawers, shelf files, or other storage containers should be clearly but briefly worded and inclusive enough to represent the contents. The containers usually have holders on the outside where card stock labels can be inserted. Various colors are available on perforated card stock sheets. ARMA guidelines recommend centering information for the container label in all caps with no punctuation. The caption on the drawer illustrated in Figure 6.7 on page 144 reads *NAMES WITH NUMBERS A–B,* indicating that records of correspondents whose names are within the A and B sections of the alphabet are stored in that drawer. Names in which the key units are numbers written as digits are filed before all alphabetic names. For example, *123 Builders* comes before *Albany Builders.*

Guide Labels

Labels on guides consist of words, letters, or numbers (or some combination of these items). In Figure 6.7, the guides shown have window tabs into which keyed captions have been inserted (NAMES WITH NUMBERS, A, APPLICATIONS, B, BAILEY, BENNETT, BOSWORTH). Some guides (alphabetic or numeric guides) are available with preprinted information. ARMA guidelines recommend placing guide captions near the left margin of the label and as near as possible to the top. Print captions in all capital letters with no punctuation. Single letters of the alphabet may be centered on guide labels if preferred.

Folder Labels

Folder labels come as pressure-sensitive adhesive labels in continuous folded strips or on sheets that can be prepared with computer software and affixed to folders. A colored stripe across the top is often used on a white or buff-colored label. Sheets of labels for computer generation usually have columns of labels across an 8½ by 11-inch sheet. Most word processing software has settings for different label sizes that match common label product numbers. Also, packaging that comes with the labels often has instructions for required software settings. Many vendors have computer software programs that generate labels, or they provide a service for custom-printed labels. Some vendors have printers that print durable laminated labels. Figure 6.18 illustrates a color-coded labeling system.

Bar codes can be generated along with a name on a label. Use of a bar code tracking system keeps a record of a file location at all times. When a file is checked out, a scanner reads the bar code. Information about the file and who checked it out is then updated and recorded in a computer program. Sometimes another label strip is generated for OUT indicators. Use of a bar code tracking system can greatly improve retrieval rates. Refer to Chapter 7 for more on bar code tracking.

Place folder labels near the left edge and as near the top of the label or the bottom of the color bar as possible. Wrap-around side-tab labels for open-sided lateral file cabinets or shelf filing are placed both above and below the color bar separator so that the information is readable from both sides of the folder. Word processing software with automatic label settings places information in the proper location on the label. For alphabetic filing, the letter of the

What format should be used for folder labels?

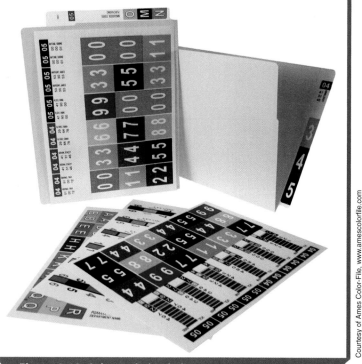

Courtesy of Ames Color-File, www.amescolorfile.com

Figure 6.18 Color-coded Labels

alphabet is keyed first, followed by about ½ inch of blank space, then the filing segment. In all cases, the label is keyed in capital letters with no punctuation as shown in Figure 6.19.

When new folders are prepared, make sure the placement of the labels and the caption format are the same as those on other folders. Consistency in the placement and format of labels helps achieve faster retrieval of a required folder. One way to achieve uniform placement of labels is as follows: When a new box of folders is opened, remove all the folders, hold them tightly together, and stand them upright on a flat surface. Place a ruler or stiff card over the tab edges at the spot where all the labels are to be affixed. Make a pencil mark across the top edge of all the tabs. A very small pencil mark will show on each of the tabs at the same place and will serve as a guide for attaching all the labels.

Sorters

A **sorter** is a device used to arrange records into alphabetic or numeric categories and to hold records temporarily prior to storage. The records are organized alphabetically in the order they will be stored to improve the speed and accuracy of actual storage in the records system. The type of sorter used depends on the volume of records in the office. Figure 6.20 on page 157 shows one sorter that accommodates records such as checks, sales slips, time cards, and correspondence.

Other specialized supplies are discussed in later chapters of the text, as their use becomes necessary. The supplies just explained and illustrated are basic ones and applicable to all storage methods.

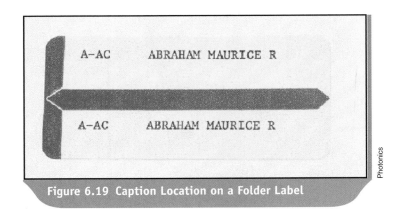

Figure 6.19 Caption Location on a Folder Label

Photonics

Figure 6.20 General-Purpose Sorter

South-Western

Selection of Storage Equipment and Supplies

Every office has its own RIM system; and the right equipment, supplies, and filing accessories can improve document-handling efficiency. Proper selection of equipment can result in saving space and time, both factors that can reduce operating costs. Records managers should keep updated on new and improved products by reading business periodicals and trade magazines; viewing vendor catalogs, brochures, and web sites; attending business shows; and participating in professional RIM association meetings.

Appropriate selection of storage equipment and supplies requires consideration of the following factors:

> **What are the benefits of using the right type and quality of storage equipment and supplies?**

1. *Type and volume of records to be stored and retrieved.* An inventory of what is to be stored is a basic step in making the best choice of storage equipment and supplies. Records in different formats or media such as papers, cards, books, computer disks, microfilm, videos, architectural drawings, or computer printouts have special storage needs. A records inventory also shows the current volume of stored records. Future volume and needs must be forecast. Chapter 7 presents more detailed information about the records inventory.

2. *Degree of required protection of records.* Confidential or classified records require equipment with locks or location in a records vault. Records vital to the operation of the business need fireproof or fire-resistant storage equipment.

3. *Efficiency and ease of use of equipment and systems.* The ease with which records can be found is a major consideration. The simpler the system is to understand, the easier it is to use. Also, less training of new employees is needed when the system is a simple one. Time saved by personnel

who store and retrieve records means dollars saved. The ease of expansion or modification of a system or the addition of compatible equipment will be important to meet the changing needs of an organization.

4. *Space considerations.* Floor-weight restrictions, use of space to the ceiling (air space), or the advisability of counter-type equipment or something in between, and the possibility of transferring part of the records to off-site storage facilities affect space which, in an office, is costly. Lateral, shelf, or rotary equipment can house more square feet of records than can conventional drawer file cabinets in the same square footage of floor space. The effect of new equipment on present layout and workflow should also be considered.

5. *Cost.* After all other criteria have been examined, cost and the company budget may be the final determinants as to which equipment and supplies may be acquired. The astute records manager realizes that the least expensive equipment and supplies may not provide the most economical records storage. Quality in construction and materials is important. Inferior materials or lightweight stock may need frequent and costly replacement. In determining costs, keep in mind the points given in Figure 6.21.

Special needs of your organization could add other factors to your list of considerations. Also, consult users of equipment under consideration for purchase to learn about benefits, problems, or special considerations associated with the equipment.

> **What factors need to be considered when choosing a storage system?**

COST CONSIDERATIONS

- Cost of personnel needed to work with the records
- Compatibility of supplies and equipment
- Benefits of using the right type and quality of storage equipment and supplies
- Cost of new storage equipment and supplies that must be purchased
- Advisability of using local vendors rather than purchasing from out-of-town vendors
- Possibility of discounts for quantity purchases
- Feasibility of choosing used rather than new equipment
- Volume of records that can be stored within the equipment

Figure 6.21 Cost Considerations

My Records

Storing Records

How and where should you store your records? What types of storage containers are needed for storing your records?

VITAL RECORDS

Vital records are usually not replaceable and require the highest degree of protection. Property deeds and wills are examples of vital records. Follow these guidelines for storing vital records:

- Store vital records in a bank safe deposit box.

- Keep the safe deposit key in a safe place accessible to you and your closest family members.

- Store copies of vital records at home in a fireproof box. Generally the more hours that records will remain below the flash point (which is 450 degrees Fahrenheit [F] for paper documents) in the container, the more the container will cost. Fireproof boxes are tested at 1700°F for 1, 2, or 3 hours. The inside temperature cannot rise above 350°F to be considered fireproof. Look for a box that meets these standards.

IMPORTANT RECORDS

Important records are usually replaceable but at considerable cost. They require a high degree of protection. Bills and receipts are examples of important records. Follow these guidelines for storing important records:

- Use a secure location near where you pay your bills to store unpaid bills. When you pay the bills, write the date and amount that you paid on your copy of the bill. Store this copy with other copies of paid bills and receipts in an alphabetic file.

- If you have a small file cabinet or a banker's box, create folders for your major bills such as your rent or mortgage, car, utilities, and so on. Store copies of paid bills and receipts in this container.

- If any of the bills you pay are tax deductible, store those receipts in a separate folder by date, with the most recent at the front. When you complete your tax return, you can find the receipts for deductions in this folder.

- If you use money management software, use the tax deduction portion of the software. Create backup copies of your data at least once a month and store the backups in a secure container.

- Consider using a bellows file to store all of the information used to file your tax return, including a copy of the return itself. Date the outside of the file and retain this container and records until it is time to dispose of the records.

USEFUL RECORDS

Useful records are usually replaceable at slight cost and require a low degree of protection. Product manuals, warranties, and routine correspondence are examples of useful records. Create separate folders to store records such as product manuals, warranties, and routine correspondence. Store the folders in a safe place that is readily accessible.

CORRESPONDENCE STORAGE PROCEDURES

This last section of the chapter looks at the advantages and disadvantages of alphabetic records management, some criteria for selecting an alphabetic storage system, and procedures for storing correspondence alphabetically.

Advantages and Disadvantages of Alphabetic Records Management

The advantages of using alphabetic records management are as follows:

- Alphabetic storage does not require an index and is, therefore, a direct access storage method. **Direct access** is a method of accessing records by going directly to the file without first referring to an index or a list of names for location in the files.
- All records for correspondent names that begin with numbers written as digits are filed before all alphabetic names according to alphabetic indexing Rule 7. Knowing this rule facilitates storage and retrieval.
- The alphabetic dictionary (A to Z) order of arrangement is simple to understand.
- Storage is easy if standard procedures are followed.
- Misfiles are easily checked by examining alphabetic sequence.
- The direct access feature can save time and, thus, reduce costs of operation.
- Related records from one name, either a company or an individual, are grouped together.

The disadvantages of alphabetic records management are as follows:

- Misfiling is prevalent if rules for alphabetic storage are not established and followed.
- Similar names may cause confusion, especially when spellings are not precise.
- Transposition of some letters of the alphabet is easy, causing filing sequence to be out of order.
- Filing under the wrong name can result in lost records.
- Names on folders are seen instantly by anyone who happens to glance at an open storage container. Consequently, confidential or classified records are not secure.
- Related records with different correspondent names are filed in more than one place.

Selection and Design of an Alphabetic Records Management System

At the time a new office is opened, managers must decide on the kind of storage system to be selected or designed. For established offices, the system in use may prove to be ineffective because it no longer serves the needs of those who request records. If records are requested by names of individuals, businesses, and organizations with few subjects, then an alphabetic system is best for that office.

When selecting the alphabetic storage method, utmost care should be exercised in the selection or design because, once installed, it is likely to be used for a long time. To select an alphabetic system, or to redesign one, the records manager should know:

- The total volume of records to be stored.
- The number of records in each alphabetic section and which letters of the alphabet contain a large number of records.
- The expected activity in the files—an estimate of how many times records may be requested.
- The length of time records are to be kept.
- The efficiency of the filing personnel.
- The time and resources available for training personnel.

In some cases, the person in charge of the records may seek the help of an RIM consultant or a representative of a filing system manufacturer to determine the best records storage system. These people study the information needs of the office, consult with the person in charge of the records, and make recommendations.

The person in charge of the records must keep the needs of the office in mind and not be swayed by the beauty of a system, the expert sales techniques of a representative, or the apparent low cost of a system. The ultimate test of any successful storage system (alphabetic or any other) is whether records that have been stored within the system can be found quickly when needed.

> **What information does a records manager need to know before talking to a manufacturer of storage systems?**

Examples of Records Storage Systems

Many different manufacturers create storage supplies and systems. The use of color enhances the effectiveness of a records storage system. For instance, all key units that begin with A are stored in white folders with red labels. If you see a yellow folder among the white folders, you know that something is misfiled, and you can immediately place the white folder with other white folders.

The use of color has two meanings: (1) **Color coding** is using color as an identifying aid in a filing system (for example, different colors might be used to divide the alphabetic sections in the storage system); and (2) **color accenting** is the consistent use of different colors for different supplies in the storage system—one color for guides, various colors for folders, one color for OUT indicators, and specific colors of labels or stripes on labels. Color coding is used in the system illustrated in Figure 6.22. Blocks of colored folders act as a visual guide to lead you quickly to a section of the alphabet. Use of a contrasting color for special folders such as key customers, current projects, or unpaid bills makes them easy to locate.

For an alphabetic system, color bars can correspond to the first letters of the correspondent's name to create blocks of colors. Another use of color shows the same first color for alphabetic letter guides and a different second color on the label for secondary guides. The use of color speeds retrieval because it eliminates the need to stop and read letters. Misfiles stand out visually when the color pattern is broken.

Many manufacturers produce trade-named alphabetic systems with special characteristics intended to speed records storage and retrieval and to provide a

How is color used in storage systems?

Esselte Corporation

Figure 6.22 Color-Coded Files

double check against misfiling. These systems use color extensively. Other trade-named alphabetic systems are available; the ones discussed here are only representative of the many systems available.

TAB Products

TAB Products is a company that provides equipment, supplies, and services for filing systems using color coding and color accenting in a variety of records systems ranging from simple to complex. *TABQUIK®* products allow you to produce and apply color-coded file folder labels. You can produce labels to color code file folders and other items, such as backup tapes, videos, books, and binders. This software can be used with a variety of printers. TAB's *File-Tracker®* software package allows you to track document location through use of bar codes and bar code readers. Bar code readers enable you to check items in or out or transfer them to a new location without manual data entry.

Smead Manufacturing Company

Smead Manufacturing Company uses color in its filing systems and products. Smead's color-coded top tab or end tab folders have a large wrap-around color bar printed on the top or end tab of each folder. Smead also offers software such as *ColorBar® Gold*. This software can be used for creating labels that include file headings, color-coded indexing, bar codes, text, images, and graphics.

Procedures for Storing Correspondence Records

The storing operation is an exacting responsibility that must be done with concentration and the knowledge that a mistake can be costly. No matter whether records storage is centralized or decentralized, the filing procedures remain the same: Records must be (1) inspected, (2) indexed, (3) coded, (4) cross-referenced if necessary, (5) sorted, and (6) stored. Therefore, the filer must enjoy detailed work, be dexterous, have a good memory, be willing to follow procedures consistently, be interested in developing new and better procedures, and realize the importance of correctly storing all records so that they may be found immediately when needed. The following sections give details about each of these steps.

Inspecting

Checking a record to determine whether it is ready to be filed is known as **inspecting.** A business record must not be stored until someone with authority marks it to be released for filing. Whatever action the record requires must be taken or noted prior to storage. Anyone storing records must be certain that action has been taken or noted in a reminder system. Notation in a reminder system assures that the record will be brought to the attention of the proper

> **How do you know when a record is ready to be stored?**

CAREER CORNER

Job Description for Records Management Specialist

The following job description is an example of a career opportunity in records management with the U.S. government. This job description information comes from USAJOBS, the official job web site of the United States government. Follow the link on the web site for this textbook to visit the USAJOBS web site and learn about more career opportunities.

JOB TITLE

Records Management Specialist, GS-0301-12/13

SALARY RANGE

$62,886.00 to $97,213.00 per year

PRINCIPAL JOB DUTIES

- Coordinate the records management activities at the Bureau of Indian Affairs offices to which assigned in order to ensure that Indian trust records in those offices are maintained in accordance with OST records management regulations, policies, and procedures.
- Serve as the Office of Trust Records liaison to local Bureau of Indian Affairs (BIA) offices.
- Disseminate guidance and information regarding records management and conduct training for local offices.
- Regularly attend meetings, training, and workshops for the purpose of staying up-to-date on changes and issues affecting records and information management.
- Ensure compliance with records management policies, assist the local office in the implementation of standard procedures for records management, and provide technical advice on all aspects of records management.

QUALIFICATIONS

To be successful in this position, you must have a high degree of interpersonal skills and the ability to communicate in a highly professional manner both orally and in writing; knowledge of general records management procedures, regulations, and practices; ability to plan, organize, and deliver training to individuals with various experience levels; and

(continued)

ability to analyze various regulations and policies specific to information resource and/or records management.

To qualify at the GS-12 grade level, applicants must have at least one year of specialized experience equivalent to the GS-11 grade level. *Specialized experience* is defined as (1) experience preparing and conducting training seminars for individuals from various experience levels; (2) experience interpreting and explaining policies and/or regulations regarding information resource and records management; and (3) experience managing the creation, storage, maintenance, use, preservation, and disposition of general trust or highly sensitive federal records.

To qualify at the GS-13 grade level, applicants must have at least one year of specialized experience equivalent to the GS-12 grade level. *Specialized experience* is defined as above, with the addition of experience developing policies and/or procedures.

person at a future date. Storing records before their contents are noted and before appropriate action has been taken can sometimes cause embarrassment to a business and can directly or indirectly result in financial loss or loss of goodwill. The copy of an outgoing letter or other communication would appear ready to be stored when it is received by the filer for storage. However, in most offices, every original (or incoming) record to be stored must bear a release mark. A **release mark** is an agreed-upon mark such as initials or a symbol placed on a record to show that the record is ready for storage (see "JJ" on Figure 6.23 on page 168). The person who prepared the reply or otherwise handled the matter usually puts this release mark on the letter.

Types of marks used are initials, a code or check mark, a punched symbol, a stamped notation, or some other agreed-upon mark. A missing mark is a signal to the filer to inquire why the release mark is missing. A date/time stamp (see OCT 23, 20-- 10:30 AM in Figure 6.23) is not a release mark. The person who opens mail often stamps the correspondence for reference purposes with a date/time stamp showing the date and time received. All filers must observe the following cardinal rule: Be sure the record to be stored has been released for storage.

Indexing

How do you index incoming and outgoing correspondence?

Because you indexed filing segments in applications for Chapters 2, 3, and 4, you know that indexing is a mental process. On correspondence, the name (filing segment) may appear in various places. As you know, the selection of the right name by which to store the record means that the record will be found quickly when it is needed. If the wrong name is selected, much time will be wasted trying to locate the record when it is eventually requested. Keep these rules in mind when indexing incoming correspondence:

1. On incoming correspondence, the name for storage purposes is usually in the letterhead.
2. If a letterhead has no relationship with the contents of the letter, the writer's name or the writer's business connection is used. The letterhead name is disregarded for filing purposes. An example is a letter written on hotel stationery by a person who is out of town on a business trip.
3. Incoming correspondence on plain paper (paper without a letterhead—usually personal) most likely will be called for by the name in the signature line, so this name is the one used for storage.
4. When both the company name and the name of the writer seem to be of equal importance, the company name is used.

Keep these rules in mind when indexing outgoing correspondence:

1. On the file copy of an outgoing letter, the most important name is usually the one contained in the letter address.
2. When both the company name and the name of an individual are contained in the letter address of the file copy of an outgoing letter, the company name is used for filing unless the letter is personal or unless a name in the body is the correct name to index.
3. On a copy of a personal letter, the writer's name is usually the most important and should be used for storage.

If a special subject is used in an alphabetic arrangement (such as Applications), the subject is given precedence over both company and individual names appearing in the correspondence. Often, the subject name is written on the correspondence at the top right.

Sometimes two names seem equally important. One name is selected as the name by which the record is to be stored and the other name is cross-referenced according to the rules learned in Chapters 2, 3, and 4. In case of real doubt about the most important name, request clarification from the records supervisor or the department from which the record came. Consult a RIM manual if one is in use in the office.

Coding

Often the filer is responsible for coding the record. The filing segment can be coded in any one of several ways. Figure 6.23 shows diagonals placed between the units, the key unit underlined, and the remaining units numbered. In some offices, a colored pencil is used for coding to make the code stand out. In other offices, coding is done with a pencil to keep distracting marks at a minimum. Coding saves time when refiling is necessary. An uncoded record removed from storage and returned at a later date to be refiled must be indexed and coded.

Cross-Referencing

The same cross-reference rules learned in Chapters 2, 3, and 4 apply for storing correspondence. For example, assume that the letter shown in Figure 6.23 on page 168 comes to the filer for storage. The record is indexed and coded for Investment Strategies, Inc., by placing diagonals between the units, underlining the key unit, and numbering the other units. The letter is then coded for cross-referencing because it is likely to be called for by Trotter Poll Company. A line is drawn under Trotter Poll Company, diagonals are placed between the units, all units are numbered, and an X is written in the margin.

A separate cross-reference sheet, as shown in Figure 6.24 on page 169, may be prepared for an alternative name, or a photocopy of the original record can be coded for cross-reference purposes. Note that the name at the top of the cross-reference sheet is coded for storage in exactly the same way as for any record—diagonals are placed between the units, the key unit is underlined, and succeeding units are numbered.

At times, a permanent cross-reference replaces an individual folder to direct the filer to the correct storage place. A **permanent cross-reference** is a guide with a tab in the same position as the tabs on the individual folders and is placed in a location that is frequently assumed to be the location of that folder. The caption on the tab of the permanent cross-reference consists of the name by which the cross-reference is filed, the word *SEE,* and the name by which the correspondence folder may be found. In Figure 6.7, a permanent cross-reference guide (BETSYS CRAFTS SEE ROSS INDUSTRIES) appears in proper alphabetic sequence in the file drawer.

A permanent cross-reference can be used, for instance, when a company changes its name. The company's folder is removed from the file, the name is changed on the folder, and the folder is refiled under the new name. A permanent cross-reference guide is prepared under the original name and is placed in the position of the original folder in the file. For example, assume that *Emory and Phillips* changes its name to *Riverside Distribution Co.* The EMORY AND PHILLIPS folder is removed from the file, the name on the folder is changed to RIVERSIDE DISTRIBUTION CO, and the folder is filed under the new name. A permanent cross-reference guide is made and filed in the E section of the file: EMORY AND PHILLIPS SEE RIVERSIDE DISTRIBUTION CO.

> **What are the advantages to coding records?**

Investment / Strategies,/Inc.

150 Salmon Ave.
Portland, OR 97202-0015
(503) 555-0192
(503) 555-0191 FAX

October 21, 20--

OCT 23, 20-- 10:30 AM

Ms. Joan Jensen, Manager
1040 Tax Express
1500 SW Cedar Ave.
Portland, OR 97204-1500

JJ

Dear Ms. Jensen

Thank you for your interest in offering investment advice to your customers. We are happy you have asked us to work with you on this new program.

We have hired the Trotter|Poll|Company to conduct a survey to help us gather information about your customers. In the near future, Trotter Poll Company will send to each of your customers a questionnaire that will provide spaces for the listing of annual income, approximate annual expenses, amount available for saving and investment, financial objectives, and other pertinent information.

X

We will analyze the data received from all those who return the questionnaire and then make recommendations for types of investments your customers should consider.

Sincerely yours

James Washington

James Washington
Investment Counselor

pas

Figure 6.23 Letter Released and Coded for Filing

Sorting

What is the difference between rough sorting and fine sorting?

Sorting is arranging records in the sequence in which they are to be filed or stored. In most instances, a sorting step precedes the actual storing. Sorting should be done as soon as possible after coding and cross-referencing, especially if storage must be delayed. Sometimes coding and rough sorting are done in sequence. **Rough sorting** is arranging records in approximately the same order as the filing system in which they will be placed. After each record has been coded, it should be rough sorted into a pile of like pieces—all As, Bs, Cs are together, all

CROSS-REFERENCE SHEET

Name or Subject

            2   3
Trotter / Poll / Company

Date of Record

October 21, 20--

Regarding

Survey of customers regarding investment objectives

SEE

Name or Subject

Investment Strategies, Inc.

Date Filed   *10/23/20 - -*   By   *J. Phelps*

Figure 6.24 Cross-Reference for Letter Shown in Figure 6.23

Ds, Es, Fs are together, and so on. Records having filing segments that are numbers written as digits are rough sorted into 100s, 200s, and so on. Coordination of inspecting, indexing, coding, and sorting means handling each record only once. If a record is needed before it has been filed, it can be found with less delay if records have been rough sorted instead of being put in a stack on a desk or in a "to-be-filed" basket. Sorting can be done on a desk or table top, with the records placed in separate piles. Use of a desktop sorter that has holders or pockets for various sections of the alphabet makes sorting easier.

After rough sorting the records according to alphabetic sections, the filer removes them section by section, alphabetizes them properly within each section, and replaces them in order in the sorter for temporary storage. This step is often called fine sorting. **Fine sorting** is arranging records in exact order of the filing system in which they will be placed. This alphabetizing of records in all sections makes them ready to be stored. Fine sorting records with numeric key units arranges them in numeric order prior to storing. Then the records are removed in sequence from all divisions of the sorter and taken to the files for storage.

Storing

What preparation is needed before a record is stored?

Storing is placing records into storage containers. Storing records correctly is very important. A misfiled record is often a lost record; and a lost record means loss of time, money, and peace of mind while searching for the record.

The time at which records are actually put into the storage containers depends on the workload during the day. In some offices, storing is the job performed first in the morning; in others, all storing is done in the early afternoon; in others, storing is the last task performed each day. In still other offices, storing is done when records are ready and when a lull in other work occurs. In a centralized filing department, storage takes place routinely throughout the day every day—along with retrieving, and re-storing.

Prior to storing records, the filer must remember to:

1. Remove paper clips from records to be stored.
2. Staple records together (if they belong together) in the upper right corner so that other records kept in the folder will not be inserted between them by mistake.
3. Mend torn records.
4. Unfold folded records to conserve storage space unless the folded records fit the container better than when unfolded.

Before placing the record into its storage location, the filer should:

1. Glance quickly at the container label to locate the place to begin storage.
2. Scan the guides until the proper file section is located.
3. Pull the guides forward with one hand, while searching for the correct folder.
4. Check for an individual or a special folder for the filing segment. If none of these folders is in the file, locate the general folder.
5. Slightly raise the folder into which the record is to be placed. Avoid pulling the folder up by its tab, however, as continual pulling will separate the tab from its folder. Raising the folder ensures that the record will be inserted into the folder and not in front of or behind it.

6. Determine the correct placement of the document in the folder because all records in the folder will bear the same coded name.

7. Place each record into the folder with its top to the left. When the folder is removed from storage and placed on a desk to be used, the folder is opened like a book with the tab edge to the right. All records in it are then in proper reading position.

8. Jog the folder to straighten the records if they are uneven before replacing the folder.

Special points to remember include:

- Never open more than one drawer in a cabinet at a time. A cabinet can fall forward when overbalanced by having two or three loaded drawers open.
- The most recently dated record in an individual folder is always placed at the front and, therefore, is on top when the folder is opened. The record bearing the oldest date is the one at the back of the folder.
- Records that are removed from a folder and later refiled must be placed in their correct chronologic sequence, not on top of the contents of the folder.
- Records within a general folder are arranged first alphabetically by correspondents' names and then by date within each correspondent's records. The most recently dated record is, therefore, on top of each group (see Figure 6.12 on page 148).

Using a Tickler File

A **tickler file** is a date-sequenced file by which matters pending are flagged for attention on the proper date. This chronologic arrangement of information "tickles" the memory and serves as a reminder that specific action must be taken on a specific date. Other names sometimes used to describe such a file are *suspense file* and *pending file*. The basic arrangement of a tickler file is always the same: chronologic by current month and day. A manual arrangement usually takes the form of a series of 12 guides with the names of the months of the year printed on their tabs. One set of guides or folders with tabs printed with 1 through 31 for the days of the month is also used. A computer tickler file is usually in the form of entries in a database with a reminder list showing on the screen or printed in sort order by action date. Figure 6.25 on page 172 shows a list of due dates for OUT files from a database. An example of a manual tickler file would be one for holding correspondence that requires specific action to be taken before being placed into the alphabetic correspondence file.

> **What is the purpose of a tickler file?**

REQUEST ID	DATE DUE	REQUESTED BY	PHONE EXT	DEPARTMENT	RECORD TYPE	CORRESPONDENT NAME	RECORD DATE
1	10/6/2007	Thomas Logan	8966	Administration	Record	Miles Law Office	1/30/2007
2	10/9/2007	Margarita Shelby	9912	Advertising	Record	WAXI Radio	5/15/2007
3	10/10/2007	Mary Neismith	8999	Accounting	Folder	Martin Auto Parts	
4	10/12/2007	David Smelson	8875	Marketing	Record	Margaret Jackson	3/17/2007
5	10/12/2007	Juan Carlos	9986	Advertising	Record	ADVO Systems	7/18/2006
6	10/13/2007	Sue Bell	3264	Accounting	Record	Mid-Atlantic Boxes Inc.	5/16/2006
7	10/17/2007	Mary Jane Hilton	7792	Purchasing	Record	Jones Supply Co.	9/16/2007
8	10/19/2007	Jack Kline	8865	Marketing	Folder	Ikohoto Trade Center	
9	10/19/2007	Wanda Adams	8921	Training	Record	Misty Waters	2/17/2005
10	10/22/2007	John Frymire	8632	Purchasing	Record	J. P. Smith	1/10/2007
(AutoNumber)							

OUT Log Tickler File : Table

Figure 6.25 Tickler Database OUT Log

Many office workers use a tickler system to remind them of events that happen yearly such as birthdays and anniversaries; membership expiration dates and dues payments; insurance premium payments; weekly, monthly, or annual meetings; subscription expiration dates; and the dates on which certificates of deposit or bonds are due. In records and information management, tickler files can be used to keep track of due dates for records that are borrowed or to keep track of records that do not have a release mark.

On the last day of each month, the person in charge of the tickler file checks through the date cards/folders to be certain that nothing has been inadvertently overlooked during the month. Then, all papers from behind the next month's guide are removed and redistributed behind the daily guides (numbered 1 through 31). At the end of October, for instance, the spaces behind all the daily guides would be checked, the October guide would be moved to the back of the file, and the November guide would be put in the front. All reminders that were filed behind November would then be redistributed behind the daily guides according to the dates on the reminders.

The tickler file must be the first item checked each day by the person in charge of it. Information on the notes found in the tickler file serves as a reminder to act or follow through on specific instructions.

> **How might a tickler file be used in a records management system?**

Misfiled and Lost Records

A lost or misplaced record can delay or affect the work of employees. If storage is done haphazardly or without following consistent procedures, lost records will be numerous. Lack of attention to spelling, careless insertion of records into the storage equipment, and distractions often cause records to be misfiled and, therefore, "lost."

Experienced filers use the following techniques in trying to find missing records:

- Look in the folders immediately in front of and behind the correct folder.
- Look between folders and under all folders in the drawer or shelf.
- Look completely through the correct folder because alphabetic or other order of sequence may have been neglected due to carelessness or haste.
- Look in the general folder in addition to searching in the individual folder.
- Check for transposition of names (DAVID MILLER instead of MILLER DAVID) and alternate spellings (JON, JOHN).
- Look for the second, third, or succeeding units of a filing segment rather than for the key unit.
- Check for transposition of numbers (35 instead of 53).
- Look in the year preceding or following the one in question.

> **What techniques are used to locate lost or misfiled records?**

- Look in a related subject if the subject method is used.
- Look in the sorter or other places that have records en route to storage.
- Ask employees who might logically have the record to look for it in their desks or folders.

If every search fails to produce the missing record, some records managers try to reconstruct the record from memory, rekeying as much as is known. This information is placed in a folder labeled LOST along with the name on the original folder. This new folder is stored in its correct place as a constant reminder to the filer to be on the alert for the missing record.

Efficient correspondence records storage is the result of:

- Good planning to choose the right equipment, supplies, and system.
- Proper training of personnel who recognize the value of the release mark, know and consistently apply the rules for alphabetic indexing, code papers carefully, prepare cross-references skillfully, invariably sort papers before storing, and carefully store records in their proper location.
- Constant concerned supervision by records managers or others responsible for the storage and retrieval functions.

Chapter Review And Applications

POINTS TO FILE AND RETRIEVE

- The volume of recorded information is rapidly increasing. More electronic records are being created, but paper records still make up a significant portion of all records.

- The four most common types of filing equipment are vertical files, lateral files, shelf files, and mobile shelf files.

- Types of supplies used for correspondence storage include guides, folders, labels, and OUT indicators.

- When selecting filing equipment and supplies, consider the type and volume of records to be stored, degree of protection required, efficiency and ease of use of equipment, space requirements, and cost.

- Alphabetic records management is appropriate for correspondence files with a low to moderate volume of records when records are requested by names of individuals, businesses, and organizations.

- Color can be used to visually separate sections of the file or to call attention to special folders.

- Filing procedures for storing correspondence records include inspecting, indexing, coding, cross-referencing, sorting, and storing.

- Tickler files can be manual or computer based and are used as a reminder for tasks to be done daily.

- Systematic search strategies should be used for finding lost or misfiled records.

IMPORTANT TERMS

alphabetic records management
bellows (expansion) folder
caption
color accenting
color coding
direct access
folder
follower block (compressor)
general folder
guide
individual folder
inspecting
label
lateral file cabinet
mobile shelving
motorized rotary storage
OUT folder
OUT guide
OUT indicator

OUT sheet
permanent cross-reference
pocket folder
position
primary guide
release mark
shelf file
sorter
special (auxiliary) guide
special folder
storage
storage procedures
storing
suspension (hanging) folder
tab
tab cut
tickler file
vertical file cabinet

REVIEW AND DISCUSSION

1. Compare and contrast the terms *storage, filing, storage method,* and *records management.* (Obj. 1)

2. List and briefly describe four kinds of commonly used storage equipment for correspondence records. (Obj. 2)

3. List and briefly describe five important supplies used in records storage. (Obj. 2)

4. Why is the straight-line arrangement of tabs on folders and guides easier to use than the staggered arrangement? (Obj. 2)

5. What five criteria should be considered when choosing storage equipment and supplies? (Obj. 3)

6. Discuss the advantages and disadvantages of the alphabetic storage method. (Obj. 4)

7. What types of information should be gathered before selecting and designing an alphabetic storage system? (Obj. 5)

8. Explain how color can be used in correspondence records storage. (Obj. 6)

9. List and briefly describe (in order) the six steps to store a record properly. (Obj. 7)

10. What kinds of release marks might you find on records ready to be stored? (Obj. 7)

11. List at least five procedures to try to locate a "lost" or a "misfiled" record. (Obj. 7)

12. What is a tickler file and how is one arranged? (Obj. 8)

APPLICATIONS

6-1 CODE CORRESPONDENCE (OBJ. 7)

DATA CD

1. Open and print the *Word* file *6-1 Coding* from the data files or write the names and addresses below on a sheet of paper.

2. Correctly index and code these names and addresses for outgoing letters to be filed in an alphabetic system. Place a diagonal between units in the filing segment. Underline the key unit and number other units in the filing segment.

Dr. Joyce Phosgene, President
Callous Records Equipment, Inc.
Coney Towers #47
Dallas, TX 75202-1847

Jaymire Communications Systems
1812 Roswell Avenue
Albuquerque, NM 87201-1254

J.C. Wilshire, Advertising Director
Johnson Office Supplies
100 Black Street
Yuma, AZ 88364-6943

1-2-3 Tailor-made Publications
87 West Second Street
Sacramento, CA 95801-9985

Oney Jasmine
205 First Street, NE
Brenham, TX 77833-5415

6-2 CHANGING STORAGE EQUIPMENT (OBJ. 2, 3, AND 5)

You and one or two of your classmates have formed a records and information management consulting company. The Wilson Charter Co. has asked your company for a consultation about their storage equipment. You and your team visited the Wilson office and noted the following:

- Correspondence is stored alphabetically in traditional four-drawer vertical file cabinets.

- Everyone in the office has access to the file cabinets.

- Ten to 20 stored records are retrieved daily, one paper at a time.

1. Along with your team members, analyze the Wilson Charter Co.'s current equipment and determine whether anything should be changed. Would open-shelf files work better? Why do you think so? What factors would contribute to your decision? What other resources are available to help your team assemble the facts needed to propose a solution for Wilson Charter Co.?

2. Create a proposal for the Wilson Charter Co. giving your team's recommendations for changing the company's filing equipment or procedures.

6-3 RESEARCH EQUIPMENT AND SUPPLIES (OBJ. 2)

1. Visit a web site for a company that sells records management equipment and supplies that use color coding or color accenting. To find sites, search using the term **records management system color** in an Internet search engine. You can also find links to sites on the web site for this textbook.

2. Prepare a brief summary that describes the types of supplies that use color that this company offers.

6-4 PREPARE FOLDER LABELS (OBJ. 9)

In this application, you will use *Access* to create folder labels for records to be filed in the J section of an alphabetic file.

1. Create a new *Access* database file named *6-4 Labels*.

2. Create a table named **Folder Labels.** Create these fields in the table: Record ID, Name, Caption. Select **AutoNumber** for the field type for the Record ID field. Select **Text** for the field type for all other fields. Set the Record ID Number field as the primary key.

3. Enter the names shown on the following page in the Folder Labels table. In the Name field, enter the complete name as written. In the Caption field, key the letter J followed by two spaces and the name in indexing order. Follow the alphabetic indexing rules studied earlier. In the Caption field, enter the data in all capitals.

4. Create a report for folder labels using the Label Wizard. Choose the **Folder Labels** table as the object the data comes from. Select **Avery Index Maker 3** for the label type (or a label of similar size, about 1 x 3 inches). Select **Arial 12** for the font. Include only the Caption field on the label and sort the labels. Name the report **Folder Labels Report.**

5. Print the labels (or print on plain paper if labels are not available).

Junk by Judy
Julie's Design Studio
Charles S. Jungworth
Christina A. Jensen
Jolly Roger Fish 'n Chips
Vernon L. Jensen, CPA
John's Jewelry Shop
Jill's Wishing Well
Jottings by Jolene
Jon Jungworth Law Firm

RECORDS MANAGEMENT SIMULATION

JOB 5 CORRESPONDENCE FILING—RULES 1-5

JOB 6 CORRESPONDENCE FILING—RULES 6-10

JOB 7 CORRESPONDENCE FILING—RULES 1-10 AND TICKLER FILE USAGE

Continue working with Auric Systems, Inc.
Complete Jobs 5, 6, and 7.

FOR MORE ACTIVITIES GO TO **http://read.swlearning.com**

Learning Objectives

1. Explain the importance of developing and implementing a records retention program.

2. List the four values of records, describe each value, and provide an example of each value.

3. Discuss the records inventory, including what it is, why it is done, and what it includes.

4. Describe a records retention schedule and explain its purpose.

5. Discuss manual and automated retrieval procedures.

6. List reasons for transferring records.

7. Discuss types of records center control files.

8. List capabilities of typical records center software.

RECORDS STORAGE

Why is a records retention program important?

Phases of the record life cycle include creation, distribution, use, maintenance, and disposition. The last two phases—*maintenance* (i.e., storing, retrieving, and protecting records) and *disposition* (i.e., transferring, retaining, or destroying records)—are discussed in this chapter.

An effective records and information management (RIM) program adheres to best practices to assure that records that continue to have value to the organization are stored and retained (kept). A **records retention program** consists of policies and procedures relating to *what* documents to keep, *where* and in what type of environment the documents are kept, and *how long* these documents are to be kept. Ideally, the time that a record should be retained is known when the record is created because the record series is listed on a **records retention schedule (RRS)**—a comprehensive list of records, indicating the time records are to be maintained.

Retention policies also allow destruction of records that no longer have value to the organization. Storing records no longer needed is costly because more floor space is used, more storage supplies and equipment are purchased (needed), and more labor is required.

The Value of Records

Records serve as the memory of an organization, and their purpose may be administrative, fiscal, legal, or historical. Classifying records by their value to an organization is useful for making retention decisions as shown in Figure 7.1.

> **What are the four categories of records values?**

RECORDS VALUES
Nonessential Records
- Not worth keeping
  - Bulk mail
  - Routine telephone messages
  - Bulletin board announcements
  - E-mail and fax messages after action is taken

Useful Records
- Short-term storage—up to three years
- Helpful in conducting business operations
- May be replaced at small cost
- Active files of:
  - Business letters
  - Memos
  - Reports
  - Bank statements

Important Records
- Long-term storage—seven to ten years
- Contain pertinent information
- Need to be recreated or replaced if lost
  - Financial data
  - Sales data
  - Credit histories
  - Statistical records

Vital Records
- Permanent Storage
- Essential for the continuation or survival of organization
- Necessary for recreating organization's legal and financial status
  - Business ownership records
  - Customer profiles
  - Student transcripts

Figure 7.1 Records Values

Once a record is stored, it may not be stored forever. One critical step in creating a records retention schedule is estimating the value of a record to an organization and determining how long the record is useful. Understanding the four categories of records values—nonessential, useful, important, and vital—is helpful when determining which records should be retained (and for how long) and which records should be destroyed. Before preparing a records retention schedule, an inventory of all records stored in an organization—in individual offices or departments, in central files areas, or in off-site storage locations—must be conducted.

Records Inventory

A **records inventory** is a detailed listing that could include the types, locations, dates, volumes, equipment, classification systems, and usage data of an organization's records. It usually involves a survey conducted by each department, with a member of each department assigned the task of inventorying its records and documenting important information about those records. Survey information from all departments is incorporated into an organization-wide records retention schedule. Some organizations use bar code and radio frequency identification (RFID) technology to speed the records inventory process. A bar code is a coding system consisting of vertical lines or bars set in a predetermined pattern that, when read by an optical reader, can be converted into machine-readable language. A bar code is shown in Figure 7.2. In records and information management, bar codes are used for tracking locations of documents, folders, or boxes of records. Bar code labels may be placed on

Figure 7.2 Bar codes

individual documents or on folder and box labels. The use of bar code technology brings improvements in data accuracy over keyboard data entry. Bar code technology is used extensively for applications such as cataloging of books and files by libraries and archives.

Radio frequency identification (RFID) is a technology that incorporates the use of an electromagnetic or electrostatic radio frequency to identify an object, animal, or person. RFID is increasingly used as an alternative to bar codes. The advantage of using RFID is that it does not require direct contact or line-of-sight scanning. An RFID system consists of three components: (1) an antenna, (2) a transceiver/reader, and (3) a transponder (the tag or chip). Using microchips to transmit encoded information wirelessly through antennae, RFID tags are activated when placed in the transmission field of a reader. These tags convey encoded information that identifies documents, folders, or boxes. Because information is transmitted automatically beyond line-of-sight, boxes do not need to be unpacked to scan individual bar code labels on folders and/or documents. The result is reduced labor costs and improved accuracy.

An example of the use of RFID is in the library of the Vatican in Italy. Two million pieces of the library's 40 million-piece collection, including 1.6 million books and centuries-old manuscripts, will be tagged with RFID chips. Library staff will be able to complete the annual inventory in 1 day. Previously, the library was closed for up to 1 month to complete the task. The RFID chips will also allow library staff to monitor the condition of the books and their locations at all times.[1]

When conducting a records inventory, a portable RFID reader as shown in Figure 7.3 can scan up to hundreds of folders in a matter of minutes. The

> **How do RFID tags on documents, folders, and boxes assist a records inventory?**

[1]Nikki Swartz, ed., "Vatican Library Tags Books," *The Information Management Journal,* Vol. 39, No. 1 January/February 2005, p. 6.

Figure 7.3 Portable RFID Reader

3M™ RFID Handheld Tracker, photo courtesy of 3M

RFID tags are read as the portable handheld reader passes within inches of the folders. Depending on the size of the file room, complete file room inventories can often be done in a matter of hours.

Why is a records inventory important?

Information collected during a records inventory includes types of records (official, record copy, or nonrecord) and their media—paper, electronic, or image. An **official record** is a significant, vital, or important record of continuing value to be protected, managed, and retained according to established retention schedules. The official record is often, but not necessarily, an original. Another name for an official record is **record copy,** or the official copy of a record that is retained for legal, operational, or historical purposes. The record copy is sometimes the original. For example, a document printed from an electronic file is often considered the official record rather than the electronic file because the print copy can be read easily. It is durable, and it is easy to use. The electronic file must still be retained for a week or two. However, the printed document may be saved for two or three years, depending on the content. The **office of record** is an office designated to maintain the *record* or *official copy* of a particular record in an organization.

A **nonrecord** is an item not usually included within the scope of official records such as a convenience file, a day file, reference materials such as dictionaries, and drafts. Nonrecords should not be retained past their usefulness. Typically, nonrecords are created, modified, and destroyed without formal RIM procedures and are not included in a records retention program.

Is listing individual records on a RRS a good practice?

Figure 7.4 on page 185 shows a sample records inventory worksheet that would be prepared for each records series retained by each department in an organization. A **records series** is a group of related records that normally are used and filed as a unit and can be evaluated as a unit to determine the records retention period. For example, purchase orders for July are a records series. Bank statements retained for a year or longer are also a records series. The **retention period** is the time that records must be kept according to operational, legal, regulatory, and fiscal requirements.

A records inventory is also a valuable tool for helping managers decide which filing method (alphabetic, subject, numeric, or geographic) to use. Information obtained from a records survey and inventory usually includes the following:

- Name and dates of records series
- Records location by department or office, then building, floor, and room, if necessary
- Equipment in which records are stored—cabinets, shelves, or vaults
- Number of cabinets, shelves, or other storage containers
- How often records are referenced—daily, weekly, monthly, or annually—and why
- Records media—paper, micrographic, electronic, or optical

RECORDS INVENTORY WORKSHEET

(Complete one form for each records series.)

Department	Person Taking Inventory	Date of Inventory
Legal	Randy Thompson	01/15/2005

Department Contact Person and Title	Telephone / Ext.	E-mail
Tiffany Smith	1153	Tiffany.smith@rmg.com

Records Series Title	Dates of Records Series	No. of Storage Containers
Townsend v Hopkins LLC	From ___Jan 1, 2002___ To ___Jan 1, 2005___	6

Description of Records Series (Contents; Purpose; Form Numbers, etc. Continue on reverse side if needed.)

Closed case files, investigation reports, forensic reports, depositions, court records

Records Format/Media
- ☒ Paper   ☒ Letter ☐ Legal
- ☐ Microform (Specify) _____
- ☐ Electronic (Specify) _____
- ☐ Optical (Specify) _____
- ☐ Publications/Books
- ☐ Maps, Drawings
- ☐ Printout
- ☐ Binders
- ☐ Video/Audio Tape
- ☐ Other _____

File Arrangement
- ☐ Alphabetic   ☐ Geographic
- ☐ Numeric   ☐ Chronologic
- ☐ Alphanumeric   ☒ Calendar Year
- ☐ Subject   ☐ Fiscal Year
- ☐ Other (Specify) _____

Volume of Records
Filing Inches _____
Cubic Feet __6__
Annual Accumulation Rate
Filing Inches _____
Cubic Feet _____

Records Value
- ☐ Nonessential
- ☐ Useful
- ☒ Important
- ☐ Vital

Reference Rate
- ☐ Daily
- ☐ Weekly
- ☐ Monthly
- ☒ Less Than Once a Month
- ☐ Annually

Storage Equipment
- ☐ Cabinet   ☒ Box
- ☐ Roll   ☐ Shelf
- ☐ Flat   ☐ Vault
- ☐ Other (Specify) _____

Current Retention Period
Active (in Office)	3 years
Inactive (in Storage)	5 years
Total	8 years

Required Retention Period—Schedule
Active	Until case closed
Inactive	10 years
Total	20 years
Destruction Date	Jan 1, 2045

Form 203 (Rev. 01/05)

Figure 7.4 Records Inventory Worksheet

- Records size—letter, legal, tab/checks, other
- Records housing—folders, binders, disks, reels, etc.
- Records value—nonessential, important, useful, vital
- Retention requirements

E-mail Records

Depending on the content of electronic mail (e-mail) messages, instant messages, or text messages sent and/or received within an organization, they may be considered records or nonrecords. Currently instant messages and text messages are more often used by employees for personal messages than for con-

Is an e-mail message ever an official record?

ducting business. However, e-mail is widely used for sending business-related messages and, therefore, records received or transmitted via e-mail are included on a records retention schedule in appropriate records series. E-mail messages are deleted from the system after a predetermined time if they no longer have value to the organization. Any important e-mail messages that need to be stored for longer periods should be printed and filed with other paper records. The original message should be deleted from the system. The printed copy becomes the official record.

Records and information managers must work with the Information Services Department in their organizations to develop official policies regarding e-mail retention. Some organizations routinely purge/delete all e-mail after 30 days. Other organizations allow each user to determine what to retain as long as the user is following the organization's policy regarding retention. E-mail users must be trained to delete unneeded documents. (See Chapter 12 for more information on e-mail policies.)

Web Records

Why should records of employee online benefit transactions be on a RRS?

Assuring that documents and information created or submitted on company web sites are included in retention policies and schedules is an important concern for many records and information managers. Records and information employees will need to determine whether a record exists only on the web site. If the same record exists in multiple locations, where is the official copy? The organization needs a policy that addresses web records. Generally, when materials are posted to an organization web site, the materials qualify as records, and the materials have not previously been stored in the RIM system, then the organization must establish a link between the web site and the RIM system. The web records are transferred into the RIM system. Web records go through the same life cycle stages as records in other formats. However, these stages are accelerated because web sites may be updated frequently.[2]

Many company web sites have some forms-based applications. Job applicants may complete job applications and submit letters of application through employer web sites. These forms may be changed or updated frequently. Additionally, employees in many organizations are able to make changes to their 401K plans, view their medical claims, and obtain other information about their company benefits online. Documents from these online transactions are included in appropriate records series, and they should be retained for the length of time required by relevant regulations, statutes, and company policies. Other organizations must keep track of sales transactions made on their web sites. One important effect of the Sarbanes-Oxley Act on organizations is that they must retain more documents and for longer periods of time than previously. No one retention period can fit all web records. Web records need to be scheduled according to function or purpose.

---

[2]Gregory S. Hunter, *The Challenges and Opportunities of Web-based Records.* ARMA Web presentation material, January 11, 2005.

After the records inventory is completed, the records and information manager determines the value of each record and then determines how long records are to be retained. Appropriate retention periods are determined and included in a records retention schedule (RRS) (see Figure 7.5 on page 188). A retention schedule contains a comprehensive list of records series titles, indicating for each series the length of time it is to be maintained. It may include retention in active office areas, inactive storage areas, and when and if such series may be destroyed or formally transferred to another facility such as an archives for historical purposes. Records destruction decisions are based on the records retention schedule. Employees do not decide, on their own, to destroy records. RIM best practices include destroying records based on an official and approved records retention schedule and in the normal course of business. Consequently, records are destroyed regularly as certain records reach the end of their usefulness. Chapter 12 contains more information about the role that records retention plays in a comprehensive RIM program.

Creating the records retention schedule is a cooperative effort among several departments in an organization: Legal, Tax, Information Management, Records Management, as well as other departments that own the records. The length of time—the retention period—may be determined by law for statutory, regulatory, or tax purposes. For other records, such as general correspondence, the length of time may be limited to the actual time of use of a record. The estimate of the frequency of use for current and anticipated business is also important. This time period usually determines how long records should be retained in offices or records centers before they are transferred to an archives or otherwise disposed of. A **records center** is a low-cost centralized area for housing and servicing inactive records whose reference rate does not warrant their retention in a prime office area.

Each department has unique needs the retention schedule must meet. Without cooperative input from all departments in an organization, the records retention schedule will not serve its purpose. In addition, the records and information manager must consider each of the following interrelated aspects when developing a records retention schedule.

1. How long will the records be used?
2. In what form should the records be kept? How accessible should the records be?
3. When should the records be determined inactive? Which records should be transferred off-site and when? How will such records be accessed? Will transferred records maintain their integrity and security?
4. What are the applicable federal, state, and local laws?
5. What are the comparative costs for keeping the records or not keeping the records?
6. When and how will the records be disposed of?

What factors influence retention periods?

Could an organization have more than one RRS?

RECORDS RETENTION SCHEDULE			
Records Series	**Years Active**	**Years Inactive**	**Total Years**
Accounting and Fiscal			
Accounts payable invoices	3	3	6
Accounts payable ledger	3	3	6
Accounts receivable ledger	3	3	6
Bank deposit records	3	3	6
Bank reconciliations and statements	3	3	6
Annual audit reports	3	P	P
Administration—Executive			
Correspondence, executive	1	1	2
Policy statements, directives	3	P	P
Advertising			
Contracts, advertising	1	2	3 years after term
Drawings and artwork	10	P	P
Samples, displays, labels	5	P	P
Human Resources			
Applications, changes, terminations	1	0	1
Attendance/vacation records	3	4	7
Medical folder, employee	While employed	0	30 years after term
Training manuals	3	P	P
Insurance			
Claims, group life/hospital	1	3	4
Claims, workers' compensation	1	9	10
Expired policies: fire, hospital, liability, life, workers' compensation	1	2	3 years after expiration
Operations			
Inventories	1	0	1
Office equipment records	3	3	6
Requisitions for supplies	1	0	1
Records Management			
Records destruction documentation	3	P	P
Records inventory	1	0	1
Records management policies	1	P	P
P = Permanent Term = Termination			
Form 220 (Rev. 01/05)			

Figure 7.5 Records Retention Schedule

Records retention schedules are based on the value of the *information* contained in the records and *not* on the storage media. Records stored on all media are included in a RRS. However, as discussed in Chapter 11, the life span of the media is important for long-term retention. In some organizations, a separate retention schedule is maintained for electronic records.

All records users need to comply with the records retention schedule adopted by their organization. Many organizations emphasize the importance of records by conducting Records Week activities centered around cleaning out old records, transferring records, and destroying records. By closely following transfer and destruction timetables, an organization can reduce clutter and improve retrieval time because fewer records will be in storage. Additional space will be available for current records needed for day-to-day decision making. The records retrieval process is discussed next.

RECORDS RETRIEVAL

Retrieval is the process of locating and removing a record or file from storage. It is also the action of recovering information on a given subject from stored records. In this section, you will learn how to retrieve records by following standard procedures and recommended best practices. Although the procedures discussed here are primarily for paper-based systems, the same procedures apply for retrieving and accessing electronic and image records. Steps for retrieving a record are shown in Figure 7.6.

> **Why are standard retrieval procedures important?**

STEPS FOR RETRIEVING A RECORD

1. Receive request for stored record or records series—requester or records center employee prepares requisition form.
2. Check index for location of stored record(s).
3. Search for record or records series.
4. Retrieve (locate) record or records series.
5. Remove record(s) from storage.
6. Charge out record(s) to requester: Insert OUT indicator in place of record(s) removed from storage; complete the charge-out log.
7. Send record(s) to requester.
8. Follow up borrowed record(s).
9. Receive record(s) for re-storage.
10. Store record(s) again. Remove OUT indicator. Update charge-out

Figure 7.6 Records Retrieval Procedure

A record or information from it may be retrieved in three ways:

1. **Manually.** A person goes to a storage container and removes by hand a record that a user has requested or makes a note of the information someone has requested from it.
2. **Mechanically.** A person uses some mechanical means such as pressing the correct buttons to rotate movable shelves to the correct location of a record, removing the record manually, or recording information requested from the record.
3. **Electronically.** A person uses some means, such as a computer, to locate a record. The requester is shown the requested information or informed on a screen in a database or in an e-mail file as to where it can be found. The physical record may not need to be removed from storage.

How are records requested?

Requests for stored records may be made orally (from the next desk, over the telephone or intercom, or by messenger) or in writing (by fax, e-mail, memo, letter, or special form). The request also may be delivered in person. A typical request, for example, might be, "Please find the most recent letter from ABC Computer Corp. that forecasts the number of silicon chips the company will produce next quarter." Or, "Please pull the DVD of the chairman's 2004 annual report to stockholders." Or, perhaps, "Please retrieve the microfiche of the current price list for auto parts." All these records have previously been stored manually according to an established method of storage. The letter, DVD, electronic record, or microfiche must be retrieved from storage and given to the requester quickly. Every minute of delay in finding a record is costly—in user or requester waiting time and in filer searching time—and could possibly lead to loss of money for the company because of a lost sale.

If filers and requesters use the same filing segment for storing and requesting a record, the system works well. If, for instance, records relating to a company named Mansfield Heat & Air were stored alphabetically under *Mansfield* but requested under *Air Conditioner Company,* the searcher would find retrieval extremely difficult because he or she would look in the A section of storage instead of the M section. Consequently, good cross-referencing is necessary for efficient retrieval.

Retrieval and Re-storage Cycle

The same steps followed for retrieving are followed for handling all manual records. Only the specific operating procedures differ. The crucial step, the point at which a problem is most likely to arise, is in Step 1 with the words used to request a record. Ideally, the person who stores a record is also the one who searches for and removes it from storage when it is requested. Realistically, however, a record may be stored by one person and retrieved by someone else when that record or information is requested.

Effective records control enables the records manager or filer to retrieve requested records on the first try and to answer correctly these questions:

1. **Who** took the records?
2. **What** records are out of storage?
3. **When** were the records taken?
4. **Where** will the records be re-filed when they are brought back to storage?
5. **How long** will the records be out of storage?

Requisition, Charge-Out, and Follow-Up Procedures

Effective records control includes following standard procedures for requesting records, charging them out, and assuring that they are returned. These procedures, referred to as *requisition, charge-out,* and *follow-up,* may be completed manually or by using an automated system. By following standard procedures consistently, the number of lost or misfiled records can be reduced or eliminated.

Requisition Procedures

Preparing a requisition is the first step in the retrieval process. A request is an in-person, mail, telephone, fax, or e-mail inquiry for information about or from records stored in a records center or an archives. A **requisition** is a written request for a record or information from a record.

> **Why is preparing a requisition form necessary?**

Even if the borrower orally requests the information or record, that request is put into writing and referred to as a requisition. The form may be prepared by the requester or completed by the filer from information given orally or in writing by the requester. An organization networked through the Internet or an intranet may post a variety of forms, including records requisition forms, that users may complete and transmit electronically. Two types of requisition forms are described next.

Requisition Form

One of the most frequently used requisition forms is a 5″ by 3″ or 6″ by 4″ card or slip of paper printed with blanks to be filled in. Figure 7.7 shows an example of a requisition form. A requester or filer may complete a similar computer-generated form in an automated system. Some RIM software, discussed later in this chapter, is capable of generating a pick list for retrieving a number of requested records. A **pick list** is a list containing specific records needed for a given program or project. A filer can use a pick list to retrieve all records on the list. The records are then sent as a group to the requester. The same list can be used to return the records to the proper files/locations.

RECORDS REQUEST	
Name on Record	**Date on Record**
Date Borrowed	**Date to be Returned**
Requester Name	**Extension**
Department	**E-mail**
Place white copy into folder. Place blue copy into tickler control file.	
Form 209 (Rev. 01/05)	

Usually prepared in duplicate — original stays in folder; copy serves as a reminder.

Figure 7.7 Requisition Form

What are some consequences of not using OUT indicators?

When a requisition form is completed, the filer will have answers to the five records retrieval questions previously discussed—Who? What? When? Where? How long? This form may be prepared in duplicate: The original stays in the folder from which the document was retrieved to serve as an OUT indicator. An OUT indicator is a form or document that describes records removed from the files and helps filers quickly find where records have been removed. The copy (usually placed into a tickler file as discussed in Chapter 6) serves as a reminder to assure the record is returned on time. A copy of a computer-generated requisition form may be printed to serve as an OUT indicator in a paper file. The filer may also be able to insert an electronic flag into the records database to indicate that a record is out of the records center. The electronic requisition form is then sent to an electronic tickler file.

On-Call (Wanted) Form

Occasionally, another user will request a record that is charged out to another user. A requisition form replacing the record in the file identifies who has the record and when it will be returned. The filer should notify the second requester that the record is on loan and state when it is scheduled for return to storage. If the second request is urgent, the filer will notify the original borrower that someone else wants the record and ask that it be returned to storage. Notification may be made orally, in writing on an on-call form or a wanted form, or by fax or e-mail. An **on-call form,** or **wanted form,** is a written request

ON CALL

WANTED BY		RECORDS WANTED		DELIVERED
DATE	**NAME**	**DATE**	**DESCRIPTION**	**DATE**
9/27	Scott R. Howard	8/17	Frost Construction File	9/30

Form 205 (Rev. 01/05)

Prepared as a duplicate—one copy to borrower; one copy attached
to the original OUT indicator in storage.

Figure 7.8 On-Call/Wanted Form

for a record that is *out* of the file (Figure 7.8). This form is similar to an OUT form. A computer-generated form may also be completed and transmitted by fax or e-mail to the records center.

Two copies of an on-call form are made—one copy goes to the borrower; the other copy is attached to the original OUT indicator in storage. When the borrowed record is returned to storage, it is charged out to the second borrower by the standard method of charge-out or by writing on the on-call form the date on which the record was delivered to the second borrower. (Note the Delivered Date column on the form in Figure 7.8.)

In some optical disk and microfilm storage systems, requested information is retrieved and sent to the requester electronically. An optical disk record is retrieved on a computer terminal and faxed or e-mailed to the requester. Microfilm is scanned into a computer terminal and faxed or e-mailed to the requester. In both cases, the official record is not removed from its file. No follow-up procedures are needed because the official record is still in storage. Requesters may be instructed to destroy the borrowed record when they have completed their work with it. Note also that manual records (paper) can be scanned and transmitted electronically by e-mail or fax. Paper records can also be faxed via a conventional fax machine. The official record is returned to the file, and the user may destroy the fax or e-mail copy of the official record after use.

Why is keeping track of requested official records important?

Why should borrowed records be controlled?

Confidential Records Requests

All stored records are considered valuable, or they would not be stored. Some are so valuable that they are stamped *Confidential, Classified, Secret, Vital,* or *Personal.* Do not release these types of records from storage without proper authorization following established procedures and best practices. In some offices, a written request bearing the signature of a designated officer of the organization is required for release of such records. In an electronic system, access to confidential records is limited to those users who know the password. If a copy of a confidential record is sent electronically, it might be encrypted (the words are scrambled into code using a software program) to prevent unauthorized access. When the requester receives the encrypted file, he or she must unscramble/decrypt the file to read it. Some records may be so valuable or confidential that they are not to be removed from storage under any circumstances. These records must be inspected only at the storage container or in a secure room. The signature of someone in authority is required before the inspection is allowed. A requisition form is usually not needed; however, a record of the persons inspecting the records may be kept.

Manual Charge-Out Procedures

Charge-out is a control procedure to establish the current location of a record when it is not in the records center or central file, which can be a manual or automated system. A record is charged out to the borrower who is held responsible for returning it to storage by an agreed-upon date. A standard procedure for charging out and following up records should be observed each time a record is borrowed, regardless of who removes material from storage. Taking less than 1 minute to note the name of a person borrowing a record will save hours spent searching for a lost or misplaced record. Borrowers seem to be more conscientious about returning records to storage when they know that records have been charged out in their names. Typically, supplies needed to charge-out records consist of the following:

1. OUT indicators to show that records have been removed from storage
2. Carrier folders to transport borrowed records while the original folder remains in the file
3. Charge-out log

Why is keeping track of who has borrowed records necessary?

OUT Indicators

When a requested record is located, it is removed from storage and an OUT form is inserted in place of the record. An OUT form shows where to re-file the record when it is returned. OUT indicators are explained in more detail in Chapter 6. If several records are removed from storage, they may be placed into a folder, referred to as a *carrier folder,* to assure the records stay together during transport to the user.

OUT Indicator Disposal

When a borrowed record is returned to storage, the OUT form inserted while the record was gone must be removed immediately. If the charge-out information was written on the OUT form, this information is crossed out, and the form is stored for reuse. In some offices, OUT forms are kept for tallying purposes— to see how many records are being requested, to determine the workload of employees, and to see which records are being used frequently and which are not. Totals may be kept daily, weekly, monthly, or yearly as determined by the standard procedure in effect. Requisition forms removed from files may be destroyed. Any forms filed in electronic tickler files may also be deleted.

Automated Charge-Out Procedures

In automated systems, completing a paper requisition form is not necessary because records may be charged out using one of two electronic methods: bar codes and RFID tags. A bar code printed on a label affixed to a record, folder, or records center storage box is similar to an electronic product code (EPC) printed on a can of food in a supermarket or on a price tag on a pair of jeans in a department store. As discussed briefly in Chapter 6, records may be indexed and bar coded to identify their places in the files and other information about the records. When a requester has presented his or her bar code identifier— often printed on an employee name tag—and the requested file is located, the bar code on the record is scanned. An electronic form is created when the bar code on the record is scanned that indicates whether the record is checked out, to whom, and for how long. Copies of the form may be printed or stored electronically. A bar code representing the electronic form may be printed and affixed to an OUT indicator and placed into the file where the requested record should be re-filed. When the record is returned, the bar code is scanned again, the OUT indicator is located, the record is returned to the file, and the requester is "cleared" of any borrowed records.

Folders and records may be rapidly checked out using RFID tags by simply passing them over the top of the reader (Figure 7.9 on page 196). Many folders can be read at once and a list of them displayed on a screen. A similar process can be used to scan folders into a box for archiving.

> **How do bar codes or RFID tages improve records charge-out?**

Follow-Up Procedures

Whoever is responsible for retrieving and charging out records from storage is also responsible for checking in the records on their return. **Follow-up** is a system for assuring the timely and proper return of materials charged out from a file. The length of time records may be borrowed from storage depends on (1) the type of business, (2) the number of requests received for the records, (3) the use of a copying machine, and (4) the value of the records.

Experience shows that the longer records remain out of the files, the more difficult their return becomes. Many organizations stipulate a week to 10 days,

> **What are some factors that affect the length of time for which records may be borrowed?**

3M™ RFID Tracking Pad, photo courtesy of 3M

Figure 7.9 Folders may be charged out by passing them over a tracking pad that reads bar codes on the folders.

with 2 weeks being the absolute maximum amount of time records may be borrowed. Other organizations allow less time because records can be copied easily and quickly, and the original may be returned to storage within a few hours. Extra copies should be destroyed when they are no longer needed. Following up on a borrowed record may mean calling a borrower, sending an e-mail, or sending a written request as a reminder that borrowed records must be returned to storage. If no other requests for the same records have been received, the date the records are to be returned may be extended.

Follow-Up for Confidential Records

The rule concerning confidential records is generally that the records (if they may be borrowed) must be returned to storage each night. A special reminder often is used to assure that these records are returned. This reminder may be a note prominently displayed, a special flag, or some other type of signal. The same charge-out procedures used for other records are also used for confidential records. However, an additional reminder to obtain the record before the end of the day also is used. Because the memory jogger must remind the filer that confidential records are out of storage and must be returned, it must be something unusual.

Charge-Out Log

Usually, an organization will have a charge-out log on which to record information for all records as they are removed from storage. A **charge-out log** is a written or electronic form used for recording the following information:

What is the purpose of a charge-out log?

1. What record was taken (correspondent name or subject title on the record and date on the record)

2. When the record was taken (date borrowed)
3. Who took the record (name of person, extension number, e-mail address)
4. Date due for returning the record
5. Date returned
6. Date overdue notice was sent
7. Extended date due

The charge-out log should be kept current and used in the follow-up procedure. Refer to Figure 7.10 for an example of a portion of a charge-out log.

RECORDS TRANSFER

As indicated on the sample records retention schedule shown in Figure 7.5 on page 188, records may be stored in an active records area for a period of time before being moved to another storage area when they are no longer accessed regularly. **Records transfer** is the act of changing the physical custody of records with or without change of legal title. In other words, records are moved from one storage area to another, but they are usually still owned by the same company. Records are transferred when they are no longer used frequently. As records age, they are less frequently accessed and become inactive. Conse-

> **Why are records transferred?**

CHARGE-OUT LOG									
Name on Record	Date on Record	Name of Person Borrowing Record	Ext. or E-mail	Date Borrowed	Date Due	Date Returned	Date Overdue Notice Sent	Extended Date Due
Hillman Equipment & Rental Sales	5/17	M. Alvarez	1153	8/19	8/26	8/26		
Buchanan Flooring, Inc.	3/3	B. Amatulli	bamatulli@xyz.net	8/21	8/28	8/25		
The Learning Center	11/30	J. Lee	1206	8/22	8/29		8/30	9/6
LeBow Salon & Day Spa	4/27	L. Davis	ldavis@xyz.net	8/31	9/7	9/6		

Form 211 (Rev. 01/05)

Figure 7.10 Charge-Out Log

What types of records are stored in an archives?

quently, dates on the records are also considered when deciding to transfer records. In most cases, the active files contain the current year's records plus those of the immediate past year.

The final phase of the records life cycle is disposition. **Records disposition** is the final destination of records after they have reached the end of their retention period in active and/or inactive storage. Records may be transferred to an archives for retention, or they may be destroyed. Inactive storage may be housed on-site or off-site. On-site storage is storage of inactive (usually) records on the premises of an organization. Off-site storage is a potentially secure location, remote from the primary location, at which inactive or vital records are stored. **Archives** are the records created or received and accumulated by a person or an organization in the conduct of affairs and preserved because of their historical or continuing value.

Archives also may refer to the building or part of a building where archival materials are located. An archives is used for permanent storage. An archivist is a person professionally educated, trained, experienced, and engaged in the administration of archival materials, including the following activities: appraisal and disposition, acquisition, preservation, arrangement and description, reference service, and outreach to historical societies and individuals or groups interested in preserving documents and other important or historical records.

The U.S. government, most U.S. states, colleges and universities, and corporations have archives where important historical records are kept. These records may include paper documents, photographs of important events, and other records media. The U.S. National Archives and Records Administration (NARA) maintains public vaults that display hundreds of records—originals or facsimiles of documents, photographs, maps, drawings, and film or audio clips that are important historical records for the nation. Visitors may view documents ranging from important treaties and legislation to letters to and from a former President and citations for military bravery. Universities in which faculty and staff researchers have made important discoveries will have copyright and patent information to protect for long periods of time. These documents and related information are stored in the universities' archives.

What happens in the disposition phase of the records life cycle?

In the disposition phase of the records life cycle, decisions are made to (1) destroy a record, (2) retain a record permanently, or (3) transfer a record to inactive storage. Records transfer is made according to an established and approved retention schedule as described earlier. If records are transferred, the main basis for making that decision is often the active or inactive use of the record. Records analysts define three groups of records according to the degree of records activity: **active records**, **inactive records**, and **archive records** (Figure 7.11 on page 200).

CAREER CORNER

Job Description for Archivist/Records Manager and Archivist / Records Analyst

The following job description is an example of a career opportunity in a large federal government agency.

GENERAL INFORMATION

These positions perform a broad range of professional duties in archives and records management with increasing administrative responsibility.

RESPONSIBILITIES

- Perform administrative work in planning, coordinating, and directing archives and records management activities
- Appraise, access, arrange, describe, catalog, make available, and perform research on records to determine their value
- Establish and periodically review and update records retention schedules to ensure records are retained and disposed of in accordance with legal requirements and business needs
- Assist in establishing efficient, cost-effective and effective records and information management by providing advice and training
- Promote public awareness of the archives and records and information management program by making oral presentations, writing articles for publication, and participating in professional organizations
- Perform other duties as required

EXPERIENCE AND EDUCATION

- Graduate level degree required
- CRM preferred

TYPICAL ANNUAL SALARIES, RELATED TO EXPERIENCE

- Archivist/Records Manager: $55,000–$74,000
- Archivist/Analyst II: $48,000–$60,000
- Archivist/Analyst I: $36,000–$46,000

RECORDS ACTIVITY

Active Records	Inactive Records	Archive Records
▪ Needed to perform current operations	▪ Do not have to be readily available	▪ Kept for their continuing or historical value
▪ Used frequently	▪ Kept for legal, fiscal, or historical purposes	▪ Preserved permanently
▪ Located near user		▪ Used to:
▪ Accessed manually or online	▪ Accessed less than fifteen times a year	• Maintain public relations
▪ Accessed three or more times a month	▪ Stored in less expensive storage area	• Prepare commemorative histories
▪ Stored in very accessible equipment in active storage area or online		• Preserve corporate history
		• Provide financial, legal, personnel, product, or research information
		• Provide policy direction
		▪ Stored in less expensive storage area, often off-site

Figure 7.11 Degrees of Records Activity

What is the difference between inactive and archive records?

Sometimes records transfer decisions are made on the basis of dates on the records. The following reasons also greatly influence when and why transfer takes place:

1. No more active records storage space is available.
2. Costs of more storage equipment and extra office space are rising, and less costly areas of nearby storage or off-site storage become attractive alternatives.
3. Stored records are no longer being requested and, therefore, are ready for transfer.
4. Workloads are lighter, and time is available for records transfer activity.
5. Case or project records have reached a closing or ending time (the contract has expired; the legal case is settled or closed).
6. Established organizational policy requires every department to transfer records at a stated time.

Transferring records that are no longer used regularly has three advantages:

1. Records transfer helps to reduce equipment costs because inactive records may be stored in less expensive cardboard containers.
2. Cabinets or shelves formerly used by the transferred files provide additional space for new active files.
3. The space in drawers, cabinets, shelves, or computer storage is increased because files are no longer crowded, which improves efficiency of storage and retrieval of active files.

Once the decision to transfer is made, the records and information manager must find answers to four important questions:

1. **What** records are to be moved?
2. **How** are the records to be prepared for transfer?
3. **When** are the records to be transferred?
4. **Where** are the transferred records to be stored?

Answers to the first three questions will depend on the transfer method selected and the organization's records retention schedule. The answer to the *where* question will depend on the method selected and on the availability of in-house (on-site) or off-site records storage areas. After answering those questions, the records and information manager then follows perpetual or periodic transfer procedures to move the selected records.

When should records be transferred?

Transfer Methods

Two of the most commonly used methods of transferring records are the perpetual transfer method and the periodic transfer method. Each method is discussed in this section, along with the procedure required to ensure efficient records transfer.

Perpetual Transfer Method

Under the **perpetual transfer method**, records are continually transferred from active to inactive storage areas whenever the records are no longer needed for reference. Examples of records that can be transferred by the perpetual method include student records after graduation; legal cases that are closed; research projects when results are finalized; medical records of cases no longer needing attention; prison and law-enforcement case records; and construction or architectural jobs that are completed.

Electronic records and nonrecords should be perpetually transferred from storage on a hard drive to storage on microfilm or optical disks (see Chapter 11

How do the perpetual and periodic transfer methods differ?

for more on microfilm and optical storage media). E-mail messages should be routinely deleted if they are not official records. The perpetual transfer method is not recommended for business correspondence or records that are referred to often and that must be available quickly.

Periodic Transfer Method

The **periodic transfer method** is a method of transferring active records at the end of a stated period of time—usually 1 year—to inactive storage. Records are moved from current files into inactive storage sites on a scheduled basis. Guides remain in the active storage containers. However, new folders are prepared for records that are then allowed to accumulate in active storage until the next transfer period. A commonly used periodic method of transferring records at the end of one period, usually once or twice a year, is called the **one-period transfer method.** Records are transferred at the end of one period (6 months or 1 year).The main advantage of this method is the ease of operation. The main disadvantage is that some frequently requested records will be in inactive storage, and users must make frequent trips to the inactive storage area. Records for some correspondents will occasionally need to be retrieved from both active and inactive storage if the requested records cover several time periods.

Transfer Procedures

After the transfer method is determined, transfer procedures are communicated to every department in the organization. Before the transfer begins, the records and information manager must ensure that adequate storage equipment is available and at the correct location to receive transferred records.

Records are transferred either to inactive or archive (permanent) storage. Inactive storage indicates the record may be infrequently referenced. At the end of the retention period, inactive records are destroyed. Records stored in an archives must be kept permanently; however, the records may still be referenced. Because some records may have historical value, a special display area may be created for those records. Often, records are transferred to a records center. Transfer procedures for inactive and archival records are the same.

Preparing records for transfer involves completing the necessary transfer forms and boxing the records for inactive or archival storage. Figure 7.12 on page 203 shows an example records transmittal form. Note that information on the form should be keyed or clearly handwritten because it will be attached to the outside of a storage box and used to locate inactive records that may be requested at a later date. Also note that information on the form is about the contents of a box such as a description of the records, the time span the records cover, the department name, and the retention information.

What is the purpose of a transmittal form?

Records Transmittal to Records Center

Department		Telephone: 1134	Date of Transfer
Legal		E-mail: jane.dorta@xyz.net	1/10/20--

Signature of Person Releasing Records
Jane D'Orta

Shaded Areas for Records Management Use Only

Box Number		Description of Records (Contents of each box)	Records Disposal Auth. No.	Department Retention Schedule Item No.	Year of Record Beg	Year of Record End	Location in Records Center	Retention Period	Disposal Year	Disposal Date
Current Year	Sequential Number									
20--	1265	Closed cases—Fraud	25	13	04	04				
20--	1266	Closed cases—Criminal	26	13	04	04				
20--	1267	Closed cases—Copyright	27	13	04	04				

DESTRUCTION OF RECORDS	The Pink Copy of this form will be sent to you when records are ready for destruction. Please sign and return the form to the Records Center. If a change in disposal method or date is necessary, attach a memo that includes the new date and/or new method of destruction and reason for the delay.		
	Approval Date	Approval Signature for Destruction	Date of Destruction	Destroyed by

Form 210 (Rev. 01/05) Distribution: White – Records Center; Yellow – Department; Pink – File Copy

Figure 7.12 Records Transmittal Form

At the time records are transferred, the transferring department completes a multicopy set of the records transfer form. Copies of the records transfer form are distributed as follows:

- The transferring department keeps one copy while the box is in transit to storage.
- The original and two copies accompany the box to inactive storage where the box is logged in, and its location on the storage shelves is noted on all copies of the transmittal form.
- One copy of the form is returned to the sending department for reference when a record from that box is requested. The copy that was first retained in the department is then destroyed because it does not contain the location of the box.

In an automated system, information from the records transfer form is either keyed or read into automatic equipment. Bar codes make this process much faster. When records are borrowed from an inactive records center or archival storage, the same controls are needed as are used in active storage—requisition, charge-out, and follow-up.

Why is uniform box size needed in a records center?

If the records center does not provide boxes of uniform size in which to store records to be transferred, the records manager must ensure that all departments use the same size box. Using uniform box sizes facilitates stacking, uses space most economically, and looks neater. A **records center box** (carton or container) is usually made of corrugated cardboard and is designed to hold approximately one cubic foot (12 inches high by 12 inches wide by 12 inches deep) of records, either legal or letter size. These boxes may have lift-up or lift-off tops or lift-out sides. Examples of recycled records center boxes are shown in Figure 7.13.

Figure 7.13 Records Center Storage Boxes

RECORDS CENTER CONTROL PROCEDURES

Whether inactive or archival records are stored off-site or within the same building as active records, several control procedures should be in place to ensure appropriate security and accession of the records (Figure 7.14).

Inactive Records Index

First and most important, records must be located. A commercial records center may house records owned by several different organizations; an in-house records center contains records for all departments of one organization. In either case, many different records series are stored on a space-available basis. Consequently, like records series with different dates probably will not be stored near each other. For example, if a request is made for an inactive accounting ledger for July 2004, the filer must locate the box of accounting records for 2004 quickly to find the requested record.

Various indexes are useful in locating stored records. An **index** is a systematic guide that allows access to specific items contained within a larger body of information. A records center will maintain an index to assist filers in locating inactive records. An **inactive records index** is an index of all records in the inactive records storage center. This index contains details about the inactive records: the dates the records were created, a description of the records series, the department that owns the records, an authorization for transfer to inactive storage, their location in the records storage center, the retention period, and the disposition date.

This information can be manually or electronically maintained and is often a continuation of the records transmittal form (Figure 7.12). The transmittal form contains all information needed for an inactive records index. A records center employee completes the location part of the form by checking

---

**RECORDS CENTER
CONTROL FILES**

Inactive Records Index	Contains a complete listing of all stored inactive records
Charge-Out and Follow-Up File	Contains requisition forms
Destruction Date File	Contains copies of transmittal form
Destruction File	Contains copies of transmittal forms after records are destroyed

Figure 7.14 Records Center Control Files

the available space in the center and assigning space for the box(es). A copy of the records transmittal form is affixed to the box containing the records, and another copy of the transmittal form is filed in the destruction date file (discussed later). If a bar code or a RFID tag is affixed to each box, it is quickly scanned into an electronic form that can be printed and affixed to the box and filed into the destruction date file. The destruction date file may also be stored electronically in an automated records center.

Charge-Out and Follow-Up File

As with active records, charge-out and follow-up procedures must be followed for inactive and archive records. When someone from the Accounting Department, for example, requests accounts payable records for July 1, 2005, through December 31, 2005, a requisition form is completed. The filer scans the inactive records index, noting the location of the requested box of records. Then the filer physically goes to that location in the records center, finds the correct box, and removes the correct record(s). One copy of the requisition form is used as an OUT indicator and is placed inside the box. Last, the requisition information is filed or entered into the charge-out and follow-up file.

A **charge-out and follow-up file** is a tickler file that contains requisition forms filed by dates that records are due back in the inactive records center. If a record is not returned by the date due, written reminders, telephone calls, faxes, or e-mail messages are used to remind the borrower to return the record(s) to the center.

Destruction Date File

How are records destroyed?

Records destruction is the disposal of records of no further value by incinerating (burning), macerating (soaking in a chemical solution to soften the paper, then bailing it), pulping (shredding and mixing with water, then bailing), or shredding. Destruction is the definitive obliteration of a record beyond any possible reconstruction—nothing can possibly be recovered from the record. Shredders that can shred records in all media formats, including disks, CDs, and micromedia, are available. Some records that do not contain confidential information may be sold for recycling. Many organizations find that contracting with service providers to destroy their records is more cost-effective than purchasing the supplies and equipment and hiring workers to carry out the destruction.

Records center control procedures include maintaining records that document when and how records are destroyed. A **destruction date file** is a tickler file containing copies of forms completed when records are received in a records center. These forms are filed by destruction dates. Destruction dates for each records series are determined when a records retention schedule is created, and these dates are recorded on records transmittal forms. Another copy of the transmittal form can be placed into the destruction date file. Documents in this file are moved into the destruction file after the documents are destroyed.

Before the destruction date arrives, the records center will notify the department that owns the records that the destruction date is approaching. A **destruction notice** is a notification (memo, listing, form, etc.) of the scheduled destruction of records. This notice reminds departmental employees that some of their records will soon be destroyed even though the department manager signed a records destruction authorization form when the records were transferred to the records center. That authorization form is kept on file in the records center. Notice that the fourth column on the records transmittal form in Figure 7.12 on page 203 identifies a records disposal authorization number. This number is assigned when the records are transferred to the records center. If a written authorization is on file, the number in that column is all that is needed to proceed with the destruction. If, after receiving the destruction notice, the department manager determines that the inactive records continue to have value, destruction may be suspended. Records retention policies and best practices should include provisions for suspending records destruction when a lawsuit or other legal actions are pending or are in process. A **destruction suspension** is a hold placed on the scheduled destruction of records that may be relevant to foreseeable or pending litigation, governmental investigation, audit, or special organizational requirements. Records for which destruction has been suspended are often referred to as *frozen records*.

> **Why are some records not destroyed on the scheduled date?**

Destruction File

Whether records are destroyed by a service provider or by records center employees, the actual destruction must be witnessed or proof provided by a certificate of destruction. A **destruction file** contains information on the actual destruction of inactive records. Usually, the type of destruction is determined at the time the records are transferred to the records center. This information is recorded on the transmittal forms in the destruction date file, which are moved to the destruction file after the records are destroyed. These forms are filed by department names and dates on which destruction was carried out. Records managers maintain and dispose of records as part of the record life cycle. Proper control procedures ensure that the right record is available to the right person at the right time and that records no longer needed are destroyed properly.

At least once a year, go through your files and safely dispose of everything that is no longer needed. Cross-cut shredding is a safe way to dispose of any paper records that contain your name, Social Security number, driver's license, account numbers, address, and bank information.

My Records

Retain and Dispose of Records

Do you have a fear of throwing away documents because you might need them some day? Do you know which records you need to keep and for how long?

To reduce the volume of your paper records, you need to dispose of records you no longer need on a regular schedule. Ask yourself these basic questions to help determine which records to keep and which ones to destroy:

- Is the information important to my life, personal interests, or job?
- Has this information become outdated? Can I find a more current document?
- How easily can I replace this document if I need the information later?

A suggested retention schedule for personal records appears below. If you have specific questions about retaining your records, ask an accountant or attorney.

File Type	Retention	File Type	Retention
Family Records		**Employment Records**	
Birth Certificate	Permanent	Contracts	4 years after completion
Diploma	Permanent		
Divorce settlement	Permanent	Correspondence	4 years after leaving job
Marriage certificate	Permanent		
Military service	Permanent	Pay stubs	1 year
Naturalization papers	Permanent		
Passport	Until receipt of renewed passport	**Taxes**	
		Federal income tax forms	7 years
Pet papers	For life of pet	State income tax forms	7 years
Social security	Permanent		
Will	Permanent	**Legal and Financial Records**	
		Deeds	Permanent
Medical Records		Contracts (mortgage, promissory notes, leases)	
Details of surgeries, diagnosis, procedures	Permanent	Still in effect	Permanent
Medicines taken	Permanent	Expired contracts	7 years
		Credit card statements	1 year
Product Receipts and Warranties		Bank statements	1 year
Currently owned	Permanent		
Sold or recycled	1 year		

RECORDS CENTER SOFTWARE

Automation in large records centers is extremely important. It improves productivity, helps center employees provide faster service, and improves system integrity. Records center software combined with bar codes or RFID tags can eliminate many manual tasks. The software should be able to perform the following main functions:

How can software improve records center efficiencies?

1. Box and/or record inventories
2. Storage management
3. Records and information searches
4. Records retention schedule correlations
5. Destruction methodology correlated with retention schedules
6. Accounting
7. User tracking

Additionally, the software can be programmed to include bar code and RFID tracking, cross-referencing, global searching, off-site storage control, label preparation, document indexing, spell-checking, report generation, audit trails, and more. (Records audits are discussed in Chapter 12.)

How can records tracking systems improve retrieval accuracy?

By incorporating bar code and RFID technology and having readers connected directly to a computer, records center automation systems can perform these additional functions:

- Locate a box on a shelf
- Check out/in a box or file
- Locate a folder in a box
- Identify a file or box for destruction
- Charge back faxing, copying, microfilm searches, and other activities to departments that requested such services[3]

Often, records tracking systems use bar codes or RFID tags to help in retrieval and to eliminate the need for keying input each time a record is requested.

Because pertinent information is not keyed each time, input errors are virtually eliminated when bar codes or RFID tags are used. Whether a record is classified as active, inactive, or archival, a tracking system allows instant recall of facts, location, and in some cases, the record itself. Most tracking systems use a database setup to manage records at the document, folder, or box level.

---

[3]ARMA International, *Records Center Operations,* 2d ed. (Lenexa, KS: ARMA International, 2002), p. 15.

Chapter Review And Applications

POINTS TO FILE AND RETRIEVE

- A records retention program establishes policies and procedures for what documents to keep, where to keep them, and how long to keep them.

- A records inventory is a survey of all records maintained by an organization.

- A retention period is the length of time that records must be retained according to operational, legal, regulatory, and fiscal requirements.

- A records retention schedule (RRS) shows how long to maintain all records.

- Retrieval is the process of locating and removing a record, a file, or information from storage.

- Follow-up is a system for assuring the timely and proper return of materials charged out from a file.

- When records are no longer used frequently, they are transferred to a records center or to an archive for permanent storage, or they are destroyed.

- Archives are the records created or received and accumulated by a person or organization and preserved because of their historical or continuing value.

- Records transfer helps reduce equipment costs because inactive records are stored in less expensive cardboard containers.

- Records center control files include an inactive records index, a charge-out and follow-up file, a destruction date file, and a destruction file.

- Records center software, along with bar codes and RFID tags, perform box inventories, charge in/out records and boxes, locate a box on a shelf, locate a record in a box, and perform numerous other important records and information functions.

IMPORTANT TERMS

active records

archive records

archives

bar code

charge-out

charge-out and follow-up file

charge-out log

destruction date file

destruction file

destruction notice

destruction suspension

follow-up

inactive records

inactive records index

index

nonrecord

office of record

official record

on-call/wanted form

one-period transfer method

periodic transfer method

perpetual transfer method

pick list

radio frequency identification (RFID)

record copy

records center

records center box

records destruction

records disposition

records inventory

records retention program

records retention schedule

records series

records transfer

requisition

retention period

retrieval

REVIEW AND DISCUSSION

1. Why is a records retention program useful to an organization? (Obj. 1)

2. List and describe each of the four values of records. Provide a record example for each value. (Obj. 2)

3. What is a records inventory? Discuss why an inventory is conducted and what is included in the inventory. (Obj. 3)

4. Describe a records retention schedule and explain why one is prepared and the purpose it serves. (Obj. 4)

5. What is records retrieval? Name at least three ways that requests for stored records may be made. (Obj. 5)

6. Explain the steps in a manual charge-out procedure. (Obj. 5)

7. Explain how records are charged out in an automated records center. (Obj. 5)

8. What is the purpose of using follow-up procedures for borrowed records? (Obj. 5)

9. List six reasons for transferring records. (Obj. 6)

10. Describe two methods of records transfer. (Obj. 6)

11. An inactive records center usually maintains four control files. Discuss these files. (Obj. 7)

12. List five capabilities of typical records center software. (Obj. 8)

APPLICATIONS

7-1 DETERMINE RETENTION PERIODS (OBJS. 1, 4)

DATA CD

ACCESS ACTIVITY

CRITICAL THINKING

1. Open the *Access* data file *7-1 Retention Schedule*. Open the Records Retention Schedule table.

2. Refer to the records retention schedule in Figure 7.5, page 188, to find retention periods for the records listed below. Enter the retention data in the Years Active, Years Inactive, and Total Years database fields.

   Records
   Expired liability policy
   Records inventory
   Bank deposits
   Advertising contracts
   Annual audit reports
   Policy statements
   Records management policies
   Requisitions for supplies
   Training manuals
   Executive correspondence

3. Sort the table by the Records Series field and then by the Record field.

4. Create and print a report to show the records retention schedule. Include all of the fields in the Records Retention Schedule table. Group the records by the **Records Series** field. Sort by the **Records** field in ascending order. Choose **Stepped** layout and **Landscape** orientation. Choose **Corporate** style. Name the report **Records Retention Schedule Report.** Print the report.

5. Create a query to show all records with **P** in the Total Years field. Display the Record Series, Record, and Total Years fields in the query results. Save the query as **Total Years Query.** Print the query results table.

7-2 SOLVE RETRIEVAL PROBLEMS (OBJS. 1, 4, 5)

COLLABORATION

CRITICAL THINKING

You and two other students have been invited to assist the owners of a small clothing company to gain better control of their records. The two owners of Creative Designs design, create, and sell silk ties for men. A variety of designs are used, including various holiday and sports themes in addition to their own creative, whimsical designs. Currently, the company consists of the two co-owners, one sales representative, and one administrative assistant. Temporary workers are often called in to help prepare a large order for shipping. The administrative assistant is responsible for preparing files for storage, filing all records, and retrieving records as needed. However, everyone in the company has access to the files, and they often remove records if the administrative assistant is helping prepare a shipment to a major retailer.

Because the company is small, few records controls are being used. Sometimes an owner will not be able to locate the sales records for a specific buyer, and no one knows who has a custom-design client's records. Misfiling occurs frequently because someone is in a hurry when records are re-filed, and file users often stack records to be re-filed wherever space is available. The administrative assistant spends unproductive time searching for misfiled records and records that should be in storage but are not.

The owners plan to expand the product line to include matching dress shirts, which will mean more employees and more records.

1. What kind of records procedures would you recommend for this growing company?

2. Would additional supplies or equipment provide adequate control of records?

3. Work with your team members to prepare a list of recommendations to help Creative Designs improve its records management.

7-3 RECOMMEND RECORDS TRANSFER METHODS (OBJ. 6)

CRITICAL THINKING

Which transfer method—perpetual, periodic, or one-period—would you recommend for each of the following records situations? Explain your decision.

1. Home improvement store: employment applications, general correspondence, property mortgage.

2. Medical clinic office: medical case files of deceased patients.

3. Law office: client folders from the past 10 years.

4. Exercise gym and spa: all folders relating to advertising activity—news releases, publicity photographs, and advertising activity reports. All records were created in the current year.

5. Condominium builder: all folders related to a high-rise condominium that has recently been completed. All units are sold, and the grand opening was held the last Saturday of last month. The folders contain records of subcontractors, new owners, insurance carriers, and governmental agencies that issued required permits.

7-4 LEARN ABOUT WEB RESOURCES RETENTION (OBJS. 1, 4)

INTERNET

National Archives in the United States and other countries provide guidance for web records retention. You will learn about guidelines provided by the National Archives of the United States, the United Kingdom, and Australia. You can find the URLs for these web sites on the Links tab at the web site for this book.

1. Access the U.S. National Archives & Records Administration web site. Click **Records Management.** Click **Policy and Guidance.** (If these links do not appear, search for *records management policy and guidance.*)

2. Which item listed under Records Management Policy and Guidance would apply to web records?

3. Access the National Archives (of the United Kingdom) web site. Click **Services for Professionals.** Click **Electronic Records Management** on the pull-down menu. Click **Advice & Guidance.** (If these links do not appear, search for *electronic records management advice and guidance.*)

4. Which of the toolkits listed under Electronic Records Toolkits applies to web records?

5. Access the National Archives of Australia web site.

6. What is the title of the guideline for web records?

RECORDS MANAGEMENT SIMULATION

JOB 8 REQUISITION AND CHARGE-OUT PROCEDURES

JOB 9 TRANSFER PROCEDURES

Continue working with Auric Systems, Inc.
Complete Jobs 8 and 9.

FOR MORE ACTIVITIES GO TO **http://read.swlearning.com**

Subject, Numeric, and Geographic Storage and Retrieval

Subject, numeric, and geographic storage methods provide security because correspondents' names are not visible on folder labels or in databases. These methods also provide almost unlimited expansion ability, which makes them the preferred storage methods for high-volume records and information management (RIM) programs. These storage methods are also alphabetic. Subjects and geographic locations are stored in alphabetic order, and a general alphabetic file is used as the index in a numeric system. Numeric records storage is an indirect system that is especially adaptable to electronic records storage. Understanding all three storage methods is essential for organizing information in a RIM program.

Subject Records Management

Learning Objectives

1. Define subject records management.

2. List advantages and disadvantages of storing and retrieving records by subject.

3. Compare the dictionary and encyclopedic subject file arrangements.

4. Describe the guides, folders, and labels used for subject records storage.

5. Describe four indexes and their use fo subject records management.

6. List the steps used when storing and trieving records stored by their subjec

7. Use computer software to prepare an index for subject records.

8. Store and retrieve records following subject records procedures.

SUBJECT RECORDS STORAGE AND RETRIEVAL

In Part 2, you studied the alphabetic method of storing and retrieving records by name—names of individuals, businesses, and organizations. Two other alphabetic storage methods—subject and geographic—are also widely used. In this chapter, you will learn how and when to arrange records by their subjects. Geographic records management, a filing method in which records are arranged by geographic location, is presented in Chapter 10.

Why store records by subject?

Subject records management is an alphabetic system of storing and retrieving records by their subject or topic. Subject filing is recommended when the range of topics used within an organization is broad and may include correspondence, reports, clippings, catalogs, research data, product development plans, and inventory lists. In such a case, a topical arrangement becomes the logical way in which to arrange information.[1] Sometimes, documents cannot be filed by any other filing characteristic.

[1]ARMA International, *Establishing Alphabetic, Numeric and Subject Filing Systems* (Lenexa, KS: ARMA International, 2005), p. 4.

File users expect records that pertain to the same subject or topic to be stored together. Consequently, subject storage is the preferred storage method in many organizations. Subject records storage is used in any type of business or organization that has a large volume of stored records. A small organization may use a limited list of subject titles (also referred to as *headings*) for coding, storing, and retrieving records. However, a large organization may have an extensive list of main subject titles as well as numerous subdivisions of those titles. Filing by subject has advantages and disadvantages as shown in Figure 8.1.

Arranging records by subject categories, such as topic, organizational function, department, service, product, or project, is logical and improves retrieval for certain records. As you study a variety of filing methods, you will learn how components of one or more filing methods can be combined for efficient records storage and retrieval. The alphabetic method is often combined with other methods. Although an organization's records may be filed alphabetically by name, some records are kept together under subject headings, such as APPLICATIONS, PURCHASE ORDERS, and RENTAL CAR CONTRACTS, because use of these records would require such groupings. Arranging records according to organizational functions, such as

SUBJECT FILING

Advantages	Disadvantages
▪ Subjects are easier to remember than names.	▪ Main subject titles and subdivisions may overlap as the list of subject titles grows.
▪ Related records are easier to find.	
▪ Related records are not scattered throughout the files.	▪ Concise, clearly defined, and uniformly stated subject titles may be difficult to select.
▪ Files can easily be expanded by adding subdivisions to main subject titles.	▪ Inconsistent subject title coding on records can make storage and retrieval difficult.
▪ Subject filing is appropriate for storing large volumes of records.	▪ Users may not remember the exact titles or be unfamiliar with the subject titles and may have more difficulty finding records.
▪ Security is provided because correspondent names are not visible to unauthorized persons who may not know the subject under which a record is filed.	▪ Planning and maintenance are required to assure that approved subject titles are used consistently.
	▪ Subject filing is the most expensive storage method because experienced filers are required.
	▪ An experienced records analyst may be required to create the subject titles to assure that the most logical subjects are selected.
	▪ Indexing, coding, and cross-referencing take more time because each record must be read carefully and thoroughly.

Figure 8.1 Advantages and Disadvantages of Filing by Subject

ACCOUNTING, HUMAN RESOURCES, MARKETING, and SALES, is often used in large organizations.

Subjects are easy to recall, and subject records storage is the only logical, efficient method of storing and retrieving certain records. Many people think records are best remembered and retrieved by subject. As a result, many types of businesses and industries file their records using the subject method. A rule of thumb for choosing an appropriate filing method is to match the method to the most logical way for file users to request records. Office workers sometimes use alternate, synonymous terms for a single topic when filing by subject. Therefore, cross-references and indexes are necessary when using subject filing. Subject indexes and cross-referencing are explained later in the chapter.

The selection of a word or phrase to use as a subject title (the filing segment) is of prime importance when using the subject storage method. One person should be responsible for selecting subject titles. That person must be thoroughly familiar with the material to be stored and have considerable knowledge of every phase of the operations and activities of the business. If all file users have authority to add subject titles to a subject filing system, the same type of record content soon becomes stored under two or more synonymous terms. Such storage of related records in two or more places separates records that should be stored together and makes retrieval of all related records difficult.

The subject title must be short and clearly descriptive of the material it represents. Once a subject title has been chosen, it must be used by everyone in the organization. Additional subject titles must be chosen so that they do not duplicate or overlap any subject previously used. Good subject selection requires agreement by file users on the subjects to be used, flexibility to allow for growth within the selected subjects and for expansion to add new material, and simplicity so that users can understand the system. Once subject titles have been selected, they must be used consistently by all file users. Preparation and use of necessary indexes ensure consistent use of selected subject titles.

Remember the following important subject filing guidelines:

1. Select subject titles that best reflect stored records, are meaningful to file users, and are easy to remember.
2. Select subject titles that have only one interpretation.
3. Use one-word subject titles whenever possible.
4. Use plural titles whenever possible.
5. Provide for the occasional use of alternate, synonymous, or related subject titles.
6. Consider combining filing methods when subdividing and subsorting records in large subject filing systems. For example, subdivide records first by subject and then alphabetically by location or name, numerically by record or document number, or chronologically by date.
7. Designate one person to manage the subject titles—to select the titles and to add new titles as needed.

Why should only one person by responsible for adding or changing subject titles?

Why is choosing subject titles so important?

My Records

Subject Filing

Would the subject method be a good way to file your personal records? How can you set up your records for filing by subject?

A purchased bellows folder with subject categories can be used to file your financial records. These folders can be used for many storage purposes. Labels include alphabetic subdivisions, subjects, and a place to write your own labels. Subject categories vary with the manufacturer of the folders and may include the following:

Automobile	Bank Records	Income Taxes	Insurance Records
Medical and Dental	Unpaid Bills and Receipts	Utilities	Miscellaneous

If you have a filing cabinet, you can also create your own folders. The following categories may serve as a guide for you:

Bank Records	Car	Charity	Education
Investments	Medical and Dental	Miscellaneous	Mortgage/Rent
Payroll	Income Taxes	Utilities	Pet Records

To help all members of your family understand your subject filing, create and print a master index of your subjects.

You and your family can brainstorm all the subjects that are likely for your family's needs. Here are some sample categories:

Family and Friends
- Family information
- Pet information
- Important phone numbers
- Frequently called numbers
- Address/phone directory
- Babysitter's checklist

Home and Automobile
- Home maintenance
- Home repairs
- Household appliances
- Vehicle maintenance
- Mileage record

Inventory
- Home inventory
- Book inventory
- Video/DVD inventory
- Audio inventory
- Photograph documentation

My Records

continued

Food and Shopping
- Groceries needed
- Meal planner
- Recipe instructions
- Mail/Internet order record
- Monthly spending record

Things to Do
- People to visit or contact
- Places to go
- Movies to see or rent
- Books to read

Cleaning and Chores
- Family chore chart
- Kids' schedule
- Cleaning checklist
- Cleaning schedule

Special Occasions
- Birthdays
- Gift ideas
- Holiday card record

Health, Exercise, and Medical
- Balanced diet log
- Nutrition worksheet
- Exercise log
- Walking log
- Quick health info
- Doctor visits
- Medication schedule

SUBJECT RECORDS ARRANGEMENTS

What is a dictionary subject arrangement?

Records may be stored in two alphabetic subject arrangements: (1) dictionary, and (2) encyclopedic. The definitions of these two terms are easy to remember when you relate them to the arrangement of words in a dictionary versus the arrangement of information in an encyclopedia. A dictionary contains a list of words in alphabetic order. An encyclopedia contains a list of words and related topics in alphabetic order. Both subject arrangements are explained and illustrated in the following paragraphs.

Dictionary Arrangement

A **dictionary arrangement** is a single alphabetic filing arrangement in which all types of entries (names, subjects, titles, etc.) are interfiled. In the subject dictionary arrangement, subject folders are arranged behind A-to-Z guides in correct alphabetic order by subject title. Generally, the dictionary subject arrangement is not recommended if the volume of records is greater than could be stored in two file drawers. However, the dictionary arrangement is used regardless of the number of records if the subject topics are easily identified without the necessity of using subdivisions. Characteristics of the dictionary arrangement are listed in Figure 8.2.

Figure 8.3 on page 222 shows a small office file arranged in straight dictionary order. A-to-Z guides are one-fifth cut and occupy first position in the file. Special guides are one-fifth cut and are in second position. Two special guides in Figure 8.3 are CUSTOMER SERVICES and SALES. These special subject guides mark exceptionally active subjects, making them conspicuous and, therefore, easier to find. All general folders labeled with subject topics and OUT guides are one-third cut. They occupy the third position in the file. So far, subdividing general subjects into more specific subdivisions has not been necessary. If records accumulate and make dividing the general subjects into more specific subdivisions necessary, the arrangement would no longer be considered a dictionary arrangement.

DICTIONARY FILE ARRANGEMENT

- Labels on primary guides are the letters A to Z in alphabetic order.
- Special guides are used to identify subject folders that are referenced often.
- General subject folders are used to store all records relating to the subject title.
- Captions on the general subject folders include the letter of the alphabet as well as the subject title.
- Subject titles are not subdivided.

Figure 8.2 Characteristics of the Dictionary File Arrangement

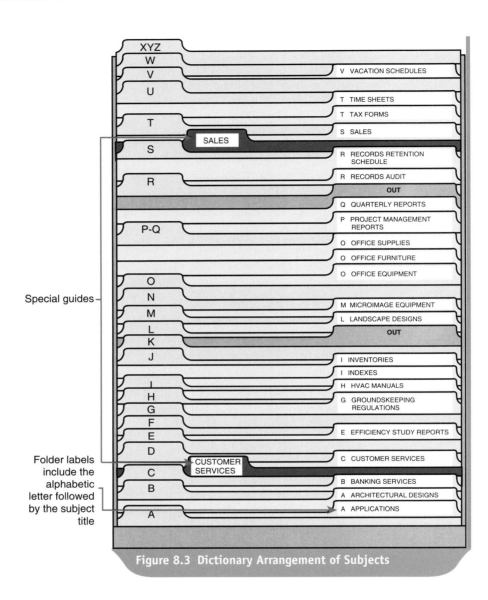

Figure 8.3 Dictionary Arrangement of Subjects

Encyclopedic Arrangement

The **encyclopedic arrangement** is a subject filing arrangement in which records are filed under broad, major subject titles and then under the specific subtitle to which they relate. Titles and subtitles are arranged alphabetically. Characteristics of the encyclopedic arrangement are listed in Figure 8.4 on page 223.

ENCYCLOPEDIC FILE ARRANGEMENT
- Primary guide captions are general subject titles.
- Secondary guide captions are subdivisions of the general subject titles.
- Folder captions include the main subject titles and the subdivisions.
- A general subject folder with the same label caption as the primary guide is inserted behind the last subdivision folder for all subjects.

Figure 8.4 Characteristics of the Encyclopedic File Arrangement

---

Figures 8.5 through 8.8 show encyclopedic arrangements of the subject file shown in Figure 8.3. As the number of records increases, the file arrangement requires specific subject subdivisions for quicker access to filed records. Study the guide and folder captions in Figures 8.5 through 8.8. *Main subjects* are printed on the label captions of the primary guides. These guides are one-fifth cut and in first-position. Secondary guides in second position also have one-fifth cut tabs. These guide labels bear the *subdivisions* of the main subjects.

Why subdivide main subject titles?

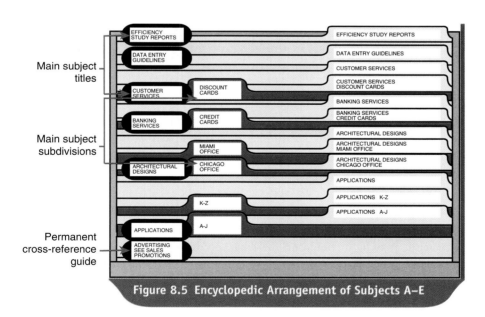

Figure 8.5 Encyclopedic Arrangement of Subjects A–E

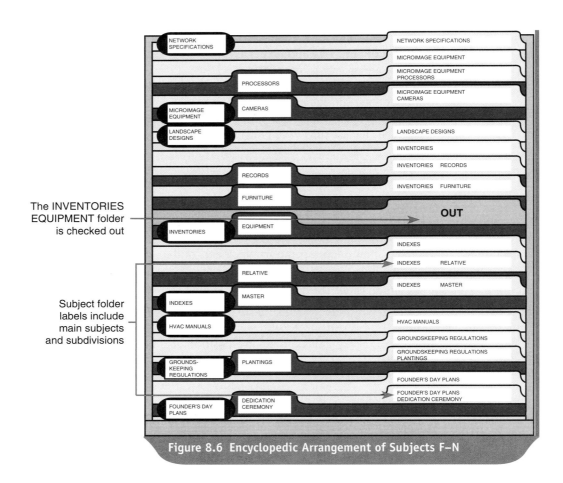

The INVENTORIES EQUIPMENT folder is checked out

Subject folder labels include main subjects and subdivisions

Figure 8.6 Encyclopedic Arrangement of Subjects F–N

The secondary guides may also include the primary guide captions such as those illustrated in Figure 8.9 on page 226. However, because guides are not removed from the file when storing and retrieving records, repeating the main subject title on the secondary guide is not necessary.

On the other hand, *folder* label captions include the main subjects and the secondary guide captions. If necessary, additional subdivisions of the first subdivision may be made for the specific subject titles. If necessary, the correspondent name may be included on the label. A comprehensive folder label helps assure that a borrowed folder will be returned to its correct file location. One-third cut folders are recommended. Once again, OUT indicators are in third position with all general folders. OUT guides, as previously discussed in Chapter 6, are usually of a distinctive color that is easily visible to show the location of a removed folder.

Most of the same general subject folders in Figure 8.3 have been maintained in the encyclopedic file arrangement shown in Figures 8.5 through 8.8 on pages 223 to 226. Specific subject folders have been added where subjects

When is a new subdivision added?

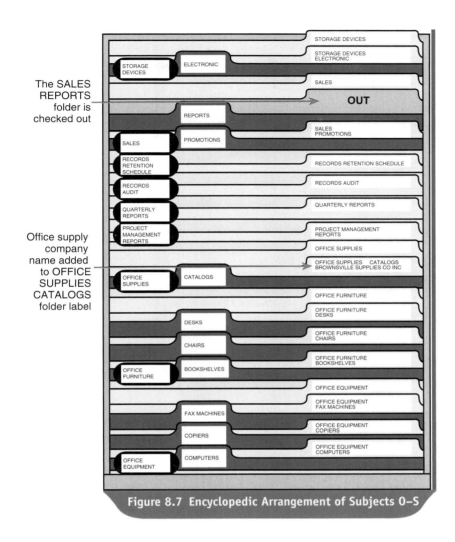

The SALES REPORTS folder is checked out

Office supply company name added to OFFICE SUPPLIES CATALOGS folder label

Figure 8.7 Encyclopedic Arrangement of Subjects O–S

are subdivided by the secondary subject guides. Note the general subject folder for BANKING SERVICES in Figure 8.5 on page 223. Although a subdivision folder for CREDIT CARDS has been added, the general BANKING SERVICES subject folder remains. The general folder holds records pertaining to other banking services information that does not fit into the credit card category.

General folders need to be checked regularly to determine whether some records could be moved into a new specific folder. When the number of records for other related subject topics has accumulated to the predetermined number that warrants a specific folder, a new subdivision should be added, the index updated immediately, a new secondary guide prepared, and a new subdivision folder prepared. General subject folders are placed after subdivision or specific subject folders so that users will first look for a subdivision to avoid filing all records in the general folder.

How should general folders be managed?

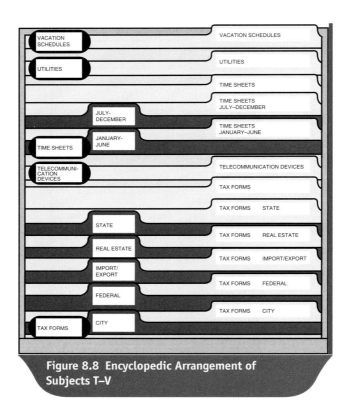

Figure 8.8 Encyclopedic Arrangement of Subjects T–V

When general folders become crowded and no specific subject subdivisions are possible, other means of subdividing records may be used. Notice that the APPLICATIONS general folders are subdivided by sections of the alphabet—A-J and K-Z in Figure 8.5. In Figure 8.6, the INVENTORIES general subject is subdivided by types of inventories—equipment, furniture, and records. The name of an office supply company catalog—Brownsville Supplies Co., Inc.—has been added to the folder label for OFFICE SUPPLIES CATALOGS in Figure 8.7.

Color can be used effectively with subject filing. Very often, each subject label will have a color band that is repeated on all guides and folders for that subject. Sometimes, all captions of one subject will be one color, the color changing when the subject title changes. A third possibility is that each subject will have guides and folders of only one color, with a change of color used for guides and folders of the next subject. Using a colored folder for all general subject folders can also be effective. Although the use of color can speed the filing process and reduce misfiles in any filing system, using color does not take the place of careful selection of meaningful subject titles in a subject filing system.

How is color used in subject filing?

SUBJECT FILING SUPPLIES

Supplies used for the subject arrangement of files include guides, folders, labels, and OUT indicators, all of which were explained in Chapter 6. The use of OUT indicators when charging in and charging out records was discussed in Chapter 7. Because more information is keyed on guide and folder label captions for subject filing than for alphabetic name files, preparing records for subject storage is slightly more challenging than for alphabetic records.

Guides and Labels

Guide labels used in subject records storage are determined by the subject titles used. If subject titles are long, subject codes or abbreviations may be used. Subject coding is explained in more detail on pages 236 to 238. Figure 8.9 shows an example of primary and secondary guides. The primary guide caption contains the main subject title; the secondary guide contains the main subject and its subdivision. Because guides are not removed from a storage container during storage and retrieval, a primary guide caption can be omitted on a secondary guide, as shown in Figures 8.5 through 8.8.

Subject filing requires customized labeling of guides and folders that matches subjects and subdivisions. Adhesive labels are available from a variety of suppliers and in a variety of sizes and colors. Packages of labels include directions for using the label function in word processing software programs. The software program label function enables preparation of many different label sizes and styles as shown in Figure 8.10 on page 228. Label templates may be downloaded from label suppliers' web sites. A template allows a user to key several captions on a template and print the entire sheet of labels or only a portion of the sheet at the same time. Blank tab inserts for one-third or one-fifth cut metal or plastic tab sizes can be purchased in strips for attaching computer-generated adhesive labels.

> **Why do subject folder captions include both main titles and subdivisions?**

> **Why does subject filing require customized guide and folder labels?**

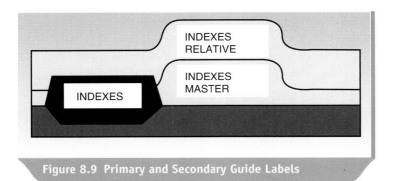

Figure 8.9 Primary and Secondary Guide Labels

INDEXES
RELATIVE

INDEXES
MASTER

INDEXES

The Smead Manufacturing Company

Figure 8.10 Computer-Generated Guide/Folder Labels

Where are captions printed on guide labels or inserts?

Captions on all guides in the records system should have consistent spacing and style. All primary guide label captions should begin near the left edge and near the top of the label. The label function of software (word processing or database) uses preset margins for each label selection. When using these settings, be sure the label captions begin at the same point on all labels.

Labels are easier to read with information in a straight line rather than staggered. Key the information in all capitals with no punctuation. Decide whether to use complete subject titles, abbreviated titles, or subject codes and follow this format consistently. Mixing styles of captions complicates filing and retrieving records.

Where are captions printed on folder labels?

Folders and Labels

Folder label captions include the primary or main subject title and all necessary subdivisions. As discussed previously, comprehensive label captions help assure that borrowed folders are returned to the correct file locations. One-third cut folders are preferred. Adhesive folder labels are available in a variety of sizes and may be printed using a laser or a deskjet printer. The label size should match the tab cut of the folder. Use the label function of word processing software for preparing labels, or follow the directions for label formatting that is packaged with the labels. The main subject title should begin near the left margin and as near as possible to the top of the label or the bottom of a

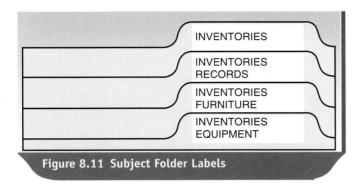

Figure 8.11 Subject Folder Labels

color bar on the label. Key the *subdivision* 0.5 inches to the right of the main subject title or under the first letter of the first line. Key the label in all capitals with no punctuation as shown in Figure 8.11. Be precise and consistent with folder label preparation. Attention to this detail creates a neat, readable, straight-line filing system.

Color code folder labels for each subject guide to reduce misfiles. Bar codes can be added for electronically tracking records. Bar codes and color codes for folders and labels in subject records storage relate to the first, second, and, sometimes, third letters in subject titles. Supplies and services for color coding and bar coding are available through companies offering records and information management products. These companies can be located through the *Yellow Pages* or on the Internet. The ARMA International web site has a buyer's guide listing vendors of filing supplies and records management products. Some of these companies offer records and information management products and services applicable to subject records systems, as well as other records systems. Their web sites not only provide information about their companies but also give helpful hints for setting up and maintaining records management systems.

OUT Indicators

An OUT guide appears in the file samples in Figures 8.3 through 8.8. You may want to review briefly OUT indicators and the charge-out and follow-up procedures discussed in Chapters 6 and 7. Follow the same procedures for subject filing that you applied in alphabetic name filing. The only difference is that you will use subject titles, rather than individual or organization names, to identify records.

> **What information should be written on an OUT guide when a subject record is borrowed?**

SUBJECT INDEXES

Why is more than one index needed for subject files?

An **index** is a systematic guide that allows access to specific items contained within a larger body of information. Because filers may not know all subjects used in a subject file, they cannot go directly to a file to locate a record. A subject file requires an index and, therefore, is considered an indirect access filing method.

Indirect access is a method of access to records that requires prior use of an external index. Users must refer to an index to determine whether a subject has been established in the system and, if it has, the location of a record before they can store or retrieve the record from the main file. Alphabetic filing is considered a direct access filing method because a specific record or correspondent name in a file can be found without first referring to an index to find its location. **Direct access** is a method of access to records without reference to an index or other finding aid.

Preparation of Indexes

Is one index more important than others in subject filing?

Indexes are electronic or printed lists. These lists are often printed on sheets of paper or on cards. Subjects listed on an index printed on sheets of paper are easier to locate at a glance than subjects printed on cards in a card index. The filer must search through several cards in order to locate the appropriate subject under which to file or locate a record. Making additions, deletions, and corrections to an index can be done quickly and easily on a computer, using either word processing or database software. Because the computer can be used to sort the index, maintaining an up-to-date index is easy. The search function of computer software also makes finding a specific subject quick and easy.

The following four types of indexes are valuable, and often necessary, when using the subject records storage method:

1. Master index
2. Relative index
3. Numeric index
4. Name index

Master Index

A **master index** is a printed alphabetic listing in file order of all subjects used as subject titles in the filing system. The master index is also referred to as the *master list, subject index,* or *subject list.* Even if computer access to the master index and relative index is available, keep an updated printed copy in the front of the file drawer with the manual files. This practice is important to maintain consistent coding and filing of records by subject. Without frequent referrals to these indexes, misfiles and duplicate subject titles are likely to occur. For a large volume of records in a complex filing system, use of electronic indexes saves time in locating specific records. The index should be updated as new subjects are added and old ones are eliminated or modified. When new subjects are added, refer to the index to avoid any subject title duplications. Figure 8.12 is a master

MASTER INDEX–SUBJECT FILE

Applications*	Landscape Designs	Storage Devices
Architectural Designs	Microimage Equipment	Electronic
Chicago Office	Cameras	Tax Forms
Miami Office	Processors	City
Banking Services	New York Branch Office	Federal
Credit Cards	Office Equipment	Import/Export
Charitable Donations	Computers	Real Estate
Customer Services	Copiers	State
Discount Cards	Fax Machines	Telecommunication Devices
Data Entry Guidelines	Office Furniture	Time Sheets*
Formatting	Bookshelves	Utilities
Keystrokes	Chairs	Vacation Schedules
Efficiency Study Reports	Credenzas	
Founder's Day Plans	Desks	
Dedication Ceremony	Office Supplies	
Groundskeeping Regulations	Catalogs	
Plantings	Invoices	
HVAC Manuals	Project Management Reports	
Indexes	Quarterly Reports	
Master	Records Audit	
Relative	Records Retention Schedule	
Inventories	Sales	
Equipment	Projections	
Furniture	Promotions	
Records	Reports	

*Divided folders do not need to be listed in the master index.

Figure 8.12 Master Index for a Subject File

index of the portion of the file illustrated in Figure 8.3. For manual filing systems, store a copy of the index, as an outline of the file contents, at the front of the file for ready access to all users. Without a master index, file users must scan all drawers or shelves of records to locate subject titles. New file users can familiarize themselves with the subject storage system quickly by referring to a master index. In addition, reference to the master index assures that only preselected subject titles are used for filing and retrieving records.

Relative Index

What is a relative index?

A more complex subject file may require a relative index. A **relative index** is a dictionary-type listing of *all* possible words and combinations of words by which records may be requested. The word *relative* is used because the index includes not only all subject titles used in the system but also synonyms for subjects or any *related* subject titles that filers might consider logical topics for storing and retrieving records.

Study the relative index in Figure 8.13 on page 233. Notice the entry for Advertising. (Advertising is not used as a subject title in the system.) The relative index refers the filer to Sales Promotions—the subject title selected for storing and retrieving advertising materials. This type of index serves as a vast cross-reference device because it contains all the subjects by which a record might be requested. When someone requests a record by a subject that is not the one selected for use in the system, check the relative index to see whether that subject title has been included. If not, add the requested subject to the index listing with the correct subject title beside it. Referencing the relative index helps filers avoid duplication of subject titles and locate subjects when records are requested by unfamiliar terms. The relative index often contains both SEE and SEE ALSO cross-references. These notations help to suggest related materials and alternative file locations.

Numeric Index

The numeric index will become more meaningful after you study Chapter 9 and learn to assign numbers to subject file headings. Filers can file and retrieve numbers faster than words or letters because they can read numbers more quickly. When numbers are used to identify specific subjects, a numeric index is needed. A **numeric index** is a current list of all files by the file numbers. Such an index shows numbers assigned to subject titles and helps filers avoid duplication of numbers when new subjects are added to the storage system.

RELATIVE INDEX–SUBJECT FILE

Subject Title	Filed Under
Advertising	Sales Promotions
Applications	Applications
Architectural Designs	Architectural Designs
Banking Services	Banking Services
Bookshelves	Office Equipment
Cameras	Microimage Equipment
Catalogs	SEE Office Supplies
Charitable Donations	Charitable Donations
Chairs	Office Furniture
Chicago Office	Architectural Designs
City Tax Forms	Tax Forms
Computers	Office Equipment
Copiers	Office Equipment
Credenzas	Office Equipment
Credit Cards	Banking Services
Customer Services	Customer Services
Data Entry Guidelines	Data Entry Guidelines
Dedication Ceremony	Founder's Day Plans
Desks	Office Equipment
Discount Cards	Customer Services
Efficiency Study Reports	Efficiency Study Reports
Electronic Storage Devices	Storage Devices
Equipment Inventory	Inventories
Fax Machines	Office Equipment
Federal Tax Forms	Tax Forms
Formatting	Data Entry Guidelines
Founder's Day Plans	Founder's Day Plans
Furniture Inventory	Inventories
Groundskeeping Regulations	Groundskeeping Regulations
HVAC Manuals	HVAC Manuals

Subject Title	Filed Under
Import/Export Tax Forms	Tax Forms
Indexes	Indexes
Inventories	Inventories
Landscape Designs	Landscape Designs
Master Index	Indexes
Miami Office	Architectural Designs
Microimage Equipment	Microimage Equipment
Network Specifications	Network Specifications
Office Equipment	Office Equipment
Office Furniture	Office Furniture
Office Supplies	Office Supplies
Plantings	Groundskeeping Regulations
Processors	Microimage Equipment
Project Management Reports	Project Management Reports
Quarterly Reports	Quarterly Reports
Real Estate Tax Forms	Tax Forms
Records Inventory	Records Inventories
Records Audit	Records Audit
Records Retention Schedule	Records Retention Schedule
Relative Index	Indexes
Sales	Sales
Sales Projections	Sales Projections
Sales Promotions	Sales Promotions
Sales Reports	Sales Reports
State Tax Forms	Tax Forms
Storage Devices	Storage Devices
Tax Forms	Tax Forms
Time Sheets	Time Sheets
Utilities	Utilities
Vacation Schedules	Vacation Schedules

Figure 8.13 Relative Index for a Subject File

Name Index

Customarily, subject records storage does not require an alphabetic index of names of individuals or companies. However, correspondence filed in a subject arrangement *does* require a name index. A **name index** is a listing of correspondents' names stored in a subject file. The name and address of each correspondent are included in the index, as well as the subject under which each name is stored. The names are arranged alphabetically on printed sheets, on cards, or in a computer file. Because records are sometimes requested by the name of an individual or a company, a name index containing this information can save time that would otherwise be spent searching for a record by subject.

STORAGE AND RETRIEVAL PROCEDURES

All the steps for storing and retrieving correspondence records studied in Chapters 6 and 7 are as important in the subject method as they are in any other storage method. A brief description of each step, together with an explanation of its application to the subject method, follows.

Inspecting

Every record in any records and information management system should be inspected to verify that it has been released for filing. Do not store a record until a written notation by someone with authority indicates that it is ready for storage. In Figure 8.14, JJ is the release mark used to indicate that the letter is ready for storage.

Indexing

Indexing, or classifying, is the mental process of determining the subject filing segment to be used in storing a record. Because each record must be read carefully, this step takes more time with the subject method than with other storage methods. If a record relates to only one subject, indexing is simple. The filer simply selects the correct subject from the master index. If someone else has previously indicated the subject under which a record is to be stored, recheck the accuracy of the subject selection. If a record contains information about more than one subject, you must determine the most important subject by which to store the record. Then cross-reference the other subject(s).

                                                                    2   3
                                                        <u>Sales</u> / Promotions /Magazine

              4   5   6
          Demirchyan/Advertising/Agency
          1530 Park Avenue, New York, NY 10128-5701
          Tele: 212.555-0177   Fax: 212.555.0136
          www.demirchyanads.com

          May 15, 20--

                                            ┌─────────────────────────────┐
                                            ¦ MAY 16, 20--   11:00 A.M. ¦
                                            └─────────────────────────────┘

          Ms. Angie Brown-Duran
          Duran Designs, Inc.
          600 E 52 St.
          New York, NY 10022-2844

          Dear Angie

          The magazine advertising media kit you requested for *Design Creator's* magazine
          is on its way. Note that the new full-color page rate is $15,650; the black/white
          page, $10,275. A copy of your ad is enclosed and ready for your approval. We
          should meet the publication deadline for the September issue with no problem.

          If you are still considering television, you might be interested in XYC-TV's
          monthly advertising schedule for June. *HGTV* and *The Garden Show* rates are
          easily within your budget. We will be happy to show you some ideas for 30-   1
          second commercials if you think you want to pursue <u>TV advertising</u>.   X   <u>Sales/</u>
                                                                                            2
          Design Creators is offering an incentive to first-time advertisers. It is offering an   <u>Promotions/</u>
          8 percent discount to all advertisers booking space in the next two issues. An 18   3
          percent discount is offered to advertisers contracting space in the next four issues. <u>Television</u>
          We can discuss these issues at our meeting on Tuesday.

          Sincerely   *JJ*

          Ani McCord

          Ani McCord
          Advertising Director

          psm

          Enclosure

Figure 8.14 Record Coded for Subject Records Storage

STEPS FOR STORING AND RETRIEVING SUBJECT RECORDS

Step 1: Inspecting
- Check for release mark.

Step 2: Indexing
- Read entire record carefully.
- Select filing segment from text.
- Verify that subject is in master index.
- Select filing segment from the master index if not in the text.

Step 3: Coding
- Code the main subject and any subdivisions where they appear in the text.
- Insert diagonals between the units, underline the key unit, and number remaining units of the filing segment.
- Write the subject at top right of record if it is not in the text.
- Underline cross-reference subjects with a wavy line, insert diagonals between the units, and number all units, starting with 1.
- Write the correct cross-reference subject title in the margin if it is not exactly right in the text. Underline it with a wavy line and number all units.
- Place an X in the margin beside the cross-reference subject.

Step 4: Cross-Referencing
- Prepare a cross-reference sheet for all alternative subjects, or photocopy the record.
- File the cross-reference sheets, or copies, under the alternative subject title(s).

Step 5: Sorting
- Sort by main subject titles, then by subdivisions.

Step 6: Storing
- File records coded for subject subdivisions in appropriate subdivision folders.
- File records coded for the main subject only into the general subject folder.
- File records in the appropriate folders in alphabetic order by correspondent names; the latest date is in the front of the folder.

Step 7: Retrieving
- Use the master or relative index to locate records.

Figure 8.15 Subject Filing Storage and Retrieval Procedures

Coding

In Chapter 2, you learned that coding means marking the filing segment on the record. Code the main subject title and any subdivisions by placing diagonals between the units, underlining the key unit, and numbering the remaining units in the filing segment where they appear on the record. Code the correspondent's name by placing diagonals between the units and continuing the numbering of the units (Figure 8.14). If the subject is not mentioned in the record, write it legibly at the top of the record. Some filers prefer to write the filing segment in color in the upper right margin of the record. The subject title is, therefore, more visible in the file. When more than one subject is indicated, code only the most important one; cross-reference all other subjects in some distinctive manner. For example, the subject to cross-reference in Figure 8.16 is underscored with a wavy line, and an X is placed in the margin

CROSS-REFERENCE SHEET

Name or Subject

        2   3   4   5

Sales/ Promotions / Television / Demirchyan / Advertising /
    6
   Agency

Date of Record

May 15, 20--

Regarding

Magazine and television advertising

SEE

Name or Subject

Sales Promotions Magazine Demirchyan Advertising Agency

Date Filed   *5/15/20 - -*   **By**   *J J*

Figure 8.16 Cross-Reference Sheet for Subject Records Storage

opposite the subject. The correct cross-reference subject title and subtitle SALES PROMOTIONS/TELEVISION are written and coded in the margin. Diagonals are placed between the units, and all filing units are numbered.

Do not rely on memory to determine the subject under which a record should be stored. Consult the master or relative index to be sure that you have selected and coded the filing segment correctly.

Coding in an alphabetic subject filing system may include an entire subject title such as PURCHASING. However, abbreviations can simplify coding in a large, complex subject filing system. Create an abbreviation with the first alphabetic character of the subject title followed by the next one or two consonants such as PRC for PURCHASING, or use the first character of each word in a multiple-word subject heading such as RRS for RECORDS RETENTION SCHEDULE. Because the codes may consist of as many as six characters, PRCH may be more easily remembered for PURCHASING than PRC. Consistency is essential when developing a subject code system in which two- to six-character abbreviations are used. Everyone using the system must understand the codes and how to develop new ones when necessary. If abbreviations are used, the master index should show codes as well as complete subject titles. Be sure to write subject letter codes on each record and include them on individual folder label captions, along with the subject title.

Cross-Referencing

Cross-references help filers locate stored records. When file users request a record under a topic other than its subject title, add a cross-reference under that topic. Code the document as suggested previously and prepare a cross-reference sheet such as the one shown in Figure 8.16 on page 237. File users looking for the document under its alternative subject title SALES PROMOTIONS/TELEVISION are sent to the original record's file location, SALES PROMOTIONS/MAGAZINE. If a record refers to several important subjects, consider filing photocopies of the record under the different subject titles involved. This procedure eliminates the need for preparing several cross-reference sheets for that record. Sometimes a permanent cross-reference guide is placed in the storage container. In Figure 8.5 on page 223, for example, a permanent guide labeled ADVERTISING, SEE SALES PROMOTIONS has been placed into the file in the primary guide position. Do not file records behind the permanent SEE guide. The SEE guide is there only to direct filers to the correct storage location.

Why would using subject codes save coding time?

In what way is subject cross-references different from alphabetic name cross-references?

CAREER CORNER

Corporate Records Manager Job Description

The following job description is an example of a career opportunity in records management at a law firm.

GENERAL INFORMATION

- Large multi-office law firm
- Travel required

RESPONSIBILITIES

- Oversee records management policies and procedures for all offices and corporate departments
- Establish policies and model procedures for the management of all formats of documents and records
- Integrate records technology with other computer applications
- Oversee records retention and destruction policies for all offices
- Establish ethics policies and procedures
- Participate in staffing and budgeting decisions relating to records and information
- Develop training modules for records and information staff
- Supervise corporate records and information staff

EXPERIENCE AND EDUCATION

- Bachelor's degree
- Five to 10 years of professional records and information management experience in law or a related area
- Ability to identify and analyze problems and to recommend and implement solutions
- Ability to manage multiple projects simultaneously
- Excellent oral, written, and interpersonal communication skills
- Strong computer proficiency in office suite applications
- Advanced database management skills
- Ability to retrieve and distribute files weighing up to 40 pounds and from shelves up to 8 feet high

Sorting

Sorting arranges records in filing order according to the records and information management system used. Use some kind of A-to-Z sorter to sort records to be stored alphabetically by subject. Sort records by main subject titles; then sort records by subdivisions as well. Time spent sorting records before filing saves filing time. Filers will be able to file and move in one direction through a filing system rather than moving backward and forward through drawers or shelves of stored records.

Storing

Storing (also called *filing*) places the hard copy into an appropriate location or saves the electronic record. For manual filing, careful placement of records into folders is always important. Be sure the subject folder label caption agrees with the filing segment coded on the record. Raise the folder slightly before inserting the record to be sure the record enters the folder completely. Remove papers that are in disarray, jog them, and return them neatly into the folder. Papers sticking out of folders can obscure guide and folder label captions.

When filing correspondence into subject folders, file records in alphabetic order according to the names of the correspondents. Then for each correspondent, arrange the records by the date of the document with the *most recent date in front.*

Retrieving

Understanding the subject records system is critical to finding and removing (retrieving) records from storage. Use indexes to help locate records. In addition, follow the retrieval procedures described in Chapter 7. As with other methods of records storage, retrieval procedures for subject records management make use of OUT indicators to show information about records that have been removed from storage. Knowing who has taken the records, the contents of those records, when the records were borrowed, and when the records will be returned is the only way to maintain control over a retrieval system. Follow-up also is necessary to assure that records are returned, to extend the charge-out time, or to direct attention to any matters needing future action or consideration.

Chapter Review And Applications

POINTS TO FILE AND RETRIEVE

- Subject records management is an alphabetic system of storing and retrieving records by their subject or topic.

- Subject records may be filed in a dictionary or an encyclopedic arrangement.

- Supplies used for the subject arrangement of files include guides, folders, labels, and OUT indicators.

- The subject records storage method requires the use of indexes and is, therefore, considered an indirect access filing method.

- The master index is an outline of the file and lists all subject titles and subdivisions in alphabetic order as they appear in the file.

- The relative index lists all subject titles and subdivisions in a straight alphabetic, dictionary order.

- When numbers are used to identify specific subjects, a numeric index—a current list of files by the file numbers—is maintained.

- Correspondence filed in a subject arrangement requires a name index.

- Maintain control over the records storage system by carefully inspecting, indexing, coding, cross-referencing, sorting, and storing records. Keep a charge-out record of all borrowed records and a follow-up system that ensures their safe return to storage.

IMPORTANT TERMS

dictionary arrangement	name index
direct access	numeric index
encyclopedic arrangement	relative index
indirect access	subject records management
master index	

REVIEW AND DISCUSSION

1. Define subject records management and explain why this system is the best choice for filing certain records. (Obj. 1)

2. Give two reasons that an organization might have a subject filing arrangement for records rather than arranging their records alphabetically by individual or company names. (Obj. 1)

3. List three advantages and three disadvantages of using the subject records storage method. (Obj. 2)

4. What do you consider the most important advantage and the greatest disadvantage to arranging records by subject? (Obj. 2)

5. Name two alphabetic arrangements of subject records storage and explain how the two arrangements are alike and how they differ. (Obj. 3)

6. What two criteria determine which alphabetic arrangement to use for a subject records system? (Obj. 3)

7. What supplies are needed when using the subject storage method? Describe the placement of subject titles on guide and folder label captions. (Obj. 4)

8. Explain how color can be used with subject labels or folders to help locate records and reduce misfiles. (Obj. 4)

9. Name and describe four indexes used with subject records storage. (Obj. 5)

10. Which two indexes are essential for all subject files? Name two types of computer software that can be used to prepare subject file indexes. (Objs. 5 and 7)

11. Explain the procedure for storing and retrieving records in a subject records storage system. (Obj. 6)

12. When filing correspondence into subject folders, how are records arranged in the folder? (Obj. 8)

APPLICATIONS

8-1 PREPARE A MASTER INDEX FOR A SUBJECT FILE (OBJS. 5 AND 7)

CRITICAL THINKING

DATA CD

ACCESS ACTIVITY

Use database software to complete a master index for subject records files for a small business. Some records have already been entered into the database. You will add records and sort the database, query the database to show only a portion of the master index, and create a report showing the complete index.

1. Locate the *Access* file *8-1 Master Index* in the data files. Copy the file to your working folder on a hard drive or removable storage device. Open the file.

2. Enter records into the Master Index table for the remaining files listed below. For records with only main subject titles, enter only the main subject title in the Main field. For records with main titles and subdivisions of main titles, enter the main title in the Main field and the subdivision title in the Sub field. (You will add subdivisions for some main titles already in the index.) Save the table.

Main Title	Subdivision
Utilities	
Utilities	Natural Gas
Utilities	Electric
Utilities	Water
Accounting	Credit Cards
Reports	
Reports	Annual Reports
Reports	Quarterly Reports
Reports	Monthly Reports
Accounting	Loans

3. Use the Advanced Filter/Sort feature to sort the Master Index table by the Main field then by the Sub field to place the index in alphabetic order.

4. Create a query based on the Master Index table. The query results should display the Main field in the first column and the Sub field in the second column. The query results should show all records that have **Office Equipment** in the Main field. Sort the Main field in ascending order and the Sub field in ascending order. Save the query as **Office Equipment Query.** Run the query and print the query results.

5. Create and save a report to show all the data in the Master Index table. The data should be sorted in ascending order by the Main field and then by the Sub field. Chose **Tabular** layout. Name the report **Master Index Report.** Print the report.

8-2 CREATE A RELATIVE INDEX (OBJS. 5 AND 7)

1. Locate the *Access* file *8-2 Relative Index* in the data files. Copy the file to your working folder on a hard drive or a removable storage device. Open the file.

CRITICAL THINKING

DATA CD

ACCESS ACTIVITY

2. Enter records into the Relative Index table for the remaining files listed below. Enter the data into the Subject Title and the Filed Under fields. Save the table.

Subject Title	Filed Under
Resumes	Applications
Cars	Vehicles
Trucks	Vehicles
Charities	Contributions
Banking	Accounting

3. Create a report to show all data in the Relative Index table. Show the Subject Title data in the first column of the report and Filed Under data in the second column of the report. Sort the Subject Title field in ascending order. Choose **Tabular** layout. Save the report as **Relative Index Report.** Print the report.

8-3 FILE OR RETRIEVE RECORDS BY THE SUBJECT METHOD (OBJ. 8)

CRITICAL THINKING

Refer to Figure 8.3 on page 222 Encyclopedic Arrangement of Subjects to file/retrieve the records described below. Indicate where each of these records would be located by writing the complete folder label caption for each. If more than one subject location is possible, list other subjects that should be used for cross-referencing. Place an X in front of each cross-reference title.

1. A new manual for the air-conditioning system

2. A report from a recent workflow efficiency study

3. A job application from Anthony Timmons

4. A letter from an office products vendor about filing supplies

5. A notice of price change on an order you have placed for filing cabinets

6. Last month's sales report

7. A memo about the date that the records audit will begin

8. Weekly time sheets for Records and Information Department employees

9. Vacation schedules for the Accounting Department

10. A price quote from a lawn and garden center to landscape a recreational area

8-4 USE THE INTERNET TO LOCATE SUPPLY VENDORS (OBJ. 4)

Office supplies needed for preparing guides and folders for a subject records management system are available from local office products stores, various discount stores, and from online vendors. You can find the URLs for two Internet search engines that will help you locate office supplies vendor web sites at the Links tab at web site for this textbook.

INTERNET

1. Locate two vendors for guides and folders and two vendors of label software.

2. Go to these vendor web sites and review their products.

3. Write a summary paragraph of what you learned by reviewing these sites.

RECORDS MANAGEMENT SIMULATION

JOB 10 SUBJECT CORRESPONDENCE FILING

Continue working with Auric Systems, Inc.
Complete Job 10.

FOR MORE ACTIVITIES GO TO **http://read.swlearning.com**

Numeric Records Management

Learning Objectives

1. Define numeric records management and list three reasons for its use.

2. List and describe the components of a consecutive numbering storage method.

3. Explain the storage and retrieval procedures for the consecutive numeric method.

4. Describe how to convert an alphabetic records arrangement to a consecutive numeric records arrangement.

5. List advantages and disadvantages of consecutive numeric records storage.

6. Compare and contrast consecutive, terminal-digit, and middle-digit numeric records storage.

7. Define chronologic records storage and explain its use.

8. Compare and contrast block-numeric, duplex-numeric, decimal-numeric, and alphanumeric coding.

9. Explain how computer indexes and database software can be used with numeric records management.

NUMERIC RECORDS STORAGE AND RETRIEVAL

The records and information management (RIM) storage methods you studied in previous chapters were alphabetic—records were arranged in alphabetic order by name or subject. In this chapter, you will learn how to store records in numeric order. As its name suggests, **numeric records management** is any classification system for arranging records that is based on numbers.

Numeric records management is often used in organizations that store and retrieve very large numbers of records and that have a need to preserve confidentiality of their records and information. Numbers used in storing records are assigned to records to identify their locations in a file. The number can be preprinted on the record (such as a purchase order or invoice number), or it may be assigned to the record based on the type of numeric filing arrangement. Records are filed by number in ascending order—from the lowest to the highest number.

Why use numeric records storage?

Numbers are impersonal; the information they represent is dependent on the numbering system and is not immediately accessible to persons other than users of the system. Anyone who happens to see an open file drawer, file shelf, or file folder cannot readily identify the contents.

The use of numbers for identification and classification of data is part of everyday work routines. Most people appreciate the speed and accuracy of using numbers. The list of numbers that each individual uses and must, therefore, remember today is long. For example, almost every U.S. citizen has a social security number, and all U.S. citizens have ZIP Codes. Citizens of other countries also have postal codes to remember. Thousands of people in the U.S. and other countries have a home telephone number, a work telephone number, at least one cellular telephone number, and maybe a pager number to remember as well. Many people also have auto license plate numbers, code numbers for entering their places of work or their condominium buildings, passwords for accessing their computers at work, and personal identification numbers (PINs) for using their debit cards. Those individuals who establish online accounts or register with various web sites have user IDs and passwords to remember. Medical office personnel ask patients for their dates of birth because patient records are stored in numeric order by dates of birth. Patient names are also on the folder labels, but the folders are stored in numeric order. When you order a pizza, the order clerk at the local pizza shop asks for your telephone number. Your name, address, and the kind of pizza you last ordered shows on the computer screen when your telephone number is entered.

In this chapter, numbering methods for numeric filing are categorized as:

- Consecutive numbering
- Nonconsecutive numbering
- Numeric coding used in combination with geographic or subject filing

The components and procedures for filing numerically are similar for all numeric records management systems. Expanding files is easy with a numeric filing system. An unlimited set of available numbers (compared with the limitation of 26 *alphabetic* characters) allows the addition of numbers, folders, and storage units without transferring current files. In an alphabetic file, adding files in one section of the alphabet requires moving folders in all drawers or on all shelves that follow the expanded section.

CONSECUTIVE NUMBERING METHOD

The most frequently used method of numbering records for storage assigns numbers to records in sequence. Also called *serial, sequential,* and *straight numeric,* the **consecutive numbering method** is a method in which consecutively numbered records are arranged in *ascending* number order—from the lowest number to the highest number. Numbers begin with 1, 100, 1000, or any

What does *consecutive* **mean?**

other number and progress upward. Office forms such as invoices, sales tickets, and purchase orders are numbered consecutively. Although these forms may be filled out at various locations within a business, they come together in the file in consecutive numeric sequence.

Consecutive numbers are often assigned to customers and clients, and their correspondence is stored by consecutive numbers. Because a record may be requested by a name or topic rather than by a number, an index must be referenced to locate a numbered record. A numeric RIM system is considered an indirect access system because an index is used to locate a record in the file. As an indirect access system, numeric filing is ideal for storing electronic records where label space for record identification is often limited. An index is prepared to show the contents of the records and their assigned file code numbers. The index lists records by name, subject, creator, date, department, location, function, or a combination of these elements. Indexes required for numeric RIM storage are discussed in detail later in the chapter.

Consecutive Numbering Components

The components of the consecutive numbering method consist of (1) a numeric file, (2) an alphabetic file, (3) an accession log, and (4) an alphabetic index. Manual files use the following supplies for this storage method:

1. Numbered guides and folders for the numeric file
2. Alphabetic guides and folders for the general alphabetic file
3. Database software (or a lined book) for an accession log
4. Database or word processing software for an alphabetic index

Numbered Guides and Folders

Figure 9.1 on page 249 shows a file drawer of consecutively numbered individual correspondent file folders in a straight-line arrangement. Primary guides, numbered 250 and 260, divide the drawer into easy-to-find numeric segments.

Consecutively numbered individual folders 250 through 259 are placed behind a corresponding guide number for Section 250.

Usually, one guide is provided for every ten folders. Folders can show the names of the correspondents to the right of the number on the label if secrecy is not a factor. However, when office policy requires names in addition to assigned code numbers, the names are not in alphabetic order. Folders are arranged in consecutive numbered order; therefore, someone with unauthorized access to files would have difficulty locating a particular person's file.

Guide captions are available in a variety of formats: (1) guides may have numbers already printed on their tabs; (2) numbered labels may be inserted

How many folders should be between guides?

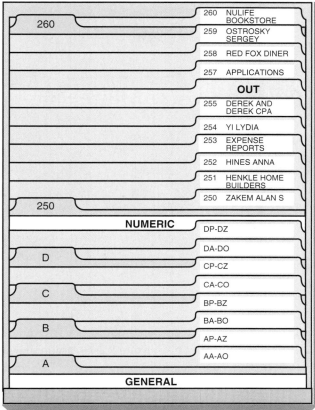

Figure 9.1 Consecutive Numbering Arrangement

into slots on the tabs; (3) self-adhesive numbers may be attached to tabs; or (4) numbers may be keyed onto guide labels. As discussed in Chapter 8, software and label templates are available for printing guide and folder label captions. RIM supply companies can also produce customized labels from an organization's database information saved to a disk or CD. Figure 9.2 on page 250 illustrates computer-generated labels with color-coded numbers. The numbers and colors call attention to misfiles, and bar codes provide electronic tracking of records. Avoid handwriting or hand printing on guide labels. Handwriting lacks uniformity of placement and style, making numbers difficult to read and unattractive.

Alphabetic Guides and Folders

Perhaps you wonder what a general alphabetic file is doing in numeric records storage. A general alphabetic file, found in many numeric arrangements, holds records of correspondents whose volume of correspondence is small. Some offices prepare individually numbered folders for correspondents as they enter the file. With this procedure, a general alphabetic file is not needed. In most

What is the purpose of the alphabetic file in a numeric system?

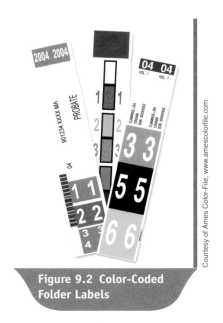

Figure 9.2 Color-Coded Folder Labels

Courtesy of Ames Color-File, www.amescolorfile.com

offices, individually numbered folders are not prepared until a predetermined number of pieces of correspondence (usually five or more) have accumulated for one correspondent or when a correspondent's file is expected to be active. Until an individual numbered folder is prepared, correspondence is stored in general alphabetic folders in a general alphabetic file in the same manner as names stored by the alphabetic method.

The general alphabetic file should be placed at the beginning of the numeric file because expansion occurs at the end of a consecutively numbered arrangement. In Figure 9.1 the general alphabetic file contains a centered primary guide labeled GENERAL. In large records systems, alphabetic-lettered guides follow this primary guide to show the alphabetic divisions. In small systems, alphabetic-lettered guides may not be needed; instead, folders with alphabetic captions are arranged in alphabetic order behind the GENERAL guide. The general alphabetic folders hold records of correspondents who have not yet been assigned numbers.

Accession Log

The **accession log**, also called an *accession book* or *numeric file list,* is a serial list of numbers assigned to records in a numeric storage system. This log provides the numeric codes assigned to correspondents, subjects, or documents and the date of the assignment. The next number available for assignment is obtained from this log. An accession log prevents a filer from assigning the same number twice. Correspondent names and subjects are entered into the accession log in indexed order. Figure 9.3 on page 251 shows an accession log created in a computer database.

What is the purpose of the accession log?

FILE NO	NAME OR SUBJECT	DATE
525	Norwood Christian Church	5/18/20--
526	Astroturf Applications	5/10/20--
527	Liang Yang	7/12/20--
528	EZ Service Center	11/22/20--
529	A1 Moving & Storage	4/21/20--
530	Unique Web Designs	2/2/20--
531	Colyer James	10/15/20--
532	Happy Time Florist	9/18/20--
533	Borrowed Time Antiques	12/2/20--
534	SmithHarrison Makita	9/1/20--
535	BT Heating & Cooling	8/17/20--

Figure 9.3 Accession Log

Although a lined book is often used for the accession log, a computer-generated log is simpler to prepare, use, and update. Database software is used in large records systems that have more than 1,000 records or several people accessing the files on a daily basis. Number code assignment can be made automatically with appropriate computer programming.[1] You can store numerous items of information about each record in one or more tables and use the Query or Report functions to generate lists or reports that show all or any part of this information. In smaller records systems, an accession log can easily be produced using a word processing program. The accession log information includes the file number, the correspondent name or subject in indexed order, and the date on which the record was added to the file.

Alphabetic Index

A numeric records storage system cannot function without an alphabetic index. An **alphabetic index** is a reference to a numeric file, organized alphabetically, that is used when the name or subject is known but not the assigned number. For a numeric-subject system, it may be called a *relative index.*[2] The index is typically a list of correspondent names or subjects for a numeric file. The assigned file codes are listed for records stored in the numbered file or a G is entered as the code for records stored in the general alphabetic file. Filers reference the alphabetic index to determine where records for correspondents are located in the filing system.

> **Why is an alphabetic index useful in a numeric storage system?**

[1]ARMA International, *Establishing Alphabetic, Numeric and Subject Filing Systems* (Lenexa, KS: ARMA International, 2005), p. 11.
[2]Ibid., p. 1.

A computer file is recommended for the alphabetic index because of its speed and efficiency in locating records. The same database table can be used to store information for an accession log and an alphabetic index. Figure 9.4 shows a partial alphabetic index generated from a database. Cross-references are in bold print.

To retrieve a record, the first source of location information is the alphabetic index to see whether a code for the subject or correspondent's name has been assigned. If a code is not found, the filer then checks the general alphabetic file to locate the record. Because rapid retrieval of a record can be important, keeping all names and subjects in one index is more efficient than looking in multiple locations. With all names and subjects in the index, a filer follows the same pattern for retrieving all records. Each correspondent and subject in the index has a different file code number or the letter G. Because the alphabetic index serves as the records location source for all file users, the index should be accurate and up-to-date.

When information about each correspondent and subject is stored in a database, locating information about that correspondent or subject is quick and easy using the database Find or Query functions. Because of the ease of obtaining information from a database, you may want to add addresses or other information. This information in a database is also useful for printing mailing labels.

NAMES AND SUBJECTS	FILE NO.	SEE
A1 Moving & Storage	529	
Astroturf Applications	526	
Borrowed Time Antiques	533	
BT Heating & Cooling	535	
Colyer James	531	
Easy Service Center	**528X**	**EZ Service Center**
EZ Service Center	528	
Happy Time Florist	532	
Harrison Makita Smith	**534X**	**SmithHarrison Makita**
Harrison Tom Mrs	**534X**	**SmithHarrison Makita**
Liang Yang	527	
Norwood Christian Church	525	
Smith Makita	**534X**	**SmithHarrison Makita**
SmithHarrison Makita	534	
Unique Web Designs	530	
Yang Liang	**527X**	**Liang Yang**

Figure 9.4 Alphabetic Index

CAREER CORNER

Medical Records Supervisor Job Description

The following job description is an example of a career opportunity in records management in a medical office.

GENERAL INFORMATION

The Medical Records Supervisor in a medical office is responsible for developing, managing and implementing the medical records system and policies as well as supervising the Records Technicians (Techs).

RESPONSIBILITIES

- Oversee clinical documentation filing, records storage and retrieval, and data reporting
- Supervise and train Records Techs who maintain accurate and timely clinical records, including heavy filing; perform chart assembly and maintenance; and maintain databases

EXPERIENCE AND EDUCATION

- Bachelor's degree
- Three years of clinical records experience
- Medical records certification preferred

SALARY

Salary is based on education and experience.

When creating a database, you can use the AutoNumber feature to assign file number codes automatically. If you want to use another numbering system, simply include a File Code Number field and enter the number. The data can be sorted on the File Code Number field in descending order so that the highest number shows on the first line of the list, allowing you to determine quickly the next number for assignment. The data can also be sorted by name to create an alphabetic name index.

The database can be used for an onscreen check of the assigned file code number for a correspondent or subject. Using the Find feature, you can go directly to a record to obtain information.

Storage and Retrieval Procedures

The steps for storage (inspecting, indexing, coding, number coding, cross-referencing, sorting, and storing) and retrieval (requisitioning, charging out, and following-up) are as important in the numeric method as they are in all other RIM storage methods. All records are inspected, indexed, and the filing segment coded before a number or a G is assigned. The procedures to follow in storing and retrieving records in numeric systems are discussed next. Steps for coding numeric records are listed in Figure 9.5.

What step is included in the storage procedures for numeric storage that is not needed in other storage methods?

Inspecting and Indexing

Inspect records for release marks. Then index to determine the filing segment by which to store each record.

Coding

Code the filing segment and identify any needed cross-references by marking an X in the margin and underlining the cross-reference name or subject with a wavy line. Sort records that do not have preprinted numbers alphabetically before consulting the alphabetic index to see whether a file code number or a G (GENERAL) has been assigned. For correspondents or subjects with numbers already assigned or preprinted on the record, code the record with the file code number by writing this number in the top right corner of the record. The letter in Figure 9.6 on page 255 shows the coded correspondent name and the

Why are records sorted more than once for numeric storage?

STEPS FOR CODING RECORDS FOR NUMERIC STORAGE

Coding
- Code the filing segment.
- Write an X in the margin beside cross-reference names or subjects.
- Underline the cross-reference name or subject with a wavy line.

Sorting
- Sort records that do not have preprinted numbers alphabetically before referencing the alphabetic index.

Number Coding
- Consult the alphabetic index for each record.
- Write the assigned file code number or a G in the upper right corner of the record.
- Assign the next available number—if a number has not been assigned—or a G.
- Enter the new file code number into the accession log.
- Write the code number or a G in the upper right corner of the record.

Figure 9.5 Coding Procedures for Numeric Records

2 3   4   5   122

L&M Advertising Agency
80 Second Avenue
New York, NY 10022-1421
Telephone: 212.555-0146   Fax: 212.555-0187
www.l&mads.com

September 24, 20--

SEP 25, 20-- 11:03 A.M.

Ms. Graciella Melena
Melena & Daughters, Inc.
600 E. 52 Street
New York, NY 10022-2844

Dear Ms. Melena

1   2   3
Your ad with Kirkman Products, Inc. is well under way. Executives at Kirkman   X
are more than a little excited about the advertising tie-in with your company. We
have a two-page ad for spring distribution we would like to share with you and
Juan Ramos, Advertising Director at Kirkman.

Juan is eager to complete the work on this campaign. By the way, Kirkman is also
willing to supply a personal appearance of one of its product designers for your
spring exhibition. Kirkman has agreed to pay $47,000 for the first spring ad if you
will handle all production costs. We can work out these arrangements in more
detail at our joint meeting.

Melena & Daughters and Kirkman Products are uniquely compatible, Graciella.
This cooperative effort creates a far more dynamic campaign for today's market
than we could have developed from an independent effort. We are eager to show
you what we have done.

I will call you next week to arrange a convenient time for a joint ad presentation.

Sincerely

L&M ADVERTISING AGENCY   RLG

J. R. McGuire

J. R. McGuire, Advertising Coordinator

kac

Figure 9.6 Coded Correspondence for Number File

code number already assigned to the name. Number 122 is written in the upper right corner of the letter.

For correspondents or subjects with the letter G already assigned, the record will be stored in the general alphabetic file. Code the record with a G in the upper right corner.

For *new* correspondents or subjects with no assigned code number, write the letter G in the upper right corner of the documents. The letter in Figure 9.7 on page 257 shows a document coded for the general alphabetic file. Make a database entry for the new correspondent or subject and indicate the file location to be G. Place the record into an alphabetic sorter for later storage in the general alphabetic file.

Number Coding

To assign file code numbers to a correspondent or subject, follow these steps:

1. When using a database accession log, create a new record. Key the correspondent's name or subject and current date (and other information) into the appropriate fields and assign the next file code number. If a database is not used, make entries into the manual accession log book to record the assigned number or the letter G for the name or subject.
2. Write the assigned number code on the record in the upper right corner.
3. If any cross-references are needed, enter the cross-reference name or subject into the database alphabetic index with the assigned file code number followed by an X at the end of the number (i.e., 122X). Key the name into the SEE field for the location of the record in the file.
4. Prepare a new folder with the file code number on its tab. Add the correspondent's name or the subject to the tab label if office policy requires this information.
5. Place the record into the folder with the top to the left, and place the folder into a number sorter for later storage in the numbered file.

Cross-Referencing

Where are cross-reference sheets filed in the numeric method?

Code all units in the cross-reference name or subject that has an X beside it in the margin. If the cross-reference name or subject does not exactly match the name or subject in the alphabetic index, write the correct cross-reference name or subject on the document, underline it with a wavy line, and number all units. Do not store cross-references in numbered file folders. File all cross-references in the general alphabetic file. Enter all cross-references into the database as described previously in Step 3. To call attention to cross-references in a database name file, consider using all capitals or bold type.

2   G

Starsound/**Recordings**
4325 21 St., New York, NY 10022-1345
Telephone: 212.555.0197   Fax: 212.555.0236

June 5, 20--

JUN 7, 20-- 12:30 PM

Ms. Graciella Melena
Melena & Daughters, Inc.
600 E. 52 Street
New York, NY 10022-2844

Dear Ms. Melena

Last week I met with your friend Diane Pruiksma regarding the renovation of our
office complex at 4325 21 St., here in the city. She suggested that I look at your
work on the Theater Arts Building because she thought it was close to the type of
makeover we are considering for our corporate offices.

Several employees from our company toured the building last week and agreed that
it is an impressive piece of work. We are interested in knowing what you and your
staff would propose for us. We have very specific needs in mind, but some creative
projects we would leave to you.

Let me know how you would like to proceed. We prefer a meeting at our location
so that we can show you the changes in layout, communication services, and office
equipment we have in mind. We are also eager to hear your suggestions and hope
that you can prepare a proposal by the end of August.

Now that we have agreed to renovate, we are eager to get started. We are looking
forward to an early meeting time that will be convenient for everyone.

Sincerely

Sumiyo Maekawa   RLG

Sumiyo Maekawa

dsr

Figure 9.7 Coded Correspondence for Alphabetic File—Numeric Method

Sorting

An initial alphabetic sorting is done before assigning file code numbers or the letter G to the records. After consulting the alphabetic index, writing assigned codes in the upper right corners of the records, and assigning all necessary codes, records are placed into numeric or alphabetic sorters. If rough sorting is done as you prepared the records, move the sorter and its contents to the storage area. However, if you prefer to perform like tasks together, sort all records after you have indexed, coded, and prepared cross-reference entries. A quick sort before storage saves time. Stacking the numbered records in random groups by hundreds, for example, eliminates moving back and forth from drawer to drawer or shelf to shelf while storing records.

Storing

Store all records coded with numbers in correspondingly numbered folders with the most recent date on top. Store records coded G in the general alphabetic folders. Store them first alphabetically according to the units in the filing segments and then by dates within each name group with the most recent date on top. File all cross-references into the alphabetic file.

Office policy determines the point at which accumulated records in the general alphabetic file require the assignment of a permanent code number. When that accumulation has occurred, remove the records from the general file and take the following steps:

1. Consult the accession log to determine the next available number. Enter the name of the correspondent or the subject and the file code number into the database file or the manual accession log. Record the current date.

2. Locate the correspondent's name in the alphabetic index. Replace the G with the file code number.

3. Locate all cross-references for the subject or correspondent's name. In the alphabetic index database, change the G on all cross-reference entries to the file code number followed by an X.

4. Re-code all records removed from the general file by crossing out the G and writing the assigned file code number above or beside it.

5. Prepare a new folder with the assigned file code on its tab (and, possibly, the correspondent's name or the subject).

6. Place all records into the new folder. Place the record with the most recent date on top.

7. Place the numbered folder in its correct numeric sequence into the number file.

Why is the accession log referenced before records are coded for numeric storage?

My Records

Home Inventory

What is a home inventory? Should you create a home inventory?

Creating a home inventory is a good idea. An inventory lists the value of your possessions and helps you keep track of the warranties, receipts, and other information about the items in your home. Use the inventory to determine your homeowner's or renter's insurance needs as well as to provide details about your possessions in case of loss.

CREATE AN INVENTORY

To create an inventory, start by listing the rooms in your home. Next list the items in each room. You can find sample home inventory sheets on the Internet by using the search term *homeowner's inventory.* Here are sample inventory headings:

Item   Model, Serial Number   Year Purchased   Cost   Present Value

MAINTAIN YOUR INVENTORY

Follow these suggestions for maintaining a home inventory:

- Keep receipts of major purchases to prove the value of an item in case of loss.

- Store warranties and/or user manuals with the receipt of the item.

- Photograph the contents of each room. Show cabinets and closets with open doors. If a closet is a walk-in, photograph inside the closet.

- Set a specific date to update the inventory annually such as the beginning or end of Daylight Savings Time or the anniversary of an important family event.

- Store the photos and a copy of your inventory sheet in a safe place such as a safety deposit box or a fire-resistant box.

- When you replace possessions, update the inventory and remove all records about the old item. Make sure the records for the new item are stored.

Don't wait for a disaster to strike before you complete a home inventory!

Retrieving

When you remove records from numeric storage, use requisitions, OUT indicators, and a charge-out log in the same way you used them for alphabetic and subject records storage. With a database table, you can include an OUT Date field, Borrower's Name field, and Date Borrowed field to record charge-out information. When a record is removed from the file, an entry is made in the database table. To ensure the safe return of borrowed records, follow the same procedures described in Chapter 7. If OUT information is kept in the database, a filter or query could be used to show all borrowed OUT files, sorted by date.

Conversion from Alphabetic Storage to Consecutive Numeric Storage

An organization may decide that a numeric arrangement would provide quicker RIM storage and retrieval than an existing alphabetic arrangement. Security may be another consideration for changing from alphabetic storage to consecutively numbered storage. A number on a storage container or file folder does not convey information to inquisitive persons. However, a name on a folder is instantly recognizable to anyone who sees it. File users may prefer an indirect access storage method that allows for a variety of useful indexes to locate stored records such as a database master index. Whatever the reason for a conversion, the procedure is time-consuming but not difficult.

> **Why would an organization change its storage system from alphabetic to numeric?**

The following steps convert an alphabetic file arrangement to a consecutively numbered arrangement:

1. Prepare numbered guides for every 10 folders in storage according to the sequence of numbers decided upon such as 1–10–20, 100–110–120, 1000–1010–1020, etc.
2. Remove each individual folder from storage and assign a file code number from the accession log. Enter the filing segment for each correspondent name or subject into the database or manual accession log beside the assigned number. Enter the date.
3. Prepare a numbered label and affix it to the folder or add the newly assigned number to the older label. *Caution:* Do not remove general folders from alphabetic storage; the reason will be explained later in the chapter.
4. Key each filing segment for cross-references into an alphabetic index database. Key the assigned file code number and an X into the database.

5. Remove and destroy all cross-reference sheets and SEE ALSO cross-references from individual folders because the database now replaces those sheets. Database records can be sorted as needed or located without sorting by using the Find function.

6. Remove any permanent cross-reference guides within the group of folders being converted to the numeric method, and make database entries for the information on the guides.

7. Code each record in every folder with its newly assigned file code number in the upper right corner of the record.

8. Return the numbered folders to storage in correct numeric sequence.

9. Create the general alphabetic file by coding all remaining records with the letter G. (All individual folders from alphabetic storage were converted to numbered folders and filed numerically.)

10. Key the name of each correspondent or subject in every general folder into the database. Database records can be sorted as needed or located with the Find function without sorting.

Advantages and Disadvantages of Consecutive Numbering

Every storage method has advantages and disadvantages. Consecutive numbering is no exception as shown in Figure 9.8 on page 262. This indirect access method has advantages for storing electronic records such as CDs and DVDs, where labeling space is often limited. A numeric code identifies the records. A database record for each item shows this number, along with the originator's name, department, subject, special project, or any other meaningful category. The database record can be as comprehensive as necessary to identify and locate records. Even when CDs and DVDs are reused, the file code number remains the same; only the information in the record fields is updated. A complete list of correspondents' names, addresses, and other information is available from the alphabetic index or a correspondent database. These database files could be searched by any of the fields of information to find a particular record. Numeric database files are used frequently for inventories of equipment and supplies. Each item is assigned an identifying number, and pertinent fields of information are added to the database for data entry and retrieval.

NONCONSECUTIVE NUMBERING METHODS

Nonconsecutive numbering is a system of numbers that has blocks of numbers omitted. Records arrangements based on these nonconsecutive numbers use a sequential order that differs from a consecutive order of numbers normally read from left to right. This section explains the use of three of these methods: terminal-digit, middle-digit, and chronologic storage.

What are nonconsecutive numbers?

CONSECUTIVE NUMERIC RECORDS STORAGE

Advantages

1. Re-filing of numerically coded records is rapid because people recognize number sequences better and faster than alphabetic sequences.
2. Expansion is easy and unlimited. New numbers can be assigned without disturbing the arrangement of existing folders or other stored records media.
3. Transfer of inactive records is easy because the lowest numbers are the oldest records and are stored together.
4. All cross-references are in the general alphabetic name database and do not congest the drawers or shelves where numbered records are filed.
5. Security is provided because names do not appear on numeric captions on guides, folders, electronic records, and other records media.
6. All records for one customer bear the same numeric code, keeping related records together.
7. Time and effort in labeling is minimized because numbers can be affixed much more quickly than names, subjects, or project titles.
8. Misfiled records are detected easily—numbers out of sequence are easier to detect than misfiled records arranged alphabetically.

Disadvantages

1. Consecutive numeric is an indirect access method that requires reference to an alphabetic index.
2. More guides are necessary for the numeric method; therefore, the cost of supplies can be higher.
3. Consecutive numeric storage is more time-consuming than other methods. Records must first be sorted alphabetically and then resorted numerically prior to storage. Resorting is eliminated with a database and use of the Find function to locate specific names or numbers in the records file.
4. Congestion occurs around the end of the file where new records are added. Records with the highest numbers are typically the most current and most active records.
5. Numbers can be easily transposed, which causes misfiles.

Figure 9.8 Advantages and Disadvantages of Consecutive Numeric Storage

Terminal-Digit Storage

Which set of digits in a terminal-digit number are the terminal digits?

Terminal-digit storage is a numeric storage method in which the last two or three digits of each number are used as the primary division under which a record is filed. Groups of numbers are read from right to left. The digits in the number are usually separated into groups by a space or hyphen.

Terminal-digit storage breaks large numbers into groups of digits and overcomes the disadvantage of congestion that can occur at the end of a consecutive numeric storage area. The terminal-digit storage method is used most effectively with thousands of folders whose numbers have reached at least five digits (10,000 or more). The words *terminal digit* refer to the end digits of a number (091 38 0297). Numbers may be assigned sequentially, or the digit groups may mean something specific. For example, the first group of numbers may be a customer identification number; the second group may indicate a sales district, salesperson, or department; the third group may indicate a date, branch office, or department.

The number may be a product number in which various groups of numbers refer to a sales department and/or a particular manufacturer or wholesaler. The numbers can have a variety of meanings, or they can be simply a sequentially assigned numeric code number.

The groups of numbers are identified as primary, secondary, and tertiary numbers reading from right to left.

Tertiary (Folder Number)	Secondary (Guide Number)	Primary (or Terminal) File Section, Drawer, or Shelf Number
35	14	65

An arrangement of numbers in terminal-digit sequence would look like the following—the numbers in bold determine the correct numeric order in the file:

```
786 67 1258 (Front of File)
231 55 2187
189 40 2891
303 99 2891
947 28 6314
287 29 6314
502 64 9284
498 64 9485
502 64 9485 (End of File)
```

Primary numbers usually indicate a drawer or shelf number. If the volume of records stored is great, more than one drawer or shelf may be needed to hold all records with numbers ending in the same terminal (or primary) digits. Figure 9.9 on page 265 shows the arrangement of folders in a portion of shelf 32. The secondary numbers determine the primary guide captions. The section of the shelf shown begins with guide 24–32. If space had permitted, the entire 32 section would show guide 00–32 at the front of the drawer. Records are arranged behind each guide by the tertiary numbers—the digits at the extreme *left* of the number.

As new folders are stored, new guides are added to separate each group of ten folders. The first section of the file shown in Figure 9.9 (the 24–32 section) has been expanded in Figure 9.10 on page 266 by the addition of folders numbered 08–24–32 through 22–24–32. The tertiary numbers have increased from 00 through 07 to 00 through 22. Therefore, secondary guides 00, 10, and 20 were added in first position, and the primary guide for 24-32 was moved to the second position of the file shelf.

When sequentially numbered records, such as 05 25 32 and 05 25 33, are added to terminal-digit storage, these new and typically more active records are filed in *different* file locations. Distributing current records throughout a storage area avoids congestion in one particular storage area. Remember that in consecutive numeric storage these records would be stored next to each other at the end of the storage area.

> **Why are records numbered 05 25 32 and 05 25 33 stored in different locations?**

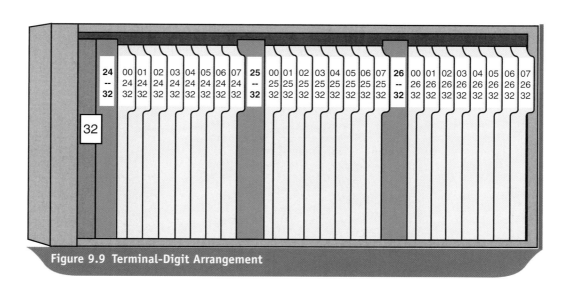

Figure 9.9 Terminal-Digit Arrangement

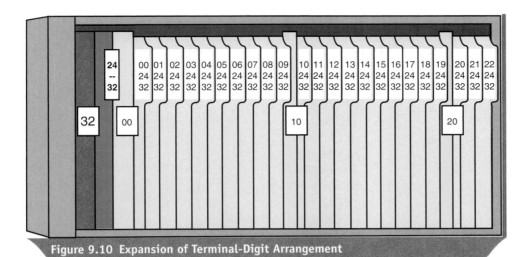

Figure 9.10 Expansion of Terminal-Digit Arrangement

Middle-Digit Storage

Middle-digit storage is another method of nonconsecutive numbering. Similar to terminal-digit storage, using this method avoids working with large numbers and overcomes the disadvantage of congestion at the end of the storage area. The words *middle-digit* refer to the middle group of digits in a large number. **Middle-digit storage** is a numeric storage method in which the middle digits are used as the finding aid to organize the filing system. It uses the middle two or three digits of each number as the primary division under which a record is filed. Groups of numbers are read from the middle to left to right. Primary numbers are in the middle, numbers to the left are secondary, and numbers to the right are tertiary, or last.

> **Which number in a middle-digit number determines the folder number?**

Secondary (Guide Number)	Primary (File Section, Drawer, or Shelf Number)	Tertiary (Folder Number)
35	14	65

An arrangement of numbers in middle-digit sequence would look like the following; the numbers in bold determine the correct numeric order:

947 **28** 6314 (Front of File)
287 **29** 6314
189 **40** 2891
231 **52** 2187
498 **64** 9485
502 64 9284
502 64 **9485**
786 **67** 1258
303 **99** 2891 (End of File)

In Figure 9.11, all records with middle digits 70 are stored in one section. The digits on the left determine record sequence within the 70 drawer, followed by the digits on the right. The left digits determine the primary guide captions **05**–70, **06**–70, and **07**–70.

In the middle-digit method, blocks of sequentially numbered records are kept together. However, records are distributed through the files in blocks of 100. Records numbered 10 70 00 to 10 70 99 are filed together in one section; 10 71 00 to 10 71 99, in the next file section. The middle-digit method has additional value when the middle digits identify someone or something specific and related records need to be kept together. If the middle digits represent a sales representative or a sales district, for example, all records for that individual or location are kept together in one block.

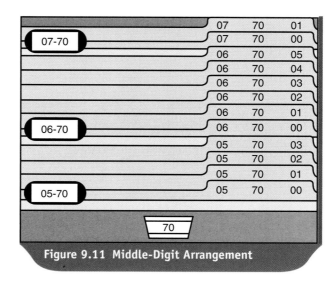

Figure 9.11 Middle-Digit Arrangement

Chronologic Storage

Chronologic storage is a method by which records are filed in date sequence, either in reverse sequence (with the most recent date on top) or forward sequence (with the earliest or oldest date on top). Users often refer to a chronologic file as a *chron file*. Exact chronologic storage is not well suited to correspondence because of the need to keep together all records from, to, and about one individual or organization. Chronologic storage is often used for daily reports, deposit slips, freight bills, statements, and order sheets that may be best stored by date.

The chronologic principle is followed in all methods of storage as records are placed into their folders. The most current records are at the front or back of the folder, thereby keeping the most recent records easily accessible. Tickler files are one form of chronologic storage. You may want to refer to the discussion of tickler files in Chapter 6.

OTHER NUMERIC CODING SYSTEMS

Numbers are sometimes added to encyclopedic arrangements of subject and geographic filing methods. Numbers help to eliminate misfiles in subject and geographic files that contain main subject divisions and numerous subdivisions. Numeric coding methods described in this section allow for coding necessary subdivisions.

Block-Numeric Coding

Block-numeric coding is a coding system based on the assignment of number ranges to subjects. Groups of numbers represent primary and secondary subjects such as the encyclopedic arrangement of a subject file discussed in Chapter 8.

The major subject divisions are assigned a block of round numbers such as 100, 200, 300. Then, each subdivision is assigned a block of numbers within the major block of round numbers such as 110, 120, 130. The more file expansion expected, the larger the blocks of numbers. The subdivision 110, for example, allows for additional subject subdivisions of subjects (111 to 119).

> **What is an important advantage of using block-numeric coding?**

Duplex-Numeric Coding

How many subdivisions are possible with duplex-numeric coding?

Like block-numeric coding, duplex-numeric coding is also used in subject or geographic filing systems that contain major categories and subdivisions. **Duplex-numeric coding** is a coding system using numbers (or sometimes letters) with two or more parts separated by a dash, space, or comma. An unlimited number of subdivisions is possible with this coding system. Subject subdivisions are added sequentially, however, and may not follow a strict alphabetic order. Notice that PAST BUDGETS comes before FUTURE NEEDS in the following example because FUTURE NEEDS was added to the file *after* PAST BUDGETS:

```
10      BUDGETS
        10–1      ACCOUNTING DEPARTMENT
                  10–1–1   PAST BUDGETS
                  10–1–2   FUTURE NEEDS
                  10–1–3   RECEIPTS
        10–2      ENGINEERING DEPARTMENT
                  10–2–1   PAST BUDGETS
                  10–2–2   FUTURE NEEDS
        10–3      INFORMATION SYSTEMS DEPARTMENT
                  10–3–1   PAST BUDGETS
```

Decimal-Numeric Coding

Where is decimal-numeric coding most often used?

Decimal-numeric coding is a numeric method of classifying records by subject in units of ten and coded for arrangement in numeric order. An unlimited number of subdivisions is permitted through the use of digits to the right of the decimal point. This method is used for classifying library materials and where large numbers of records arranged by subject or geographic location must be permanently grouped and when these records are subdivided into smaller groups.[3] It is called the *Dewey Decimal Classification (DDC) System.*

The system has nine general classes or main divisions (100–900). A tenth division (000) is used for records too general to be placed in any of the nine main divisions. Each main division can be divided into nine or fewer parts (110, 120, to 190). These nine parts can be divided further into nine additional groups (111, 112, to 119). Decimals are added for further divisions

[3]ARMA International, *Establishing Alphabetic, Numeric and Subject Filing Systems* (Lenexa, KS: ARMA International, 2005), p. 11.

(111.1, 111.1.1). The DDC is not commonly used in an office. However, the use of decimals to subdivide records is a practical alternative to the dashes, spaces, and commas used in duplex-numeric coding to subdivide records.

Alphanumeric Coding

Alphanumeric coding is a coding system that combines letters and numbers, in combination with punctuation marks, to develop codes for classifying and retrieving information. Main subjects are arranged alphabetically, and their subdivisions are assigned a number. After all main subjects are determined, they are given a number (usually in groups of 10 or 100 to provide for expansion). More elaborate variations of this system may use both letters and numbers and have numerous subdivisions.

```
MGT–MANAGEMENT
     MGT-01   RECORDS MANAGEMENT
          MGT-01-01      STORAGE EQUIPMENT
          MGT-01-02      FILING SYSTEMS
               MGT-01-02-01      PAPER
               MGT-01-02-02      ELECTRONIC
               MGT-01-02-03      PROCEDURES MANUAL
          MGT-01-03      ELECTRONIC RECORDS RETENTION SCHEDULE
          MGT-01-04      VITAL RECORDS RETENTION SCHEDULE
     MGT-02      SALES MANAGEMENT
          MGT-02-01      ADVERTISING
```

DATABASES FOR NUMERIC STORAGE

Earlier in this chapter, you read how database software can simplify creating the accession log and the alphabetic index required for a numeric file. All necessary information can be kept in one table for ready access and updating. When you design database queries to sort file code numbers for the accession log, remember that the computer sorts within a database field from left to right. With terminal-digit or middle-digit numeric storage, use a separate field for each part of the number to aid in sorting and preparing the accession log and alphabetic index. For example, with terminal-digit numbering, set up three fields in the database table for the numeric code: Tertiary, Secondary, and

How does using a database benefit numeric storage and retrieval?

Primary. Enter the numeric code for each group of numbers in its correct field. Data entry is simplified and less prone to error if the order of the numeric codes in the table matches the normal left-to-right reading sequence.

To sort these numbers as an accession log and determine the next number to be assigned, create a query to display fields in this order: Primary, Secondary, and Tertiary. Then sort each of these three columns in descending order. The query results would be displayed as shown in Figure 9.12 on page 271.

Note that the numbers in the query results are in reverse order to the numeric file code to allow the last four digits (Primary field) to be sorted first, the middle digits (Secondary field), second, and the first three digits (Tertiary field), last. The last number assigned—502 64 9485—is shown at the top of the list. The next number available for assignment is 503 64 9485.

A list similar to that used for terminal-digit numbering can be generated to produce a sorted list of numeric codes for middle-digit numbering. Numeric codes for middle-digit numbering would be entered on the query design with the middle set of numbers (Primary field) first; the left-most set of numbers (Secondary field), second; and the last group of numbers (Tertiary field), third. Sorting for these three fields would follow the same order. The middle-digit numbers could be sorted from only two fields (by combining the Primary and Secondary numbers into one field because they read from left to right and would be sorted in that order). However, using the same practice for either method of numbering reduces confusion, and also increases the flexibility to change later to terminal-digit or consecutive numbering without changing the table.

When using the accession log for a nonconsecutive numbering system, the number on the top line of the query results table may not show the next number to be assigned. Remember that in a particular office, the Primary number may indicate a drawer or shelf; the Secondary number, the section of the shelf or drawer; and the tertiary number, the order of the file in that section. Another

Primary	Secondary	Tertiary	Name or Subject	Date
9485	64	502	WXTV	9/30/20--
9485	64	498	Cleaning Supplies	9/14/20--
9284	64	502	Chou Meiling	10/02/20--
6314	29	287	Balawi Vincent	10/03/20--
6314	28	947	GlorePost Dorothy CPA	9/24/20--
2891	99	303	LaPlata Motor Sports	9/04/20--
2891	40	189	McCutchen Alex Jr	9/17/20--
2187	55	231	Brentwood Apartments	9/18/20--
1258	67	786	Applications	9/04/20--

Figure 9.12 Terminal-Digit Accession Log Query Results

office may have different categories assigned for the number groupings. For example, the first group of numbers could indicate a customer identification number; the second, a branch office; and the third, a department. A specific record's appropriate grouping would determine where to look on the database-generated accession log to locate the next number to be assigned. For a large volume of records, however, you may need to use the database Filter function to show only the categories that pertain to the group of records that you are coding. Another convenient feature of the Sort function for database records is the ability to sort and print mailing labels. Mailing labels must be pre-sorted to take advantage of bulk mailing rates. Computer-generated mailing labels can be sorted by ZIP Code without entering parts of the ZIP Code into separate fields because these numbers are sorted in sequential order as read from left to right.

Chapter Review And Applications

POINTS TO FILE AND RETRIEVE

- Records can be numbered consecutively, numbered in combination with geographic locations or subjects, or stored in nonconsecutive filing arrangements.

- Components of the consecutive numbering method include (1) a numbered file, (2) an alphabetic file, (3) an accession log, and (4) an alphabetic index.

- The accession log is a serial list of numbers assigned to records in a numeric storage system. It also provides the next number available for assignment.

- The alphabetic index is a reference to a numeric file, arranged alphabetically. It is used when the number code for a name or subject is not known. Because the index must be referenced before storing or retrieving a record, numeric records storage is an indirect access method.

- Steps for storing records in a numeric system include inspecting, indexing, coding, number coding, cross-referencing, sorting, and storing.

- Terminal-digit storage creates an even distribution of consecutively numbered records throughout a numeric system, and middle-digit storage allows blocks of related records to be stored together sequentially.

- Chronologic storage is used in some aspect of almost every filing method. Records from the same correspondent are arranged in folders by date, and tickler files are arranged by date to serve as reminders of due dates.

- Block-numeric coding and duplex-numeric coding combine numeric codes with subject or geographic categories, and alphanumeric coding uses alphabetic subject abbreviations with a numbering system.

- Computer databases are important for efficient numeric records storage. Improved efficiency of records management derives from the computer's ability to select particular records quickly, to identify their numeric code, to sort records so that a specific record or numeric code is located quickly, and to prepare lists and reports from stored information in a variety of formats.

IMPORTANT TERMS

accession log

alphabetic index

alphanumeric coding

block-numeric coding

chronologic storage

consecutive numbering method

decimal-numeric coding

duplex-numeric coding

middle-digit storage

nonconsecutive numbering

numeric records management

terminal-digit storage

REVIEW AND DISCUSSION

1. Define numeric records management and list three reasons for storing records by the numeric method. (Obj. 1)

2. Why is expansion easier with numeric than with subject filing? (Obj. 1)

3. List and describe the components of consecutive numeric storage. (Obj. 2)

4. What are the steps used when preparing records for numeric storage? (Obj. 3)

5. Explain why records in numeric storage may be coded with either the letter G or a number. (Obj. 3)

6. When are records transferred from the general alphabetic file to the numbered file? (Obj. 3)

7. Why should a general alphabetic file be placed at the beginning, rather than at the end, of a consecutively numbered storage arrangement? (Obj. 3)

8. How are cross-references prepared in the consecutive numbering method? How are they numbered? (Obj. 3)

9. When an alphabetic arrangement is converted to a consecutively numbered arrangement, where will the general folders in the alphabetic file be located in the numeric storage arrangement? Will records in these folders be coded with a number? Why or why not? (Obj. 4)

10. List at least three advantages and three disadvantages of consecutive numeric records storage. (Obj. 5)

11. Explain how numbers are sorted in consecutive numbering, terminal-digit numbering, and middle-digit numbering. (Obj. 6)

12. Give at least one way that terminal-digit and middle-digit numbering are alike and one way that they are different. (Obj. 6)

13. Define chronologic storage and explain how it is used. (Obj. 7)

14. Give at least one way that block-numeric, duplex-numeric, decimal-numeric, and alphanumeric coding are alike and one way that they are different. (Obj. 8)

15. What are two ways that database software makes numeric data storage and use easy and fast? (Obj. 9)

APPLICATIONS

9-1 ARRANGE MANUAL FILES BY TERMINAL-DIGIT, MIDDLE-DIGIT, AND CONSECUTIVE NUMBERING (OBJ. 6)

CRITICAL THINKING

1. Manually arrange the numbers below in terminal-digit order.

2. Manually arrange the numbers below in middle-digit order.

3. Manually arrange the numbers below in consecutive order.

24 15 38	18 03 01	16 74 34	17 34 60	27 11 82	21 32 71
21 33 71	26 00 02	17 33 60	19 31 01	27 10 82	20 33 70
29 17 50	16 74 32	29 17 51	18 31 02	17 31 01	27 11 42

9-2 SORT DATABASE RECORDS FOR TERMINAL-DIGIT, MIDDLE-DIGIT, AND CONSECUTIVE NUMBERS (OBJ. 6)

DATA CD

CRITICAL THINKING

ACCESS ACTIVITY

The numbers in Application 9-1 have been entered into a database table so that they can be sorted for terminal-digit, middle-digit, and consecutive numbering.

The first group of two digits is in the Group 1 field, the second group of two digits is in the Group 2 field, and the third group of two digits is in the Group 3 field.

1. Locate the *Access* file *9-2 Number Arrangements* in the data files. Copy the file to your working folder on a hard drive or removable storage device. Open the file.

2. Create a query based on the Number Arrangements table to sort the numbers in terminal-digit filing order. Sort in descending order. Save the query as **Terminal-Digit Order.** Print the query results.

3. Create a query based on the Number Arrangements table to sort the numbers in middle-digit filing order. Sort in descending order. Save the query as **Middle-Digit Order.** Print the query results.

4. Create a query based on the Number Arrangements table to sort the numbers in consecutive filing order. Sort in descending order. Save the query as **Consecutive Order.** Print the query results.

5. Use the query results to check your answers for Steps 1–3 in Application 9-1.

9-3 LEARN MORE ABOUT DECIMAL-NUMERIC CODING (OBJ. 8)

Decimal-numeric coding, or the Dewey Decimal Classification (DDC) System, as stated earlier, is used in libraries and other organizations. You can find the URL for learning more about the DDC at the Online Computer Library Center web site. A link to this site it provided under Links on the web site for this textbook. Answer the following questions based on information found on the web site.

1. Where is the Online Computer Library Center organization located?

2. What is the purpose of this organization?

3. What are the four areas of information provided on the organization's web site?

4. Search the site using the search term *DDC*. What is the current edition of the DDC?

5. What is Open WorldCat?

RECORDS MANAGEMENT SIMULATION

JOB 11 CONSECUTIVE NUMBER CORRESPONDENCE FILING

JOB 12 TERMINAL-DIGIT NUMERIC CORRESPONDENCE FILING

Continue working with Auric Systems, Inc.
Complete Jobs 11 and 12.

FOR MORE ACTIVITIES GO TO **http://read.swlearning.com**

Geographic Records Management

Learning Objectives

1. Explain the need for geographic records management.

2. Name the kinds of businesses that might use the geographic method of storage.

3. List advantages and disadvantages of geographic records management.

4. Compare dictionary and encyclopedic arrangements of geographic records.

5. Explain the differences between the lettered guide plan and the location name guide plan.

6. Describe an arrangement of guides and folders in the geographic storage method.

7. Explain the use of an alphabetic index in the geographic storage method.

8. Describe how indexing and coding for the geographic storage method differ from indexing and coding for the alphabetic storage method.

9. List the types of cross-references used in the geographic storage method and how they are stored.

10. Describe how files are arranged using compass terms and how this method differs from general alphabetic filing.

THE GEOGRAPHIC RECORDS STORAGE METHOD

In this part of the textbook, you have already studied subject and numeric records management. In this chapter, you will learn a third storage method closely related to subject records management that uses alphabetic and numeric filing and indexing rules. Some types of information, especially in specialized activities, are more easily accessed based on location within a facility, a locality, a state or province, a country, or a continent. Business activities spanning wide geographic areas demand intelligent business decisions based on location. Specialized fields such as natural sciences, the oil and gas industry, property records in city/county/state or federal governments, and the facility management profession use storage methods based on location.

You have already studied numeric storage and alphabetic storage by name and by subject. **Geographic records management** is a method of storing and retrieving records by location using a geographic filing system. A **geographic filing system** is the classification of records by geographic location usually arranged by numeric code or in alphabetic order.[1]

In this age of e-commerce and dot.com companies, communication and commerce, even for small businesses, can involve a worldwide audience. The automobile industry is an example of a widespread international business operation. American automobile manufacturers, such as General Motors and Ford, do not limit their markets or purchase of components to this country, and companies from countries, such as Japan, produce and sell a variety of cars in the United States. Even state and local governments establish branch offices in other countries to promote foreign trade. Clearly, the global economy creates business opportunities that extend to locations all around the world. High-tech communications and satellite networks facilitate interactions for multiple locations worldwide.

Scientific institutions that conduct research and house the results of the research may use geographic storage for documentation as well as specimens collected in the field. For example, a large natural sciences academy includes a herbarium that houses plant collections. It is the primary repository and source of information for many well-known botanists. The herbarium uses a regional geographic filing system for the materials about specimens collected from around the world and housed at the herbarium. The file plan includes local (nearby states alphabetic by name), other North America north of Mexico (with states then provinces in alphabetic order), Latin America (all of western hemisphere from Mexico south), Europe and the Middle East, Africa, Asia, and the Pacific Islands (including Australia and New Zealand). Figure 10.1 on page 278 shows the arrangement of records by region for the specimen files. The materials are also used to generate color-coded maps of the geographic system.

In another example, a major oceanography library has an outstanding collection of expedition reports and over 78,000 maps. The map collection includes a large collection of hydrographic/bathymetric charts. The map collection is arranged alphabetically by national hydrographic agency and then in a geographic filing arrangement within each agency.

The oil and gas industry needs to track oil and gas resources by location worldwide. A major oil company files its information related to specific oil wells by a standard numbering system, established by the American Petroleum Institute, that is used to code the material by location. The ID

> **What are some business activities that require decisions based on location?**

[1]ARMA International, *Glossary of Records and Information Management Terms* (Prairie Village, KS: ARMA International, 2000), p. 11.

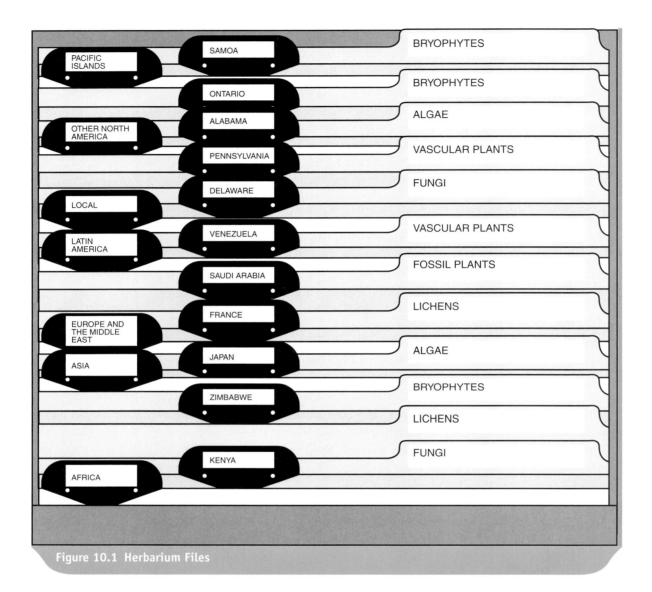

Figure 10.1 Herbarium Files

number includes codes for state, county, and oil well number. For example, ID#42-501-12345 would be state #42 (Texas), county #501 (Harris County), and Oil Well # 12345.

Records of property such as homes, businesses, new developments, parks, and government offices are important for proving ownership, for obtaining necessary permits, and for responding to 911 calls or other emergencies. Finding ownership, responding to emergencies, or issuing permits is faster and more efficient when the records are arranged by location.

Some large corporations, government agencies, and universities monitor and track the maintenance of a great number of buildings, grounds, and

How does geographic records management help facilities management?

© Getty Images/PhotoDisc

Figure 10.2 Petroleum companies may use geographic records management.

equipment through facility management. In addition, new construction or re-construction must also be monitored and related to existing records. For example, a large university tracks construction projects on campus. The campus map is divided into 26 alphabetic sectors, starting in the east with A and ended in the west with Z. Each time a building was added in a sector, a new code was created, A01, A02, A03 through Z07, etc. The building codes translated into coordinates, such as A1 or B52, and so on. To track projects, a number is added to the end of the building code. For example, A01-04 is the fourth renovation on building A01 (Science Center). The codes include the type of construction. For example, 1 is off campus, 2 is renovation, 3 is original construction, and 4 is infrastructure (across sectors/buildings). A project code that reads 3-Z01, is the original construction of the first building in sector Z, which coordinates with a particular building such as the Medical Center.

A similar example is a large gas and electric utility that uses coordinates internal to the plant to identify the location of equipment (fittings, valves, subsystems, pipe runs, compressors, etc.) and each piece of equipment or pipe run has a *tag number* associated with it. The tag number is entered into a database, and it accesses the specification sheet, drawing, bill of materials, and Operations & Maintenance manual for the item. The tag number is comprised of several components. It includes the area number of the gas plant (170), then the system type (s=steam, o=oil, g=gas), then the line number or system number it was located on (221), and finally a size and item number (8-1234). So a tag # 170-G-221-8-1234 is:

- in gas plant area 170
- a gas system (G)
- gas line number 221
- 8 inch
- item #1234

Other examples of businesses that may store records by the geographic method include:

- Multinational companies with plants, divisions, and customers outside the boundaries of the United States
- E-commerce businesses that need information about customer locations and target sales areas
- Businesses that have many branches (possibly sales offices) at different geographic locations within the United States and have a high volume of intra-company correspondence
- Insurance companies, franchised operations, banks, and investment firms that are licensed to operate in specific states and whose records are kept according to those states
- Utility companies (electricity, gas, telephone, water) whose utility facilities and services and customers are listed by location within their service area
- Real estate agencies that list their properties by areas such as foreign countries, divisions of countries or cities, groupings of subdivision names, or streets within a metropolitan area
- Scientific and other publications that file photographs and slides by location

Who uses geographic records storage?

What is a geographic information system?

Many geographic filing systems are used to support an internal geographic information system. A **geographic information system** (GIS) is a computer system designed to allow users to collect, manage, and analyze large volumes of data referenced to a geographic location by some type of geographic coordinates such as longitude and latitude. It lets the user query or analyze a database and receive the results in the form of a map. Geographic information systems are increasingly considered essential components of effective engineering, planning, and emergency management operations.

ADVANTAGES AND DISADVANTAGES OF GEOGRAPHIC RECORDS STORAGE

Like any records system, geographic records management has advantages and disadvantages; however, when information is requested and referenced by location, records need to be stored by location. In these situations, the advantages outweigh the disadvantages. This section describes advantages and disadvantages of geographic records management.

Advantages

The principal advantage of geographic storage is that operations relating to a specific location are filed together. It provides reference to information specific to certain geographic areas for making decisions about those locations or for compiling statistics relative to the locations. For example, storing records by building name and location is a means of monitoring all the maintenance activity for that building. An analysis of records can be used constructively to note (1) the types of equipment that must be maintained and how often maintenance is done; (2) the kinds of maintenance or operational problems have occurred most often and how soon equipment must be replaced; (3) the buildings that require the most maintenance and resources to do that maintenance; or (4) the buildings that must be updated to meet new codes. If equipment is moved from one building to another, geographic file guides and folders are easily rearranged. Each geographic area in storage is a unit or a group, and the shift of groups of records is easily accomplished by moving an entire group from one file location to another.

Why use geographic records storage?

Disadvantages

The principal disadvantage of geographic storage is that the user must know the geographic location, or an index must be created and maintained. For instance, customer records filed by location require an alphabetic index of all correspondents' names and addresses. If the location of a correspondent is not known, an alphabetic index must be referenced to learn the location before a record can be filed or retrieved from the geographic file. Like the subject and numeric storage methods, geographic storage may require two operations to store and retrieve a record—a check of the index for the correct file location and then the actual search of the file.

Another disadvantage of the geographic method is the complexity of the guide and folder arrangements that may be required in some large systems. For example, a geographic arrangement takes more time to establish than an alphabetic name or subject file when the nature of the organization requires many subdivisions. Storing and retrieving records can be more time-consuming, too, because reference must be made first to an area (such as a state), then to a location within that area (such as a city), and finally to a correspondent's name and address.

Cross-references are necessary in the geographic storage system for both alphabetic filing methods and numeric filing methods. Alphabetic cross-references may include, for example, names of organizations having more than one address or organizations located at one address and doing business under other names at other locations. Although place names are typically sequenced alphabetically, geographic arrangements sometimes combine alphabetic and numeric arrangements. Records from global locations are sometimes written in the native language of the country producing the record. At the very least, city and country names are written in the native language. In some instances, the English language equivalent of the city/country name may be different. For instance, Mumbai, India is known in many U.S. organizations as Bombay, India and Firenze, Italia is known as Florence, Italy. The records are usually filed in the order of the U.S. known name, so a cross-reference to other languages is required.

The advantages of using geographic records management outweigh these disadvantages for business operations requiring information accessed by geographic location.

GEOGRAPHIC RECORDS STORAGE ARRANGEMENTS

The geographic arrangement of records in an office depends on the following:

- The type of business
- The way reference is made to records (i.e., by building, by state, by ZIP Code, by geographic region, by country)
- The geographic areas related to records

The geographic arrangement can be as simple as a file of city streets or countries of the world. More complex systems include subdivisions and are arranged in order from major to minor geographic units; for example, (1) country name, (2) state name or state equivalent (provinces, for example), (3) city name, and (4) correspondent's name. In general, the filing segment in geographic records storage includes geographic filing units first, followed by the correspondent's name. If geographic areas are subdivided by subject such as Accounts Receivable, Sales, or Purchasing, the subject area would be considered second and then the correspondent's name. Subdivisions by subject may be appropriate for centralized records in a company that maintains extensive

My Records

Organizing Photographs

How do you organize your photos? Can you find a particular photo quickly? Are your photos stored safely?

If you are like many people, you have photos both in printed and digital form. Are your printed photos in a shoe box, a drawer, or stacks on a shelf? How about your digital pictures—are they scattered on your hard drive or several removable storage devices? Are you able to find and view the photos within a few minutes when you want to see particular photos?

ORGANIZE PRINTED PHOTOS

Follow these guidelines to organize your printed photos:

- Organize your printed photos by location, subject, date, or event.

- Organize and store negatives using the same system as the printed photos.

- Store photos in plastic enclosures made of uncoated polyester, polypropylene, or polyethylene.

- Create albums of your photos using the plastic enclosures stored in a three-ring binder.

- If you place photos in a scrapbook, avoid using adhesives that may cause chemical damage to the photo. Rubber cement and self-stick "magnetic" pages are particularly damaging to photos.[2]

ORGANIZE DIGITAL PHOTOS

Follow these guidelines to organize your digital photos:

- Centralize your photos for a particular location, subject, date, or event. *Windows* creates a My Pictures folder inside the My Documents folder. Create appropriate folders inside the My Pictures folder or on your hard drive or removable storage device.

- Make a back-up copy of your picture folders to a CD or to a large flash drive.

- Use photo software that comes with your digital camera to help you organize pictures into albums.

- Internet companies have photo web sites where you can post your pictures—not all are free. Use these sites to post picturing for sharing with friends.

[2]Northeast Document Conservation Center, *Care of Photographs,* <http://www.nedcc.org/leaflets/phocar.htm> (accessed July 19, 2005).

business operations through branch offices in different locations. The location of the branch office could be subdivided by operational functions and then by correspondent names. Most likely, such centralization of records would be through centralized electronic records accessed in various company sites through an intranet.

Compass Terms

Some records and file guides in geographic filing use compass point terms. A **compass point** is any of 32 horizontal directions indicated on the card of a compass.[3] A **compass term** uses compass points as part of the company or subject name. When filing records with compass terms, each word or unit in a filing segment containing compass terms is considered a separate filing unit. If the term includes more than one compass point, the term should be treated as it is written.[4] This is same procedure you learned earlier for filing company or organization names. The table below shows examples of indexed names that contain compass terms.

Examples of Names with Compass Terms

Filing Segment	Indexing Order of Units			
Name As Written	**Key Unit**	**Unit 2**	**Unit 3**	**Unit 4**
1. North West Plumbing Inc.	North	West	Plumbing	Inc
2. North Western Imaging	North	Western	Imaging	
3. North-West Computer Co.	Northwest	Computer	Co	
4. Northwest Kitchens	Northwest	Kitchens		
5. Northwestern Refrigeration Co.	Northwestern	Refrigeration	Co	

---

[3]Dictionary.com, <http://dictionary.reference.com/search?r=2&q=compass%20point> (accessed August 30, 2005).
[4]ARMA International, *Establishing Alphabetic, Numeric and Subject Filing Systems* (Lenexa, KS: ARMA International, 2005), p. 21.

Compass terms are frequently applied to technical studies conducted by geographers, geologists, geophysicists, and other scientists studying the earth's surface. To maintain a geographically organized file in these circumstances, the compass term is treated as an adjective and is placed after the name. Again, this procedure is used **only** in scientific document filing. The table below shows examples of names that contain compass terms indexed for scientific document filing.

Who uses compass terms?

Examples of Names with Compass Terms

Filing Segment	Indexing Order of Units for Scientific Document Filing		
Name As Written	Key Unit	Unit 2	Unit 3
1. North Andreas Fault	Andreas	Fault	North
2. Northwest Mackinaw Island	Mackinaw	Island	Northwest
3. Ohio	Ohio		
4. Eastern Pacific Rim	Pacific	Rim	Eastern

Dictionary Storage Arrangement

A **dictionary arrangement** for geographic records is an arrangement of records in alphabetic order (A–Z). Use the dictionary arrangement when filing single geographic units such as all streets, all cities, all states, or all countries. Two guide plans may be used: the lettered guide plan or the location name guide plan.

Lettered Guide Plan

A **lettered guide plan** is an arrangement of geographic records with primary guides labeled with alphabetic letters. The lettered guide plan can be used in any geographic arrangement. For a large volume of records stored geographically, alphabetic guides cut storage and retrieval time by guiding the eye quickly to the correct alphabetic section of storage.

Figure 10.3 on page 286 shows a dictionary arrangement of records by country in a lettered guide plan. The primary guides are one-fifth cut lettered guides arranged in a straight line in the first file drawer position (from left to right). The general country folders are third-cut folders arranged in a straight line in the third folder tab position (far right) in the file drawer. As you can see, a lettered guide plan may be excessive in a file consisting of only a few, diverse names.

What are two commonly used guide plans?

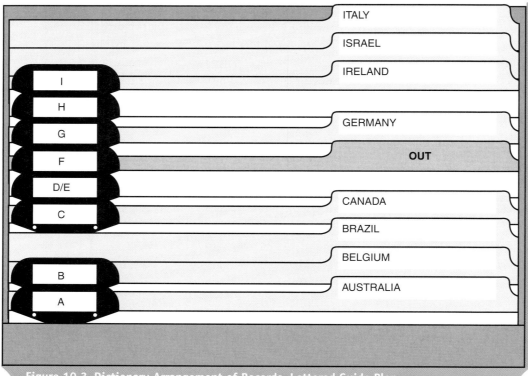

Figure 10.3 Dictionary Arrangement of Records, Lettered Guide Plan

Location Name Guide Plan

A **location name guide plan** is an arrangement of geographic records with primary guides labeled with location names. When location names are few but diverse, use the location name guide plan.

Figure 10.4 on page 287 shows a location name guide plan in a dictionary arrangement of foreign country names. The primary guides are one-fifth cut country name guides arranged in a straight line in the file drawer first position. The general country folders are one-third cut folders arranged in a straight line in the file drawer with a third-position tab location (far right side). Figures 10.3 and 10.4 show the different guide plans in a dictionary arrangement of identical records.

Encyclopedic Storage Arrangement

An **encyclopedic arrangement** is the alphabetic arrangement of major geographic divisions plus one or more geographic subdivisions also arranged in alphabetic order. Similar to the dictionary storage arrangement, the encyclopedic arrangement makes use of either a lettered guide plan or a location name guide plan.

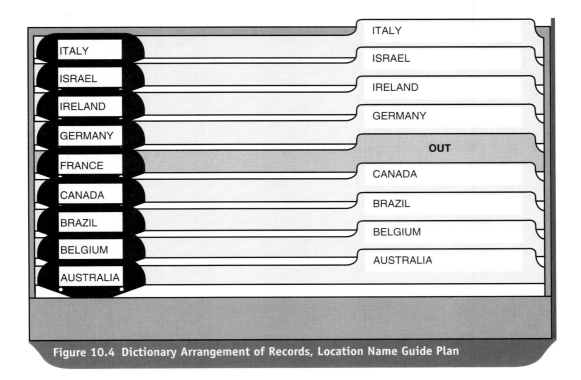

Figure 10.4 Dictionary Arrangement of Records, Location Name Guide Plan

Guides in a storage system provide sufficient guidance to speed the storage and retrieval of records. Guides should not dominate a storage area and become an efficiency barrier.

Although lettered guides with closed captions require more thought when filing (i.e., A–D, E–H, I–P), they provide a means of using fewer lettered guides. Figures 10.5 and 10.6 (pages 288 and 289) illustrate geographic records storage in an encyclopedic arrangement. Compare the guide plans used for these identical records: Figure 10.5 uses a lettered guide plan and Figure 10.6 uses a location name guide plan. The major geographic units in the illustrations are state names; the subdivisions are city names. Refer to the illustrations as you study the following detailed explanations of the file arrangements, the guide plans, and the folder contents.

Lettered Guide Plan

Figure 10.5 shows part of a drawer of New York and North Carolina records stored by the lettered guide plan. Refer to Figure 10.5 as you study the following arrangement description:

1. In first position in the drawer are fifth-cut, primary guides for the state names NEW YORK and NORTH CAROLINA, the largest geographic division in this storage plan.

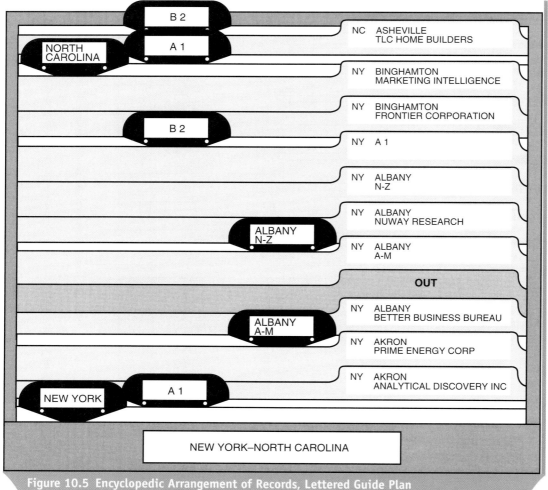

Figure 10.5 Encyclopedic Arrangement of Records, Lettered Guide Plan

2. In second position are the secondary guides. The secondary guides are fifth-cut alphabetic guides that divide the states into alphabetic sections. Each guide indicates the alphabetic section within which records with city names beginning with that letter are stored. The guide tabs are numbered consecutively so that they will be kept in correct order.

3. In third position are special guides. Special city guides indicate cities with a high volume of records. The guides ALBANY A–M and ALBANY N–Z provide a separation of correspondents' names in the city section. These guides are fifth-cut.

4. In fourth position as your eye moves left to right across the contents of the file are the folders. Folders are one-third cut, third position tab folders arranged in a straight line at the right of the file drawer. Notice the

What kinds of guides and folders are needed?

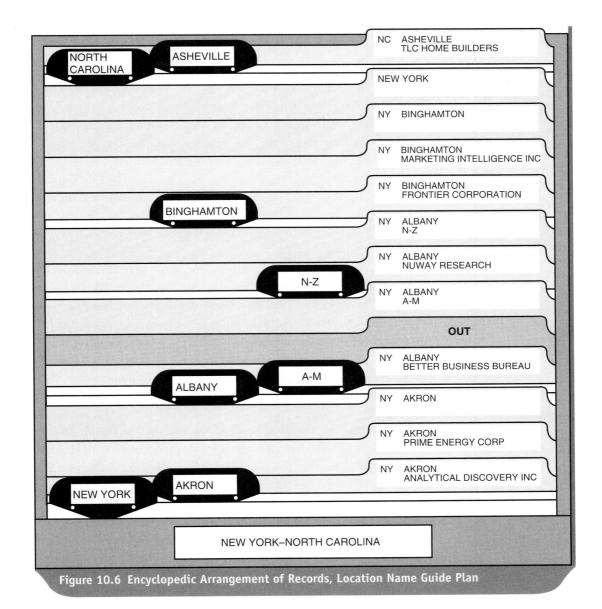

Figure 10.6 Encyclopedic Arrangement of Records, Location Name Guide Plan

three kinds of folders used in this file arrangement: general alphabetic state folders, special city folders, and individual folders.

5. Each secondary guide is accompanied by a corresponding general alphabetic city folder, which is placed at the end of that alphabetic section. The folder has the same caption as that of the secondary guide. Each general alphabetic folder contains records from correspondents located in cities with names beginning with the letter of the alphabet on the folder. For instance, the general A 1 folder might contain correspondence from organizations and individuals in New York cities such as

Adams, Akron, Alabama, and Amsterdam but not from Albany because that city has its own special city folders.

6. The special city folders accompany the special city guides (NY ALBANY A–M and NY ALBANY N–Z).

7. Individual folders for correspondents are arranged alphabetically by city and then by correspondents' names. The label caption for individual folders includes the name of the correspondent's state and city on the first line. The correspondent's name is on the second line.

8. Also in fourth position in the drawer are OUT guides. The OUT guides are third-cut, third-position guides and mark the location of a borrowed folder.

Location Name Guide Plan

Probably the most frequently used location name guide plan arrangement is one that uses state names as the first filing segment (or country names for international operations). Figure 10.6 shows part of a drawer of New York and North Carolina records stored by the location name guide plan. Refer to Figure 10.6 as you study the following arrangement description:

1. In first position in the drawer are primary guides for state names NEW YORK and NORTH CAROLINA. The guides are one-fifth cut, first-position guides.

2. In second position are city guides. AKRON is the first city guide after the NEW YORK state guide. Because the city guides stay in the drawer in their correct positions, they do not need to include the name of the state. The guides are one-fifth cut, second-position guides.

3. In third position are special lettered guides A–M and N–Z. These special guides show an alphabetic division of correspondents' names in the city of ALBANY section. Special guides speed the location of active or high-volume records. The guides are one-fifth cut, third position guides.

4. In fourth position in the drawer are all folders. General folders are shaded in the illustration to distinguish them from individual folders. The folders are one-third cut, third-position folders. Notice that a general city folder bearing the same caption as the city guide comes at the end of the folders behind each guide.

5. The general state folder for NEW YORK is at the end of the NEW YORK section. File correspondence from New York in this general state folder when no general folder for that city is in the file. Arrange the records alphabetically in the general state folder by city name first, followed by the correspondent's name. If correspondents' names are identical, use the street name and house number to determine correct order. Store all records from the same correspondent in chronologic order with the most recent record in front.

> **How are special guides used?**

6. A general city folder is used for every city guide used in the file drawer. Place the general city folder at the end of the city subdivision. ALBANY has two general city folders, one for correspondents' names beginning with A to M and a second general city folder for correspondents' names beginning with N to Z. Store all records in general city folders alphabetically by correspondent's name. Arrange records from the same correspondent with the most recent record in front. When records begin to accumulate for one correspondent, say five or more, consider opening an individual folder for that correspondent.

7. Individual folders for correspondents are arranged alphabetically by name within their state and city sections. The folder label captions include the state and city locations as well as the correspondents' names. Because folders will be removed from the file, the comprehensive caption helps to prevent misfiles when borrowed records are returned to storage. Arrange records in individual folders with the most recent record in front. Be sure to store all records in folders with the top of the document at the left of the folder.

8. Also in fourth position in the file drawer are one-third cut OUT guides, which show the location of borrowed records.

GEOGRAPHIC RECORDS STORAGE INDEXES

You are already familiar with indexes because you studied the use of alphabetic and master indexes in Chapter 8, Subject Records Management, and alphabetic indexes and accession logs in Chapter 9, Numeric Records Management. Because geographic records are arranged first by location and then by company or individual names, the correspondent's location must be known before a record can be located. If the location of a correspondent is not known, the file user must use an alphabetic index.

Numeric File List

As you learned in Chapter 9, a numeric file list, also called an accession log, is a serial list of the numbers assigned to records in a numeric storage system. The list is used to determine the next number available for assignment. In the examples described on pages 279 and 280 of this chapter, a numeric list would be used to determine the next oil well number, the next building number, the next project number, or the next equipment item number.

CAREER CORNER

Job Description for Curatorial Assistant

The following job description is an example of an opportunity to work in geographic records management in a botanical garden in the United States.

JOB TITLE

Curatorial Assistant, Botany

SALARY RANGE

$24,000.00 to $32,000.00 per year

PRINCIPAL JOB DUTIES

- Work with curators and collection manager to plan for each phase of projects including preparing storage plan for specimens.
- Assist in the reorganization of the herbarium to streamline the taxonomic and geographic filing system.
- Implement the plan devised with curators and collection manager. This will include moving herbarium specimens in an organized fashion to temporary storage, placing specimens into newly renovated areas, reorganizing the taxonomic and geographic filing system, and tracking the status of the specimens.
- Supervise the work of students and volunteers who will help with above.
- Help with routine herbarium management tasks including processing loans, making labels, mounting plants, accessioning specimens, filing specimens using the geographic filing system, and preparing specimens for freezing.

QUALIFICATIONS

- A college degree and some expertise in botany are preferred. The ideal candidate will know enough about plant identification to recognize likely errors in filing and identification.
- Experience working in a herbarium and with specimens is preferred; familiarity with computers and database programs is highly desirable; good organization skills and attention to detail are essential; ability to work both independently and collaboratively with a diversity of colleagues is required.
- Must be organized and familiar with scientific plant names and other biological information, geography, and geographic filing systems. Must be accurate and efficient in data entry of botanical and geographic information.

Alphabetic Index

The alphabetic index lists all correspondents or subjects in geographic storage. This index can be a computer database index or a printed list.

For numeric files, the alphabetic index includes the assigned file codes for records stored in a numbered file. The index would include an entry for each of the identification numbers assigned to each file (i.e., account number, oil well number, customer number). Figure 10.7 shows an example of the alphabetic index for numeric geographic files.

However the index is maintained, the index must be easy to update and keep current. Names or subjects will be added, deleted, or changed. The index should include appropriate information. For example, in an alphabetic index, the correspondent's name and full address or the full subject name should be used. Figure 10.8 on page 294 is a database alphabetic index for geographic records storage. The correspondents' names are in alphabetic order in column one. The state, city, and street locations are shown in the remaining columns. All correspondents are listed in the index, including correspondents whose records are stored in general city and state folders.

When the information for an index is stored in a database, users can access an individual name on the screen without looking for the name on a printed list. Even with the capability to check electronic indexes, a printed copy of the index should be available.

Why is an alphabetic index needed?

Master Index

A master index is a complete listing of all filing segments in the filing system. Figure 10.9 on page 294 is a database master index for correspondents. States were sorted first, then the city names, and finally the correspondents' names.

The master index shows at a glance the geographic units covered in the filing system and is especially useful to new file users. A printed copy of the index is kept in the front of the file drawer or another readily accessible location.

What is a master index?

Alphabetic Index for Oil Wells	
Oil Well	**Number**
Harris County, Texas, Oil well #12345	42-501-12345
Harris County, Texas, Oil well #13567	42-501-13567
Jones County, Oklahoma, Oil well #6789	40-403-6789
Rainer Parish, Louisiana, Oil well #2468	45-203-2468

Figure 10.7 Alphabetic Index for Numeric Geographic Files

Alphabetic Index

Indexed Name	State	City	Bldg	Street	See Also
Analytical Discovery Inc	NY	Akron	4873	Center St.	
Armor Supply Center	NY	Cortland	1601	Fourth St.	
Better Business Bureau	NC	Asheville	389	Main St.	NY Albany
Better Business Bureau	NY	Albany	150	Rowan St.	NC Asheville
Computer Magic	NY	Geneseo	38	Main St.	
Echo Power Equipment	NY	Cherokee	174	Military Rd.	
Frontier Corporation	NY	Binghamton	20	Shuman Blvd.	
Kerry Company The	NY	Albany	204	Delaware Ave.	
Marketing Intelligence Inc	NY	Binghampton	451	Dunbar Rd.	
Nuway Research	NY	Albany	44	Broadway	
Prime Energy Corp	NY	Akron	2470	Miles Rd.	
TLC Home Builders	NC	Asheville	20	River Dr.	

Figure 10.8 Alphabetic Index for Geographic Files

Master Index

State	City	Indexed Name	Bldg	Street
NC	Asheville	Better Business Bureau	389	Main St.
NC	Asheville	TLC Home Builders	20	River Dr.
NY	Akron	Analytical Discovery Inc	4873	Center St.
NY	Akron	Prime Energy Corp	2470	Miles Rd.
NY	Albany	Better Business Bureau	150	Rowan St.
NY	Albany	Kerry Company The	204	Delaware Ave.
NY	Albany	Nuway Research	44	Broadway
NY	Bath	Marketing Intelligence Inc	451	Dunbar Rd.
NY	Binghamton	Frontier Corporation	20	Shuman Blvd.
NY	Cherokee	Echo Power Equipment	174	Military Rd.
NY	Cortland	Armor Supply Center	1601	Fourth St.
NY	Geneseo	Computer Magic	38	Main St.

Figure 10.9 Master Index for Geographic Files

If the alphabetic index is prepared with database software and names are kept updated, queries can be created for viewing or printing an updated alphabetic or master index at any time; or an individual record can be viewed or printed. Other software packages that allow resorting and moving of columns can also produce a master index.

GEOGRAPHIC RECORDS STORAGE AND RETRIEVAL PROCEDURES

Supplies used in the geographic method are similar to those used in other storage methods. These supplies consist of guides, folders, and OUT indicators. You may want to review the section on filing supplies in Chapter 6 before continuing with the discussion of storage and retrieval procedures.

The same basic steps for storing records in alphabetic, subject, and numeric methods (inspecting, indexing, coding, cross-referencing, sorting, and storing) are also followed in the geographic method. Minor differences are explained in the following paragraphs. Retrieval procedures (requisitioning, charging out, and following up) are also basically the same.

Inspecting and Indexing

Check to see that the record has been released for storage (inspect) and scan the letter for content to determine its proper place in storage (index). In Figure 10.10 on page 296, the handwritten letters *JK* indicate that the letter is released for storage.

Coding

Code the document for geographic storage by marking the correspondents' *location* (address) first. Code by underlining the filing segment (see Figure 10.10, Raleigh, NC). Write numbers above or below the filing segment to show the order of indexing and alphabetizing units. Then code the name of the correspondent by underlining the name, placing diagonals between the units, and numbering the succeeding units. Figure 10.10 shows a letter coded for the geographic storage method.

After coding documents, consult the alphabetic index to see if the correspondent is currently in the system. If not, add the new correspondent's name and address to the index.

3 4 5
Stratford/Group,/Inc.
Educational Consultants

2 1
49 Kimberly Lane, Raleigh, /NC 76000-4127
PHONE: (919) 555-0143 FAX: (919) 555-0123

May 4, 20--

MAY 07, 20-- 11:05 A.M.

Dr. Michael L. Kelley
Alfred State College
Alfred, NY 14802-3643

Dear Dr. Kelley

Your request for 50 brochures explaining in detail the programmed learning
materials we have available for use in summer workshop programs has been
referred to our Burbank, California, office.

Interest in this exciting and novel material has been extremely high, and we are
pleased that professors are finding it so worthwhile. Because of the extraordinary
number of requests for this brochure, it is temporarily out of stock. We expect a
new supply within the next two weeks, however, and will send you 50 copies as
soon as we receive them.

Thanks for letting us provide you with helpful materials for your workshop.

Sincerely   JK

Johandra Linfoot

Johandra Linfoot
Educational Consultant

dw

2 /1
Branch Office: 2964 Broadway, Burbank,/CA 91500-1217 X

Figure 10.10 Letter Coded for Geographic Filing

Cross-Referencing

Cross-referencing is as necessary in the geographic storage method as it is in the alphabetic or numeric storage methods. In Chapters 2, 3, and 4, personal and business names are listed that may require cross-references. In this chapter, additional cross-references may be needed for (1) names of organizations having more than one address, and (2) organizations located at one address and doing business under other names at other locations. When a foreign country name is translated into its English equivalent, a cross-reference to the other language is also required.

In the geographic storage method, insert cross-references in both the alphabetic or numeric index and the storage file. In the numeric index, prepare an entry for each of the identification numbers assigned to each file (i.e., account number, oil well number, customer number). In the alphabetic index, prepare an entry for every name by which a correspondent may be known or by which records may be requested. For the letter shown in Figure 10.10, a cross-reference shows a branch office located in another city. A filer might look for a record from the Stratford Group, Inc. in either of these two locations.

In the file, three types of cross-references can be used: (1) cross-reference sheets that are stored in folders to refer the filer to specific records, (2) cross-reference guides that are placed in storage as permanent cross-references, and (3) SEE ALSO cross-reference notations on sheets or on folder tabs. Each of these cross-references is explained in the following paragraphs.

A **cross-reference sheet** is a sheet placed in an alternate location in the file that directs the filer to a specific record stored in a different location other than where the filer is searching. The cross-reference sheet in Figure 10.11 on page 298 is made for the branch office indicated on the letter shown in Figure 10.10. The original letter is stored in the N section of geographic storage (NORTH CAROLINA), but the cross-reference sheet is stored in the C section (CALIFORNIA).

A **cross-reference guide** is a special guide that serves as a permanent marker in storage indicating that all records pertaining to a correspondent are stored elsewhere. For example, the cross-reference guide in Figure 10.12 on page 298 shows that all records for Lockwood, Inc. are stored under the home office location in Ann Arbor, MI, not the branch office location in St. Clair Shores, MI. The words *Ann Arbor* must be written on each record when it is coded. The cross-reference guide is stored according to the location on the top line of its caption in alphabetic order with other geographically labeled guides and folders.

A **SEE ALSO cross-reference** is a notation on a folder tab or cross-reference sheet that directs the filer to multiple locations for related information. If a company has two addresses and records are stored under both addresses, two SEE ALSO cross-references would be used. For example, if Windsor Publishing

What names require cross-referencing?

How are SEE ALSO cross-references prepared?

CROSS-REFERENCE SHEET

Name or Subject

2
_CA_ /Burbank
3   4   5
Stratford / Group, / Inc.
2964 Broadway

Date of Record

May 4, 20--

Regarding

Program learning materials for summer workshop

SEE

Name or Subject

NC Raleigh
Stratford Group, Inc.
49 Kimberly Lane.

Date Filed _5/7/20 - -_   **By** _J K_

Figure 10.11 Cross-Reference Sheet for Geographic Method

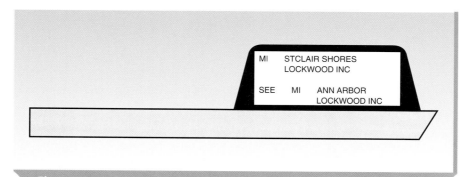

MI   STCLAIR SHORES
        LOCKWOOD INC

SEE   MI   ANN ARBOR
                LOCKWOOD INC

Figure 10.12 Cross-Reference Guide for Geographic Method

Co., Inc. conducts business in Houston, TX, and also in Milan, Italy, the references would indicate that information for this company can be found in two storage locations. If these SEE ALSO cross-references are sheets of paper, they are kept as the first items in their respective folders so that they will not be overlooked (see Figures 10.13 and 10.14 on pages 299 and 300). Instead of being written on separate cross-reference sheets, this SEE ALSO information may be keyed on the tabs of the two folders for the Windsor Publishing Co., Inc. (see Figure 10.15 on page 300). Figure 10.16 on page 301 shows a cross-reference entry in a database record.

> How does this cross-reference sheet differ from the one shown in Figure 10.11?

CROSS-REFERENCE SHEET

Name or Subject

2
TX / Houston
3   4   5   6
Windsor / Publishing / Co., / Inc.

1313 North Sixth Street

Date of Record

Regarding

SEE ALSO

Name or Subject

TX Wichita Falls
Windsor Publishing Co., Inc.
2264 Evanston Avenue

Date Filed *11/4/20 - -*   **By** *J K*

Figure 10.13 Cross-Reference Sheet for SEE ALSO References

CROSS-REFERENCE SHEET

Name or Subject

$\quad\quad\quad$ 2 $\quad\quad\quad$ 3

TX / Wichita / Falls

$\quad$ 4 $\quad\quad\quad$ 5 $\quad\quad$ 6 $\quad$ 7

Windsor / Publishing / Co., / Inc.

2264 Evanston Avenue

Date of Record

Regarding

SEE ALSO

Name or Subject

TX Houston

Windsor Publishing Co., Inc.

1313 North Sixth Street

Date Filed $\quad$ _11/4/20 - -_ $\quad\quad$ By $\quad$ _J K_

Figure 10.14 Cross-Reference Sheet for SEE ALSO References

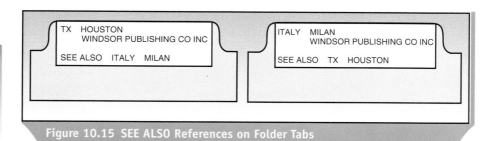

TX   HOUSTON
$\quad\quad$ WINDSOR PUBLISHING CO INC

SEE ALSO   ITALY   MILAN

ITALY   MILAN
$\quad\quad$ WINDSOR PUBLISHING CO INC

SEE ALSO   TX   HOUSTON

Figure 10.15 SEE ALSO References on Folder Tabs

What is the advantage to placing SEE ALSO cross-reference information on folder labels?

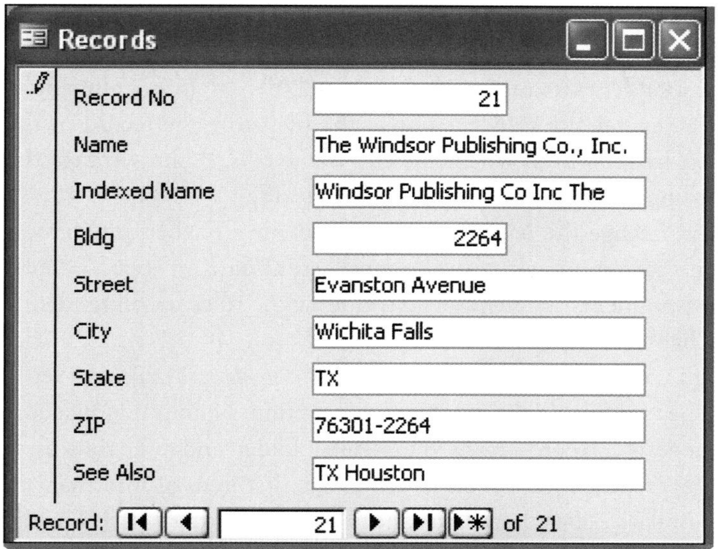

Records

Record No	21
Name	The Windsor Publishing Co., Inc.
Indexed Name	Windsor Publishing Co Inc The
Bldg	2264
Street	Evanston Avenue
City	Wichita Falls
State	TX
ZIP	76301-2264
See Also	TX Houston

Record: 21 of 21

Figure 10.16 Cross-Reference in a Database Record

Sorting

Sort records numerically by file code or alphabetically by location. If alphabetic, sort first by the largest geographic unit such as country or state name; then sort by the first subdivision such as state equivalent or city; finally sort by the names of the correspondents, in alphabetic order.

Storing

Individual correspondents' folders, special city folders, alphabetic subdivisions of cities with their corresponding general folders, general folders for alphabetic grouping of cities, and general state or regional folders may be part of a geographic records storage arrangement. Therefore, placing a record in the wrong folder is easy to do. Because of the complexity of a geographic arrangement, be extremely careful when storing.

Lettered Guide Plan

Assuming that the alphabetic arrangement is by state and city, look for the primary state guide. Then use the lettered guides to locate the alphabetic state section within which the city name falls. After finding that section, look for an individual correspondent's folder. If you find one, store the record in that folder in chronologic order with the most recent record on top.

If an individual folder for the correspondent is not in the file, look for a general city folder. If a general city folder is in the file, store the record according to the correspondent's name in the same manner as in an alphabetic arrangement. If a general city folder is not in the file, store the record in the general alphabetic folder within which the city name falls. Again, arrange the city names according to the rules for alphabetic indexing.

Within a city, arrange the names of correspondents alphabetically; group the records of one correspondent with the most recent date on top. If identically named correspondents reside in one city, follow the rules for filing identical names (see Chapter 4 for review).

When enough correspondence has accumulated to warrant making a separate folder for a specific city, a specific geographic section, or an individual correspondent, remove the records from the general folder and prepare a new folder with the geographic location on its tab as the first item of information. Then prepare a similarly labeled guide, if one is needed, for the folder. Finally, place the folder and guide in their alphabetic positions in storage.

Although requirements for preparing a separate folder for a specific geographic location vary, a good rule of thumb is this: When five or more records accumulate that pertain to one specific geographic location (such as a state, city, or a region), prepare a separate folder for that location.

What procedures are followed to create a folder for an individual correspondent?

Location Name Guide Plan

Again, assuming that the arrangement is by state and city, find the primary state guide and look for the correct city name on a secondary guide. If a city guide is present, search for an individual correspondent's folder. If one exists, store the record in the folder according to date.

If an individual folder is not in the file, store the record in the correct general city folder according to the geographic location of the correspondent and then by name, in alphabetic order with the other records within the folder. If more than one record is stored for a correspondent, arrange the records chronologically with the most recent date on top.

If a general city folder is not in the file, place the record in the general state folder, first according to the alphabetic order of the city name and then by correspondent's name and street address (if necessary), according to the rules for alphabetic indexing.

Retrieving

Retrieving a record from a geographic file involves these five steps:

What are the retrieval procedures?

1. Asking for the record (requisition)
2. Checking the alphabetic or numeric index to determine the location of the record
3. Removing the record from the files
4. Completing charge-out documentation for the record
5. Following up to see that the record is returned to storage within a specified time

Requisition

Requests for a record stored by geographic arrangement may identify it by location, by numeric file code, or by correspondent's name. If the request is made by location, finding the record should be simple. If the request is made by name or number, however, refer to the alphabetic index or a computer database to locate the file used to store the record.

Charge-Out

After you have located and retrieved the record, charge it out in the same manner that you charge out records from any other storage method. Be sure to insert an OUT indicator at the storage position of the record. A Charge-Out field can be added in a records database and shown in the alphabetic index.

Follow-Up

The follow-up procedures used to secure the return of borrowed records are the same for the geographic method as those used with any other storage method. Use a tickler file or another reminder system to be sure that records are returned to storage at designated times and to remind yourself of records that need to be brought to someone's attention in the future. If OUT information is recorded in a database table, this information can be sorted by date and used as a tickler file.

Chapter Review And Applications

POINTS TO FILE AND RETRIEVE

- Geographic records management is grouping and storing records by location.

- Companies that need information by location to make good business decisions are likely to choose geographic records management. This filing method is important to multi-location businesses as well as specialized fields such as natural sciences, the oil and gas industry, and the facility management profession.

- Many geographic filing systems are used to support an internal geographic information system.

- Geographic records storage requires a more complex system of guides and folders than other types of records storage, and storing and retrieving records can be more time consuming.

- Some records and files in geographic filing use compass point terms which require the use of unique filing rules.

- Two basic arrangements are commonly used in geographic storage: the dictionary arrangement and the encyclopedic arrangement. The arrangement used depends on whether subdivisions of the geographic units are necessary.

- Either the lettered guide plan or the location name guide plan can be used. Whether the files contain a small number of diverse names or a large number of similar names will likely determine the guide plan.

- Because geographic records are arranged first by location, then by company or subject, and then by individual names, the correspondent's location must be known before a record can be located.

- An alphabetic index lists all correspondents or subjects in geographic storage. For numeric files, the alphabetic index includes the assigned file codes for records stored in a numbered file.

- A master index, which shows at a glance the geographic units covered in the filing system, is also helpful and is especially useful to new file users.

- Except for indexing and coding, the storage and retrieval procedures for geographic records storage are similar to those used for other storage methods.

- Indexing and coding require looking first at the location of the document and then at the name, the document subject, or project title being stored.

- Cross-references should be placed in both the alphabetic index and the storage file.

IMPORTANT TERMS

compass point

compass terms

cross-reference guide

cross-reference sheet

dictionary arrangement

encyclopedic arrangement

geographic records management

geographic filing system

geographic information system

lettered guide plan

location name guide plan

SEE ALSO cross-reference

REVIEW AND DISCUSSION

1. Why is it important to arrange records by location? (Obj. 1)

2. Name three kinds of businesses that are likely to use the geographic method of storage. (Obj. 2)

3. What are the advantages and disadvantages of the geographic storage method? (Obj. 3)

4. Explain how the dictionary and encyclopedic arrangements of geographic records differ. (Obj.4)

5. Explain the difference between the lettered guide plan and the location name guide plan. (Obj. 5)

6. Describe the arrangement of guides and folders in an encyclopedic arrangement of a geographic file using the lettered guide plan. The geographic units covered in the arrangement are state names and city names. (Obj. 6)

7. Explain how an alphabetic index is used in geographic records storage. (Obj. 7)

8. Explain how indexing and coding for the geographic method are different from indexing and coding for the alphabetic method of records storage. (Obj. 8)

9. List three types of cross-references used in the geographic method and state where they are placed or stored in the filing system. (Obj. 9)

10. When may files be arranged using compass terms? How does using compass terms to arrange files differ from general alphabetic filing methods? (Obj. 10)

APPLICATIONS

10-1 SELECTING A GEOGRAPHIC ARRANGEMENT (OBJS. 4, 5, AND 6)

CRITICAL THINKING

For each of the following scenarios, identify the most efficient geographic arrangements and explain the reasons for your choices. Identification of this arrangement should include as many of the following elements as appropriate: major and minor geographic units, encyclopedic or dictionary arrangement, lettered guide plan or location name guide plan.

1. A large aerospace company keeps its facility and equipment maintenance records by building code. The buildings and equipment include:
   Assembly Plant: Belt 1, Belt 2, Motor 456, Motor 123, Lathe 3
   Research Center: Computer 72, Mega Server 6, Small printer, Large printer
   Fire Station: Hose 3, Hose 5, Extinguisher 23, Ladder 9
   North Testing Laboratory: Oven 17, Microscope 43, Centrifuge 12
   South Testing Laboratory: Oven 18, Microscope 21, Centrifuge 5

2. The home office of a large food processing/packing plant is located in Iowa. The company maintains correspondence and records to branch offices in three regions of the United States—Western, Northeast, and South Central—as well as in Japan, Canada, and England.

3. A newspaper publisher in Scranton, PA, maintains a file of all streets in the city. The street name file identifies paper carriers who distribute home delivery to those locations. The newspaper also has mail subscribers in the states of Pennsylvania, New York, Ohio, and West Virginia.

4. A garment manufacturer maintains records by its operations in ten cities. City locations include the following:

   United States
   Los Angeles, CA
   Philadelphia, PA
   Detroit, MI

   Canada
   Calgary, Alberta
   Montréal, Quebec
   London, Ontario

   Central America
   Managua, Nicaragua
   León, Nicaragua

   South America
   Cuernavaca, Morelos, Mexico
   Zamora, Michoacan, Mexico

10-2 COMPASS TERMS (OBJ. 10)

1. Assume the names listed below are to be filed in a scientific document file that uses compass terms. Key or write each name and indicate the indexing order. The indexing order of the first name is shown below as an example. Number the names to show the order in which they would be placed in the files.

Key Unit	Unit 2	Unit 3
Mackinaw	Island	Southwest

a. East Cumberland Lake
b. Eastern Shore Park
c. East Avon Park
d. North River Preserve
e. Northern Plateau

f. Southwest Mackinaw Island
g. Northern Ohio Fault
h. East Ridder Fault
i. Western Pacific Rim

2. Assume the names listed above are to be filed in an alphabetic subject file (not a scientific document file). Key or write each name and indicate the indexing order. Number the names to show the order in which they would be placed in the files.

10-3 GEOGRAPHIC INDEXES (OBJS. 8 AND 9)

1. Create a new *Access* database file named *CH10 Indexes*. Create a table named **Records.** Create the following fields in the table and set the primary key.

ACCESS ACTIVITY

Field Name	Field Type
Record No	Number (primary key)
Name	Text
Indexed Name	Text
Bldg	Number
Street	Text
City	Text
State	Text
ZIP	Text
See Also	Text

2. Enter records for names shown on page 308 in the Records table. For names with more than one address, enter each record separately and enter cross-reference information in the See Also field. (This information may seem unnecessary when all records are viewed. When an individual record or a subset of the records is viewed, however, this data alerts users that the same name is filed in another location.)

3. Create a query named **Alphabetic Index** based on the Records table. Include the Indexed Name, State, City, Bldg, Street, and See Also field in the query results. Design the query to sort by Indexed Name, then by State, then by City, and then by Street fields. Print the query results table.

4. Create a query named **Master Index** based on the Records table. Include the State, City, Indexed Name, Bldg, Street, and See Also fields. Design the query to sort by State, then by City, then by Indexed Name, and then by Street fields. Print the query results table.

Records:

Record No	Name and Address	Record No	Name and Address
1	John Powers Electronics 24 Delaware Ave. Rochester, NY 14623-2944	11	Wilkes Tree Farm 400 Stanton Christiana Rd. Newark, DE 19713-0401
2	Indian River Community College 3209 Virginia Ave. Fort Pierce, FL 34982-3209	12	Beverly Plumbing 1000 Gordon Rd. Rochester, NY 14623-1089
3	Computer Land, Inc. 30 Shepherd Rd. Springfield, IL 62708-0101	13	Electric City, Inc. 3201 Southwest Traffic Way Kansas City, MO 64111-3201
4	Portland Cement Co. 12000 Lakeville Rd. Portland, OR 97219-4233	14	Abba D Plumbing 901 S. National Ave. Springfield, MO 65804-0910
5	Penn Valley Community College 3300 Southwest Traffic Way Kansas City, MO 64111-3300	15	Pioneer Center Furniture 560 Westport Rd. Kansas City, MO 64111-0568
6	Cerre Ceramic Studios 7250 State Ave. Kansas City, KS 66112-7255	16	Amy's Sports Center 874 Dillingham Blvd. Honolulu, HI 96817-8743
7	Toby Leese Tack Shop 175 University Ave. Newark, NJ 07102-1175	17	Genesis Cinema 1325 Lynch St. Jackson, MS 39203-1325
8	John Powers Electronics 10 State St. Rochester, NY 14623-2944	18	Computer Magic 84 Center St. Springfield, MA 01101-2028
9	City Office Supplies 4281 Drake St. Rochester, MI 48306-0698	19	Computer Magic 24 Fourth Ave. New York, NY 10018-4826
10	Armstrong State College 11935 Abercorn St. Savannah, GA 31419-1092	20	The Computer Store 2847 14th St. New York, NY 10018-2032

10-4 RESEARCH GEOGRAPHIC FILING USES (OBJS. 1 AND 2)

INTERNET

1. Access a search engine on the Internet. Search using the exact phrase *geographic filing system*.

2. From the results list, find sites for at least two businesses or institutions that describe their use of a geographic filing system. Do not include course outlines or course descriptions at colleges or universities.

3. Follow the links to the business or institution web site. Read and summarize the use of a geographic filing system for the business or institution.

4. Send an e-mail to your instructor with a summary of your findings.

RECORDS MANAGEMENT SIMULATION

JOB 13 GEOGRAPHIC FILING

Continue working with Auric Systems, Inc.
Complete Job 13.

FOR MORE ACTIVITIES GO TO **http://read.swlearning.com**

Technology and the RIM Program

| Chapter 11 | Electronic and Image Records |
| Chapter 12 | The Records and Information Management Program |

Electronic records may be stored on magnetic or optical media. Optical media is an electronic and image media. Image media, such as microforms, may be scanned and viewed on a computer screen. Because of this close relationship between electronic and image records media, the storage and retrieval capabilities of the records and information management function is greatly expanded. Records and information management (RIM) departments are able to provide a wide array of services to meet the needs of an organization.

A well-developed and managed RIM program includes policies for sending and storing e-mail messages, retention and disposition, and disaster preparedness and prevention.

Electronic and Image Records

Learning Objectives

1. Define *electronic record* and *image record* and describe the relationship between the two records media.

2. Define *magnetic media* and *optical media* and list three types of each media.

3. List data input devices and discuss storage and retrieval procedures for electronic media.

4. Discuss issues that affect records retention—duplicate records, media compatibility and stability, access, and e-mail.

5. Discuss retention for active and inactive electronic records.

6. Discuss records safety and security.

7. List and describe four types of microforms and four factors related to microfilm quality.

8. Discuss microfilming procedures and equipment.

9. Discuss microfilm processing and duplicating equipment and commercial imaging services.

10. Describe microform storage, retrieval, and storage environments.

11. Discuss retention for image records.

12. Discuss RIM software for electronic and image records.

13. Add records to an electronic and image records database and print a report.

14. Search the Internet for information on electronic and image records topics.

THE RELATIONSHIP BETWEEN ELECTRONIC AND IMAGE RECORDS

How are electronic and image records related?

Although some records are stored only on electronic media, image records may be stored on image media or on electronic media. Most paper records can be stored on electronic or image media. However, some larger image records, such as medical testing films, movies, and photographs, are stored on electronic media because of the larger storage capacity of such media.

An **electronic record** is a record stored on electronic storage media that can be readily accessed or changed. An electronic record is often referred to as a *machine-readable record*—digitized and coded information that must be translated by a computer or other type of equipment before it can be understood. An **image record** is a digital or photographic representation of a record on any medium such as microfilm or optical disk.

Electronic records may contain quantitative data, text, images, or sounds that originate as an electronic signal. A memorandum created with word processing software and stored as a computer file is an electronic record. A printed copy of that memorandum is not an electronic record; it is a paper record. A database index of a subject filing system is an electronic record. A computer-generated copy of the subject index printed on paper or microfiche is not an electronic record.

> **What is a machine-readable record?**

ELECTRONIC MEDIA

Electronic media include magnetic media and optical media. Optical media are also electronic image media. Magnetic recording is the most widely used technology for video and audio recordings. Magnetic media can store and retrieve a document faster than other storage media. Because the moving parts of magnetic media are subject to failure, backups are regularly scheduled. When erased or damaged, data on magnetic media can be restored from backups.

> **What is the most widely used medium for video and audio recordings?**

Magnetic and Optical Media

Magnetic media are a variety of magnetically coated materials used by computers for data storage. Types of widely used magnetic media are listed in Figure 11.1 on page 314. **Optical media** is a high-density information storage medium where digitally encoded information is both written and read by means of a laser. Optical media include optical disks, compact disks (CDs), computer output to laser disk (COLD), digital videodisks (DVDs), and optical cards. An optical disk is a platter-shaped disk coated with optical recording material.

The floppy disk is enclosed in a plastic case. Diskettes are widely used removable magnetic disks for microcomputers. The hard disk is usually called a *hard drive* because the storage device and the recording medium are considered as one unit. Hard disks in a variety of storage capacities are installed into most microcomputers. They may also be removable external drives as discussed later in this chapter.

Magnetic tape on reels or in cartridges is often used for storing backups of data. Magnetic tape is a preferred long-term and archival storage medium. RAID configurations provide mass storage with the advantage of spreading

---

MAGNETIC MEDIA

- Floppy disk, or diskette—A piece of round plastic that stores data and records by electromagnetic charges.
- Hard disk—A thin, rigid metal platter covered with a substance that holds data in the form of magnetized spots.
- Magnetic tape—A long strip of polyester film coated with magnetizable recording material, capable of storing information in the form of electromagnetic signals.
- Redundant array of independent disks (RAID)—A computer storage system consisting of over 100 hard disk drives contained in a single cabinet that simultaneously send data to a computer over parallel paths.
- Videotape—A magnetic tape on which visual images are electronically recorded, with or without sound.

Figure 11.1 Magnetic Media

---

data across an array of hard drives, which reduces the chance that if one drive fails, all data will be lost. Desktop units are also available. Videotapes are used for recording personal activities and television programming.

Electronic document formats include digitized images generated by document scanners and character-coded data or text produced by word processing software, e-mail systems, or other computer programs. Each format (paper, photographic, and electronic) has distinct attributes that can satisfy specific life-cycle and records retention requirements. However, no format is superior in every circumstance.

Optical disks are electronic image media. The high storage capacity and durability of optical disks allow the capture of text as well as graphic, photographic, and animation images for viewing on a computer screen. More commonly used types of optical disks are listed in Figure 11.2 on page 315.

CD-ROM disks were developed first for audio storage, and they gradually evolved to data storage. Additional CD formats—CD-R (recordable) and CD-RW (rewritable)—have contributed more options for records and information management storage applications. CDs provide safe and reliable media that can store images for long periods of time, sometimes up to 100 years. CDs store databases, documents, directories, publications, and archival records that do not need alteration. CDs do not require special hardware or software to retrieve information; however, the storage capacity is limited. A standard CD can hold from 12,000 to 15,000 documents. Because CDs can be stored in a jukebox that can hold as many as 500 CDs, a larger number of documents can be stored on a large number of CDs.

> **What is the difference between a CD-R disk and a CD-RW disk?**

OPTICAL MEDIA

- Compact disk–read-only memory (CD-ROM) disk—A high-density digital disk storage medium that can be read only. It cannot be written on.
- Compact disk–recordable (CD-R) disk—A write-once optical disk.
- Compact disk–rewritable (CD-RW) disk—An erasable optical disk.
- Computer output to laser disk (COLD)—A technique for the transfer of computer-generated output to optical disk so that it can be viewed or printed without using the original program.
- Digital videodisk or digital versatile disk (DVD)—A read-only optical storage medium that stores approximately 130 minutes of full-motion video.
- Digital videodisk-Recordable (DVD-R)—A recordable DVD.
- Digital videodisk-rewritable (DVD-RW)—A rewritable DVD.
- Optical card—A small electronic device about the size of a credit card that contains electronic memory and possibly an imbedded integrated circuit. This card is also known as an *optical memory card,* an *optical digital data card,* and a *smart card.*

Figure 11.2 Optical Media

COLD technology combines the capabilities of scanning paper documents created on another system and linking them to COLD documents (computer-created records saved by laser to optical disks). This combination of digital image scanning of paper documents, optical disk storage, and search capabilities of database software facilitates development of a computerized records storage and retrieval system for both active and long-term records. Full-motion video requires huge amounts of storage space. One solution to the high-storage capacity needed for multimedia is the digital videodisk (DVD). DVDs are also used in some long-term data storage applications. DVD-R and DVD-RW media have extended their use to include data storage.

Smart cards may be used for secure access to buildings, for student IDs, and to store automobile service histories. They may be preloaded with specific currency amounts for use in ATMs and debit card purchases. When that amount is depleted, the card may be reloaded with the same or a larger amount. Optical memory cards are currently being used to store medical images and personal medical records; for high-security driver's licenses and access/entry cards; and for immigrant ID cards.

Removable Data Storage Devices

When fixed magnetic disks become full, they must be replaced with higher capacity drives or additional hard drives must be purchased. A large-capacity external hard drive is shown in Figure 11.3. External ZIP™ drives, especially those with USB cables, are used for backing up computer files and graphics. Using hard drives with removable media or using external hard drives has several advantages:

What are the advantages of using removable disks?

- Removable media can be stored in locked cabinets, vaults, or other secure locations to prevent unauthorized access.
- Removable disks can be used in other computer systems with compatible drives.
- Removable disks can be used to back up conventional hard drives and to restore electronic records if a hard drive fails.
- Removable hard disks can be used with an identical device if a removable hard drive fails.

Why use a flash drive instead of another type of external hard drive?

Small portable drives, such as flash drives, make carrying data for use on multiple computers very easy. A **flash drive** is a read write device that attaches to a computer and is usable as a standard hard drive. The drive consists of a small printed circuit board encased in a hard plastic covering as shown in Figure 11.4 on page 317. These devices are provided by a variety of vendors and have various names. Storage capacities range from 128 MB to 4 GB. They may be carried in pockets, attached to key rings, or worn around the neck. They can plug into a USB port directly, or attached to a lanyard plugged into a USB

Courtesy of Maxtor Corporation

Figure 11.3 Removable Hard Drive

Courtesy of Hewlett-Packard

Figure 11.4 Flash Drive

port. A **lanyard** is a cord that can be attached to the USB port on a microcomputer or laptop.[1] A desktop docking station is available for some flash drives. Fingerprint recognition for security is available on some flash drive models as well. Flash drives may be used to carry files to another computer for working in another location or to back up computer data. With sufficient memory, a flash drive can be used to back up an entire microcomputer hard drive.

Data Input

Computer data entry most often is done through a computer keyboard. However, other input devices such as scanners, bar codes, optical character recognition (OCR), fax machines, and various handheld devices are also used. Remember that hard disks, floppy disks, and other removable disks are also input devices. With voice-recognition software and a microphone, users may enter data by dictating letters, memos, messages, or other documents into a computer or by speaking commands to a computer. This technology is especially helpful to individuals who do not have full use of their hands.

A **scanner** is a device that converts an image (text, graphic, or photograph) of a document into electronic form for processing and storage. A scanner passes light over a document or object and converts it to dark and light dots that become digital code. Scanners may be handheld devices that are passed

Where are bar codes used in addition to RIM data input?

How does a scanner enter data?

[1]"USB Flash Drive," *Wikipedia, The Free Encyclopedia,* <http://en.wikipedia.org/wiki/Flash_drive> (accessed May 25, 2005).

over an item to be entered or desktop models that scan a document from a flat surface. A desktop scanner is shown in Figure 11.5. A desktop document scanner used in RIM applications must have an automatic document feeder, which will allow a stack of paper to be placed into a tray and automatically brought into the scanner one page at a time. Scanners that do not have an automatic document feeder are designed for graphics and require each page to be manually placed onto the scanner.

Bar code and radio frequency identification (RFID) technology, previously discussed in Chapters 6 and 7, are also types of scanned data entry. *Bar code* is a coding system consisting of vertical lines or bars set in a predetermined pattern that, when read by an optical reader, can be converted into machine-readable language. In records and information management, bar codes and RFID tags are used for tracking locations of documents, files, or boxes of records. With bar code software, users can print labels from a computer or from a dedicated bar code printer. Bar code labels are placed onto each document or onto the first page of a multipage document that is scanned into a computer. With appropriate software, scanned documents can be separated and assigned to folders much faster than can be done manually. Information assigned to the bar codes can be used for indexing, tracking, and retrieval. Bar codes and RFID tags are also used to check out items in libraries, to record items shipped and received, and to record items stocked on shelves in supermarkets. A bar code reader is a photoelectric scanner that translates bar code symbols into digital forms so that they can be read by a computer.

Optical character recognition (OCR) is machine-reading of printed or written characters through the use of light-sensitive materials or devices. A device, such as a wand, is used to read special preprinted characters and to convert them into digital form for computer data entry. For example, a department store associate uses OCR scanning to enter prices from a product. A desktop

What happens when a bar code is scanned?

Figure 11.5 Desktop Document Scanner

Courtesy of Hewlett-Packard

fax machine scans an image and converts it into digital code enabling transmission to another fax machine or to a computer with an internal fax modem and fax software. A fax modem and fax software may be installed as part of a computer system to simulate a desktop fax machine's input and output.

Mobile communication devices are handheld computers that may be controlled by a stylus-type pen or by user's thumbs to select menu items. Users also use their thumbs to key messages on a BlackBerry® device, shown in Figure 11.6. The Blackberry and the Treo™ by Palm® are examples of an integrated device that will handle telephone, wireless e-mail, Internet browser, and organizer functions. A personal digital assistant (PDA) is a similar handheld computer, but it does not have telephone capabilities. Several brands of PDAs are available. Devices that have both PDA features and telephone capabilities are commonly called smart phones.

Smartphones and other types of computers can use push technology to deliver e-mail and other data. **Push technology** automatically delivers e-mail and other data to a device based on the user's profile and request for specific data. Users do not have to search for information or to retrieve e-mail, it arrives when the push software locates it on the Internet or an e-mail message arrives. "Companies are currently using push to issue information to employees, such as automatic updating of business manuals, parts inventories, and policies."[2]

> **What benefit does push technology provide?**

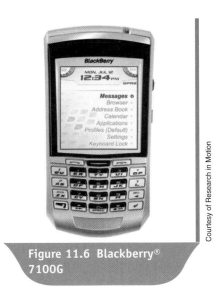

Courtesy of Research in Motion

**Figure 11.6 Blackberry®
7100G**

[2]Kim Guenther, "What is Push Technology," Darwin, Information for Executives, June 1, 2000, <http://www.darwinmag.com/learn/curve/column.html?ArticleID=43> (accessed May 21, 2005).

Storage and Retrieval Procedures

As the use of electronic records has made electronic media a primary records storage media, storage and retrieval of these records has presented new concerns. Indexing electronic records is just as important as indexing manual records and for the same reason—to locate and retrieve records or information. For electronic records, retrieval is a records retention issue. Information redundancy, media compatibility and stability, and access are also related to records retention.

Indexing

The value of records increases when users are assured that they can be retrieved when needed, especially electronic records. Indexing provides the means to locate, group, retrieve, and manage documents. Having well-indexed records reduces financial and legal risks, improves standards compliance, and enhances productivity. Unless a good quality indexing system is built into a document or records and information management computing application, the system will fail to perform one of its primary purposes—locating and retrieving the document-based information.

Indexing should not be taken lightly. Indexing involves planning and making decisions such as what to index and which index terms to use. In paper-based storage systems, indexing involves units and sometimes subjects. Indexing computer-based records is similar in that *units* become *fields* and *subjects* become *keywords*. Index fields can be used to categorize documents, to track creation or retention dates, or to enter subject matter. As in a paper-based system, indexing electronic records is essential for finding and retrieving the *right* information.

Indexing a computer record is the mental process of deciding the name or code by which it will be stored and retrieved. Coding the record is entering the record identifier code or filename for storage. Electronic files, particularly those files on diskettes, are often carelessly identified with abbreviations as filenames that only the record creator could interpret. The filename *bodmtgmins* illustrates a filename that means nothing to anyone other than the person creating it. *Board Meeting Minutes 5-25-05* would be a much clearer filename and would aid retrieval.

Full-text indexing provided by OCR-capable software eliminates the need for someone to read and manually index documents using keywords. OCR software "reads" a scanned document or page and indexes every word to track its location. Consequently, documents can be found using any word or phrase in them.

Paper records are located by looking into a particular file cabinet, into a certain drawer, and into a specific file folder. An electronic storage system

Why are electronic records indexed?

What is another name for subjects in a computer-based records system?

should be able to recreate this same type of hierarchical system through multiple levels of nested folders, or directories and subdirectories, as described in Chapter 5, can be created in the electronic storage system. A well-designed and organized electronic records system makes retrieval of electronic records easy.

Retrieval

Electronic information is stored on a network hard disk, a user's local hard disk, an optical disk, a diskette, or on a removable drive. These files must be identified so that they can be easily retrieved, used, and dispositioned. Consequently, users need to identify the categories and subcategories to which the electronic information belongs. They also need to create matching directories and subdirectories on their computers where the information will be stored. Consistency in naming directories, subdirectories, and files is necessary for locating computer records. An index or log of directories, subdirectories, and filename categories should be kept up-to-date and accessible to employees creating and storing electronic records. The *Board Meeting Minutes 5-25-05* file discussed previously could be in a directory named *Board of Directors* with a subdirectory named *Minutes.* The filename could be the specific meeting date. The index or log would show all subdirectory names under the main directory—*Board of Directors*—and would give the uniform file extensions for files in that directory.

Operating system software, such as *Microsoft Windows,* automatically maintains a directory and filename index of files. Computer storage peripherals, such as removable hard drives, floppy drives, and optical disk drives, are often represented by labeled icons on a computer's desktop. Storage peripherals and their fixed or removable media are computer-based equivalents of file cabinets. When a storage device is selected, a directory of the device's recording medium is displayed. The root directory is displayed first and provides an overview of the contents. The root directory typically contains subdirectories that are identified by folder icons. Large magnetic tape libraries use similar indexing and retrieval methods; however, files stored on large magnetic tape reels may be indexed by batches or groups of files. For example, one tape may be labeled *accounts receivable records 2005--2006.* An online index for offline records speeds retrieval considerably. Software can identify the location of a tape and guide a robotic arm to retrieve the tape in a tape library.

A **data warehouse** is a collection of data designed to support management decision making. Data warehouses contain data that present a clear picture of business conditions at a single point in time. A data warehouse includes systems to extract data from operating systems and a warehouse database system that provides flexible access to the data. *Data warehousing,* or *data mining* as it is sometimes called, generally refers to combining many different databases across an entire organization. Records can be assembled from various applications, platforms (operating systems), and storage devices into formats for

How do directories, subdirectories, and files benefit electronic records retrieval?

Why is a data warehouse an important RIM support device?

presentations to management for decision making or other business purposes. For example, executives may retrieve and assemble electronic records from several departments that will help them assess the profitability of their organization.

Diskettes, magnetic tape cartridges, CDs, DVDs, or other removable data storage devices must be clearly labeled for accurate storage and retrieval. In centralized data processing facilities, much more information may be required on media labels. Information that should be included on these media labels is listed in Figure 11.7. All this information will not fit onto small labels. Consequently, label contents may be limited to brief identifiers with more complete information recorded manually into a logbook.

Why is clear and comprehensive labeling of media important?

RETENTION AND DISPOSITION

As discussed in Chapter 7 and earlier in this chapter, electronic records must be included on an organization's records retention schedule and destroyed according to the schedule. Records and information managers have long recognized the importance of records retention for visible records media such as paper and microfilm. The same controls need to be applied to electronic records as well.

Duplicate Records

What is information redundancy?

In many organizations, users may be able to access the same information in machine-readable and human-readable formats. Storing duplicate copies of the same information is called *information redundancy.* Word processing documents may be created on a computer and revised and edited through several

---

LABEL INFORMATION FOR ELECTRONIC RECORDS

Removable Data Storage Devices
1. Department, unit, or organization that created the records
2. Name of records series
3. Inclusive dates, numeric series, or other identifying information
4. Type of computer on which records were created
5. Software name and version used to create the records

Centralized Data Processing Facilities
1. Complete listing of files contained on the medium
2. Manufacture date for the medium
3. Security precautions and access restrictions
4. Type of copy—working or storage
5. Any special attributes of the medium

Figure 11.7 Label Information—Electronic Records

versions before a final document is produced. These versions may be retained to provide a history of development of the document. Each version may be printed for review and corrections. The computer files may also be backed up for protection and retention. Consequently, one document may be available in several versions and formats, which means redundant information and redundant recordkeeping. RIM is affected by space needs—file cabinet, floor space, and media space for electronic records. During the discovery phase of a lawsuit, electronic records, paper records, and microfilm records may be subject to review by opposing parties. Paper records may be routinely purged and destroyed, but electronic records may not be subject to the same controls. Records retention schedules and policies must apply to electronic records as well records in other formats.

Media Compatibility and Stability

If you have worked with computers for a number of years, you have probably witnessed changes in electronic storage media. For example, many new microcomputers no longer have floppy drives. They have CD or DVD drives. Records that are on 5.25-inch floppy disks that are in long-term storage may not be recoverable unless an organization has also stored an older working computer that has a compatible drive and software.

Software also can become obsolete or be discontinued, or an organization can change the software used across the organization. Media compatibility refers to how well the media and the equipment needed to access information stored on the media work together. Records created in an obsolete or discontinued software program may no longer be accessible. New software programs that provide backward compatibility with older versions help overcome some software upgrade problems. Current media may not be compatible with future equipment or software. Operating systems may also change, which will prevent access and retrieval. A *Microsoft Windows* operating system may be replaced by a *Linux*® operating system or a newer operating system. RIM managers must look toward the future when selecting storage media and equipment. They need to consider whether what they purchase in 2006 will be compatible with records stored in 2010.

Media stability refers to the length of time the media will maintain its original quality so that it can continue to be used. The useful life of paper and photographic media is longer than the retention periods for the information stored in these formats. The useful life of electronic media depends on the number of times the media is accessed. The stable life expectancy of electronic records is often shorter than the required retention period for the information stored on the media. The following practices help to preserve electronic records for longer periods.

> **Why is media compatibility important?**

> **What happens when media are unstable?**

1. Magnetic and optical media should be inspected regularly. Samples may be inspected in large storage collections. Inspection should include a visual inspection as well as retrieval and playback of the information.
2. Diskettes may be refreshed by using defragmentation or disk scanning software.
3. Magnetic tapes should undergo a slow unwind/rewind cycle (called *retensioning*) to obtain an evenly tensioned tape before they are stored to extend their useful life.
4. Other electronic records can be recopied onto new media at predetermined intervals to extend their lives for the required retention period. Periodic recopying is known as *renewing* the media.
5. Copying can also be used to transfer information from deteriorating or obsolete media. Digitally coded information can be copied an indefinite number of times without degrading the quality. However, video and audio recordings based on analog signals lose image and/or sound quality with copying. Recopying makes managing electronic records difficult and requires a future commitment of labor and resources with no certainty that the technology needed to recopy records onto new media will be available (i.e., media compatibility).
6. **Migration** is the process of moving data from one electronic system to another, usually in upgrading hardware or software, without having to undergo a major conversion or re-inputting of data. Electronic records should be inspected and migrated regularly.

What is the process of moving data from one electronic storage system to another called?

Access

Users can access paper records by going to storage areas and retrieving them. Paper can be removed from cabinets and other storage containers for reference or taken to another work area for use (charged out). Electronic records, however, may be stored in remote locations where users cannot see the records or know what type of media is used.

Remote workstations connected by a network or intranet allow many users to access data at the same time. Organizations connected to the Internet may allow access by customers and employees to forms and other information. Customers may complete forms online and submit them to the organization much faster than by conventional means.

Internet or intranet access also provides the opportunity for creating new records such as online forms. These new records must be incorporated into the records and information management system and retention periods assigned. Freedom of access also raises safety and security concerns, which are discussed later in this chapter.

E-mail Records

E-mail messages transmitted through an organization's e-mail system are usually considered the organization's property and, therefore, are subject to management under an organization's RIM program.[3] E-mail and Internet use is monitored in many organizations. If e-mail messages contain information about programs, policies, decisions, and important transactions; document oral conversations or meetings during which policy was discussed or formulated; or document planning, discussion, or transaction of other business, they may have ongoing value. Consequently, records retention policies may apply. Users decide whether a message is a record or a nonrecord, based on the information in the message, and file it in appropriate directories and subdirectories.

> **When is an e-mail message a record?**

An e-mail system may provide a way to arrange messages into folders, but it is not a records system. E-mail messages must be transferred to a proper recordkeeping system for long-term storage. Although e-mail messages may be copied and saved into a *Word* file, some of the metadata will be lost. When e-mail messages are part of an organization's records system—paper or electronic—users may transfer e-mail to a subdirectory (folder) on a local hard drive, network drive, diskette, or other electronic storage medium. If RIM software is used to manage and identify information, then appropriate metadata must be entered into the records management system when an e-mail message is placed into it. **Metadata** is data about data. Metadata describes how, when, and by whom a particular set of data (an e-mail message, for example) was collected, and how the data is formatted. It also includes sender and receiver information, as well as the date and time the message was sent. Metadata is essential for understanding information stored in data warehouses.

> **What information is included in metadata?**

Active Records Storage

Data is a valuable organizational resource, and users want and need to have access to that data from many locations, sometimes in different time zones. For effective storage management of electronic media, storage copies need to be differentiated from working copies. *Working copies* are intended for ongoing information processing and reference requirements. *Storage copies* are created to satisfy retention requirements. The most active or working copies of electronic records are usually stored where they can be quickly accessed. That location may be inside a computer on a hard drive or on diskettes or CDs that are stored nearby. Diskettes may be stored in desktop containers or media pages that may be inserted into three-ring binders or folders. CDs may be stored in

> **What are working and storage copies?**

[3]David O. Stephens and Roderick C. Wallace, *Electronic Records Retention: New Strategies for Data Life Cycle Management* (Lenexa, KS: ARMA International, 2003), p. 25.

desktop storage boxes or towers or media pages. Optical disk cartridges may also be stored in towers. Desktop diskette and CD storage containers are shown in Figure 11.8.

Inactive Records Storage and Archives

Why are master copies not used in daily operations?

When records are transferred to inactive files or archives, systematic storage according to standard filing procedures apply. Storage copies, sometimes called *master copies,* of electronic records are usually recorded onto removable magnetic or optical media. These copies often contain inactive records that have been transferred from hard drives, and they are seldom referenced. Use of storage copies may be limited to making additional working copies if existing working copies are damaged. These copies also are used to recover and restore information if a system failure or other disaster occurs. The long-term quality of magnetic storage media has not been determined. Because magnetic records can be damaged by extreme temperature or proximity to magnetic charges, vital records should be stored on a more permanent medium for archival storage.

Although optical disks have a predicted life expectancy of approximately 100 years, retrieving records from optical disk storage requires computer equipment and software. Computer equipment and software can become obsolete, which affects retrieval of records created on that hardware and software. Newer versions of some software and hardware accept earlier versions and save the records in the new version. However, media format or size may change, which will make locating the specific type of disk drive difficult. For these reasons, microfilm remains a popular medium for long-term storage of vital records. Although many media formats and equipment have been replaced or become obsolete, older media will often be located when a records inventory is

Courtesy of Fellowes, Inc.

Figure 11.8 Desktop Media Storage Containers

conducted. Maintaining a current inventory of electronic records helps records and information managers develop effective retention schedules for those records. They are also better able to make data migration decisions—which records need to be migrated and to what media they need to be migrated. State-of-the-art technology is sometimes state-of-the-art for a short time.

Records and information managers should develop total life cycle retention periods. *Online retention* reflects the length of time the data should remain on primary storage devices, usually magnetic disks. The online retention period may be a few days, weeks, or months, but rarely more than a year. *Nearline retention* reflects the length of time data needs to remain onsite but offline in secondary storage devices, usually optical media. Nearline retention also is usually a short period of time, a few months or a year or so. *Offline retention* reflects the length of time the data needs to be offline, usually offsite, and usually on magnetic tapes. Retention periods should be assigned according to the records series stored on the tapes. A *total retention* period, required for most records retention schedules, reflects the length of time the data should remain in computer-processible form. After that time has expired, all data should be purged from all storage devices supporting the system.[4]

If electronic information is in directories and subdirectories, a software file manager can sort the files by date and identify records due for disposition (retain or destroy). Ways to dispose of electronic records are presented in Figure 11.9.

> **What are total life cycle retention periods?**

DISPOSITION PROCEDURES FOR ELECTRONIC RECORDS

- Magnetic disks—Delete file(s) from the disk and overwrite the space with new information. Defragmentation and disk scanning software can overwrite areas of a hard disk or diskette that are no longer being used.
- Magnetic tapes—Mark files for deletion and overwrite the space. Usually, all files must be restored to a hard disk, the marked files deleted, and the remaining files written to the tape. Delete the files restored from the hard disk after they are written to the tape. Use defragmentation and disk scanning software to overwrite the disk.
- CD-ROM disks—Restore all files to a hard drive, delete selected files, write remaining files onto a new CD-ROM. Destroy original CD-ROM by shredding.
- CD-R, CD-RW disks—Restore all files to a hard drive, delete selected files, rewrite remaining files to the same disk.

Figure 11.9 Disposition of Electronic Records

---

[4]Ibid.

How are files and information on magnetic disks erased?

To dispose of information on a magnetic disk, the file(s) must be deleted from the disk, and the space the files occupied must be overwritten to make recovering the information almost impossible. When users delete files, the space is marked for re-use, but the information is not physically removed or erased from a disk. With the help of commonly used utility programs, a user may restore deleted files that have not been overwritten. Procedures for disposition of electronic files are presented in Figure 11.9.

RECORDS SAFETY AND SECURITY

Safeguarding records against intentional or unintentional destruction or damage and protecting records confidentiality is known as *records protection.* Protecting records, regardless of their media, and their proper use and control are essential. Networked computer records systems are vulnerable to outside intruders through Internet access. Safety and security of electronic records are discussed in this section.

Records Safety

What is records safety?

Records safety refers to protecting records from physical hazards existing in an office environment such as electrical surges, physical damage to diskettes and CDs, high humidity, extreme heat or cold, and natural disasters. The procedures discussed in the following sections apply to controlling and protecting records from physical hazards.

Protective Measures

Users should adopt protective measures for hardware, software, and media. These measures include using surge protectors to protect computer equipment from changes (surges) in electrical voltage and affixing locks to areas containing computer files and equipment to protect against misuse or theft.

Why should you take care when filling out an online registration form?

Optical and magnetic media should not be stored in direct sunlight, placed near radiators, or exposed to heat sources. CD-R media that are not housed in cartridges may be damaged by exposure to light. They should be stored in containers that are stored in closed cabinets. High humidity, extreme heat or cold, exposure to light, electromagnetic sources, dust, smoke, and various storage conditions can damage electronic records; therefore, controlling temperature and humidity and other storage conditions helps protect these records. Dust and other contaminants can infiltrate high-density media housings and render portions of recorded information unreadable. Air conditioning is usually required to control temperature and humidity and to remove pollutants. Media storage areas should be cleaned regularly.

My Records

Reduce the Flow of Unsolicited Information

Is your e-mail in-box overflowing with unwanted offers? Are telemarketers calling at all hours?

While you may not be able to stop completely the ever-increasing flood of information, taking the following steps will help to reduce the volume of unwanted junk mail, spam, and telemarketing calls you receive:

DECREASE JUNK MAIL

- Write to the Direct Marketing Association Mail Preference Service to add your name and address to the residential file of customers who do not wish to receive promotional mail at home. The file is updated four times a year.

- When you enter a sweepstakes, fill out product warranty cards, or provide personal information on a form for any reason, write on the form: "Please do not sell my name or address."

DECREASE SPAM

- Do not fill out an on-line registration form (newsletters and mailing lists usually require them) unless the site's privacy policy clearly says that the data will not be shared with other people without your approval.

- Read any online form carefully before you transmit personal information through a web site. Some sites require you to de-select a check box to opt out of future communications with that particular company or related companies.

- Don't display your e-mail address in public forums such as newsgroup postings, chat rooms, or web sites.

- Use two e-mail addresses—one for personal messages and one for newsgroups and chat rooms.

- Report unwanted spam e-mail to the Federal Trade Commission, and send a copy of the offending e-mail to your ISP (internet service provider).

STOP UNWANTED TELEMARKETING CALLS

- Register your telephone number(s) on the National Do-Not-Call Registry to block calls for five years. Remember to include your cell phone number. A link to this site is provided on the web site for this textbook.

- If you receive an unwanted telemarketer call, interrupt the caller and say, "Please permanently remove me from your calling list." If the same company calls again, they are violating the law.

Adequate preparation for and protection from natural disasters, such as floods, fires, and earthquakes, should be provided. Protection from natural disasters involves advance planning to select a second equipment site for emergency operation and for making duplicate copies of vital records for the alternate location. See Chapter 12 for more on disaster preparation and recovery.

Records Conversion and Backup

Records stored on magnetic media should be converted to hard copy, optical disks, or microforms (Figure 11.10) for long-term storage. The life expectancy of magnetic records may be limited, depending on storage conditions. Therefore, careful attention must be made to environmental conditions for long-term storage of magnetic tapes. Vital records should not be on magnetic media for long-term storage.

Users should protect against loss of files by establishing a policy of backing up computer files and storing the copies in fireproof cabinets or in an offsite location. Duplicate electronic records made from back-up copies can be created quickly and inexpensively. Backing up records is good insurance that records will be available when needed.

Protection Against Computer Viruses

Taking measures to prevent computer viruses from destroying data is an essential part of records security. A **virus** is a computer program that replicates itself into other programs that are shared among systems with the intention of causing damage. The opportunity for the introduction of viruses increases when

South-Western/Thomson Learning

Figure 11.10A Microfiche is popular for long-term records storage.

Figure 11.10B Roll microfilm is often used for long-term records storage.

computer users access electronic records from remote locations. Viruses transmitted over the Internet and through e-mail can be particularly destructive. Safety measures involve (a) using virus detection software programs regularly, (b) making back-up copies of new software programs onto large storage capacity ZIP™ disks or CD-R or CD-RW disks before installing them onto a computer, and (c) making daily back-up copies of data entered. Always checking for viruses on data disks from outside sources helps eliminate data damage from viruses. Users need to update virus detection software regularly from the detection software company's web site.

Records Security

Records security refers to protecting records from unauthorized access. Electronic transmission and distribution of records require special security precautions. With wide use of the Internet to conduct business, organizations take careful measures to provide records security and protection from unauthorized access to the information stored on electronic media. Generally accepted safety measures are discussed in the following sections.

Why do electronic records transmitted over the Internet require security precautions?

Security Policies and Checks

Implementing a security policy helps to ensure safe, reliable operation of the records system. Such a policy is based on a detailed study of equipment used, records functions performed, information contained in the principal records, employees having access to the records, and current security devices.

Conducting security checks and, when necessary, bonding personnel who use hardware and software in the system help ensure the safety of records. The electronic records security policy should include close supervision of records work plus holding employees personally accountable for the proper maintenance of company equipment and information.

Security Measures

As a deterrent to crime, some firms have a security warning programmed into their computers for display onto terminal screens. An effective method of controlling access to a computer room is a card reader/combination lock system into which employees must insert their access cards and key in a personal code before the door will open. Other security systems scan and save the scan of each person's eyes, which is matched each time the same person tries to enter a secure area. Voice prints are also used in a similar manner. Individuals may pass their hands under scanners or place their thumbs on a thumb pad to gain approval for access to secure areas.

A **firewall** is a combination hardware and software buffer that many organizations place between their internal networks and the Internet. A firewall allows only specific kinds of messages from the Internet to flow in and out of the internal network. This limitation protects the internal network from intruders or hackers who might try to use the Internet to break into these systems. To prevent spyware from being secretly installed onto computers, many companies incorporate spy detection software as part of their system security measures.

Data Protection

To protect data stored on disks or tapes against unauthorized use, safeguards such as passwords, digital signatures, encryption, or call-back may be used.

- A **password** is a string of characters known to the computer system and a user, who must specify it to gain access to the system. It may be a special word, code, or symbol that is required to access a computer system. Passwords are not sufficient protection because they can be stolen or guessed. You should not use a real word or variation of your name, date of birth, a word that can be found in a dictionary, or a word that might logically be guessed. The best password is a mix of letters, numbers, and punctuation marks in a random sequence of at least eight characters. Some security experts recommend developing a meaningful sentence and selecting a combination of letter, numbers, and symbols to represent that sentence in one word—your password.

- A **digital signature,** or *e-signature,* consists of a string of characters and numbers added as a code on electronic documents being transmitted by computer. The receiving computer's special software performs a mathematical operation on the character string to verify its validity. The Electronics Signature in Global and National Commerce Act, passed in 2000, sets national standards for electronic signatures and records and gives them the same legal validity as written contracts and documents. The law

What is the purpose of a firewall?

provides that no contract, signature, or record shall be denied legally binding status just because it is in electronic form. A contract must still be in a format capable of being retained and accurately reproduced. Credit card companies accept e-signatures at check-out counters in supermarkets, department stores, and other point-of-sale locations.

- **Encryption** is a method of scrambling data in a predetermined manner at the sending point to protect confidential records. The destination computer decodes the data. Encryption is the process of converting meaningful information into a numeric code that is only understood by the intended recipient of the information. The receiving computer and Internet browser understand the mathematical formulas that turn the information into numeric code and back again into meaningful information. *International-Grade encryption,* also called *40-bit encryption,* uses billions of possible keys to secure information. *Domestic-Grade encryption,* also called *128-bit encryption,* uses thousands of times more key combinations than International-Grade encryption. As the Internet has become a major vehicle for commercial, proprietary, or sensitive information transmission, the perceived need for encryption or other security measures has risen accordingly. With encryption, organizations can use EDI to transmit highly sensitive information.

    After several major organizations suffered serious online security breaches, data encryption has become a vital security measure. Organizations are, however, being selective in determining which data to encrypt. The most identity-sensitive data are encrypted first. Encrypting data backups that will be shipped offsite is a priority.[5]

- A **call-back system** is a records protection procedure requiring an individual requesting data from a computer system to hang up after making a telephone request and wait for the computer to call back. In call-back systems, telephone numbers are checked by the computer before information is released to the requesting party to be sure that only authorized persons have access to the requested information.

> **What kind of data might an organization want to encrypt before sending it over the Internet?**

Security for Faxed Documents

Transmitting documents by fax has become one of the most widely used methods of correspondence between companies, medical offices, hospitals, and other types of organizations. Unfortunately, many workers in offices where medical documents and other confidential information are received fail to take necessary precautions to prevent unauthorized individuals from access to the fax machine. A fax machine dedicated for confidential material only and located in a less open area or calling ahead to alert the message receiver to watch for a fax provides some security.

[5]Sandra Gittlen, *Network World,* (06/27/05) Vol. 22, No. 25, p. 58, <http://www.networkworld.com/supp/2005/ndc4/062705-storage-encryption.html> (accessed August 2, 2005).

E-mail Retention Policies

As mentioned previously, e-mail messages may be obtained as evidence in lawsuits. Damaging evidence can often be found in messages that senders or receivers thought were deleted. Because the main computer makes daily backups of all files, including e-mail, copies of messages sent and deleted may still be in the back-up file. In addition, software programs often make several copies of files and place them in different addresses. Computer experts may be able to recover these files.

Security issues stemming from unsuspected file copies call for the following measures: (1) Implement an organization-wide e-mail policy that requires regular purging of files that are no longer active nor needed for future operations or historical records. (2) Follow the established e-mail policy and do not put anything into an e-mail message that you would not want repeated or used in court. (3) Protect your password. (4) Always log off (sign off) the system properly so that no one else can create, change, or damage records on your computer.

IMAGE MEDIA

What organizations are likely users of microfilm records?

As you have already learned, records or documents may be stored in paper or electronic formats. Records may also be stored in photographic format. Conventional photographic negatives and medical X-rays are examples of photographic documents. Microforms are photographic document storage media. **Microform** is the collective term for all microimages such as microfilm, microfiche, aperture cards, and microfilm jackets. Microfilm is a photographic reproduction of a document greatly reduced in size from the original on fine grain, high-resolution film that requires a reader for viewing. Because the photographic image is greatly reduced in size, it is called a *microimage,* and it cannot be read without magnification. The miniaturized image of a document is called

South-Western/Thomson Learning

Figure 11.11 An aperture card has an opening designed as a carrier for film image(s).

CAREER CORNER

Records Clerk Job Description

The following job description is an example of a career opportunity in records management in a legal office.

GENERAL INFORMATION

This position is in a legal services organization.

RESPONSIBILITIES

- Creating, maintaining, and tracking firm records stored onsite and offsite using records management software
- Creating files
- Filing/indexing documents
- Retrieving, delivering, and sorting active and inactive files
- Preparing files for offsite storage
- Performing special projects

REQUIREMENTS

- Good communication skills (oral and written)
- Ability to type 30 words per minute
- Ability to lift 40 lbs
- Ability to work effectively on a team
- Basic PC proficiency

EDUCATION AND EXPERIENCE

- High school diploma
- At least 1 year work experience
- Previous law firm and well-known legal software experience

a *microrecord. Microfilming* is the process of photographing documents to reduce their size. Microforms offer compact storage for active and inactive phases of the records life cycle.

All microforms originate from roll microfilm. Microforms can be produced from paper documents, called *source documents,* or from computer-generated information. The most common microforms are roll film (open reels and cartridges) and unitized or flat microforms (microfiche, microfilm jackets, and aperture cards). These flat forms contain one unit of information such as one report or one document. Because roll film can hold a large number of images, unrelated documents may be stored on one roll. Therefore, microfilm on reels or cartridges are nonunitized microforms. The main advantage of using microforms is that they provide compact storage and, therefore, reduce storage space requirements.

Many organizations use microforms for long-term records storage. They may produce their microforms in an in-house micrographics department or send documents to outside vendors to produce their microforms. **Micrographics** is the technology by which recorded information can be quickly reduced to a microform, stored conveniently, and then easily retrieved for reference and use. Micrographics technology miniaturizes recorded information. Because space is an important business resource, reducing storage space requirements is often the main reason for implementing micrographics technology. Equipment costs to produce microform records are the major implementation costs for these records systems. For long-term storage, equipment costs may be offset by savings in storage cost and retrieval efficiency. Types of microforms are listed in Figure 11.12 on page 337.

Important considerations for using microfilm include size and quality, which is determined by the resolution, density, reduction ratio, and magnification ratio of the microfilm. **Resolution** is a measure of the sharpness or fine detail of an image. Good resolution requires high-quality film and a camera with a good lens. High resolution means that a microimage is clear and easily readable when magnified on a reader with a viewing screen and a light source or when printed from the reader.

Density is the degree of optical opacity of a material that determines the amount of light that will pass through it or reflect from it. A densitometer is used to measure the contrast between the dark and light areas of microfilm. A high-quality microimage has a wide variation in the dark and light areas of the microfilm. *Line density* indicates the opacity of characters, lines, or other information in a microimage. *Background density* refers to the opacity of noninformation areas. The higher the contrast, the easier the images are to read. If too little difference exists between line and background densities, microimages may look faded. If background density is too high, fine lines may widen, and interline spaces may fill in. Uniform densities are important for microforms used in automated duplicators, enlarger/printers, and scanners. Contrast

---

Which microforms are flat microforms?

Why are resolution and density important when producing microfilm?

MICROFORMS

- Roll microfilm—The most widely used and least expensive microform to create.
  - Records are placed in sequential order on the microfilm.
  - Roll microfilm is available in 16mm (millimeter), 35mm, and 105mm widths.
    - Microfilm in 16mm width is preferred for documents measuring up to 11″ by 17″.
    - Microfiche is created on 105mm microfilm.
    - Microfilm in 35mm width is primarily used for engineering drawings.
- Microfiche—A microform in the shape of a rectangular sheet having one or more microimages arranged in a grid pattern with a heading area across the top. The eye-readable heading strip is called a *header;* it does not require magnification. Also called simply *fiche* (pronounced as "feesh").
  - Microfiche is created from 105mm width microfilm cut into 148mm lengths.
  - Fiche is a unitized microform because it contains one unit of information such as a financial report. It is good for grouping information.
    - Records are arranged on the fiche by filming documents in a continuous series by rows.
    - The index is usually in the lower right corner.
- Microfilm jacket—A flat, transparent, plastic carrier with single or multiple film channels made to hold single or multiple film strips.
  - A jacket has one or more sleeves or channels for inserting and protecting strips of 16- or 35-mm microfilm.
  - Jackets can be updated by inserting new microfilm into a channel.
  - Jackets keep related records together.
- Aperture card—An electronic data processing card (7 3/8″ by 3 1/4″) with a rectangular hole (aperture) specifically designed as a carrier for a film image(s).
  - Aperture cards are used primarily for holding engineering drawings or blueprints on 35-mm microfilm.
  - A record is easily updated by removing an obsolete card and inserting a new one into the storage unit.
- Computer-output microform or microfilm (COM)—Computer output converted directly into microform without a paper printout as an intermediary. Using a tape-to-film photographic device called a *recorder,* computer records on magnetic tape are converted into a microimage on roll film or microfiche.
  - COM is used for long-term data retention.
  - COM is popular for archival storage.

Figure 11.12 Types of Microforms

sharpness depends on the quality of the source document as well as the proper lighting during filming.

The **reduction ratio** is the relationship between the dimensions of the original or master and the corresponding dimensions of the photographed image. The ratio also is a measure of the number of times a dimension of a document is reduced when photographed. For example, a reduction ratio expressed as 1:24 (or 24×) means that the image is 1/24th the size of the original record, both horizontally and vertically.

Reduction ratios range from 5× to 2400×, with 24× being the most commonly used reduction. Higher reduction ratios result in smaller images; consequently, a greater number of images can be photographed on one square inch of microfilm. For example, 8,100 regular-size bank checks can be photographed on 100 feet of microfilm at 24× reduction; 16,600 checks, at 50×. Banks use microfilm in 2,000-foot lengths. For easy retrieval, however, the film is cut into 100-foot or 215-foot lengths after developing.

A microimage must be enlarged or magnified for reading. Magnification is the opposite of reduction. It measures the relationship between a given linear dimension of an enlarged microimage as displayed on a screen or printed on paper and the corresponding dimensions of the microimage itself. Magnification is expressed as 24×, 48×, and so on. Magnification can also be expressed as a ratio—1:24, 1:48, and so on. The **magnification ratio,** also called the *enlargement ratio,* is a method of describing the relationship between the size of an image and the original record when viewed on a microfilm reader screen. For example, a one-inch square microrecord that is magnified ten times (10×) appears in its enlarged form as ten square inches. An image filmed at 24× reduction must be magnified at 24× to produce an original-size copy.

Is a high reduction ratio helpful when microfilming records?

Why is the magnification ratio important when viewing microimages?

Microfilming Procedures and Equipment

An image system is a combination of procedures and equipment that form an efficient unit for creating and using records in microform or electronic images. Figure 11.13 on page 339 identifies records procedures used in the three stages of an image records system: preparation, processing, and use of records. The procedures and equipment used in an image system are described in the next section.

Document Preparation

Why do sticky notes have to be removed before microfilming documents?

Preparing source documents for microfilming is one of the most time-consuming and labor-intensive aspects of microfilming. Document preparation is entirely manual work necessary for preparing documents and placing them into proper sequence for filming. Correspondence and other documents must be removed from file cabinets or other containers and folders and stacked neatly in correct sequence. Documents must be checked carefully; all paper

---

STAGES OF AN IMAGE SYSTEM

- Preparation
  - Prepare records for imaging
- Processing
  - Index and code records
  - Microfilm or scan records
  - Process microfilm
  - Make duplicate copies for use
- Use
  - Store records
  - Retrieve records
  - View/read records
  - Print hard copy (optional)

Figure 11.13 Stages of an Image System

---

clips and staples removed; torn pages mended; and attachments to records, such as envelopes, routing slips, and sticky notes, removed. Source documents are usually prepared for microfilming in batches so that an entire 100- or 215-foot roll can be filmed at one time.

Indexing Procedures

Recording information to serve as a location directory for microforms or electronic records is referred to as *indexing.* An index attaches identification data, called an *address,* to microrecords or electronic records. In micrographics technology, the term *index* refers to a list of microrecords on roll film, microfiche, microfilm jackets, or aperture cards. An index may be handwritten or created with a computer. Microrecord indexing may be prepared manually during filming or after filming.

To index manually during filming, a computer operator stationed beside a microfilm camera assigns identifiers during filming. To index microrecords after filming, an operator places a roll of microfilm into a reader, views each image, and assigns an identifier by keying the identifier and sequential number of the microimage into a computer. Commonly used methods of indexing roll microfilm during filming include:

1. **Flash target indexing**—Specially prepared pages, called *flash targets,* are inserted between source documents during preparation. The targets precede and describe the microimages that follow them.
2. **Sequential frame numbering**—Sequential numbers are assigned to each frame within a 16mm or 35mm microfilm reel or a 16mm cartridge for manual retrieval of microimages. A two-part number identifies the roll and frame address of each microimage. For example, the number

What is an index of microrecords?

What type of information is on a flash target?

12-3276 identifies a microimage recorded on reel or cartridge number 12 at frame number 3276. The next image would be numbered 12-3277.

What is the difference between a blip code and a bar code?

3. **Blip coding**—An optical mark, usually rectangular, is recorded on microfilm, appearing below each image. The mark is used for counting images or frames automatically for specially designed retrieval devices. Blip coding is an automated variation of sequential frame numbering.

4. **Bar coding**—Bar codes help automate the indexing for scanned or microfilmed documents. Bar code labels may be affixed to documents before they are scanned or microfilmed. If the identifiers are sequential numbers, bar code labels can be computer-generated in order and printed on adhesive tape or printed on a bar code printer.

Unitized or flat microforms may be indexed in various ways. Microfiche, jackets, and aperture cards can be indexed by adding a title (header) at the top of the microform. The header usually includes the name of the document and microrecord sequence number. A bar code may also be affixed to the header. Microfiche and jackets may have a color band on the header for color coding. A color code represents a batch of records or an entire file and identifies a particular type of record. Color coding helps filers locate misfiled microrecords quickly.

Microfilming Equipment

Records are captured on microfilm through the use of microfilm cameras. The following cameras are commonly used.

1. **Rotary camera**—A microfilm camera that uses rotating belts to carry documents through the camera. It makes images on 16-mm film at a speed of over 500 documents a minute. Rotary cameras are used primarily for filming large-volume records such as checks and invoices.

2. **Planetary camera**—A microfilm camera that uses 35-mm microfilm to film large engineering drawings, hardbound books, and other large documents. Documents are placed on a flat (plane) surface for filming. Because documents remain stationary during filming and are photographed one at a time, microfilming is slower with a planetary camera.

3. **Step-and-repeat camera**—A microfilm camera that produces a series of separate images on 16- or 35-mm film, usually in orderly rows and columns, to produce microfiche. An updatable microfiche camera may be used to add new images to a previously prepared microfiche if any unexposed space is available on the fiche. This camera can also overprint existing images with *VOID* or *PAID* if desired.

4. **Aperture card camera**—A microfilm camera that records miniaturized images of engineering drawings or other large source documents onto

35-mm film frames that are premounted into tabulating-size cards. The camera cards contain unexposed film that the camera uses to photograph a drawing or other source document. A source document is placed face-up onto a flat copyboard, and the camera takes a picture of it. After exposure, the camera card passes through a processing chamber and is delivered, fully developed, in about 1 minute.

5. **Filmer/Scanner**—A microfilm camera that can also operate as a scanner. It is also called a *camera/scanner* or *scanner/filmer.* Source documents are microfilmed and digitized in one operation. Microfilm images can be scanned at the same time they are filmed. This dual process updates the electronic image file as it produces microfilm rolls for legal, archival, or historic purposes. Electronic images provide immediate access; the microfilm provides a record for long-term retention.

Processing, Duplicating, and Production Equipment

After records are microfilmed, the film is processed. A microfilm processor applies heat and chemical treatments to make microimages visible for display, printing, or other purposes. Because exposed film is protected by a cover on the processor, a darkroom is not required.

A master microform may be a camera-original microform produced directly from source documents or a copy that is one or more generations removed from the original. The term *generation* is used to indicate the relationship of a copy to the original source document. Camera-original microforms are first-generation microforms. Copies made from camera-original microforms are second-generation microforms. Copies of those copies are third-generation microforms, and so on. The master microform is the storage copy, and it is not circulated for use. Duplicates are used as working copies. Working copies may be distributed for use or serve as intermediate copies from which more copies will be produced. A duplicate may also be made by simultaneously exposing two rolls of film in the film unit of the camera.

> **What is a second-generation microform?**

The most frequently used method of making multiple copies of microforms is contact printing. This process makes a duplicate copy of microfilm by placing the emulsion side of the developed original film in contact with the emulsion side of the copy film and directing a light beam through the original image to the copy. Developing the copy film then produces a duplicate. *Print films* or *copy films* are used for microform duplication.

> **What type of film is used for filming duplicate microforms?**

After 16-mm roll microfilm is processed and duplicated, it may be inserted into cartridges. A jacket viewer/scanner, viewer/filler, or a reader/filler is used to identify microimages for insertion into microfilm jackets. Magnified images are displayed onto a screen for examination and selection. When the last image to be inserted is displayed, the operator pushes a button or presses a lever that activates a knife. The knife cuts the film and pushes it into the jacket sleeve.

This process is repeated until all sleeves or channels are filled. Aperture card mounters operate in a similar manner.

Commercial Imaging Services

What benefits do commercial imaging service companies offer organizations?

Because equipment costs necessary for in-house microfilming and processing can be quite high, commercial service bureaus provide a practical alternative. Such a service may offer microfilming, processing, duplicating, inspecting and testing, cartridge loading and labeling, and producing microfilm jackets and aperture cards. Micrographics service bureaus are often used for microform scanning and related services to integrate micrographics and electronic document imaging technologies. Commercial records storage centers often are used to store the master copies of vital records.

Microform Storing, Retrieving, and Viewing

Microform storage copies are intended for retention purposes, and they are seldom referenced. Working copies are prepared for reference and use. Figure 11.14 contains information about storing microforms.

Because working copies are used to conduct normal work activities, they are subjected to dust, skin oils, fingerprints, liquid spills, contamination by foreign materials, and exposure to excessive light and temperatures. Microfiche

Why is stacking microforms harmful to them?

MICROFORM STORAGE RECOMMENDATIONS

- Store storage and working microform copies in a vertical, upright position to prevent warping.
- Avoid stacking or subjecting microforms to pressure or weight.
- Use drawer cabinets for microform reels and cartridges.
- Store microfilm reels and cartridges in boxes on shelves or in drawer cabinets partitioned to fit the boxes.
- Store cartridges in carousels partitioned to fit the boxes.
- Store flat microforms in drawer cabinets, separated by tabbed dividers similar to guides in paper records files.
- Store flat microforms upright in open or closed trays for desktop use or place them into cabinets for security.
- Use microform storage panels with pockets to insert microfiche or microfilm jackets (optional). Multiple panels may be inserted into binders.

Figure 11.14 Microform Storage Recommendations

may be folded or torn. Microfilm in jackets or aperture cards may become separated from their carriers. Microfilm cartridges can crack or come apart. All microforms may be damaged by readers or display devices, printing equipment, duplicators, scanners, or storage equipment. Additionally, environmental conditions can affect the long-term storage of microfilm and microforms. Environmental and other storage recommendations are listed in Figure 11.15.

Microforms are duplicated so that one or more working copies are created for viewing, printing, or scanning. Special equipment is necessary for viewing, printing, and scanning microforms. Microforms must be removed from their storage containers before they can be viewed, printed, or scanned. For manual location of microforms on reels and cartridges, extra equipment is not required. Human-readable headers on flat microforms—microfiche, microfilm jackets, and aperture cards—make retrieval easy, and no special equipment is necessary

> **Why do microform storage areas need to be environmentally controlled?**

> **How are flat microforms retrieved?**

STORAGE ENVIRONMENT RECOMMENDATIONS

1. Microform work areas—Prohibit eating, drinking, and smoking. Keep storage containers and equipment clean when using working copies.
2. Microrecord long-term retention storage conditions—Maintain a maximum temperature of 70 degrees Fahrenheit and relative humidity less than 50 percent. Assure constant temperatures between 50 and 70 degrees Fahrenheit and humidity between 20 and 40 percent. Any change in temperature in a 24-hr. period should not be greater than 10 degrees or 5 degrees humidity.
3. Microfilm medium-term retention storage conditions—Maintain a maximum temperature no greater than 77 degrees Fahrenheit (preferably 70° F.). Relative humidity may range from 20 to 50 percent; variations not to exceed 10 percent a day.
4. Microform storage copies—Store in a fire-resistant room or vault. Use noncombustible and noncorrosive storage equipment. Vital microrecord storage copies may be stored in insulated cabinets within fire-resistant storage areas. Store duplicate vital microform copies in another location with the same storage conditions for the retention period for maximum protection.
5. Microfilm storage copies—Store in closed containers such as drawer cabinets or shelving units with doors to prevent damage by light. Store in boxes if open shelving or storage racks are used. Use an air-conditioning or air-filtration system that will remove abrasive particles and gaseous impurities that can harm the film.
6. Film reels, storage boxes, and paper enclosures or attachments—Use acid-free products because acids and other contaminants can cause destructive chemical reactions on film.
7. Deteriorating microforms—Remove from storage areas immediately. Replace with duplicate copies as soon as deterioration is noticed.
8. Microfilm safety and security—Use the same safety and security protection for storage copies as for other types of records. Limit access to authorized users. Safeguard procedures against damage or loss must be in place for storage or master copies.

Figure 11.15 Storage Environment Recommendations

for manual retrieval. Computers may be used to locate and/or retrieve microforms as well as electronic records. Microforms may be stored onto and retrieved from a microfilm drive, called an *M drive,* in a microcomputer. Images are displayed onto a computer screen for viewing and selection for printing. Types of display devices for microforms are listed in Figure 11.16 on page 345.

RETENTION

The life span of microfilm is as long as the life span of paper records. Microfilm records in a carefully controlled environment can be protected and preserved for decades with estimates extending to hundreds of years. Optical disks, including CDs and DVDs, have useful life spans ranging from 10 to 100 years. To ensure protection of microfilm or electronic records, the master copies of these records are not circulated for use. Working copies are made for everyday use or for loan. In some organizations, optical disk records are transferred to new disks every ten years to assure their continued high-quality condition. The process of making new copies of the master record is called *remastering,* and it helps extend the life span of electronic records.

Additional retention guidelines include:

- Records kept for three years or less may be kept as paper records or on magnetic or optical disk storage.
- Records kept from 7 to 15 years should be considered for optical disk storage or microfilming. These records can be kept accessible and stored in less space.
- Vital and archival records are often kept on microfilm because of its established durability.

Microfilm records remain in original text format, just reduced in size. Reading the text requires only projection and magnification. The standardized format of microfilm protects records from technological obsolescence that could occur over long periods with electronic records. In addition, long-standing federal law permits acceptance of microfilmed records as legal documents, admissible as evidence in a court of law. Multimedia storage containers, similar to the one shown in Figure 11.17 on page 346, are used to store electronic and image media.

Why is microfilm often used for vital records storage?

SOFTWARE

RIM software has the capability to track and manage paper, electronic, and image records. Records centers or RIM departments usually have one software program that performs all necessary functions for the records system. However, some organizations may use a retention software program in addition to

What RIM functions can be done by using software?

DISPLAY DEVICES FOR MICROFORMS

Display Device	Description
Microform Reader	An optical device for viewing a projected and enlarged microimage. The image is displayed onto a screen for viewing. A reader is the most important display device and has the broadest application.
Single-Purpose Reader	A microform reader that accepts only one type of microform.
Multipurpose Reader	A microform reader that accepts more than one type of microform but not all microforms. Some readers will accommodate interchangeable carriers that will allow different types of microforms.
Stationary Reader	A reader that provides a large screen for viewing and a wide choice of optional features such as a hood to reduce glare.
Microform Viewer	A hand-held, or portable, magnifier for microfiche, microfilm jackets, or aperture cards. A microform is inserted into a slot and manually positioned for viewing.
Microform Projector	A device that magnifies microimages for display onto a wall or a wall-mounted screen. These projectors are readers without screens that allow microforms to be used during group presentations.
Reader/Printer	A microform reader that is also capable of reproducing an enlarged microimage in hard copy. Hard copies generally range in size from 8.5″ by 11″ to 18″ by 24″. An enlarger/printer is used if larger sizes are needed. Reader/printers are the most widely used type of microform printers. They may be single- or multipurpose devices, depending on the types of microforms they will accept.
Universal Reader/Printer	A reader/printer that uses interchangeable carriers for roll and flat microforms.
Reader/Scanner	A microform reader that combines the capabilities of a reader and an image digitizer. Also known as a *digital microimage workstation,* it produces electronic document images from magnified microimages. Digitized microimages may be distributed over networks, attached to e-mail messages, used for OCR, and used for input into desktop publishing programs.
Microfilm Drive (M Drive)	A computer peripheral device that retrieves and digitizes microimages for display on a microcomputer to which it is connected. It accepts 16mm microfilm cartridges that are manually loaded into the drive. The computer directs the drive to advance the microfilm to the desired frame.

Figure 11.16 Display Devices for Microforms

Courtesy of Russ Bassett

Figure 11.17 Multimedia Storage Containers

a RIM program. A software program may allow users to build a representation of a microfilm storage unit on a computer screen and assign numbers or bar codes to microfilm boxes and other records storage boxes. Indexes for paper, electronic, and microfilm records may be stored online as part of the indexing function. Using software to manage electronic records provides much needed control. Because most of these records are not visible, superior management tools are needed. The control of records through computer software increases rapid access to records and reduces the number of misplaced records. RIM software packages or customized software developed for an organization can be used to maintain records location files, charge-out files, and retention and destruction records. Less work is involved with charging out microimage records because microforms are copied for use.

Software programs may be single-function programs that manage only one aspect of the records management area such as offsite records storage. Other software options include integrated packages that address the total records management of an organization and modular programs that have separate modules for each records system function. Selection of appropriate software should be determined by several factors:

1. Complexity of the software and amount of training required for employee proficiency
2. Well-written training manuals that accompany the software
3. Reliability and experience of the vendor
4. Initial cost and future costs of the software and installation
5. Maintenance, backup, and support services offered

Chapter Review And Applications

POINTS TO FILE AND RETRIEVE

- An electronic record is a record stored on electronic storage media that can be easily accessed or changed.

- An image record is a digital or photographic representation of a record on any medium such as microfilm or optical disk.

- Electronic media include magnetic and optical media.

- Electronic records must be included on an organization's records retention schedule and destroyed according to the schedule.

- Safeguarding records against intentional or unintentional destruction or damage and protecting records confidentiality are known as records protection.

- Microforms are photographic document storage media.

- The life span of microfilm is as long as the life span of paper records.

- RIM software may be used with electronic and image media.

IMPORTANT TERMS

call-back system
data warehouse
density
digital signature
electronic record
encryption
firewall
flash drive
image record
lanyard
magnetic media
magnification ratio
media compatibility

media stability
metadata
microform
micrographics
migration
optical character recognition (OCR)
optical media
password
push technology
reduction ratio
resolution
scanner
virus

REVIEW AND DISCUSSION

1. Define *electronic record* and *image record* and describe the relationship between the two records media. (Obj. 1)

2. Define *magnetic media* and *optical media* and list three types of each media. (Obj. 2)

3. List two advantages of using removable data storage devices. (Obj. 2)

4. What is a flash drive, and what benefits does using one provide? (Obj. 2)

5. List four devices that may be used for data input and discuss how electronic records are indexed and retrieved. (Obj. 3)

6. Discuss how duplicate records, media compatibility and stability, access, and e-mail relate to records retention. (Obj. 4)

7. Discuss retention for active and inactive electronic records. (Obj. 5)

8. What steps can be taken to protect records? List two ways of providing records safety and two methods of assuring records security. (Obj. 6)

9. List and describe four types of microforms and four factors related to microfilm quality. (Obj. 7)

10. How are documents prepared for microfilming, what types of cameras are used for microfilm, and how are electronic and image records indexed? (Obj. 8)

11. How are microforms typically stored, and what environmental concerns need to be monitored? (Obj. 9)

12. What types of retrieving and viewing equipment are used with microforms? (Obj. 10)

13. Prepare a list of three retention guidelines for long-term retention of image records. (Obj. 11)

14. List three functions typically served by RIM software used for electronic and image records. (Obj. 12)

APPLICATIONS

11-1 ELECTRONIC RECORDS RETENTION ISSUES (OBJS. 3-5)

COLLABORATION

CRITICAL THINKING

You are an employee in an organization that recently organized its electronic records and installed RIM software. Your assignment is to identify issues that will affect retrieval and retention of the records.

1. Work with another student in your class to complete this application.

2. Prepare a list of issues that will affect access, retrieval, and long-term retention of the electronic records. These listed items should relate to one or more of the following: hardware, software, and/or procedures for records and information management.

11-2 CLASSIFY E-MAIL MESSAGES (OBJ. 4)

E-mail messages may be considered records or nonrecords depending on their content and continuing value to an organization. Work with a classmate to complete the following:

CRITICAL THINKING

COLLABORATION

1. Read the description of each e-mail message below and decide whether the message should be considered a record and stored in the records and information system.

2. Create a directory system for storing the e-mail files you decide are records. For all these messages, create a meaningful filename for the record and a meaningful name for the directory where the record will be stored on a hard drive. Assume that your operating system allows the use of long filenames.

Message Date	Message Contents
a. 11/04/--	Message from a coworker indicated that a meeting at 9 a.m. next Friday is convenient for her
b. 11/04/--	Message from your supervisor describing new procedures for handling purchase orders
c. 11/04/--	Message from the vice president of Human Resources explaining the new personal savings plans available to all employees
d. 11/05/--	Message from a coworker wishing you happy birthday
e. 11/05/--	Message from a coworker providing routing instructions for a report you are preparing
f. 11/05/--	Message from a vendor, Broadway Computer Services, Inc. listing details of a new contract being negotiated
g. 11/06/--	Message from an outside contractor, Kingsmill Roofing, giving an estimate for completing a roofing project
h. 11/06/--	Message from a coworker who is having trouble accessing online files and wonders whether you are having the same problem
i. 11/07/--	Message to Broadway Computer Services, Inc. with questions regarding the contract being negotiated
j. 11/07/--	Message from the Finance Department's administrative assistant summarizing decisions made at a department meeting and listing action items
k. 11/07/--	Message to Monica Ortega, CPA, requesting a bid for the annual tax audit
l. 11/07/--	Message from your supervisor informing all employees that she will be out of the office next Wednesday

11-3 ELECTRONIC AND IMAGE RECORDS DATABASE (OBJ. 13)

DATA CD

ACCESS ACTIVITY

Key the following index information into a database used for locating electronic and image records.

1. Locate the *Access* file *11-3 Records Index* in the data files. Copy the file to your working folder on a hard drive or removable storage device. Open the file.

2. Add the following records to the Electronic and Image Records Index database table. Two records are provided in the database table as examples. Record ID is an AutoNumber field and will be filled automatically by the software.

3. Use the Report Wizard to create a report based on the Electronic and Images Records Index table. Include all the fields in the report. Group data by the Media field and then by the Location field. Sort the records in ascending order by the Name field. Choose **Stepped** layout and **Landscape** orientation. Save the report as **Electronic and Image Records Index Report.**

4. Change the report margins or style, if needed, so the report fits on one page. Print the report.

Name	Record Date	Storage Date	Media	Location
Pradhan Bipin	05-24-2000	06-01-2001	Microfilm	Offsite
Santoro Renovation Drawing	07-23-2005	07-25-2005	Aperture Card	Active
Santoro Engineering Services	06-15-2005	06-17-2005	CD-ROM	Active
Tecumseh Engineering Services	05-14-2005	05-17-2005	CD-ROM	Active
FDC Technology	03-21-2002	04-01-2003	Microfiche	Offsite
Articles of Incorporation	11-15-1995	12-01-2005	Microfilm	Archives
Franz Auto Parts	12-26-2005	12-26-2005	Microfiche	Active
Tecumseh Renovation Drawing	08-20-2005	08-23-2005	Aperture Card	Active

11-4 RESEARCH ELECTRONIC AND IMAGE RECORDS TOPICS (OBJ. 14)

INTERNET

Using the search engine of your choice, search the Internet for information on RAID and microforms.

1. Look for new information about RAID (redundant array of independent disks) that is not provided in this chapter. Write a brief paragraph about what you find.

2. Search for information about government agencies, libraries, or companies that use microforms. Write a brief paragraph about what these organizations store on microforms.

FOR MORE ACTIVITIES GO TO **http://read.swlearning.com**

The Records and Information Management Program

Learning Objectives

1. List components of a records information management (RIM) program.

2. Define and describe efficiency ratios useful in RIM.

3. List responsibilities of a RIM program.

4. Define and describe the purpose of a records audit.

5. Explain the purpose of a records and information manual.

6. List goals of a forms management program.

7. List guidelines for constructing a well-designed form.

8. Explain the phases of a disaster recovery plan.

9. Define and describe knowledge management.

10. Discuss the use of RIM software.

11. List actions taken to implement a retention schedule.

RIM PROGRAM COMPONENTS

A comprehensive RIM program includes responsibility for storing records on all media; records retention and destruction; compliance with laws and regulations, managing active and inactive records, and protecting vital records.[1] Other responsibilities may include micrographics technology (discussed in Chapter 11); the records audit; correspondence, copy-making, and forms management; disaster prevention, preparation, and recovery; knowledge management; RIM software selection, implementation, and management; and RIM policy implementation and enforcement.

[1] William Saffady, *Records and Information Management: Fundamentals of Professional Practice* (Lenexa, KS: ARMA International, 2004), p. 9.

What is the basis for records storage?

Records Storage

The records storage component of the RIM program is based on the record life cycle presented in Chapter 1. The storage method—alphabetic, subject, numeric, or geographic—is determined after a records inventory is completed. (See Chapter 7 for more on the records inventory.) Managing records storage includes not only making decisions about storage supplies and equipment for storing active and inactive records, but also managing the safety, security, and the environment for all stored records. Active records are consulted frequently soon after they are created. However, they are consulted less often as they age. As records become inactive, the concern becomes records preservation, space conservation, and reduced storage costs. Offsite storage and microfilming provide solutions that address these concerns.

Why is having a records retention schedule important?

Records Retention and Destruction

Determining which records should be kept, how long they should be kept, and how they are dispositioned (destroyed or stored permanently) are critical activities that are governed by approved policies and procedures. Records retention procedures and policies are valuable components of a comprehensive RIM program. Through these procedures and policies, an organization can assure that records are available for recommended periods.

A basic records control tool is the records retention schedule, which is a listing of an organization's records along with the stated time categories of records must be kept. The records retention schedule is illustrated and discussed in Chapter 7.

Records Retention Schedule Development

After records inventory surveys completed by each department in an organization are collected, a tentative records retention schedule is prepared. Members of each department, members of the legal staff, and others involved with regulatory requirements review the schedule and verify suggested retention periods. When all parties agree, the records retention schedule is finalized and approved by senior management.

Records Retention Schedule Implementation

To assure that all organization members are aware of and adhere to records retention schedules, they are distributed to each department along with detailed instructions for their use. Special meetings may be held to explain further if necessary.

Compliance

As stated previously in this text, various laws and regulations have an impact on records and information management. In addition to meeting records retention requirements to comply with local, state, and federal tax laws, the Health Insurance Portability and Accountability Act (HIPAA) of 1996, the Privacy Rule of 2001, and the Sarbanes-Oxley Act of 2002, also affect RIM. (See Chapter 1, page 17, for more details about these important acts.) Other regulations are specific to certain industries. As a consequence of the need to comply with appropriate laws and regulations, organizations must develop and implement policies and procedures to assure compliance.

Many organizations have also made adjustments to their policies and procedures to adhere to ISO 15489, the international records management standard. If an organization is involved in international trade, it must adhere to ISO 9000 guidelines. These guidelines specify how product development procedures are documented and how the records are maintained. Emphasis is placed on quality.

What is the meaning of compliance?

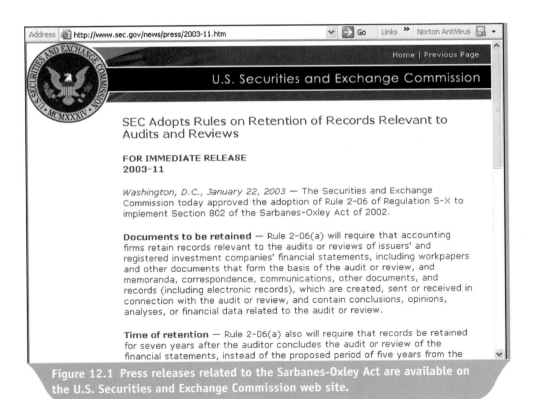

Figure 12.1 Press releases related to the Sarbanes-Oxley Act are available on the U.S. Securities and Exchange Commission web site.

Source: U.S. Securities and Exchange Commission <http://www.sec.gov/news/press/2003-11.htm> (accessed September 26, 2005).

Active Records Management

Effective management of active records involves three types of ongoing controls: (1) cost containment; (2) efficiency controls, ratios, and standards; and (3) performance standards. When these controls are applied to people, storage space and equipment, and routine procedures, they become key elements that make a RIM program function effectively. All three controls are based on the **cost-benefit ratio**—a comparison to determine that every cost (input) results in an equal or greater benefit (output). When applied, the cost-benefit ratio gives guidance and purpose to the process of cost, efficiency, and performance controls.

Cost Containment

Managing the volume of paper records, as pointed out in Chapters 1 and 7, carries with it tremendous costs. These costs include salaries, storage space, equipment, and supplies.

Labor costs represent the largest percentage of total RIM costs. The human resources cost factor includes managerial, supervisory, and operating personnel salaries along with employee benefits such as retirement plans, social security contributions, and various types of insurance. Installing automated RIM systems can help reduce long-term labor costs. Electronic media costs have declined, but storage and management costs have increased. A clearly defined and implemented records retention policy prevents an organization from retaining unnecessary data that keeps storage costs high.

Steps commonly taken to reduce costs include:

> **Which cost item represents the largest percentage of RIM costs?**

1. Identify and assign cost figures to the four main cost categories— salaries, space, equipment, and supplies. These elements include hourly rates for all records personnel, cost of equipment, and cost of the space that equipment occupies. Then, the costs of maintaining typical files (such as five-drawer vertical file cabinets) can be calculated and used in cost-reduction studies.
2. Compare labor costs for storing and retrieving records in-house and using offsite or commercial storage facilities. For example, apply the cost-benefit ratio to using a commercial records center. Evaluate the cost of picking up records, storing records, using a pick list to retrieve records, delivering records to the company, and destroying records. Include costs incurred by emergency records requests and fast delivery.

Costs of equipment, space, salaries, and supplies can be controlled by (1) eliminating unnecessary records, (2) carefully supervising the use of equipment and supplies, and (3) selecting equipment and media that require less space and less time to operate. Implementing efficiency and performance standards can also reduce labor costs when employee efficiency and performance are measured and evaluated against these standards.

Efficiency Controls

An **efficiency control** is a method for evaluating the ability to produce a desired effect with a minimum expenditure of time, energy, and space. When efficiency controls are applied to storage and electronic equipment, many possibilities surface for delivering faster data output, documents, and paper records while conserving time, energy, and space.

Efficiency controls also include measuring filers' speed and accuracy and developing standards from such measurements. Practical standards for storing and retrieving records are developed by answering three important questions: (1) How much time is required to store a record from the time such storage is authorized? (2) How much time is required to retrieve a record from storage? (3) What is the expected turnaround time—the time required to find and deliver a record to a requester after a request for a record has been made? Time standards depend on whether a task is performed manually or electronically. In addition, times may vary among organizations because of differences in types of records stored, storage facilities and equipment, and filers' skills. The three questions can be directly related to published standards for manual storage and retrieval systems, such as those listed in Figure 12.2, that large firms and standards associations have developed. Efficiency controls have value and include not only efficiency standards but also efficiency ratios.

Why measure RIM program efficiency?

Task	Time Unit
Manual Systems:	
Code one-page letter	200 per hour
Key folder labels	100 per hour
Sort invoices into 3-digit numeric sequence	1,500 per hour
Sort coded letters	250 per hour
Place records into subject file	150 per hour
Place invoices into numeric file	250 per hour
Retrieve records from color-coded file	2.5 per minute
Retrieve correspondence and prepare charge-out records	70 per hour
Electronic Systems:	
Store and retrieve files: Depends on access time—microseconds of time required for a computer to store and retrieve data.	

Figure 12.2 Records Storage and Retrieval Standards

Efficiency Standards

Because providing needed information is the main function of any RIM program, the most important test of any records system is the speed with which stored information is located. Efficiency standards used to measure filers' ability to locate information include:

1. The number of misfiles—usually about 3 percent of the total number of records filed
2. The number of "can't find" records—should be less than 1 percent
3. The time required to find a record—should never exceed 2 to 3 minutes

What is the purpose of efficiency standards?

At least once a year, a RIM manager should check the efficiency of the program. In addition to the three efficiency standards mentioned previously, other measures to check include:

1. The number of records retrieved compared to the total cubic feet of stored records
2. The number of records received—in number of records or in cubic feet of space occupied
3. The amount of space being used for records compared to the total square feet of floor space
4. The amount of unused space available
5. How often records are requested from the files
6. How much equipment is (or is not) being used
7. How many records have been destroyed or transferred from active to inactive storage

Efficiency Ratios

An **efficiency ratio** is a standard for measuring the efficiency of various aspects of records systems. Ratios provide RIM managers with a quantifiable means of measuring efficiency. They can then establish an efficiency standard, set a baseline, and thereafter measure its progress or decline. Efficiency ratios in one organization may be compared with efficiency ratios of other organizations as well. The most useful ratios are: (1) the **activity ratio**, (2) the **accuracy ratio**, and (3) the **retrieval efficiency ratio**. These ratios are explained in Figure 12.3 on page 357.

What are three types of efficiency ratios?

Performance Standards

The attitudes that each records employee brings to the job affect performance standards. In addition to the efficiency and cost controls discussed earlier, each of the following aspects of human behavior needs to be understood and controlled:

1. Poor attendance—frequent tardiness and absences
2. Excessive need for overtime work

Why do managers need to understand performance standards?

Type of Ratio	Formula	Example
1. Activity ratio—measures the frequency of records use	$\dfrac{\text{Number of records requested}}{\text{Number of records filed}}$	Requested 500 records; filed 5,000 records—a 10% activity ratio
		When the ratio is below 5%, transfer all records that fall below 5% to inactive storage or destroy them.
2. Accuracy ratio—measures the ability of filers to find requested records	$\dfrac{\text{Number of records found}}{\text{Number of records requested}}$	Found 5,950 records; requested 6,000 records—a 99.17% accuracy ratio
		When the ratio falls below 97%, the records system needs immediate attention.
3. Retrieval efficiency ratio—measures the speed with which records are found and verifies how filers spend their time	$\dfrac{\text{Time to locate records}}{\text{Number of records retrieved}}$	A ratio of 75% (retrieving 80 records in 60 minutes) suggests an efficient records system and productive filers, depending on the type of files and filing conditions.

Figure 12.3 Records System Efficiency Ratio Formulas

3. Numbers and patterns of errors in the work of each employee
4. Slow response to work assignments
5. Low morale and lack of interest in work assignments
6. Lack of concern for, or inability to follow, budget limits
7. Repeated failure to meet performance standards

Supervisors should discuss these performance problems with their employees. By working together, solutions can be developed for increasing productivity in the records system.

Inactive Records Management

As you studied in Chapter 7, inactive records are not accessed frequently. Consequently, they do not need to be stored near filers and users. They may be stored in a records center—either in-house, offsite, or in a commercial records storage facility. By implementing and adhering to established retention and destruction schedules, inactive records that need to be available for long periods are maintained for the time periods dictated by the schedules.

What are mission-critical records?

Vital Records Protection

First mentioned in Chapter 1 and discussed again in Chapter 7, vital records are sometimes described as *mission-critical records* because their existence is critical for the continued operations and purposes of an organization. As a consequence of their importance, organizations implement special procedures for protecting those vital records. Vital records stored on microfilm or electronic media are subjected to specific environmental, security, and safety controls to assure their continued usefulness for as long as they are needed—permanently for some documents and records. As discussed later in this chapter, developing and implementing a disaster preparedness and prevention program is part of the protection plans for all stored records.

RIM PROGRAM RESPONSIBILITIES

A RIM program in a large organization encompasses a variety of responsibilities, including the records audit; preparation and distribution of the RIM manual; disaster preparedness, prevention, and recovery; knowledge management; RIM software selection, implementation, and management; and RIM policy implementation and enforcement. Each of these responsibilities is discussed in the following sections.

Why is a records audit performed?

Records Audit

A **records audit** is a periodic inspection to verify that an operation is in compliance with a records and information management program. From the audit, managers hope to find ways of improving the program's performance. Large organizations may use their own trained staff to undertake such an audit, or they may hire outside consultants (usually having more objectivity and expertise) for this purpose. Small firms often use outside auditors because they usually do not have a qualified records auditor on staff.

A records audit provides three kinds of information about a records and information management program:

1. **Information about current operations.** This information includes how well the objectives are being achieved, whether written policies and procedures are available and followed by all personnel, whether policies and procedures reflect the way documents are processed, and the scope of RIM activities and any problems associated with them.
2. **Analysis of the current system and its needs.** This analysis includes the layout of files, effectiveness and validity of policies and procedures,

qualifications of the staff, uses of available equipment, active and inactive storage systems, costs of operating the system versus projected costs, and security measures for preserving and protecting records.

3. **Recommended solutions for improving the RIM program.** These solutions also include cost estimates for implementing the recommendations.

Software can be used to provide audit trails for tracking document use and, consequently, staff productivity. A system administrator can monitor electronic image and electronic records use by determining who has been viewing which documents, where, and when. Monitoring sensitive case documents that need to be kept secure, tracking staff productivity, and tracking search activity among public records can be done using audit logs generated by the software.

Records and Information Manual

The most important reference for a RIM staff is a records and information manual. This manual contains all information necessary for managing the RIM program in an organization (e.g., policy statements; records retention schedules; indexing, coding, and filing procedures; vital records procedures; records inventory procedures; general policies and procedures; records and information manual distribution and use; administrative responsibilities; disaster prevention and recovery plan; and so on).

> **Why is a records and information manual needed?**

Especially useful in conducting the records audit, this manual is the official handbook of approved policies and procedures for operating the RIM program. Responsibility for various phases of the program, standard operating procedures, and aids for training employees are included in the manual. Some organizations may also include information about their knowledge management and ISO 9000 activities. The contents of a typical records and information manual are listed in Figure 12.4 on page 360.

Correspondence, Copy, and Forms Management

Ideally, the records and information manager is involved with records from their creation to their destruction. Unfortunately, this situation does not always occur. If it did, a records and information manager's involvement with records creation would begin by managing paper selection. To manage records creation beyond paper selection, the RIM manager must influence those who are responsible for creating and using the records; namely, the records originators, records receivers, and the administrative staff that distribute and manage the records. Managing correspondence creation, copy creation, and forms is discussed in this section.

Main Sections	Contents
1. RIM program overview	Definition, goals, policies, personnel responsibilities, records retention schedules, disaster prevention and recovery plan
2. Classification system	Records classifications—transaction and reference documents; internal and external records; important, useful, nonessential, and vital records—alphabetic, master, and relative indexes; subject records classification codes; retention and disposition codes
3. Storage procedures for records on all media	What records to store and when, preparing records for storage, classifying and coding, preparing cross-references, sorting, storing, restricting access, retrieving, charging-out, following up borrowed records, maintaining folders and containers
4. Records retention schedules	Short-term and long-term retention periods, retention schedules for specific departments, electronic records retention (if necessary), guidelines for retaining e-mail messages and web site records
5. Storage locations	Department sites, central sites, offsite locations
6. Annual program evaluation or audit	Purposes and requirements for each program evaluation or audit
7. Records disposition	Disposition functions, implementing records retention schedules, packing records, labeling boxes, transferring records, retrieving inactive records, destroying inactive records
8. Disaster recovery plan	Preparation steps for potential disasters, plan activation, recovery and resumption of operations
9. RIM software	Summary of software capabilities and uses

Figure 12.4 Records and Information Manual Contents

Correspondence Management

Why should correspondence creation be controlled?

The goal of controlling correspondence is to reduce the number of records that must be stored and maintained. Records originators need to be reminded that the most expensive cost in a record's life cycle is incurred at its creation stage. Records receivers and administrative staff need to distinguish between records required for documentation from those that may be destroyed. The easiest way to control records costs is to reduce the number of records that enter the system by destroying those records that are **not** needed and controlling only those that are needed for business or historical purposes.

Controlling correspondence includes evaluating the tasks of creating, distributing, using, storing, and eventually disposing of correspondence and then looking for the most economical ways of accomplishing these tasks. Many automatic features of word processing software save valuable time for office staff. Using form letters saves the time of correspondence originators. Digitized letterheads, commonly used paragraphs, special letter parts, special forms, and a

Job Description for Records Center Supervisor

The following job description is an example of a career opportunity in a corporate records center.

GENERAL INFORMATION

The Records Center Supervisor coordinates and supervises the records center staff who are responsible for maintaining systems and procedures that facilitate efficient retention and disposition of internal customer records.

RESPONSIBILITIES

- Plans, schedules, and assigns work tasks according to customer direction
- Coordinates and supervises Records Center staff
- Performs quality checks of work performed by Records Center staff
- Ensures security and preservation of records in the Records Center
- Trains Records Center staff
- Provides information and training for internal customers as required
- Documents policies and procedures and ensures they are up-to-date
- Works with customers on research and retrieval projects
- Ensures adherence to retention schedules
- Gathers data and prepares reports on all phases of the RIM program as required
- Coordinates information creation, receipt, storage, retrieval, and disposition activities

EXPERIENCE AND EDUCATION

- Two years of college with specialized course work in records management, business law, and computer technology
- One to two years' experience in a records environment
- Previous supervisory experience
- Strong oral and written communication skills
- Excellent customer service skills
- Self-motivation and ability to work independently
- Ability to perceive and analyze problems, develop alternatives, and make or recommend sound decisions
- Membership in professional organizations
- Thorough knowledge of retention schedules, with ability to conduct research
- Knowledge of relevant technology systems and applications
- *Microsoft Office* and *Microsoft Access* database management experience

variety of text data and graphics can be indexed and stored in word processing files and retrieved as needed. The user selects a number of paragraphs to include in a letter, memo, fax, or e-mail message. The paragraphs may be selected from a binder containing copies of printed letter parts or from an electronic file for cutting and pasting into a document. The document is printed for a signature or signed electronically.

Copy Management

A photocopier can create many copies with great speed. Because producing extra copies of documents and reports can easily become standard practice in an office, photocopying control is an important part of the total control process. Many organizations and universities program departmental user codes into photocopiers so that users must enter a proper code before copies may be made. Numbers of copies made are automatically charged to the departments using the copiers; this procedure is called chargeback. These departments are billed regularly, such as monthly, bimonthly, or perhaps every 6 months. They also receive periodic reports of photocopier use.

RIM employees need to identify all costs of creating and copying records—personnel, equipment, supplies, space, and so on. In addition, they should uncover hidden costs, including the costs of ordering supplies, purchasing records storage equipment, and mailing.

Easily implemented ways to control copy-making costs include:

- Select the most suitable—and least expensive—methods and supplies.
- Use only one or two copier models to reduce maintenance costs.
- Calculate per-copy costs regularly.
- Use charge-back procedures to charge all copy-making costs to the department involved.

Even tighter controls over copiers are possible by requiring employees to obtain approval from a supervisor before making copies and by installing copiers that require a key or access card to unlock and use them. These copiers may also record the job number, the number of copies made, and a reference for charging the copy costs to the using department. These copiers can then regularly process usage reports.

Forms Management

A **form** is a fixed arrangement of predetermined spaces designed for entering and extracting prescribed information on a paper or electronic document (Figure 12.5 on page 363). A RIM manager's responsibilities include forms management to assure consistency across all departments in an organization. In large corporations, schools, universities, and other organizations that use many forms, this responsibility may be delegated to a forms manager and staff who are part of the RIM program.

> **What is the meaning of *chargeback*?**

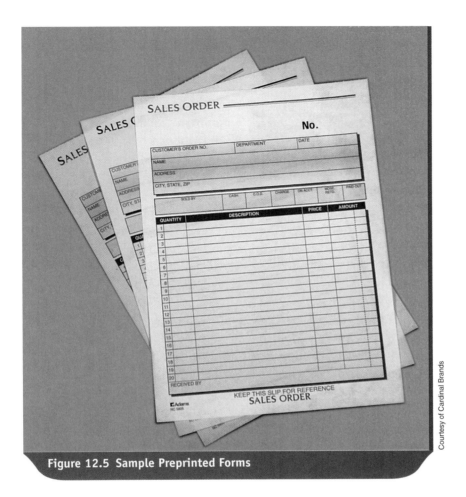

Courtesy of Cardinal Brands

Figure 12.5 Sample Preprinted Forms

A form contains two types of data:

1. **Constant data** are data that are preprinted on a form. Constant data do not require rewriting each time the form is filled in. Examples of constant data include the word *Date* and the phrase *Pay to the order of* on a bank check, and the words *Quantity, Description, Price,* and *Amount* on an invoice.
2. **Variable data** are data that change each time a form is filled in. Examples of variable data on a bank check are the filled-in date, the payee's name, the amount of money, and the signature.

Typical goals of forms management are to:

1. **Determine the number and use of forms.** This information is obtained as a part of a records inventory.

What types of data are included in a form?

2. **Eliminate unnecessary forms.** This goal includes: (a) eliminating forms that overlap or duplicate each other by combining them, (b) eliminating forms that collect unused information, and (c) eliminating forms no longer needed.
3. **Standardize form size, paper quality, typefaces, and design features such as company logos and form numbers.** Standardization results in lower form costs because one type and size of paper can be used throughout the organization.
4. **Ensure efficient forms design.** Apply sound design principles (see Figure 12.6 on page 365).
5. **Establish efficient, economical procedures for printing, storing, and distributing forms.** These procedures should include an inventory control program to allow sufficient time to revise forms before reordering them.

Types of Forms

What are some commonly used single-copy forms?

Single-copy forms, such as telephone message forms, are used within one department for its own needs. Multicopy forms, such as a four-copy purchase order, are used to transmit information outside the creating department. These preassembled sets of forms are glued together at the top for easy removal of each copy. In automated records systems, electronic forms appear on terminal screens for data input from a keyboard. These forms are created using special forms design software or programs such as *Microsoft Word* or *Microsoft Access*. Unlike paper forms, electronic forms are not printed and stocked. Instead, after they are designed, they may be filled in online, and either transmitted to another workstation or printed. If additional copies are needed, they are printed or made on photocopiers.

Buying standard forms from an office supply store is less expensive than custom-designed forms as long as a standard form meets the needs of an office. Standardized forms are used in large numbers because they are capable of handling large quantities of information in the least amount of time, effort, and space. As forms continue to be an efficient way of gathering and transmitting information, their design, use, cost, and storage require managerial approval and periodic evaluation. Forms management features of software can help users design or modify forms. Well-designed forms assist in maintaining an efficient and productive forms management program.

Forms Design

A forms designer needs to know: (1) how the form will be used; (2) the types of items to be filled in and their sequence; (3) the size, color, and weight of paper stock to be used; and (4) the amount of space needed for each fill-in item.

The main objectives in forms design are to make the form efficient to fill in—manually or electronically, efficient to read and understand, and efficient to store and retrieve. These objectives can be met by applying the design guidelines shown in Figure 12.6. Ideally, in multicopy form sets, each receiving department copy is a different color. However, when forms are downloaded from web sites, they are usually printed on white paper and photocopied for other departments. Forms design books and office suite software programs help office workers design professional-quality forms. Programs that have forms templates can be used to design commonly used forms such as invoices and purchase orders. An example of an invoice template is shown in Figure 12.7 on page 366.

GUIDELINES

- Eliminate excessive graphic features such as borders or drawings.
- Avoid requesting unnecessary or unlawful information.
  - Ask for age **or** date of birth, not both.
  - Avoid asking for personal information or information that could be used illegally such as religion or ethnicity.
- Eliminate horizontal lines when the form will be filled in on a computer.
- Give each form a name that indicates its function; "form" is not a necessary part of a form name—Application, not Application Form.
- Assign each form a sequential number within the creating department.
- Include the revision date with the form number—RM205 Rev. 05/05.
- Arrange items in the normal reading pattern of left to right and top to bottom.
- Arrange items in the same order in which data will be filled in or extracted.
- Use black ink to facilitate scanning or microfilming.
- Use a small font size such as 10 point for captions.
- Allow sufficient space for fill-ins.
- Use check boxes to save user time.
- Use box design style for constant data.

Name

- Place instructions for filling in at the top of the form.
- Place distribution and filing information at the bottom of the form.
- Key instructions consisting of several lines or paragraphs in lowercase and initial caps.

Figure 12.6 Forms Design Guidelines

Source: Adapted from Marvin Jacobs and Linda I. Studer, *Forms Design II: The Course for Paper and Electronic Forms* (N. Olmstead, OH: Words and Pictures Publishing, 1991).

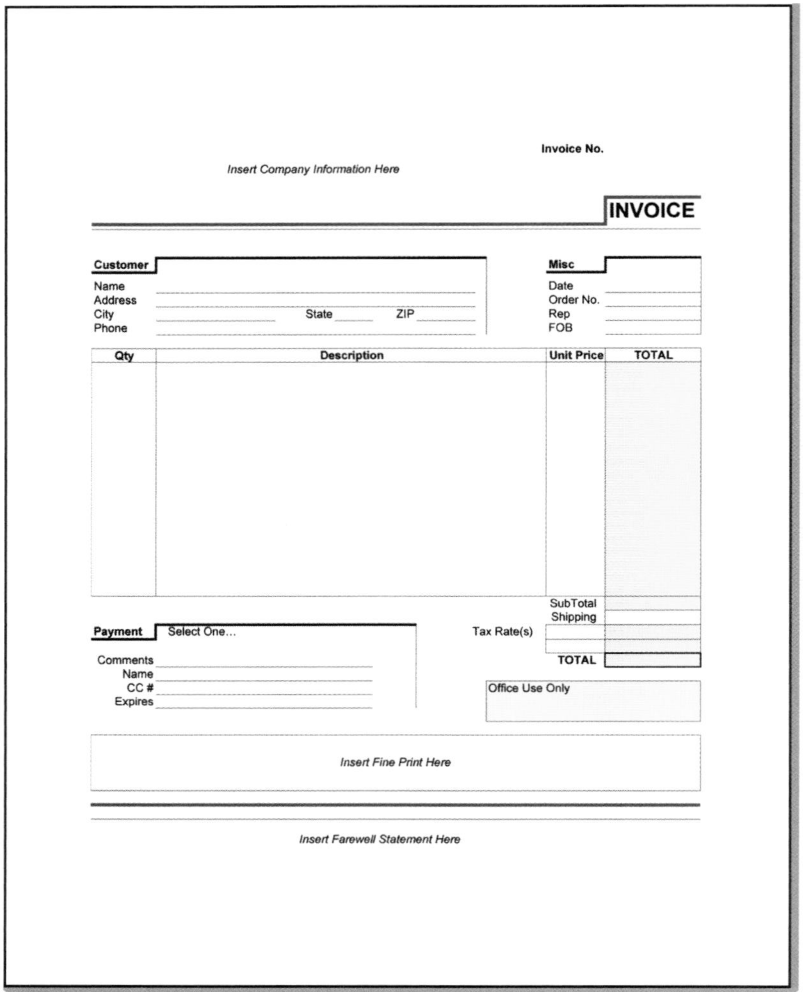

Invoice No.

Insert Company Information Here

INVOICE

Customer
Name
Address
City State ZIP
Phone

Misc
Date
Order No.
Rep
FOB

Qty	Description	Unit Price	TOTAL
		SubTotal	
		Shipping	
	Tax Rate(s)		
		TOTAL	

Payment Select One...
Comments
Name
CC #
Expires

Office Use Only

Insert Fine Print Here

Insert Farewell Statement Here

Figure 12.7 ***Microsoft Excel*** **Invoice Template**

Disaster Prevention, Preparedness, and Recovery

Organizations all over the world adopt plans for dealing with emergencies caused by weather disasters or other events as well as internal emergencies such as broken water pipes and small electrical fires. Some organizations have developed plans for terrorist attacks. **Disaster recovery plans** may also be referred to as contingency plans, emergency plans, or disaster plans. Whatever their title, these plans are developed and implemented to provide guidance for protecting records and information and continuing business operations when emergencies and disasters occur.

An emergency is an unforeseen event that calls for immediate action. Examples of an emergency include a broken water pipe, a bomb threat, or a sudden storm that require actions but do not usually result in major loss or disruption of operations for an organization. A disaster is a sudden emergency event that results in major loss of resources or disruption of operations for an organization. Disasters can result in significant financial damage. Examples of disasters include a destructive fire, a flood causing major facility or product loss, or a tornado that causes major damage to one or more facilities.

Disaster prevention is the first phase of the disaster plan in which measures are taken to reduce the probability of loss resulting from an emergency. If an emergency occurs, these measures reduce the likelihood that they will turn into RIM disasters.[2]

Preparedness, the second phase, is simply being prepared to respond when an emergency occurs. Once an emergency is recognized, personnel know what to do and whom to call. Preparedness activities include developing a response team, developing and updating the plan, testing emergency systems, training employees, stocking emergency supplies, arranging for recovery vendors, and establishing hot sites (locations where a complete computer operation is set up and ready). Responding to an emergency event means activating resources necessary to protect the organization from loss. These activities occur before, during, or directly after an emergency and include contacting the response team, notifying appropriate authorities, securing facilities, and notifying RIM recovery vendors.

Recovery, the third phase, involves necessary activities to restore operations quickly, especially vital systems and processes that will keep producing products and services as well as retaining customers. These activities include dehumidifying records, restoring data onto computers, and returning vital records from offsite storage.[3] A disaster recovery plan is a written and approved course of action to take when disaster strikes, ensuring an organization's ability to respond to an interruption in services by restoring critical business functions. The plan also details how records will be handled before and during a disaster and after in the recovery stage. Procedures for the immediate resumption of business operations after a disaster are included as well. How an organization prepares for a disruption to its business determines how well, or if, it survives. Flooding from leaking roofs, leaking air conditioners, overflowing toilets, broken water mains, broken water pipes, overflowing sewer systems, and other water sources is a commonly occurring type of business interruption. Equipment outages and power outages are also common causes of interruption to business activity. Fire or explosion, earthquake, hurricane, and building outage

> **What is an emergency?**

> **What activities take place in the recovery phase?**

[2]Virginia A. Jones and Kris E. Keyes, *Emergency Management for Records and Information Management Programs* (Prairie Village, KS: ARMA International, 2001), p. 5.
[3]Ibid., p. 6.

resulting from construction or environmental problems are more serious causes of business interruption. Hurricanes, earthquakes, and the well-publicized bombings in major cities and in federal office buildings have alerted all businesses to the critical importance of a disaster recovery plan.

A disaster recovery plan is the basis for the following activities:

1. Identifying preventive measures against records and information loss
2. Initiating a company-wide response to disasters that threaten records and information
3. Identifying response personnel and their roles
4. Estimating cost of and various types and lengths of business disruptions
5. Providing offsite storage for vital records and backup computer data storage
6. Designating alternative sites for mission-critical tasks including computer-related operations
7. Establishing recovery procedures for damaged records and information
8. Establishing recovery priorities
9. Identifying sources of supplies, equipment, and services for recovery and restoration of damaged records and media
10. Testing the plan through mock disasters and making appropriate changes

What are some ways to protect electronic records?

Records can be lost and/or damaged when necessary precautions are not taken to protect them. Routine precautions are taken to protect electronic data such as controlling extremes in temperature and humidity, backing up valuable data, installing antivirus programs that detect and remove computer viruses, installing firewall programs to prevent unauthorized network intrusions, installing surge protectors to minimize damage caused by electrical variances, and removing magnetic items from around hard drives and floppy disks. Discussions in Chapter 11 include procedures for controlling and protecting records from physical hazards, controlling environmental conditions necessary to ensure safe storage of all records, and protecting records from unauthorized access. The test of a sound disaster recovery plan—and any other precautionary procedures and safety measures taken to protect records and business operations—is whether it allows business activity to resume within a few days after a disaster. Such a plan includes not only a recovery of records but also a recovery of the work site, essential equipment, and the work force.

Records Safety in an Emergency

My Records

If the fire alarm went off in your home, which records would you decide to save? If you must be evacuated from your home, what records should you take with you?

The most important task in any emergency is for the personal safety of you and your family. The American Red Cross web site contains many suggestions for coping with emergencies, including how to prepare for them.

Throughout this text, the *My Records* sections have given tips about managing your personal records. These tips are helpful to you in case of an emergency. The next step in safeguarding your records is to act on the tips.

- Identify your vital records and make certified copies (see Chapter 1 My Records on page 10).

- Document the original vital records (and you may have many) with addresses, phone numbers, contact people, and the location where you have stored these records off-site.

- Store the originals in a safety deposit box or similarly safe offsite location (see Chapter 6 My Records on page 159).

- Store the certified copies in a weather-proof container that you can take with you as you leave your house.

- Store the container that holds the copies with your personal survival kits stocked with food, water, medical supplies, and a change of clothing.

- Store the most recent computer backup in the same weather-proof container.

- Update the records in the storage container at least once a month.

Be prepared: Plan and then implement the plan.

Knowledge Management

If an organization recognizes that it is a part of the knowledge economy and that it employs knowledge workers, it may be engaged in knowledge management activities to make effective use of its knowledge resources.

Knowledge management is an interdisciplinary field that is concerned with systematic, effective management and utilization of an organization's knowledge resources. It encompasses creation, storage, retrieval, and distribution of an organization's knowledge—similar to records and information management.

Why is managing knowledge important?

A knowledge resource may be explicit knowledge or tacit knowledge. Explicit knowledge is contained in documents, databases, e-mail, or other records. Tacit knowledge is acquired through observation, practice, and imitation. It relies on experience, judgment, and intuition and is exhibited through employee skills or "know-how."[4] Employee knowledge, skills, and experience are valuable resources that, with proper management, can be fully utilized. The first step in managing knowledge is to conduct a knowledge inventory to determine what knowledge, skills, and experience employees have and where they are located. Once that information is collected, organized, and stored in a knowledge database, employees can be used in areas where their knowledge, skills, and experience are needed. Sometimes a department or office borrows an employee from another department for a short time to perform specialized duties.

RIM Software

What is the main objective for using RIM software?

As discussed previously in this book, automating many of the manual processes in the RIM function is the main objective in choosing a software program. Small RIM departments and small organizations may use word processing or database software to prepare searchable databases. They may also select a vendor system for a specific function of their RIM program. Large organizations that have large volumes of records are more likely to use integrated software programs to administer several processes involved in the RIM function. Some RIM software, such as *Accutrac*™, provides organizations with more options for automating physical (paper) and electronic records and information management throughout the record life cycle.

RIM software allows users to automate manual functions for paper, electronic, image, and e-mail records. Some programs provide access to an organization's records database via the Internet and allow user-defined enterprise records management applications. Some features that may be provided with RIM software are listed below.

Can retention schedules be developed with the aid of RIM software?

- Eliminates the need to prepare records transmittal forms manually
- Allows integration with the an e-mail system and classification of e-mail messages
- Allows management of e-mail, images, and faxes, and other electronic documents in the same manner as paper records
- Automates the records retention process and assures implementation and compliance of an organization's records retention policy
- Allows tracking of patent, trademark, and copyright records
- Allows printing of color-coded labels

[4]William Saffady, *Knowledge Management: A Manager's Briefing* (Prairie Village, KS: ARMA International, 1998), p. 4.

- Provides statutory and regulatory research needed for preparing and up-dating records retention schedules
- Allows use of handheld and stationary bar code readers

Some programs are organized into modules that provide different features. Organizations may purchase only those modules needed in their organizations.

Policy Implementation and Enforcement

A records retention program includes not only retention and destruction schedules but also policies for implementing those schedules. In organizations in which records retention policies have been established, the RIM manager is responsible for implementing the policies and assuring that all employees are complying with the policies. In order to achieve organization-wide implementation, each department may appoint RIM coordinators to assume responsibility for organizing and supervising retention activities in that department. Possible retention actions are listed in Figure 12.8.

Records coordinators will locate records eligible for retention actions and remove them from cabinets, shelves, and other containers. They will locate electronic records in hard drive directories and subdirectories. These manual activities are time-consuming and labor intensive. To comply with specified retention periods, records in some records series will need to be subdivided by dates such as the end of a calendar or fiscal year.[7]

Implementing and enforcing the e-mail policy may also be the RIM manager's responsibility. An e-mail policy may include the following statements:

- All e-mail is the property of the organization and is subject to management controls.

> **What types of policies are implemented and enforced as part of the RIM program?**

> **What tasks do records coordinators perform?**

RETENTION SCHEDULE IMPLEMENTATION

- Identify records series eligible for retention actions
- Destroy records with elapsed retention periods
- Transfer inactive paper or photographic records to offsite storage
- Transfer inactive electronic records from hard drives to removable media for offline or offsite storage
- Destroy paper copies after records are microfilmed or scanned

Figure 12.8 Retention Implementation Actions

Source: Adapted from William Saffady, *Records and Information Management: Fundamentals of Professional Practice* (Lenexa, KS: ARMA International, 2004), p. 6-7.

---

[7]David O. Stephens and Roderick C. Wallace, *Electronic Records Retention: New Strategies for Data Life Cycle Management* (Lenexa, KS: ARMA International, 2003), p. 48-49.

- Employees can assume no right to privacy regarding e-mail—the organization has the right to inspect all e-mail files.
- E-mail must be professional and must not include any derogatory remarks.
- E-mail will be retained for 30 days (or 60, or 90) after it is opened, read, and acted on. E-mail older than the specified retention period will be automatically purged (deleted).
- E-mail to be retained longer than the specified retention period needs to be printed and stored into an appropriate paper file, or migrated from the e-mail active files to inactive storage, and kept for the retention period indicated on the records retention schedule.
- Any e-mail related to current or pending litigation may not be destroyed without approval from the organization's Legal Department.
- Employees who violate these rules are subject to disciplinary action.[8]

RIM employees who have studied and gained experience in all topics discussed in RECORDS MANAGEMENT, Eighth Edition, can look forward to long, successful careers in the records and information management profession.

---

[8]Ibid.

Chapter Review And Applications

POINTS TO FILE AND RETRIEVE

- RIM program components include records storage, records retention and destruction, compliance, active and inactive records management, and protecting vital records.

- Records storage is based on the record life cycle.

- The records retention schedule is a basic records control tool.

- Many organizations must manage their RIM function to comply with federal and state laws and regulations.

- The RIM program is responsible for conducting the records audit; preparing and distributing the records and information manual; and managing correspondence, copy-making, and forms.

- Preparing a disaster recovery plan and implementing it in the event of a disaster is another responsibility of the RIM program.

- Knowledge management helps an organization fully use all skills and abilities of its employees.

- Integrated RIM software can automate many manual RIM processes and control records throughout their life cycle.

- RIM policy implementation and enforcement are important responsibilities of the RIM program.

IMPORTANT TERMS

accuracy ratio
activity ratio
constant data
cost-benefit ratio
disaster recovery plan
efficiency control

efficiency ratio
form
knowledge management
records audit
retrieval efficiency ratio
variable data

REVIEW AND DISCUSSION

1. List three elements of a comprehensive records and information management program. (Obj. 1)

2. Define activity, accuracy, and records retrieval efficiency ratios and describe the purpose of each ratio. How is each ratio calculated? (Obj. 2)

3. List three responsibilities of the RIM program. (Obj. 3)

4. Define *records audit* and describe its purpose. (Obj. 4)

5. Explain the purpose of a records and information manual. List at least three items included in the manual. (Obj. 5)

6. List three goals of forms management. (Obj. 6)

7. List at least three guidelines to follow when constructing a well-designed form. (Obj. 7)

8. What are the phases in a disaster recovery plan? Explain what occurs during each phase. (Obj. 8)

9. What is knowledge management? Describe explicit knowledge and implicit knowledge. (Obj. 9)

10. Discuss the use of RIM software. What is the main reason for using RIM software? (Obj. 10)

11. List three actions necessary for implementing a records retention schedule. (Obj. 11)

APPLICATIONS

12-1 DESIGN AN INFORMATION FORM (OBJS. 6 AND 7)

CRITICAL THINKING

Assume that you are a property manager for a condominium complex called Green Gables. You need to collect information about the automobiles owned by condo residents. Your goal is to keep track of all automobiles that regularly park in the condo parking lot by issuing preprinted parking stickers for each vehicle. Review the guidelines for creating forms in Figure 12.6 to help you complete this application.

1. Design a form that will be printed and given to residents to complete by hand. Include the complex name and the form title **Automobile Registration** at the top of the page.

2. Provide brief instructions for completing the form and indicate that the completed form should be returned to the management office. Indicate that residents should complete and submit a form for each vehicle that will be parked in the condo complex parking lot. Remind residents to submit new forms if they change vehicles.

3. Provide space on the form for residents to write the following information:
   - Current Date
   - Owner Name
   - Unit No.
   - Telephone No.
   - Automobile Make
   - Automobile Model
   - Automobile Color
   - License Plate No.
   - State of Registration

4. Include a space for the parking sticker number to be recorded and indicate that the number will be assigned by the management.

5. At the bottom of the form, key the form identification code **AUTO** and the current month and year as the revision date. For example: AUTO Rev. 05/06. Save the form as *12-1 Auto Form*. Print the form.

12-2 ENTER DATA USING A DATABASE FORM (OBJS. 6 AND 7)

In application 12-1, you created a form to collect data for the Green Gables condo complex. Now you will create an *Access* database to store and organize the automobile information.

ACCESS ACTIVITY

COLLABORATION

1. Create a new database file named *12-2 Automobile Registration*.

2. Create a new database table named **Automobile Registration.** Include the following fields in the table: Form Date, Owner Name, Unit #, Telephone #, Make, Model, Color, Plate #, State, Sticker #. Select **Number** as the field type for the Unit # and Sticker # fields. Select **Text** as the field type for all other fields. Select **Sticker #** as the primary key.

3. Create an AutoForm based on the Automobile Registration table. Enter the data shown on page 376 for six residents using the AutoForm. Enter the current year in dates.

4. Add two more records using the AutoForm. Assume that two of your classmates live in Units # 403 and 708. Interview your classmates and enter their auto information using the form. Assign sticker numbers 158 and 159 to their autos. Close the form without saving it.

5. Create a report based on the Automobile Registration table using the Report Wizard. Include all fields in the report except the Form Date field. Sort by the Unit # field in ascending order. Choose **Landscape** orientation, if needed, to have all fields show on one page. Name the report **Automobile Registration.** Print the report.

Form Date: 05/06/--
Owner Name: Jose Rodriguez
Unit #: 907
Telephone #: 513.555.0198
Make: Toyota
Model: Camry
Color: White
Plate #: CRL 5534
State: OH
Sticker #: 153

Form Date: 05/04/--
Owner Name: Andrea Phillips
Unit #: 312
Telephone #: 513.555.0120
Make: Jeep
Model: Cherokee
Color: White
Plate #: DDM 6589
State: KY
Sticker #: 155

Form Date: 05/05/--
Owner Name: Joshua Gibson
Unit #: 401
Telephone #: 513.555.0156
Make: Ford
Model: Focus
Color: Silver
Plate #: 23 DV 56
State: IN
Sticker #: 154

Form Date: 05/06/--
Owner Name: Sarah Fields
Unit #: 611
Telephone #: 513.555.0134
Make: Chevrolet
Model: Impala
Color: Black
Plate #: ORK 3448
State: OH
Sticker #: 152

Form Date: 05/07/--
Owner Name: C. J. Andrews
Unit #: 205
Telephone #: 513.555.0167
Make: Ford
Model: 500
Color: Navy Blue
Plate #: RCT 1562
State: KY
Sticker #: 156

Form Date: 05/05/--
Owner Name: Frank Patruso
Unit #: 710
Telephone #: 513.555.0123
Make: Lexus
Model: ES300
Color: Pearl White
Plate #: XMV 2198
State: OH
Sticker #: 157

12-3 LEARN MORE ABOUT RIM SOFTWARE

INTERNET

Some information about the RIM software *Accutrac* is presented in this chapter. More information about RIM software is available on the vendor web sites.

1. Access the *Accutrac* web site. You can find the URL for the *Accutrac* web site at the Links tab at the web site for this textbook. If you cannot access the *Accutrac* web site, use a search engine to find a web site for another RIM software.

2. Click an appropriate link to learn about the company's products. Read the information provided about the software and view any illustrations that are provided. You may need to click an illustration to enlarge it so that you can view it more clearly.

3. Look specifically for information about software features related to retention management. Write a brief paragraph that summarizes the information provided.

4. Look specifically for information about how bar code readers can be used with the software. Write a brief paragraph that summarizes the information provided.

FOR MORE ACTIVITIES GO TO **http://read.swlearning.com**

Appendix

Rule 1: Indexing Order of Units

A. Personal Names

A personal name is indexed in this manner: (1) the surname (last name) is the key unit, (2) the given name (first name) or initial is the second unit, and (3) the middle name or initial is the third unit. If determining the surname is difficult, consider the last name written as the surname. (You will learn how to handle titles that appear with names in a later rule.)

A unit consisting of just an initial precedes a unit that consists of a complete name beginning with the same letter—*nothing before something*. Punctuation is omitted. Remember, the underscored letter in the example shows the correct order. For example, 1 and 2 below have the same Key Unit *(Sample)*. The underscored "D" in *Darin* shows the alphabetic difference between the two names.

B. Business Names

Business names are indexed *as written* using letterheads or trademarks as guides. Each word in a business name is a separate unit. Business names containing personal names are indexed as written.

Rule 2: Minor Words and Symbols in Business Names

Articles, prepositions, conjunctions, and symbols are considered separate indexing units. Symbols are considered as spelled in full. When the word *The* appears as the first word of a business name, it is considered the last indexing unit.

Articles:	a, an, the
Prepositions:	at, in, out, on, off, by, to, with, for, of, over
Conjunctions:	and, but, or, nor
Symbols:	&, ¢, $, #, % (and, cent *or* cents, dollar *or* dollars, number *or* pound, percent)

Rule 3: Punctuation and Possessives

All punctuation is disregarded when indexing personal and business names. Commas, periods, hyphens, apostrophes, dashes, exclamation points, question marks, quotation marks, underscores, and diagonals (/) are disregarded, and names are indexed as written.

Rule 4: Single Letters and Abbreviations

A. Personal Names

Initials in personal names are considered separate indexing units. Abbreviations of personal names (Wm., Jos., Thos.) and nicknames (Liz, Bill) are indexed as they are written.

B. Business Names

Single letters in business and organization names are indexed as written. If single letters are separated by spaces, index each letter as a separate unit. An acronym (a word formed from the first, or first few, letters of several words, such as NASDAQ and ARCO) is indexed as one unit regardless of punctuation or spacing. Abbreviated words (Mfg., Corp., Inc.) and names (IBM, GE) are indexed as one unit regardless of punctuation or spacing. Radio and television station call letters (KDKA, WNBC) are indexed as one unit.

Rule 5: Titles and Suffixes

A. Personal Names

A title before a name (Dr., Miss, Mr., Mrs., Ms., Professor, Sir, Sister), a seniority suffix (II, III, Jr., Sr.), or a professional suffix (CRM, DDS, Mayor, M.D., Ph.D., Senator) after a name is the last indexing unit.

Numeric suffixes (II, III) are filed before alphabetic suffixes (Jr., Mayor, Senator, Sr.). If a name contains a title and a suffix (Ms. Lucy Wheeler, DVM), the title *Ms* is the last unit.

Royal and religious titles followed by either a given name or a surname only (Princess Anne, Father Leo) are indexed and filed as written.

B. Business Names

Titles in business names (Capt. Hook's Bait Shop) are indexed as written. Remember, the word *The* is considered the last indexing unit when it appears as the first word of a business name.

Rule 6: Prefixes, Articles, and Particles

A foreign article or particle in a personal or business name is combined with the part of the name following it to form a single indexing unit. The indexing order is not affected by a space between a prefix and the rest of the name (Alexander La Guardia), and the space is disregarded when indexing.

Examples of articles and particles are: a la, D,' Da, De, Del, De La, Della, Den, Des, Di, Dos, Du, E,' El, Fitz, Il, L,' La, Las, Le, Les, Lo, Los, M,' Mac, Mc, O,' Per, Saint, San, Santa, Santo, St., Ste., Te, Ten, Ter, Van, Van de, Van der, Von, Von der.

Rule 7: Numbers in Business Names

Numbers spelled out (Seven Lakes Nursery) in business names are filed alphabetically. Numbers written in digits are filed before alphabetic letters or words (B4 Photographers comes before Beleau Building and Loan).

Names with numbers written in digits in the first units are filed in ascending order (lowest to highest number) before alphabetic names (229 Club, 534 Shop, First National Bank of Chicago). Arabic numerals are filed before Roman numerals (2 Brothers Deli, 5 Cities Transit, XII Knights Inn).

Names with inclusive numbers (20-39 Singles Club) are arranged by the first digit(s) only (20). Names with numbers appearing in other than the first position (Pier 36 Cafe) are filed alphabetically and immediately before a similar name without a number (Pier 36 Cafe comes before Pier and Port Cafe).

When indexing names with numbers written in digit form that contain *st, d,* and *th* (1st. Mortgage Co., 2d Avenue Cinemas, 3d Street Pest Control), ignore the letter endings and consider only the digits (1, 2, 3).

When indexing names with a number (in figures or words) linked by a hyphen to a letter or word (A-1 Laundry, Fifty-Eight Auto Body, 10-Minute Photo), ignore the hyphen and treat it as a single unit (A1, FiftyEight, 10Minute).

When indexing names with a number plus a symbol (55+ Social Center), treat it as a single unit (55Plus).

Rule 8: Organizations and Institutions

Banks and other financial institutions, clubs, colleges, hospitals, hotels, lodges, magazines, motels, museums, newspapers, religious institutions, schools, unions, universities, and other organizations and institutions are indexed and filed according to the names written on their letterheads.

Rule 9: Identical Names

Retrieving the correct record when there are identical names of people or businesses is easy when using a computer database. A records management database typically contains a unique field with information specific to a particular person or business name—often a phone number, a special identification number, or an assigned number generated by the database software. Because each person or business has a unique identifier, there is no need to look for other information to determine which person is which.

In correspondence files, determining which person or business is the correct one when there are others with identical names can be a challenge. When personal names and names of businesses, institutions, and organizations are identical (including titles as explained in Rule 5), the filing order is determined by the addresses. Compare addresses in the following order:

1. City names.
2. State or province names (if city names are identical).
3. Street names, including *Avenue, Boulevard, Drive,* and *Street* (if city and state names are identical).
   a. When the first units of street names are written in digits (18th Street), the names are considered in ascending numeric order (1, 2, 3) and placed together before alphabetic street names (18th Street, 24th Avenue, Academy Circle).
   b. Street names written as digits are filed before street names written as words (22nd Street, 34th Avenue, First Street, Second Avenue).
   c. Street names with compass directions (North, South, East, and West) are considered as written (SE Park Avenue, South Park Avenue).
   d. Street names with numbers written as digits after compass directions are considered before alphabetic names (East 8th Street, East Main Street, Sandusky Drive, South Eighth Avenue).
4. House or building numbers (if city, state, and street names are identical).
   a. House and building numbers written as digits are considered in ascending numeric order (8 Riverside Terrace, 912 Riverside Terrace) and placed together before spelled-out building names (The Riverside Terrace).
   b. House and building numbers written as words are filed after house and building numbers written as digits (11 Park Avenue South, One Park Avenue).
   c. If a street address and a building name are included in an address, disregard the building name.
   d. ZIP Codes are not considered in determining filing order.

Rule 10: Government Names

Government names are indexed first by the name of the governmental unit—city, county, state, or country. Next, index the distinctive name of the department, bureau, office, or board. A discussion of local and regional, state, federal, and foreign government names follows.

A. Local and Regional Government Names

The first indexing unit is the name of the county, city, town, township, or village. *Charlotte Sanitation Department* is an example. *Charlotte* (a city) would be the first indexing unit. Next, index the most distinctive name of the department, board, bureau, office, or government/political division. In this case, *Sanitation* would be the most distinctive name of the department. The words *County of, City of, Department of, Office of,* etc., are retained for clarity and are considered separate indexing units. If *of* is not a part of the official name as written, it is not added as an indexing unit.

B. State Government Names

Similar to local and regional political/governmental agencies, the first indexing unit is the name of the state or province. Then index the most distinctive name of the department, board, bureau, office, or government/political division. The words *State of, Province of, Department of,* etc., are retained for clarity and are considered separate indexing units. If *of* is not a part of the official name as written, it is not added as an indexing unit.

C. Federal Government Names

Use three indexing "levels" (rather than units) for the United States federal government. Consider *United States Government* as the first level. The second level is the name of a department; for example, *Department of Agriculture.* Level three is the next most distinctive name; for example, *Forest Service.* The words *of* and *of the* are extraneous and should <u>not</u> be considered when indexing. In the following examples, note that *United States Government* is the first level in all cases.

D. Foreign Government Names

The name of a foreign government and its agencies is often written in a foreign language. When indexing foreign names, begin by writing the English translation of the government name on the document. The English name is the first indexing unit. Then index the balance of the formal name of the government, if needed, or if it is in the official name (China Republic of). Branches, departments, and divisions follow in order by their distinctive names. States, colonies, provinces, cities, and other divisions of foreign governments are followed by their distinctive or official names as spelled in English.

CROSS-REFERENCING

Some records of persons and businesses may be requested by a name that is different from the one by which it was stored. This is particularly true if the key unit is difficult to determine. When a record is likely to be requested by more than one name, an aid called a cross-reference is prepared. A **cross-reference** shows the name in a form other than that used on the original record, and it indicates the storage location of the original record. The filer can then find requested records regardless of the name used in the request for those records.

Cross-references for data stored in an electronic database are often not needed. Because the search features of database software are extensive, a record can usually be found easily using any part of the filing segment. Also, entire records are often visible when a search result shows on the screen. There may be instances, however, when a cross-reference is needed under an entirely different name. In these instances a cross-reference database record can be created.

Four types of personal names should be cross-referenced:

1. Unusual names
2. Hyphenated surnames
3. Alternate names
4. Similar names

Also, nine types of business names should be cross-referenced. Two will be presented in this chapter; the remainder, in Chapters 3 and 4.

1. Compound names
2. Names with abbreviations and acronyms

Glossary

a

accession log   A serial list of numbers assigned to records in a numeric storage system. Also called an *accession book* or *numeric file list*.

accuracy ratio   A measure of filers' ability to find requested records.

active records   Records needed to perform current operations. They are subject to frequent use and are usually located near the user. They can be accessed manually or online via a computer system. They are used three or more times a month.

activity ratio   A measure of the frequency of records use.

alphabetic index   A reference to a numeric file, organized alphabetically, that is used when the name or subject is known but not the assigned number.

alphabetic records management   A method of storing and arranging records according to the letters of the alphabet.

alphanumeric coding   A coding system that combines letters and numbers, in combination with punctuation marks, to develop codes for classifying and retrieving information. Main subjects are arranged alphabetically, and their subdivisions are assigned a number.

archive record   A record that has continuing or historical value and is preserved permanently by an organization.

archives   Records created or received and accumulated by a person or organization in the course of the conduct of affairs and preserved because of their historical or continuing value.
   The building or part of a building where archival materials are located.

ARMA International   A professional group interested in improving educational programs in schools and industry and providing on-the-job knowledge about records and information management.

ASCII   An acronym for the American Standard Code for Information Interchange. The code assigns specific numeric values to the first 128 characters of the 256 possible character combinations.

b

backup   A copy of electronic files and/or folders made as a precaution against the loss or damage of the original data.

bellows (expansion) folder   A folder that has a top flap and sides to enclose records in a case with creases along its bottom and sides that allow it to expand.

block-numeric coding   A coding system based on the assignment of number ranges to subjects. Groups of numbers represent primary and secondary subjects.

c

call-back system   A records protection procedure requiring an individual requesting data from a computer system to hang up after making a telephone request and wait for the computer to call back.

caption   A title, heading, short explanation, or description of a document or records.

charge-out   A control procedure to establish the current location of a record when it is not in the records center or central file, which can be a manual or automated system.

charge-out and follow-up file A tickler file that contains requisition forms filed by dates that records are due back in the inactive records center.

charge-out log A written or electronic form used for recording the record taken, when it was taken, who took it, the due date, the date it was returned, the date an overdue notice was sent, and if necessary, an extended due date.

chronologic storage A method by which records are filed in date sequence, either in reverse sequence (with the most recent date on top) or forward sequence (with the earliest or oldest date on top).

coding The act of assigning a file designation to records as they are classified.

color accenting The consistent use of different colors for different supplies in the storage system.

color coding Using color as an identifying aid in a filing system.

compass point Any of 32 horizontal directions indicated on the card of a compass.

compass terms Compass points used as part of the company or subject name.

consecutive numbering method A method in which consecutively numbered records are arranged in *ascending* number order—from the lowest number to the highest number.

constant data Data that remain the same such as preprinted data on a form. They do not require rewriting each time a form is filled in.

cost-benefit ratio A comparison to determine that every cost (input) results in an equal or greater benefit (output).

cross-reference A notation in a file or list showing that a record has been stored elsewhere; an entry directing attention to one or more related items.

cross-reference guide A special guide that serves as a permanent marker in storage indicating that all records pertaining to a correspondent are stored elsewhere.

cross-reference sheet A sheet placed in an alternate location in the file that directs the filer to a specific record stored in a different location other than where the filer is searching.

d

data warehouse A collection of data designed to support management decision-making.

database A collection of related data stored on a computer system. Databases are organized especially for rapid search and retrieval of specific facts or information.

decimal-numeric coding A numeric method of classifying records by subject in units of ten and coded for arrangement in numeric order.

density The degree of optical opacity of material that determines the amount of light that will pass through it or reflect from it.

destruction date file A tickler file containing copies of forms completed when records are received in a records center.

destruction file A file that contains information on the actual destruction of inactive records.

destruction notice A notification (memo, listing, form, etc.) of the scheduled destruction of records.

destruction suspension A hold placed on the scheduled destruction of records that may be relevant to foreseeable or pending litigation, governmental investigation, audit, or special organizational requirements.

dictionary arrangement A single alphabetic filing arrangement in which all types of entries (names, subjects, titles, etc.) are interfiled.

An arrangement of records in alphabetic order (A–Z).

digital signature A string of characters and numbers added as a code on electronic documents being transmitted by computer; also called *e-signature*.

direct access A method of accessing records by going directly to the file without first referring to an index or a list of names for location in the files.

direct access A method of access to records without reference to an index or other finding aid.

directory A subdivision of a storage device such as a hard drive created using the operating system of a computer.

disaster recovery plan A written and approved course of action to take when disaster strikes, ensuring an organization's ability to respond to an interruption in services by restoring critical business functions.

document imaging An automated system for scanning, storing, retrieving, and managing images of paper records in an electronic format.

duplex-numeric coding A coding system using numbers (or sometimes letters) with two or more parts separated by a dash, space, or comma.

e

e-commerce An electronic method to conduct business communication and transactions over networks and through computers.

efficiency control A method for evaluating the ability to produce a desired effect with a minimum expenditure of time, energy, and space.

efficiency ratio A standard for measuring the efficiency of various aspects of records systems.

electronic data interchange (EDI) A communication procedure between two companies that allows the exchange of standardized documents (most commonly invoices or purchase orders) through computers.

electronic fund transfer (EFT) A system and procedures that provide for electronic payments and collections.

electronic mail (e-mail) A system that enables users to compose, transmit, receive, and manage electronic documents and images across networks.

electronic record Data stored on electronic media that can be readily accessed or changed. A piece of equipment is required to view and read electronic records.

encryption The process of converting meaningful information into a numeric code that is only understood by the intended recipient of the information; any procedure used in cryptography to prevent unauthorized use.

encyclopedic arrangement A subject filing arrangement in which records are filed under broad, major subject titles and then under the specific subtitle to which they relate.

The alphabetic arrangement of major geographic divisions plus one or more geographic subdivisions also arranged in alphabetic order.

enterprise content management (ECM) Technologies, tools, and methods used to capture, manage, store, preserve, and deliver content across an enterprise.

external record A record created for use outside an organization.

f

field A set of one or more characters treated as a unit of information and part of a record in a database.

filename A unique name given to a file stored for computer use that must follow the computer's operating system rules.

filing (storage) method The way records are stored in a container, such as a filing cabinet.

filing segment The name by which a record is stored and requested.

firewall A combination hardware and software buffer that many organizations place between their internal network and the Internet to protect the internal network from outside intrusion.

flash drive A read/write device that attaches to a computer and is usable as a standard hard drive. The drive consists of a small printed circuit board encased in a hard plastic covering.

folder A subdivision of a storage device such as a hard drive created using the operating system of a computer.

A container used to hold and protect the contents of a file together and separate from other files.

follower block (compressor) A device at the back of a file drawer that can be moved to allow contraction or expansion of the drawer contents.

follow-up A system for assuring the timely and proper return of materials charged out from a file.

form A fixed arrangement of predetermined spaces designed for entering and extracting prescribed information on a paper or electronic document.

g

general folder A folder for records to and from correspondents with a small volume of records that does not require an individual folder.

geographic filing system The classification of records by geographic location usually arranged by numeric code or in alphabetic order.

geographic information system A computer system designed to allow users to collect, manage, and analyze large volumes of data referenced to a geographical location by some type of geographical coordinates such as longitude and latitude.

geographic records management A method of storing and retrieving records by location using a geographic filing system.

guide A rigid divider used to identify a section in a file and to facilitate reference to a particular record location.

i

image record A digital or photographic representation of a record on any medium such as microfilm or optical disk.

important records Records that assist in performing a firm's business operations and, if destroyed, are replaceable, but only at great cost.

inactive records Records that do not have to be readily available but which must be kept for legal, fiscal, or historical purposes; referred to less than fifteen times a year.

inactive records index An index of all records in the inactive records storage center.

index   A systematic guide that allows access to specific items contained within a larger body of information.

indexing   The mental process of determining the filing segment (or name) by which a record is to be stored and the placing or listing of items in an order that follows a particular system.

indexing order   The order in which units of the filing segment are considered when a record is stored.

indexing rules   Written procedures that describe how the filing segments are ordered.

indexing units   The various words, numbers, and symbols that make up a filing segment.

indirect access   A method of access to records that requires prior use of an external index.

individual folder   A folder used to store the records of an individual correspondent with enough records to warrant a separate folder.

inspecting   Checking a record to determine whether it is ready to be filed.

internal record   A record that contains information needed to operate an organization.

Internet   A worldwide network of computers that allows public access to send, store, and receive electronic information over public networks.

ISO 15489   A standard for records management policies and procedures.

k

key unit   The first unit of the filing segment.

knowledge management   An interdisciplinary field that is concerned with systematic, effective management and use of an organization's knowledge resources, including the knowledge and experience of its employees.

l

label   A device that contains the name of the subject or a number given to the file folder or section contents.

lanyard   A cord that can be attached to the USB port on a microcomputer or laptop. A flash drive or other USB device can be attached to the other end of the cord.

lateral file cabinet   Storage equipment that is wider than it is deep and that allows access to records from the side (horizontally).

leading zero   A zero added to the front of a number so that all numbers align on the right and will be sorted in consecutive order by a computer.

lettered guide plan   An arrangement of geographic records with primary guides labeled with alphabetic letters.

location name guide plan   An arrangement of geographic records with primary guides labeled with location names.

m

magnetic media   A variety of magnetically coated materials used for computers for data storage; e.g., floppy disk, hard disk, magnetic tape, redundant array of independent disks (RAID), videotape.

magnification ratio   A method of describing the relationship between the size of an image and the original record when viewed on a microfilm reader screen. Also called the *enlargement ratio*.

management   The process of using an organization's resources to achieve specific goals through the functions of planning, organizing, leading and controlling.

master index   A printed alphabetic listing in file order of all subjects used as subject titles in the filing system.

media compatibility   How well the media and the equipment needed to access information stored on the media work together.

media stability   The time the media will maintain its original quality so that it can continue to be used.

metadata   Data about data. It describes how, when, and by whom a particular set of data was collected, and how the data is formatted.

microform   The collective term for all microimages such as microfilm, microfiche, aperture card, microfilm jacket, or microfilm roll.

micrographics   The technology by which recorded information can be quickly reduced to a microform, stored conveniently, and then easily retrieved for reference and use.

middle-digit storage   A numeric storage method in which the middle digits are used as the finding aid to organize the filing system. It uses the middle two or three digits of each number as the primary division under which a record is filed.

migration   The process of moving data from one electronic system to another, usually in upgrading hardware and software, without having to undergo a major conversion or re-inputting of data.

mobile shelving   Series of shelving units that move on tracks attached to the floor for access to files.

motorized rotary storage   A storage unit that rotates shelves in the unit around a central hub to bring the files to the operator.

n

name index   A listing of correspondents' names stored in a subject file.

nonconsecutive numbering   A system of numbers that has blocks of numbers omitted.

nonessential records   Records that have no predictable value to the organization after their initial use and should be destroyed after use.

nonrecord   An item that is not usually included within the scope of official records such as a convenience file, day file, reference materials, drafts, etc. These records are not required to be retained and therefore do not appear on a records retention schedule.

numeric index   A current list of all files by the file numbers. It shows numbers assigned to subject titles, which helps avoid duplication of numbers.

numeric records management   Any classification system for arranging records that is based on numbers.

o

office of record   An office designated to maintain the *record* or *official* copy of a particular record in an organization.

official record   A significant, vital, or important record of continuing value to be protected, managed, and retained according to established retention schedules. It is often, but not necessarily, an original record. In law, an official record has the legally recognized and judicially enforceable quality of establishing some fact.

on-call/wanted form   A written request for a record that is *out* of the file.

one-period transfer method   A method of transferring records from active storage at the end of one period of time, usually once or twice a year, to inactive storage.

operating system An organized collection of software that controls the overall operations of a computer. The computer's link between the computer hardware, the user, and the application software.

optical character recognition Machine-reading of printed or written characters through the use of light-sensitive materials or devices.

optical media A high-density information storage medium where digitally encoded information is both written and read by means of a laser.

OUT folder A special folder used to replace a complete folder that has been removed from storage.

OUT guide A special guide used to replace any record that has been removed from storage and to indicate what was taken and by whom.

OUT indicator A control device that shows the location of borrowed records; can be a guide, folder, or sheet.

OUT sheet A form that is inserted in place of a record removed from a folder.

p

password A string of characters known to the computer system and a user, who must specify it to gain access to the system.

path A notation that includes a drive designation and the folders that indicate the location of a computer file.

periodic transfer method A method of transferring active records at the end of a stated period, usually one year, to inactive storage.

permanent cross-reference A guide that replaces an individual folder to direct the filer to the correct storage place.

perpetual transfer method A method of transferring records continuously from active to inactive storage areas whenever they are no longer needed for reference. Records are removed from current files into inactive storage sites on a scheduled basis.

personal digital assistant (PDA) A handheld computer that is portable, easy to use, and capable of sharing information with a desktop or notebook computer.

pick list A list containing specific records needed for a given program or project. A filer can use the list to retrieve all records on it.

pocket folder A folder with partially enclosed sides and more expansion at the bottom than an ordinary folder.

position The location of the tab across the top or down one side of a guide or folder.

primary guide A divider that identifies a main division or section of a file and always precedes all other material in a section.

push technology Technology that automatically delivers e-mail and other data to a device based on the user's profile and request for specific data.

q

query A database object used to instruct the program to find specific information.

r

radio frequency identification (RFID) A technology that incorporates the use of an electromagnetic or electrostatic radio frequency to identify an object, animal, or person. Used as an alternative to bar codes.

record Stored information, regardless of media or characteristics, made or received by an organization that is evidence of its operations and has value requiring its retention for a specific time.

A database element, part of a table, containing all the fields related to one person or topic.

record copy Another name for an official record, it is the official copy of a record that is retained for legal, operational, or historical purposes.

record life cycle The life span of a record as expressed in the five phases of creation, distribution, use, maintenance, and final disposition.

records audit A periodic inspection to verify that an operation is in compliance with a records and information management program.

records center A low-cost centralized area for housing and servicing inactive records whose reference rates do not warrant their retention in a prime office space.

records center box A box, usually made of corrugated cardboard, that is designed to hold approximately one cubic foot (12 inches high by 12 inches wide by 12 inches deep) of records, either legal or letter size.

records destruction The disposal of records of no further value by incineration, maceration, pulping, or shredding. Complete obliteration of a record beyond any possible reconstitution.

records disposition The final destination of records after they have reached the end of their retention period in active and/or inactive storage; they may be transferred to an archives for retention or be destroyed.

records inventory A detailed listing that could include the types, locations, dates, volumes, equipment, classification systems, and usage data of an organization's records.

records management The systematic control of all records from their creation or receipt, through their processing, distribution, organization, storage, and retrieval, to their ultimate disposition.

records retention program A program established and maintained to provide retention periods for records in an organization.

records retention schedule A comprehensive list of records series titles, indicating for each series the length of

time it is to be maintained. It may include retention in active office areas, inactive storage areas, and when and if such series may be destroyed or formally transferred to another entity such as an archives for historical purposes.

records series A group of related records filed and used together as a unit and evaluated as a unit for retention purposes.

records system A group of interrelated resources— people, equipment and supplies, space, procedures, and information—acting together according to a plan to accomplish the goals of the records and information management program.

records transfer The act of changing the physical custody of records with or without change of legal title. Relocating records from one storage area to another.

reduction ratio The relationship between the dimensions of the original or master and the corresponding dimensions of the photographed image.

reference document A document that contains information needed to carry on the operations of a firm over long periods of time.

relative index A dictionary-type listing of all possible words and combinations of words by which records may be requested.

release mark An agreed-upon mark such as initials or a symbol placed on a record to show that the record is ready for storage.

requisition A written request for a record or for information from a record.

resolution A measure of the sharpness or fine detail of an image.

retention period The time that records must be kept according to operational, legal, regulatory, and fiscal requirements.

retrieval The process of locating and withdrawing a record from a filing system or records center. Also, the action of accessing information from stored data on a computer system.

retrieval efficiency ratio A measure of the speed with which records are found and that verifies how filers spend their time.

s

scanner A device that converts an image of a document to electronic form for processing and storage.

SEE ALSO cross-reference A notation on a folder tab or cross-reference sheet that directs the filer to multiple locations for related information.

shelf file Open-shelving equipment in which records are accessed horizontally from the open side; may be an open style or have roll-back fronts.

sorter A device used to arrange records into alphabetic or numeric categories and to hold records temporarily prior to storage.

sorting Arranging the records in the sequence in which they are to be stored.

special (auxiliary) guide A divider used to lead the eye quickly to a specific place in a file.

special folder A folder that follows a special guide in an alphabetic filing arrangement.

storage The placement of records, according to a plan, on a shelf or in a file drawer or electronically saving a record to a medium readable by a computer.

storage procedures Steps for the orderly arrangement of records as required by a specific storage method or system.

storing Placing records into storage containers.

subject records management An alphabetic system of storing and retrieving records by their subject or topic.

suspension (hanging) folder A folder with built-in hooks on each side that hang from parallel metal rails on each side of a file drawer or other storage equipment.

synchronization The process bringing items into agreement. In case of PDAs and personal computers, this means updating the data on the PC and the PDA so that both contain the same data.

t

tab A projection for a caption on a folder or guide that extends above the regular height or beyond the regular width of the folder or guide.

tab cut The length of the tab expressed as a proportion of the width or height of the folder or guide.

table A database element containing a group of records related to one subject or topic.

terminal-digit storage A numeric storage method in which the last two or three digits of each number are used as the primary division under which a record is filed. Groups of numbers are read from right to left.

tickler file   A date-sequenced file by which matters pending are flagged for attention on the proper date.

transaction document   A record used in an organization's day-to-day operations.

u

useful records   Records that are helpful in conducting business operations and may, if destroyed, be replaced at slight cost.

v

variable data   Data that change such as data entered each time a form is filled in.

vertical file cabinet   Storage equipment that is deeper than it is wide. Generally, the arrangement of folders in the file drawers is from front to back.

virus   A computer program that replicates itself into other programs that are shared among systems with the intention of causing damage.

vital records   Records, usually irreplaceable, which are necessary to the continued operation of an organization.

w

World Wide Web   A part of the Internet that contains HTML documents that can be displayed and searched using web browser programs.

Index